TIME IS LUCK:
THE CINEMA OF
MICHAEL MANN

TIME IS LUCK:
THE CINEMA OF
MICHAEL MANN

James Slaymaker

First published in 2022 by
Telos Publishing, 139 Whitstable Road, Canterbury, Kent CT2 8EQ

Telos Publishing values feedback. If you have any comments about this book
please e-mail feedback@telos.co.uk

Time is Luck: The Cinema of Michael Mann © 2022 James Slaymaker

ISBN: 978-1-84583-207-0

Cover design: David J Howe

Contents

Introduction

'There's people who live life authentically and there's people who live a life of fabrication. And it begins with the question of how you're gonna do your time' –
Michael Mann (Tucker, 2012)

Like many of Mann's protagonists, Vincent (Tom Cruise), the terminally alienated assassin at the centre of *Collateral* (2004), meets his fate within a space of mass transit. He arrived at Los Angeles International Airport the previous evening with a clear plan of action: he was going to carry out five hits at five different locations around the city, working through a list given to him by a local drug baron, before boarding a plane at dawn to move on to his next assignment. Despite the violent nature of his work, Vincent approaches it with the composure and self-assurance of a consummate professional. He's honed his craft over many decades, and he now prides himself on his ability to complete every job on schedule, with minimum fuss, and with no trace of evidence left behind at any of the crime scenes. In order to function at this high level, Vincent deems it a necessity to devote every aspect of his life to his work. He does not maintain any personal relationships, has no fixed residence, and views everything – and *everyone* – around him through a lens of emotional detachment.

For Vincent, these sacrifices are acceptable because they enable him to live a life that is determined purely on his own terms. While the other inhabitants of the city are consumed by illusory notions of 'right' and 'wrong', obsessed with social conventions, and driven by materialistic desires, Vincent lives according to his own code of conduct – and he believes that his total commitment to his personal philosophy elevates him above the masses. Shortly after hailing a ride with cab driver Max (Jamie Foxx), who does not yet know of his client's nefarious reasons for being in the area, Vincent details his pessimistic view of modern urban living. Gazing at the passing streets of LA, he pontificates: '17 million people. If this were a country, it would be the fifth-biggest economy in the world. But nobody knows each other. I read about this guy. Gets on the MTA, here, and dies. Six hours he's riding the subway before anybody notices. This corpse doing laps around LA, people on and off, sitting next to him, nobody notices.' Vincent reasons that there is little point in leading one's life according to conventional standards of social etiquette within an environment that, in actuality, is deeply indifferent to human life. The individual must figure out for themselves which values and principles they wish to govern their behaviour – and then pursue a lifestyle that is rooted in these values, regardless of what anybody else thinks.

In the end, Vincent is fatally shot by Max on an empty subway cart circling the city on a never-ending loop. Realising that he has no chance of survival, Vincent does not express any sense of anger at his killer. He sits down on a vacant seat and, acknowledging the irony of the situation, asks Max: 'think anybody will notice?' The life drains out of his body, and he slumps forward, the lights of the city visible behind him. Vincent accepts his death calmly because it represents the logical endpoint for his existential journey. He has pursued his professional goals up to the very final moment, struck down in the process of completing the fifth and final hit on the list. For Vincent, everybody who is enmeshed in such a hyper-modern urban environment is destined to end up precisely the same way: seamlessly slipping out of existence while the rhythms of a vast and inhuman city continue to run unaffected by the loss. To die young, knowing that he never sacrificed his integrity, is a preferable fate to him than leading a life that is stifled by compromise.

The quest to maintain personal autonomy within a de-humanising, technologically advanced metropolis is one of the central recurring themes across Mann's entire oeuvre: Frank (James Caan), the preternaturally skilled safecracker from his theatrical debut *Thief* (1981), fights to retain control over his working practices after agreeing to collaborate with Leo (Robert Prosky), the authoritarian boss of a rapidly expanding crime syndicate; biochemical researcher Jeffery Wigand (Russell Crowe) resists being treated as a pawn of either the tobacco industry or the state-affiliated media in *The Insider* (1999); Depression-era gangster John Dillinger (Johnny Depp) struggles to avoid incarceration after becoming the subject of an extensive, heavily publicised manhunt orchestrated by J Edgar Hoover (Billy Crudup) in *Public Enemies* (2009); computer hacker Nick Hathaway (Chris Hemsworth) uses his technological prowess to evade detection from a sprawling surveillance network in *Blackhat* (2015).

When we look over the trajectory of Mann's career, it makes sense why he has such an affinity for idiosyncratic outsiders and mavericks that must fight to hold on to their individuality within environments that are often hostile to personal expression. Mann began his filmmaking career with politically radical documentary short films such as *Jaunpuri* (1969), a portrait of student activists during the May '68 protests in Paris, and *17 Days Down the Line* (1972), a study of militant groups in Biafra and Northern Ireland. These shorts played several prestigious film festivals and soon caught the eye of network television executives, leading to Mann being offered scriptwriting and directing assignments for a variety of drama series, including *Hawaii Five-O* (1968-1980), *Starsky & Hutch* (1975-1979), *Vega$* (1978-1981) and *Police Story* (1973-1987). Mann's next major breakthrough came when he was hired to work on a script rewrite for the Ulu Grosbard-directed film *Straight Time* (1978). The project, which revolves around a petty thief who faces difficulty adapting to civilian life after serving a six-year jail sentence, required Mann to conduct extensive research at Folsom state prison. This experience inspired executives at ABC to bring Mann on to assist with the pre-production process on *The Jericho Mile* (1979), a TV film based on a spec script by literature professor Patrick Nolan which had languished in development hell for years before being picked out by actor Peter Strauss as a potential star vehicle for himself. Reportedly, Strauss was so impressed by Mann's rewrite of Nolan's script that he personally requested that he be given the opportunity to direct the feature.

Although *The Jericho Mile* was produced as a television feature and lacks the formal rigour of Mann's later films, it exhibits, in a rough form, many of the thematic preoccupations which he would go on to develop and refine in his theatrical work. The plot of *The Jericho Mile* revolves around Larry Murphy (Peter Strauss), a young inmate serving a life sentence at Folsom prison after fatally shooting his abusive father. Murphy openly admits that he was responsible for the crime but refuses to apologise for it, as he acted to protect his younger stepsister from further mistreatment at the hands of the family patriarch. He also asserts that he knew life imprisonment would be the price he'd have to pay for committing the murder beforehand. Therefore, he made the conscious decision that the protection of his sibling was more important than his freedom. Murphy lives as a loner within the walls of Folsom, refusing to become involved with the gang system and determined to avoid conflicts with the other convicts. Murphy, instead, whiles away his time by practising the solitary sport of sprinting. Murphy always runs alone, refusing to race other athletes or even keep track of his timing because he needs no external validation. However, when the prison wardens notice just how adept Murphy is becoming at the sport, they recruit the state track-and-field coach to train him, in the hopes that he may represent Folsom in the Olympics. Throughout, Murphy remains deeply sceptical of the warden's plans to turn him into an international sports sensation, reiterating that he does not desire money, or fame, or public recognition; he runs for private reasons that he will not disclose to anybody, and he does not need any external reward. Murphy's disinterest in exploiting his skills for material gain seems incomprehensible to the guards, to the other inmates, and to the prison psychologist, none of whom can understand why Murphy would dedicate so much of his life to physical activity if he is not working toward any clear target. Although Murphy feels pressured to go along with the intentions of the wardens at first, he reaches a breaking point when he is asked to make a public apology for the murder of his father in the presence of the US Olympic board. Faced with the option of living an inauthentic life of material success, which would require him to publicly express regret over a crime he still believes to be ethically justified, or returning to the prison yard to spend the rest of his days in anonymity, Murphy does not hesitate in choosing the latter option. He may be in physical captivity, but he alone gets to decide what he places value on and how he deals with his life sentence. In this sense, Murphy manages to establish a decent degree of freedom despite his adverse circumstances.

Even at this early stage, then, Mann was establishing a clear set of idiosyncratic thematic interests – and he was doing so within the constraints of American network television. The critical commercial success of *The Jericho Mile* (which received, among other honours, an Emmy Award for Outstanding Writing in a Limited Series or a Special, and a Directors Guild of America award for Outstanding Directorial Achievement in Specials for TV/Actuality), enabled Mann to make the leap to the silver screen with *Thief*, a loose adaptation of Frank Hohmier's novel *The Home Invaders: Confessions of a Cat Burglar* (1975). It was at this point that Mann truly began to develop a mature aesthetic style with distinct formal features that would recur across his later projects: the treatment of the city as a monolithic, ultra-modern force that threatens to engulf the main characters; the interplay between objective and subjective points of view as protagonists struggle to remain afloat within grand urban structures which threaten to de-humanise them; the blending together of private and public spaces; the palpable sense of melancholia and alienation which haunts his characters; the emphasis on new technologies and their impact on our perceptual relationship with the world; the combination of visceral violence and romantic longing; the use of long lenses and methodical camera movements to transform concrete structures into abstract washes of colour and light. *Thief* also announced a key issue that would come to play a central role in all of Mann's subsequent films: work. Whether they are criminals or police officers, journalists or historians, boxers or computer hackers, every one of Mann's protagonists is deeply preoccupied with their profession, and their struggle for self-determination is intrinsically intertwined with the pressures and expectations imposed upon them by their work. For some, their profession becomes an albatross around their neck, forcing them to compromise on their ideals and perform tasks that have a negative impact on the wider population; for others, their profession is the one part of their life that brings them a genuine sense of fulfilment, as they manage to establish a decent degree of agency within the confines of their work. When this sense of freedom is achieved, however, it is hard-earned and usually comes at a high personal cost – the Mannian protagonist must actively resist a multitude of entities that seek to crush them into submission, quell their individuality, and reduce them to just another cog in the system. The structures of late capitalist America are actively hostile to difference, and fighting against these structures necessitates a strenuous effort that requires every ounce of the protagonist's strength. Consequently, they typically have little energy left to devote to romantic or familial relationships. Though Mann's characters often long for the pleasures of a stable romantic life, they are – for the most part – fundamentally incapable of sustaining one. In *Thief*, Frank abandons his wife Jessie (Tuesday Weld) and adopted child to escape the increasingly controlling grasp of Leo's syndicate and returns to running a solo crime operation. In *Heat* (1995), master thief Neil McCauley (Robert De Niro) comes close to fleeing the city and forming a family with local bookstore clerk Eady (Amy Brenneman). However, on their way to the airport, McCauley makes a sudden detour to exact revenge on the traitor who fed information about him and his gang to the feds. This decision – to place more importance on upholding his professional code of ethics than on ensuring the safety of his romantic partner – is what ultimately brings about his demise, though, like Vincent, McCauley takes some degree of satisfaction in the knowledge that he has lived his life completely on his own terms.

This tension between the desire to maintain control over one's life and work and the desire to forge loving relationships is at the centre of the aura of melancholy that pervades Mann's cinema. Mann's work paints a portrait of a dystopian America in which individuals drift like spectres through a network of freeways, skyscrapers, lobbies, diners, anonymous hotel rooms, warehouses, airport lounges, and subway stations. Landscapes of steel and neon signs and luminescent streetlights block the night sky, leaving the individual feeling as though they are enclosed from all sides by man-made structures. Mann's urban environments are featureless, inhuman spaces, scrubbed free of any real indication of cultural or national specificity; these spaces simultaneously make their inhabitants feel claustrophobic and dwarfed by their sheer enormity. Walls of glass make it hard to distinguish interior from exterior, and public and private spaces blend together to the point that they become hard to tell apart. In *Manhunter* (1986), an intimate discussion between father and son takes place in the middle of an aisle of a sterile, blindingly white supermarket; visually, it resembles the high-security prison in which a serial killer was interrogated earlier in the film. The living spaces in *Heat* are indistinguishable from hotel rooms – minimalistic, antiseptic, functional places to eat and sleep, not homes. At one point, McCauley even clarifies that he purposefully keeps his apartment free of permanent possessions to make it easier for him to make a quick escape if the cops ever track him down – openly acknowledging that he views his apartment as a transitional space, not a permanent residence. When Vincent Hanna (Al Pacino) is kicked out of his familial home by his wife late into the narrative and moves into a deluxe hotel suite, the change barely registers. Mann's cinema presents a frictionless, globalised world without clear borders, and yet, paradoxically, every location resembles a prison in which every character is trapped.

And so Mann's films revolve around figures drawn to the periphery of society, who value their autonomy over easy assimilation and are therefore marked as maladjusted threats to the stability of the dominant social system. Often, the characters are swept up within a current of technological and social change which they are incompatible with. As a result, they must make the most of the small amount of time they have left before they are either snuffed out by the system (*Thief, Heat, Collateral, Public Enemies*) or subsumed within the very social structure which creates their sense of dissatisfaction (*Manhunter, Miami Vice* (2006)). Everything moves too rapidly for the protagonists to keep up with. They latch onto moments of quiet reflection to re-orientate themselves, usually accompanied by images of the natural world – the essential elements of land, water, and air that remain constant as the artificial constructions surrounding them perpetually shift and evolve. Max keeps a photograph of the Maldives islands taped to the windshield of his cab, so he can take in the beauty of the landscape for a few minutes when the demands of his work become overwhelming: 'My own private getaway. When things get too heavy for me, I take five minutes out, and I just go there. And I just concentrate on absolutely nothing.' But these retreats always turn out to be short-lived. There is always another fare to collect, another score to pull off, another criminal to apprehend. Sonny Crockett (Colin Farrell) transgresses professional boundaries by embarking on a relationship with Isabella (Gong Li), the lover of a powerful cartel leader. Although the relationship provides him with the only source of authentic emotional connection he feels throughout the entire film, the social pressure ultimately becomes too much for him to tolerate and he cuts ties with Isabella for good. 'Remember what you told me, time is luck,' Isabella tells Crockett during their final meeting. 'Well, luck ran out,' Crockett replies. 'It was too good to last.' For Crockett, the sacrifices he must make to live an authentic life are too much to bear, and he makes the painful choice to return to the flux. Others have greater determination and hold out until they are forcibly expelled from the system – like Dillinger, shot dead on the street outside a screening of W S Van Dyke's *Manhattan Melodrama* (1934) by two of Hoover's right-hand men. Before his demise, Dillinger is shown watching the scene in which Clark Gable's gangster Blackie Gallagher is calmly lead to the electric chair. His final words seem to have particular resonance for Dillinger: 'Die the way you lived, all of a sudden, that's the way to go. Don't drag it out. Living like that doesn't mean a thing.' Dillinger gazes at the screen with rapt attention and an implicit sense of self-recognition: He realises that an idealistic outcast such as himself cannot survive long within Hoover's new world of perpetual surveillance and draconian state control, and he quietly accepts his fate.

Close bonds in Mann's cinema often develop between individuals who, at first glance, should be fundamentally opposed to one another: serial killer Francis Dollarhyde (Tom Noonan) and Will Graham (William Petersen), the FBI agent assigned to hunt him down in *Manhunter*; McCauley and LAPD officer Hanna in *Heat*; socially conscious computer hacker Hathaway and cyber-terrorist Sadak (Yorick van Wageningen) in *Blackhat*. These characters may not spend much time on screen together, but they are connected through acts of aesthetic and narrative doubling which emphasise their status as mirror images of one another. This kinship between the protagonist and their perverse double is often presented as being more substantial than the superficial relationships they share with their friends and family members. These characters are isolated, obsessive, disaffected, and unable to blend into the societal mainstream. Unable to establish healthy social lives, they fixate on their doubles, others struck by the same malaise as they. Because of their unwavering commitment to their own, specific moral code, these doubles often find themselves at odds with one another, pushed into a position where, to complete their professional mission, they are forced to kill their double. This act does not typically bring satisfaction or a feeling of balance; on the contrary, the survivor is left with a strange sensation of emptiness, now more alone than ever.

There are, however, some notable instances in which Mann's protagonists are able to triumph above their circumstances – though, even in these cases, there remains a sense that these moments of victory may turn out to be fleeting. In *The Insider*, Wigand and CBS journalist Lowell Bergman (Al Pacino) manage to successfully air Wigand's testimony against the tobacco giant Brown & Williamson aired on broadcast television, but this individual accomplishment only hammers home just how difficult it is for genuine dissent to be expressed within a mediasphere corrupted by corporate interests. Bergman realises that he cannot practice his craft in good faith while still working for CBS, so turns his back on the company. He knows that he must find an outlet that will allow him to voice his genuine viewpoints without fear of censorship or manipulation, but he is left uncertain as to whether he can sustain his honour within the field of journalism, no matter which publication he moves on to. At the end of *Blackhat*, Hathaway, along with his romantic and professional partner Chen Lien (Tang Wei), have foiled the plot of a nefarious gang of computer hackers while simultaneously avoiding capture from the US and Chinese authorities. As they walk towards freedom, however, Mann's camera pulls back to reveal that their movements are being captured by CCTV cameras that feed into a large security office. The pair are still marked as wanted felons, and within a culture of such pervasive state surveillance, they risk being apprehended if they let their guard down for even a second.

As Mann entered the 21st century, his practice became dominated by a dual quest to explore ways in which digital technologies are intensifying state mechanisms of surveillance and control and, simultaneously, to discover the poetic, sensual and painterly possibilities of new digital filmmaking equipment. While the majority of Hollywood auteurs have incorporated digital technologies in their craft primarily for cost-effectiveness and ease-of-use, essentially composing their features in the same way as they would have if they had been shooting on photochemical film (at times, even going so far as to add artificial film grain to the image to mimic the materiality of celluloid reels), Mann utilised these tools to experiment with how they may be able to register the real world in a manner that is qualitatively different from analogue film capture. As Mann explained, when asked about his choice to shoot *Collateral* on HD digital cameras:

'[M]y reason for choosing DV wasn't economy but was to do with the fact that the entire movie takes place in one city, on one night, and you can't see the city at night on motion-picture film the way you can on digital video. And I like the truth-telling feeling I receive when there's very little light on the actors' faces – I think this is the first serious major motion picture done in digital video that is photoreal, rather than using it for effects. DV is also a more painterly medium: you can see what you've done as you shoot because you have the end product sitting in front of you on a Sony high-def monitor, so I could change the contrast to affect the mood, add colour, do all kinds of things you can't do with film.' (Olsen, 2004: 81-82)

As Mann's comments illustrate, his attraction to the medium was based on two factors: on the one hand, the portability, miniature size, and outstanding light-capturing capacity of the digital apparatus allowed Mann to capture locations, actions, and stray details in a more immediate manner than possible with analogue film production; on the other hand, Mann was entranced by the possibility for DV to be mobilised to create 'painterly' effects. Mann's digital images appear to get closer to the reality of the world, which exists beyond the frame (responding intuitively to unexpected moments of action, relying less on artificial light sources, and eager to enter into perilous terrain), but the overall effect is not one of documentary verisimilitude. They are hyperreal, warping space and colour to render his chosen environments otherworldly. At times, the screen becomes obscured by digital noise: smeary, pixelated textures produce pictorial abstractions which make the viewer conscious of the material qualities of the mediating apparatus.

Mann's characters experience an unshakable feeling of elegiac mourning for an idyllic lost era as they fail to find a foothold within a harsh technological present. Mann's digital projects powerfully articulate the affective structure of feeling which emerges from a life immersed within the hyper-accelerated rhythms of contemporary culture, while also expressing resistance to these negative forces: by focusing on visceral sensation to puncture the widespread de-materialisation fostered by computerisation; by dramatising how mechanisms of digital surveillance may be turned against their operators to empower the individual; and by crafting moments which realise the sensual qualities of the digital image as a means to counteract the medium's cultural association with coldness and inhumanity – this is often achieved by intentionally incorporating ostensible technological 'glitches' into his formal style. Mann, then, materially engages with the very technologies of communication which he reflexively critiques to make the viewer aware of the extent to which digitality has impacted our relationship with other people, our labour practices, and our environment, while also pointing to the ways in which such technology may be re-purposed to challenge hegemonic hierarchies of power and control.

Over the span of five decades and twelve feature films, Michael Mann has firmly established himself as one of the most distinctive artistic voices in modern American cinema. Despite remaining within the studio system for the vast bulk of his career, Mann has managed to imprint a singular authorial signature on every project he has helmed, maintaining a striking formal and thematic consistency across his work in a diverse range of genres: from neo-noir crime films to frontier Westerns; from sports biopics to conspiracy thrillers; from gangster features to horror films. In each case, Mann draws upon a recognisable generic vernacular while also revising and updating elements we associate with the form to transform it into a vehicle for exploring his personal philosophical, political and social concerns. This book contributes to the growing collection of literature that treats Mann as a serious and vital artist whose body of work contemplates many of the most pressing cultural dilemmas of the new millennium.

Due, in large part, to his status as a commercially successfully filmmaker who operates within the sphere of mainstream Hollywood cinema, it has taken a while for Mann to receive substantial recognition by critics. However, the tide has started to shift in recent years, as evidenced by the small collection of book-length studies that have been published about his work over the past two decades. Mark Steensland's *Pocket Essentials guide to Mann's cinema* (2002) provides a broad overview of Mann's life and career up until the release of *Ali* (2001). However, as the title indicates, this book offers more of a broad introduction to Mann's filmography than a critical analysis. Although the biographical information and behind-the-scenes details provided by Steensland are illuminating, there is little attempt here to unpack the driving themes and formal preoccupations of Mann's work. F X Feeney and Paul Duncan's Taschen release *Michael Mann* (2006) is a handsomely designed tome that showcases a valuable array of production photos, notes, and screenshots, though, again, it is light on textual analysis. The book only offers a broad description of each of Mann's films, with some linkages between the various stages of Mann's career noted but not explored extensively. Jonathan Rayner's *The Cinema of Michael Mann: Vice and Vindication* provides a more robust analysis of Mann's career, discussing his films primarily in relation to the history of American genre cinema. Rayner's work perceptively contextualises Mann's work within wider cinematic traditions, pointing out the ways in which his films either conform to or deviate from generic frameworks, ranging from the gangster film to the historical epic to expressionistic horror. Rayner sketches a useful theoretical prism through which Mann's films may be approached, though, unfortunately, the passages of textual analysis he applies to the films themselves tend to be short and lacking in detail.

The collection *The Philosophy of Michael Mann* (2014), edited by Steven Sanders, Aeon J Skoble, and R Barton Palmer, surveys a multitude of philosophical approaches with which one may approach the filmography of Michael Mann, featuring a diverse range of essays that deal with issues including the treatment of existentialism across the filmmaker's body of work, Mann's formal exploration of urban architecture, and post-classical composition in Mann's digital features. Though this book contains many interesting perspectives on Mann's body of work, others are less persuasive, and, as is often the case with essay collections of this kind, the pieces do not cohere into any single, overarching theoretical argument. Mark E Wildermuth's *Blood in the Moonlight: Michael Mann and Information Age Cinema* (2005) examines the thematisation of computer media and informatics throughout Michael Mann's oeuvre, examining Mann's strategies of constructing technologically advanced landscapes in which his characters long for phenomenological experience and human connection. Wildermuth's analysis is insightful and invigorating, as he sheds light on an aspect of Mann's work that has, thus far, been under-explored: its critical engagement with technological change and how his protagonists struggle to navigate these transformations. It is unfortunate that Wildermuth's book was published before Mann's major 21st century digital works were released, as these later features develop the themes that the author delves into here in fascinating ways.

Vincent M Gaine takes a similar approach of interrogating, in-depth, a single thematic strand across Mann's entire body of work in *Existentialism and Social Engagement in the Films of Michael Mann* (2011). Gaine reads all of Mann's films through the lens of existential philosophy, arguing that each of his protagonists experiences an existential struggle to assign meaning to their lives. This struggle either leads them to insular self-obsession or productive social engagement. Gaine supports his thesis with lengthy breakdowns of each film, dissecting the psychological makeup of notable characters and demonstrating how the machinations of Mann's plots are designed to dramatise different aspects of existential philosophy. Gaine's scholarly tome is intricate and perceptive. His focus on the interconnections across different films offers an exciting way to think about Mann's work as a unified, ongoing project offering variations on recurrent themes and ideas, rather than a series of discrete texts to be studied in isolation. Finally, there is Steven Rybin's *Michael Mann: Crime Auteur* (2013) – arguably the richest and most complete study of Mann's work released so far. Rybin's rigorously researched analysis covers each of Mann's films in detail, from *The Jericho Mile* to *Public Enemies*, focusing on the director's engagement with film history, his complex relationship with genre tropes, and the minutiae of his formal style. What I find striking about Rybin's work is the meticulous detail with which he examines key scenes from Mann's oeuvre; placing carefully selected sequences under the microscope, Rybin painstakingly explores the nuances of composition, performance, colour scheme, camera movement and montage.

Time is Luck: The Cinema of Michael Mann explores Mann's work in relation to transformations in labour practices, technologies of vision, and strategies of dissent that have occurred over the late 20th and early 21st centuries. Applying extensive textual analysis to each of Mann's features, this study explores how these transformations are reflected in the filmmaker's output, formally and thematically. I pay particular attention to Mann's late features, illustrating how Mann's experimentation with digital filmmaking equipment informs his critique of the intensification of state control over the lives of individuals, the corporatisation of criminal activity, the de-materialisation of work, and the erasure of national and cultural boundaries. However, I also believe that it is important to note that, although Mann expresses anguish at the pervasive nature of technologically advanced systems which exist to exploit the common man, curtail civil liberties, and prop up corrupt regimes, there always remains space for protest and resistance in his cinema. This aspect of Mann's art is essential to keep in mind and is too often ignored by critics, who have often accused the filmmaker of cynicism or even anti-humanism. This book argues that Mann's films also remind us of the necessity of holding onto our humanity, seeking out meaningful interpersonal relationships, and asserting our individual agency within a world that can seem overwhelmingly unjust, oppressive and alienating.

My Life to Live:
The Jericho Mile (1979)

Michael Mann's debut feature, *The Jericho Mile,* exemplifies legendary filmmaker Jean Renoir's theory that 'a director makes only one movie in his life. Then he breaks it into pieces and makes it again' (Ó Maoilearca, 2015). Although it is slightly rough around the edges and lacking in the complexity of narrative and form which characterises Mann's theatrical work, *The Jericho Mile* contains the seeds of themes and obsessions which Mann would go on to develop and refine across his mature projects: the tension between living life on one's own terms and conforming to social expectations, the interpersonal bonds which emerge on the margins of society, the exploitative nature of American institutions, and the nature of masculinity. This is not to say, however, that *The Jericho Mile* is only valuable insofar as it prefigures Mann's mature style. Even though it was produced for broadcast on network television, and, inevitably, this meant that many restrictions were placed on Mann during production, *The Jericho Mile* is a nuanced, confident debut which raises vital questions about the nature of success, how an individual defines themselves in relation to their surroundings, and the mechanisms through which a repressive organisation may exert power over those in its grasp.

The Jericho Mile began life as a spec script that had been languishing in development hell in the backroom of ABC studios for years before actor Peter Strauss – who was much in-demand following the success of the miniseries *Rich Man, Poor Man* (1976) – handpicked it to be his next project. At this point, Mann was virtually unknown in the industry, having only directed a few short documentary projects and some episodes of episodic crime and drama serials. What convinced Strauss to select this young novice to helm his chosen project was Mann's experience conducting extensive research in Folsom prison while performing an uncredited rewrite of the Grosbard film *Straight Time*. During this period, Mann developed a fascination with the social infrastructure of the inmates at the penitentiary, coming to view it as a microcosm of the United States as a whole. As Mann commented in a retrospective interview: 'It was as if the whole of our body politic, our culture, our society had all been compressed and into a geographically compressed space. Almost like a lab experiment. A bad lab experiment. And so all the dynamics that were outside were inside on steroids' (Appelo, 2014). As this description makes clear, the primary point of fascination for Mann was not the relationship between the inmates and the guards, nor the inner workings of the justice system itself, but the ways in which the inmates strived to assert some level of individual agency and self-expression even though so many freedoms have been taken from them – for some of the men, this was a case of forming their own subcultures, rules, and traditions, while for others it meant devoting themselves to solitary tasks in which they found a great deal of value.

This first-hand research influenced Mann greatly when he was fleshing out Nolan's spec script. Actual details, behaviours, and attitudes observed by Mann during his time at Folsom were added to the material to make the portrayal of the prison appear more authentic and lived-in. Scenes such as the one where inmate R C Stiles (Richard Lawson) explains his habit of taping photographs of his civilian life onto the walls of his cell to envision what his future will be like upon his release, and the sequence in which various prisoners express their respect for Rain Murphy by silently approaching him in the cafeteria hall and placing items of food on his plate, were based on real incidents that Mann observed during his time in Folsom. The high level of attention paid by Mann to mundane daily rituals, pockets of dead time, and small behavioural details creates an indelible impression of what everyday life behind bars is genuinely like, and differentiates *The Jericho Mile* from paint-by-numbers on-screen portrayals of prison life. Strauss was so impressed by the intricacy of the rewritten script that he recommended to ABC bosses that Mann be allowed to direct it as well. ABC granted his request, and Mann's first step was to secure permission to shoot on location within Folsom. The prison wardens accepted, but gave Mann a strict 19-day production window, and warned him that his crew may encounter antagonistic or otherwise dangerous behaviour from the inmates. Mann was warned that if the film crew's presence inspired any mass-scale rioting, or if an inter-gang war broke out, production would have to shut down immediately. But Mann, who had already produced footage under challenging conditions while making his early documentary shorts, was willing to accept the risk. As Mann explained, making the film within the actual space of the prison served as a constant – and vital – reminder of the instability of life as an inmate: 'We had 13 stabbings and one killing during the 19 days in which we were shooting. So it was obviously a dangerous place' (Tucker, 2012). Mann's commitment to filming within the actual jail certainly paid off: the volatile energy of the space, the sense that we're witnessing a living, breathing environment which may collapse into violence at any moment, infuses every frame of *The Jericho Mile*.

How does an individual adapt to life in jail without losing his sanity? How does one retain a sense of freedom within an environment in which he is constantly under surveillance and subject to strict rules? How do the men forced into these conditions relate to one another and develop their own sub-cultures and power hierarchies? These issues, central to the film, are established in the first sequence. *The Jericho Mile* opens with a vibrant montage that introduces the prison population as a dynamic community consisting of various sub-cultures. Despite being confined by the literal barriers of the prison walls, the inmates have transformed the yard into a dynamic and varied space within which each man engages in their own strategies of self-expression *and* self-assertion. Some of the inmates search for fulfilment by attaching themselves to a larger group, while others pursue isolated pastimes: an inmate dances alone while carrying a boom box; a group of inmates play chess; a gang gather around a poker table; men lift weights; a man styles another man's hair; a basketball game takes place. Along with these brief snapshots of activity, Mann inserts shots of tattoos, murals and other material totems which indicate various gang affiliations. Murphy, the film's protagonist, is introduced in an unceremonious fashion. He is first seen sprinting alongside Stiles in a brief tracking shot inserted into this montage – there is, at this point, little to indicate that he is deserving of more attention than any of the other inmates. He appears as just another figure amongst the group of inmates whiling away their time on the courtyard, and, as Mann integrates his running into the collage of different leisure pursuits, there is nothing that immediately distinguishes him from the rest of the population. However, as the sequence goes on, Mann's camera keeps returning to him, and the initial collective viewpoint of the yard gradually zeroes in to a focus on one individual. Although Stiles and

Murphy initially seem to be running together as part of a shared pursuit, Murphy pushes forward on his own after Stiles becomes too exhausted to continue. Stiles calls out for Murphy, but he is so absorbed in his physical activity that he does not seem to be aware that he is now running alone.

This sequence is rooted upon a tension between collective and individual experiences. Prison inmates are typically depicted in American media as a homogenous mass forced to comply with the same regulations, eat the same food, wear the same clothes, and live in identical quarters. Mann's montage subverts this popular image of the conformity of prison life to reveal the heterogeneous array of hobbies, cultural affiliations, and coping strategies that exist within the prison community. Because these men are physically restricted, it becomes essential for them to determine how they spend their own time within the confines of the jail – when one has had so many freedoms forcibly taken from them, the question of what tasks and goals the individual regards as valuable takes on monumental significance. For Murphy, this activity is running, and his all-consuming commitment to this solitary sport is treated as, as Jonathan Rayner observes, 'the fact and symbol of his apartness' (2013: 45). Murphy dedicates himself to an ethos of individualism within the prison which keeps him from joining any communal activity, gang, or other sub-culture. His complete immersion in his chosen sport helps him to detach from the prison environment, which, as we soon learn, is an essential expression of his individualism and his primary strategy for survival.

The opening montage abruptly ends with the deafening sound of the prison alarm system and a shot of the monolithic guard tower which looms over the courtyard. As the alarm sounds, Mann cuts to a series of images that show the courtyard from a high angle. We no longer perceive the yard from the perspective of the inmates; we, instead, adopt the viewpoint of the guards, and the delimited structure of the yard is now clearly delineated. The scene then cuts to a lengthy image of an unnamed guard gazing down at Murphy from his desk in the tower. The head of the guard fills the centre foreground of the frame, while Murphy is pushed into the middle-ground, framed behind a wire fence. Now we can see the entire space of the yard, the race track looks surprisingly small, and the physical restriction placed on Murphy's movement is emphasised – before, we could not see the edges of the race track, but now they become apparent, and we realise that Murphy was, in fact, moving around a narrow area of land. This tension between internal freedom and material constraint will come to the fore later in the narrative.

Although *The Jericho Mile* remains the only Mann film set entirely within prison walls, many of his later works focus on ex-convicts whose mentalities have been irrevocably shaped by the time they spent on the inside. *Thief*, *Heat*, *Public Enemies* and *Blackhat* all focus on ex-convicts who view the time they spent in jail as being instrumental in shaping their worldviews. They tend to be incapable of entirely breaking out of the behaviours they developed behind bars even after being released into the outside world. Across Mann's body of work, there are two differing approaches to surviving in prison demonstrated by his protagonists. Some spend their time in incarceration focused entirely on planning the life they intend to lead once they make it back into the civilian population. Others adapt to incarceration by committing to a rigorous self-improvement programme. Frank, the protagonist of *Thief*, Mann's follow-up to *The Jericho Mile*, exhibits the former trait. He feels that a massive amount of time has been 'robbed' from him by the state, and so, after release, he feels pressured to pursue his life goals as fast as possible. As we later discover, Frank devoted the bulk of his time in jail to creating an idyllic vision of what his life would be like following his release – he externalises this fantasy through a makeshift collage composed on a piece of card, depicting a suburban tract home, a beautiful wife, a sports car, and a child. As he explains to his prospective love interest Jesse: 'I have run out of time. I have lost it all. So, I can't work fast enough to catch up. I can't run fast enough to catch up. The only thing that catches me up is doing my magic act.' *Thief* illustrates the destructive consequences that result when an ex-con systematically forces others to fit into a narcissistic fantasy crafted by a single individual in isolation. Frank's erratic behaviour in *Thief* is primarily caused by his determination to actualise this dream, which leads him to manipulate and mislead those around him with little consideration of the long-term consequences which may result from the shortcuts he's taking.

Blackhat's Hathaway belongs to the second category. After being furloughed by the FBI in exchange for helping them to hunt down a cyber-terrorist, Hathaway states that he accepted the sentence given to him by the US government (he, after all, did breach the law by breaking into the mainframes of several financial institutions, and never makes any attempt to claim innocence), but it was always of the utmost importance to him that he had control over the interests and pursuits he devoted his time to while constrained in his small holding cell. During the few glimpses we get of Hathaway's time in prison, we see him exercising, listening to music, and reading books on post-structuralist philosophy and new media theory. Later in the narrative, Hathaway describes these actions as components of an intensive training program he devised to expand his mental and physical capacities. In doing so, Hathaway explained, he altered his perception of his imprisonment from being a punishment to being an opportunity to better himself. This was Hathaway's strategy to avoid the de-humanising effects of incarceration. As Hathaway phrases it: 'I did the crime, I'm doing the time. Time isn't doing me. I do my own time, not the institution's. See, to hold on to who you are in there, you dedicate yourself to your program. You work out on your body and your mind.' In *The Jericho Mile*, the difference between these two perspectives is thematised through the ideological split between Murphy and Stiles. If Stiles, like Frank, exerts all his mental energy on pining for the civilian life he'll return to upon release, then Murphy, like Hathaway, adapts to prison life more effectively by treating his incarceration as an opportunity to work on his self-improvement. Because he focuses so vigorously on his chosen sport, Murphy feels as though he is reclaiming his agency. Hathaway's stated ambition to 'do my own time, not the institution's' feels as though it could have been said by Murphy to describe his philosophical outlook.

Murphy offers a fascinating prototype of the Mannian loner. Though he evidently exhibits many characteristics associated with these later protagonists because he spends the entire narrative in prison, he never experiences the tension between dogged self-determination and participation within mainstream society that these other characters do. While characters like Frank and Hathaway are tasked with the difficult task of re-entering the civilian population, Murphy has long accepted that he will never leave Folsom. He openly acknowledges that he has committed pre-meditated first-degree murder and is adamant that he will not apologise for his decision. He firmly believes that this act was morally justified: he killed his abusive father after finding out that he was sexually assaulting his stepsister on a regular basis. The murder was not an act of passion, perpetrated in the heat of the moment. Murphy knew that he would receive life imprisonment if he committed this crime. He carefully weighed the consequences he would inevitably face against his sense of moral duty to protect his stepsister from further harm. Although he asserts that the murder was absolutely necessary, Murphy never tries to appeal his sentence. Murphy made the decision entirely on his own terms, and he now wants to deal with the repercussions on his own terms. He rebuffs all attempts by the prison psychologist, Dr Bill Janowski (Geoffrey Lewis), to make him confess remorse over the crime and scoffs at the idea that the prison system can 'rehabilitate' him. As Murphy asserts during a heated exchange: 'I am convicted, murder one. I did it. Now, I am doing my own time. I mess with no one. No one messes with me. I did what I did. It's over. That's it.' Like many later Mann protagonists, he manages to cope with life in prison by devoting himself entirely, body and soul, to honing a particular skill. But, unlike many of the others, he never views this skill as something that may have practical application in the outside world.

The only social bond that Murphy has with another human being is his friendship with Stiles, who occupies a neighbouring cell and shares Murphy's reluctance to integrate into the prison gang system. Murphy views gangs as offering only a false illusion of community and camaraderie, and that committing to any one of them would betray the individualist ethos which he has adopted to survive life behind bars (it should be noted that, although the gang run by Dr D is portrayed as mercenary, nefarious and destructive, the film's overall treatment of prison sub-cultures is more multifaceted than Murphy's absolutely cynical view of them, as Mann recognises that, in some instances, these groups provide a vital sense of belonging and a space in which the individual's prized cultural traditions and rituals may be articulated). On the other hand, Stiles disengages from the gang system because he does not see himself as being part of the inmate population. Stiles is never truly 'present' during his time in prison; his thoughts are perpetually directed towards his idealised idea of what his life was like and his vision of what it will be like again after his release. Murphy makes a conscious choice to reject the hierarchal communities which structure the inmate community. On the other hand, Stiles drifts amongst the different sub-cultures but is not interested in asserting his allegiance to any of them.

Murphy and Stiles, therefore, employ vastly different techniques to cope with the monotony and isolation of prison life. Whereas Stiles keeps himself sane by directing his attention entirely towards the world outside, Murphy prefers to ignore the existence of an external world altogether, focusing his attention intensely on the perfection of a single task. Stiles fills his cell with material reminders of his previous life: photos, letters, and trinkets. Murphy's cell, in contrast, is completely plain: the only item adorning its blank blue walls is a single exercise bar stretching across the top of the space. His intense, unwavering commitment to his 'program', to borrow Hathaway's terminology, allows Murphy to block out the outside world; he does not have to think about all he is missing out on and all he has left behind if he can keep his mind occupied on a particular activity. When the prison mail is delivered, Stiles is ecstatic to receive a letter from his wife informing him that his new baby has been born; she includes new photos to add to his collage. Stiles re-reads the letter incessantly, imagines the future he will share with his family, and shows the images to the other inmates, indicating Stiles' reliance on personal relationships and emotional attachments. In contrast, Murphy is captured in a series of one-shots as he performs a series of exercises alone in his cell. Murphy even goes as far as to rudely push Stiles away when he comes to tell him about his good news. Murphy refuses to gaze at the photo, telling him, 'I'm warming down, man.'

The framing emphasises the narrowness of Murphy's world, but also his agility and freedom of movement within these confines; Stiles, in contrast, refuses to accept the limitations forced on him by his situation and loses himself in the illusion of escape represented by the photo.

From Murphy's perspective, Stiles' obsession with the outside world can only bring him pain. The visits he receives from his family are the highlight of Stiles' existence, but they only occur once every three months, and he must relive the agony of separation every time they leave. Stiles claims to love receiving updates from his family, but they also serve as painful reminders of all the significant events he is unable to participate in – he finds hearing about milestones in his young daughter's life especially painful, knowing that he wasn't present to witness them in person and that they can never be experienced again. The overwhelming suffering that Stiles feels as a result of his obsessive fixation on all the blessings his captivity is preventing him from enjoying only reinforces Murphy's assurance that a man must detach from all emotional ties if he hopes to maintain his sanity while in jail. The contrast between the two inmates' worldviews is underlined during a highly charged verbal confrontation that occurs close to the film's midpoint. Frustrated with listening to Stiles complain about his inability to see his wife for another three months, Murphy snaps at him: 'If you can't handle the time, don't do the crime.' Murphy takes pride in his ability to accept responsibility for his previous actions, which, in his eyes, necessitates dealing with the punishment without protest; as Stiles bemoans the 'unfairness' of his sentence, Murphy believes that he is failing to take the same level of responsibility, instead choosing to wallow in pointless self-pity. Stiles' retort, however, makes it clear that he views Murphy's stoic disconnection not as a sign of emotional strength but of thinly veiled vulnerability: 'That's our difference. You don't need nobody. You run until you zone out like a glue-sniffer, till you can't talk. Until then you tired enough to get some sleep. Until the next day when you gotta go through the same thing again. No, Mr Murphy, you don't need nobody [...] You gotta be the luckiest man alive.' Murphy has cut himself off not only from the prison population – refusing to take part in team sports, gang affiliations, and prison jobs – but also from all pre-existing relationships on the outside. Although his resistance to submitting to the demands of the corrupt authorities is admirable, the extent to which he blocks out those who may potentially hurt him means that, in Stiles' viewpoint, he is also blocking out those who may potentially bring him emotionally satisfaction. Stiles' description of Murphy as 'the luckiest man alive' is deeply ironic – for Stiles, to be alive means opening himself up to the pleasure *and* the pain of engaging with loved ones. To completely cut himself off would be unthinkable, even if his physical separation from them causes him grief.

We learn almost nothing of Murphy's upbringing, education, or career. Even though he clearly felt a deep connection to his stepsister at some point earlier in his life, there is no indication that they remained in contact after his sentencing. Murphy consciously throws himself into the immediate moment with such intensity that he feels no need to dwell on his past or future. Janowski indicates that Murphy once demonstrated a far more erratic, highly charged personality when he comments that a previous psychologist wrote in Murphy's file: 'explosions of violence, volatile personality [...] Indicates potential for explosive rage.' This description seems like a far cry from the subdued behaviour he exhibits during the events depicted throughout the narrative. Murphy does not refute any of these claims, nor does he say he has reformed any aspect of his personality; he simply reiterates that he does not believe in counselling, with the implicit message that any issues he has had in the past have been dealt with by himself – without any outside help. Mann's portrayal of Murphy is not straightforward: his determination to resist the efforts by prison officials to break his spirit so that he may be a more pliable, manipulable member of the community is treated as admirable (as the remainder of this chapter will illustrate, these officials are acting solely out of self-interest), though it is also clear that Murphy's total disconnection from everybody around him takes a heavy emotional toll.

Notably, it is Janowski who first notices Murphy's aptitude for sprinting, instantly recognising that Murphy may hold the potential to be a serious, professional-level athlete; knowing that Murphy may be reluctant to partake in organised sport, he convinces the warden Earl Gulliver (Billy Green Bush) to start secretly recording his times and comparing them to national records. Amazed at just how rapidly Murphy can run the mile distance, Janowski, in collaboration with Gulliver and the state track and field coach Jerry Beloit, hatch a plan to enter him into the upcoming Olympics trials. In their eyes, entering Murphy into the US Olympic team will be mutually beneficial for the inmate *and* the institution: it would provide considerable positive press and financial reward for the prison, plus offer Murphy the opportunity to gain some recognition for his gift. Gulliver soon becomes enamoured with the idea of Murphy's triumph on the field becoming internationally recognised as evidence of the potential of Folsom to rehabilitate dangerous criminals – this is ironic, considering that Murphy repeatedly rejects narratives of rehabilitation, and that, even if Murphy did repudiate his crimes, he would still be forced to carry out a life sentence.

Just as Murphy refuses to accept advice from the prison counsellor, he also refuses to take tips from the visiting coach. After easily beating a group of professional sprinters brought in from the state team, Beloit speaks to Murphy in private and is baffled to hear that Murphy has never subscribed to any conventional athletics routine. 'You gonna teach me how to run right, professor?' Murphy asks mockingly, fully confident that he is a more proficient athlete than Beloit and any of the athletes he's previously trained. Beloit is an intelligent man and attempts to defuse Murphy's hostility by telling him that his ambition as an athletics trainer is to bring out the best in his pupils, not to tell them what to do: 'There's no right. It's what's right for you, what's natural. Your own style. We're just going to take you to a faster, stronger more powerful place.' What Beloit does not understand is that not only is Murphy already performing at the highest level he possibly can, but that, for Murphy, running is fundamentally an expression of his selfhood.

He tells Beloit that he has never followed professional advice, has no careerist ambitions, and does not even pay attention to how fast he's going. He managed to hone his skill purely by going into the yard and running every day without fail. Statistics and records mean nothing to him. If Murphy were to compromise in this regard and allow another individual to dictate how he practices this craft, he would lose interest in it and no longer be able to perform.

Janowski, Gulliver and Beloit cannot comprehend Murphy's insistence that he does not require external validation to justify the large amount of time he has dedicated to running because they have no idea what it feels like to be facing a life prison sentence. Murphy does not practice his chosen sport to gain wealth, attract popularity, or win medals. He conducts his athletics purely for his own benefit, to give his life a sense of purpose while he's behind bars. But he does not need anybody else to recognise that this pursuit is purposeful, and he does not need to receive a material reward to prove that this pursuit is purposeful. The free men are embedded in a culture that privileges material gain above all else, so they see no point in Murphy devoting so much of his time to perfecting a craft unless it can generate money or social capital (It is no coincidence that the first shot of the outside world depicts a woman on a game show being given increasing handfuls of dollar bills). But such trappings have little value for Murphy, a man who has firmly resigned himself to the fact that he will spend the rest of his life locked up in a place where he does not truly own any possessions and the standard notions of respectability and social mobility do not exist. All that Murphy has (and all that Murphy will ever have) is his integrity and freedom to determine his own values. Murphy feels pressured to go along with the training at first, but he always regards Janowski, Gulliver and Beloit with scepticism. The emphasis they place on material reward is fundamentally opposed to his own focus on personal, self-defined fulfilment, and they view one another through a lens of mutual incomprehension. This tension grows as Murphy is increasingly asked to compromise his own carefully determined principles, reaching a final breaking point when he is requested to do something which, for him, is completely unthinkable: to ensure that he receives a place on the Olympic team, he must publicly apologise for the murder of his father. If Murphy were to give in to this demand, he would guarantee himself a shot at Olympic glory, winning the admiration of the prison staff the mainstream population. But, he would also have to tell an egregious lie about the most significant incident that has occurred in his entire life. To portray himself as a remorseful prisoner looking for redemption would be fundamentally antithetical to the way he actually views himself, and he bravely refuses to comply with this request. Murphy can tolerate the physical restriction of prison, but he cannot stand the possibility.

While Murphy becomes entangled in a plot by the prison staff to exploit his skill on the field for their own material gain, the threat to Stiles comes from another part of the prison community. Noticing the depth of Stiles' desperation to see his family, Dr D (Brian Dennehy), the leader of a highly powerful, white supremacist gang who presides over several illegal operations inside the jail, including drug running and contraband trading, manipulates his emotional fragility to draw him into a deal which predictably turns sour: Dr D offers to use his influence amongst the prison staff to get Stiles' conjugal visit moved forward to the next weekend. In return, Dr D wants Stiles to agree to carry out an unspecified favour for him in the future. Stiles is naturally suspicious of the offer, but Dr D breaks down his defences by disingenuously appealing to some vague sense of camaraderie which, he says, all inmates should feel towards one another. 'Do I look like I'm the FBI, baby?' Dr D asks Stiles, when he expresses his reluctance to enter an 'open-ended jailhouse obligation.' 'What's wrong with you?' Dr D continues, 'If we can't help each other do easy time who is? The man?' This line of rhetoric is deeply ironic, as Dr D is closely aligned with the prison guards, offering them material bribes in return for their silence over the transgressions he commits on the inside. He is, therefore, aligned more closely with those in power than he is with his fellow inmates. The guards turn a blind eye to Dr D's offences not only because he offers them monetary bribes but also because the racist ideology he subscribes to is endemic within the official American justice system (this aspect of *The Jericho Mile*, it should be noted, remains fairly under-developed, but it prefigures more complex explorations of the connections between material power and race in *The Last of the Mohicans* (1992) and *Ali*).

Stiles never truly places his trust in Dr D, but his insatiable desire to see his wife as soon as possible overwhelms his reason, and he reluctantly agrees to the proposition. Stiles is so blinded by his excitement for the visit that he does not think to ask how Dr D will organise this visit, nor does he enquire further about the nature of the task he will be expected to perform in return. Moreover, Stiles does not consider the fact that that his alliance with Dr D will be perceived as a betrayal by the other African American members of the prison community. Branded a traitor, Stiles is ostracised by the black community once word of this agreement spreads, who express no sympathy for his burning desire to reconnect with his loved ones on the outside. 'All you got in here are brothers, and the only brothers you need are black,' a member of the Black Brotherhood tells Stiles, in a moment that seems to make him realise just how offensive his actions have been and how misguided he was to assume that he could accept this deal without suffering extremely negative consequences.

And, sure enough, the promised conjugal visit turns out to be a ruse. Arriving at their designated meeting spot, Stiles is not greeted by his wife but by a prostitute hired by Dr D's men. He then realises that he has been followed closely by a member of Dr D's gang, who whispers to Stiles, 'Make like she's your woman,' and then hands a rolled-up wad of banknotes to the prostitute. It becomes clear to Stiles that Dr D has fundamentally misunderstood the nature of Stiles' pining for his visit; he believes that Stiles was only interested in sexual release and that it doesn't matter who he receives this sexual release from. For Dr D, sex can be completely divorced from emotional attachment, so it should not matter to Stiles if this encounter is transparently transactional. The hooker then role-plays as though she is Stiles' wife, embracing him and then telling him to 'make like you believe it' – echoing the words of Dr D's henchman – to avoid rousing the suspicion of the nearby guards. She then tells Stiles that, after they have had sex, she has been instructed to give him two balloons of smack for him to transport inside the jail – and it becomes clear that this is the aforementioned favour Dr D expects him to carry out. The simulacrum of affection offered by the hooker will, Stiles recognises, only heighten the agony of his familial separation, and the fact that he is being asked to act as a pawn in their narcotics scheme at the very same time as the visit makes explicit just how much contempt Dr D truly has for him. Stiles refuses to play ball and storms away from the encounter. This is Stiles' forceful assertion of self, as he refuses to submit to Dr D's nefarious scheme despite his awareness that Dr D will likely seek to exact revenge on him if he does not fulfil his end of the bargain.

When Murphy finds out about this incident, he expresses admiration for Stiles' resistance to Dr D's scheme and acknowledges that urgent action must be taken if Stiles is to escape the gang's wrath. Believing that Stiles will be killed if he remains in the main prison population, Murphy hastily devises an escape plan. Murphy tells Stiles that if he makes a dash for the guard's tower immediately after the lunch bell rings – while the other prisoners are making the way to the cafeteria and the wardens are distracted – he may stand a chance of breaking out of the facility undetected. Murphy recognises that this is a risky idea, so he promises to accompany Stiles to the exit to provide with protection if he is spotted by an adversary along the way. Due to the extensive influence of Dr D's gang, however, word of the escape is soon passed on to Dr D through an unspecified eavesdropper, and the plan is sabotaged: an inmate working on postal delivery duty places a lock on the door of Murphy's cell, preventing him from joining Stiles in his bolt to the exit. As this tragic chain of events unfolds, Mann cross-cuts between three points of action that occur concurrently: Stiles running through the packed prison corridors; Murphy desperately trying to break the padlock off; and two members of Dr D's gang waiting near the entrance of the guard tower to ambush Stiles. When Murphy finally breaks out of his cell, it is already too late – Stiles's route has been intercepted and he has fallen into the hands of Dr D's henchmen. The motion of Murphy flinging open his cell door is edited so that it directly rhymes with the motion of one of the attacker's knife being pulled out of its holster, implicitly connecting Stiles' death to Murphy's failure. Once Stiles has been cornered, little struggle takes place. He is immediately held against a mesh wire fence by two assailants and stabbed multiple times in the back.

Stiles' death is framed in a lengthy wide shot, a mesh wire fence creating a physical barrier in the foreground. Stiles appears head-on as he is penetrated, and Mann lingers on the sight of his body slowly sinking to the floor while the perpetrators run out of frame. This staging lends Stiles' death a great sense of emotional weight. Mann does not allow the viewer to feel any vicarious sense of excitement – he never uses any shot that would align our perspective with Stiles' killers. Instead, he emphasises only the sense of defeat that overcomes Stiles as he realises that he will never see his family again. Mann then cuts across the 90-degree lines as Murphy finally makes it to the scene. Stiles' bloodied corpse is sprawled across the frame's foreground as Murphy enters in the background. A despondent Murphy walks across the Z-axis to the spot where Stiles is lying face-down on the ground, and he respectfully turns his body over. As he does this, Murphy notices that the bag of family photos Stiles was carrying with him was punctured during the attack. Mann cuts to an insert shot of the images splayed on the ground, many of them crumpled and stained with Stiles' blood. It's a haunting image, encapsulating the desire for an idealised familial life so powerful it led Stiles to risk everything he had to pursue it. This motif of still photographs representing idyllic but unattainable escape from adverse conditions will reappear throughout Mann's later films: in *Thief*, Frank visualises his dream suburban life on a collage composed of picture elements he has extracted from magazines, flyers, and personal photographs; in *Collateral*, Max keeps a postcard of the Maldives islands in his cab that he can gaze at and fantasise about a less hectic life, whenever the pressures of his profession start to suffocate him.

Murphy is so incensed by Stiles' murder that he takes it upon himself to exact revenge against Dr D. Motivated by a combination of grief, guilt and anger, Murphy makes the fateful choice to represent Folsom in try-outs for the Olympic team, on the condition that he be granted half an hour of unsupervised time in the metal works room in return. Murphy uses this opportunity to seize the satchel of money that Dr D keeps stashed inside, dump it on the ground of the courtyard in full view of the gang, and ceremoniously set it on fire. This is not only an act of vengeance against the men who took his companion's life, it is also a forceful symbolic expression of his contempt towards the prison's gang culture and the all-consuming lust for power which turns men like Dr D into monsters. An enraged Dr D repeatedly tells Murphy 'I'm talking to a dead man,' while Mann cuts to images of the burning cash. For Murphy, Stiles' murder reaffirms several beliefs that he has held since the beginning of the film: that for an individual to compromise their own sense of right and wrong, as Stiles did, can only lead to tragedy; that all figures of power must be distrusted on principle; and that the single-minded pursuit of money will corrupt an individual's soul beyond repair. The image of Murphy burning the notes underlines this final point in a particularly potent way.

It is ironic, then, that Murphy can only make this bold statement by agreeing to attend the Olympic trials – an act he has been avoiding for the entire narrative and one that is fundamentally at odds with his principles. However, Murphy can only stomach the arrangement for a short period of time, as when he attends the organised meeting with the Olympics board it becomes painfully clear to him that they intend to exploit him for their own material gain, in much the same way that Stiles had been exploited by Dr D's gang. The board inform Murphy, bluntly, and with Gulliver and Janowski present, that the corporate sponsors of the US team have expressed unease about being associated with a convicted felon currently serving time. However, they add that their sponsor's concerns may be quelled if Murphy were to announce, publicly, that he regrets his crime and that, if he were placed in the same situation again, he would not have murdered his father. This, the head of the board claims, would illustrate conclusively that Murphy had been indeed 'rehabilitated'. But, for Murphy, the prospect of transforming his life story into a false tale of redemption to appease a board of sponsors is unacceptable. Equally unacceptable is the claim by Janowski, made sitting at the same table, that Murphy should not be forced to answer this question because his mental faculties were compromised at the time of the murder – and, Janowski asserts, this meant that Murphy was not truly responsible for the crime. Murphy knows this to be untrue, as he has asserted time and time again that the killing of his father was a conscious decision that he still views as being ethically sound. Murphy is a man who has been stripped of his freedom, of his possessions and any hope of a future outside of captivity. If he were to sacrifice his integrity at this moment, he would lose the only thing left in his life that holds value to him. 'I hate what happened,' Murphy tells the board, 'but I will not repudiate what happened, and I will not repudiate what happened because all I have is my name and my face. In the same place, in the same time in the same conditions I would blow him away all over again.' Murphy steadfastly refuses to allow his image to be warped into a corporate product for easy consumption, even though he knows that this assertion of his authentic self will put an end to his athletic career before it has even started.

And so Murphy ends up just as he began: doomed to remain locked in Folsom for the rest of his life, alone, fine-tuning his sprinting skills for no other reason than because it's what gives him the sense of purpose he needs to survive imprisonment. Murphy has achieved no concrete goals – his athletic career will never take off, he has built no significant relationships and his sentence remains the same. The only thing that Murphy has accomplished is a more intricate understanding of his own fundamental values. To emphasise the circularity of the narrative, the final sequence of *The Jericho Mile* is a direct parallel of its opening: a fast-paced montage of varied activities being practised by the inmates in the courtyard. Once again, shots of Murphy racing around the track are interspersed with these snapshots of disparate pastimes. However, this time, the other men gradually stop what they're doing and gather around the track to cheer Murphy on. Murphy himself does not notice their presence – indeed, Mann frames much of the sequence in tight profile close-ups of Murphy's face, which abstract the crowd into a hazy blur of colour. After finishing his lap of the track, Murphy pulls out a stopwatch and checks his time. He sees that he has beaten the recorded time accomplished by the athlete who was selected to represent the US in the Olympics after Murphy was disqualified. This is the first instance in which Murphy records his own running time in the film, and it may seem to be antithetical to his stated belief that he does not view his sprinting in competitive terms. However, rather than celebrating this significant feat, Murphy symbolically tosses the watch at the wall of the prison, causing it to break irreparably. Murphy thus acknowledges that he *can* meet the standards set up by professional athletes, but he is uninterested in compromising his ideals to join the professional field of organised sports. Murphy's official time and his ranking amongst other runners mean nothing to him – ultimately, he and the other prisoners recognise, too, that the values of personal integrity and self-determination are of greater importance than any monetary achievements or public recognition that Murphy may have garnered had he stuck with the Olympic program. As the prisoners gather around Murphy in applause, we witness a personal victory of the kind that is rare to find in Mann's cinema. However, this victory is an inherently fleeting one. There has been no substantial change in the structure or the running of the prison system, and Murphy's situation remains the same as it was at the start of the narrative. Murphy knows that he may serve the remainder of his sentence on his own terms, and takes a certain degree of comfort in that knowledge, but he still remains trapped inside the institution and is haunted by the sense of melancholy that his solitary lifestyle entails. Mann undercuts the upbeat tone of this final sequence by closing the film on a freeze-frame of Murphy's face, giving us a bittersweet reminder that, that his life will always be defined by physical confinement and stasis.

I opened this chapter by arguing that *The Jericho Mile* deserves to be considered as a serious work of cinematic art in its own right rather than a minor footnote in an otherwise substantial oeuvre. This close textual analysis has illuminated the intricacies of Mann's handling of character, narrative, and formal design in this work, despite working within the boundaries of the television studio system. However, I feel that it is necessary to point out that many of the themes touched upon within Mann's feature debut would go on to be revisited in greater depth in the director's later features. The impact of incarceration on an individual's psyche is treated with more insight in *Thief* and *Blackhat*; the devastating effects of self-imposed isolation are handled with greater emotional impact in *Heat* and *Collateral*; *Ali* and *The Last of Mohicans* are more nuanced in their portrayal of systemic racial oppression; *The Insider* and *Public Enemies* are more complex in their critiques of the attempts of the US government to force perceived dissidents into submissions. So, while I reiterate that *The Jericho Mile* deserves to be appreciated on its own terms, it is fascinating to witness how quickly Mann develops his style and fleshes out these early preoccupations.

Frontier of the Dawn:
Thief (1981)

Although *The Jericho Mile* contains the seeds of the aesthetic and thematic interests that would come to define Mann's career, *Thief* represents a significant step forward in terms of formal ambition and thematic sophistication. Following the significant critical success of *The Jericho Mile*, Mann found himself in high demand. Reportedly, he received over twenty financially lucrative offers from enthusiastic television producers who longed to secure his talents for projects already in development. Mann, however, had grown stifled by the restrictions of the television film and set his sights on the silver screen. Eschewing the offers given to him by TV execs, the filmmaker used this newfound position of prestige to helm his passion project – a film based on the life of real-life jewel thief John Seybold, who had recounted his exploits in the book *The Home Invaders: Confessions of a Cat Burglar* (1975). Oddly, though *Thief* is now held in far higher esteem than its predecessor, the reaction to the film at the time of its release was much more muted that the ecstatic praise that greeted *The Jericho Mile*. Although far from a total failure, the film was not a massive commercial sensation upon release. It earned a modest $11.5 million at the box office against a $5.5 million budget, which was respectable business, but did not indicate the enormous box office draw that Mann would become a decade later, with more epically scaled projects like *The Last of the Mohicans* and *Heat*. For the most part, the critical reactions to the film were modest, with the consensus being that *Thief* was a handsomely mounted, if insubstantial, theatrical debut that cemented Mann's status as a distinctive young stylist – though who had still to live up to his full potential. Gary Arnold's assessment for *The Washington Post* encapsulates the attitude with which reviewers greeted *Thief*: '[T]he new crime melodrama *Thief* promises to be a remarkably evocative and stylish feat of moviemaking. Impressed by the obvious graphic and kinetic flair demonstrated by director Michael Mann and his crew, you'd prefer to suppress the suspicion that this dynamic style, paced to a throbbing rock theme by Tangerine Dream, could be the prelude to a thematic letdown. Ultimately, a rude awakening is inescapable.' In the decades that followed, however, *Thief* has grown in reputation and is now rightly considered a classic of 1980s genre cinema.

In many ways, *Thief*'s protagonist, referred to only as Frank, expresses a comparable philosophical perspective to Murphy's: he is firmly committed to an ethos of individualism and believes that it is of the utmost importance that he lives his life entirely according to his own, self-determined philosophy of being. However, this commitment to a solitary lifestyle leads to an unshakeable sense of loneliness and dissatisfaction. This internal friction between Frank's need to exert complete control over every aspect of his own life and his desire to forge meaningful interpersonal connections causes a sense of discontent that he tries to resolve over the course of the narrative. However, the way he goes about achieving this goal is misguided as it requires him to give up his agency over his work and become indebted to a tyrannical authority figure who wishes to exploit his considerable gifts for his own personal monetary gain. Frank ultimately realises that, despite the superficial material rewards that a life of suburban affluence may offer him, it is fundamentally opposed to his deeper ideological values – and, like Murphy, he makes the conscious choice to return to his earlier state of being.

Like Murphy, Frank is a highly dexterous individual who has devoted enormous time to perfecting his craft. Frank also takes considerable pride in his talent and believes that he must work alone, lest the purity of the craft and the lifestyle he has carefully cultivated be jeopardised. Although Frank often has to cooperate with other people when conducting his robberies, he keeps himself emotionally distant from them. He takes on associates on a temporary basis, keeping details about his private life concealed so that he avoids becoming entangled in long-standing working relationships which may potentially make it easier for the authorities to track him down. The robberies occur in silence, with each man pulling off his role perfectly like cogs in a well-oiled machine. As an independent jewel thief, Frank's all-consuming passion may not have the legitimacy of Murphy's, but he too operates according to a strict moral code. He avoids committing acts of violence, unless it is absolutely necessary to prevent violence being inflicted upon himself, will only target institutions that will not be substantially affected by the loss of funds, and while conducting heists, he will not commit home break-ins. During his first meeting with mafia boss Leo, Frank keeps his guard up, explaining his distrust of syndicates: 'I am self-employed. I don't deal with egos […] So what the fuck do I have to work for you for?' Frank, like Murphy, knows that tying himself to a wider organisation will require him to sacrifice his autonomy over his work and become subordinate to others – and so he consciously avoids becoming ensnared in such a system.

Frank increasingly feels the pressure to acquiesce, however, as he discovers that it is becoming near-impossible to maintain his individualist approach to his professional life in the face of Leo's insatiable ambition to monopolise the city's criminal sphere. Leo's sprawling, hugely powerful crime syndicate increasingly branches out into all areas of illegal activity in Chicago over the course of the film, and it subsumes nearly all petty thieves and independent operations as it does so. Frank and Leo are diametrically opposed in terms of their attitude towards criminal activity. Whereas Frank views it as a necessity to be an outsider, live off the grid, and position himself in opposition to 'official' forms of state power, Leo aligns himself with the establishment. Leo's deep connection to the establishment is evidenced by the fact that he owns a large share of the shopping mall – the ultimate centre of late capitalist consumer culture – and holds influence over other government institutions such as adoption and real estate agencies. While Frank has trained himself to become a master of his craft, performing meticulous physical labour at every job he takes on, Leo operates his criminal enterprise as though he were the CEO of a large corporation. He hires underlings to do the practical work, filling his own time with the management of these workers and the money they gain through their labour.

Frank always regards Leo and his offer of a partnership with a sense of scepticism, but he naively agrees to strike up a deal in the hopes that he can amass a considerable sum of money in a short span of time, which he then plans to use to fund the dream life he envisioned while incarcerated. Frank devoted his time behind bars to building up a mental image of the ideal life he hoped to build for himself after his release. Visually represented by a makeshift collage pieced together by Frank out of 'found' images, this fantasy appears somewhat generic, a familiar suburban idyll consisting of a doting wife, white picket fence, and child to raise in his own image. What is most disconcerting about Frank's obsession with constructing this life is that he will not allow it to happen organically. Unlike *The Jericho Mile*'s Stiles, Frank does not fall in love with somebody and then envision a life with them; he visualises a fantasy and then searches for somebody he can mould to fit this vision. When Frank chooses to fixate on Jessie, a newly single diner waitress, we get the impression that he is not truly interested in her as an individual, but as an idealised embodiment of his dream woman. He proposes the idea of embarking on this suburban idyll with her very early into their courtship and she, wrapped up in the intensity of the moment, impulsively agrees. Yet, there is little sense of true communication between them throughout the film. He constantly lies and withholds important details of his life from her, heightening the impression that he is not interested in having a true life partner so much as he is eager to attach himself to anybody who may assist in the actualisation of his fantasy. What Frank fails to consider, however, is just how difficult it will be to escape the clutches of Leo's gang. After conducting a large heist for Leo at the mid-point of the narrative, Frank reaches the high point of his emotional arc. He has made enough money to retire to the life of domestic bliss he envisioned while in prison, has a new family, and appears to have broken free of Leo's control. But Leo is not content to allow Frank to enjoy his retirement. He soon makes an attempt to coerce Frank to carry out more jobs for him, threatening to take away all the comforts of Frank's suburban life if he refuses. Realising the extent to which he has surrender his autonomy to Leo, Frank knows that the only possible course of action is to gradually cut himself free from the relationships, possessions, and professional ties he spent the first half of the film developing. Thus, like Murphy, Frank essentially ends up in the same situation he was in at the beginning of the film. After sending Jessie and their adopted baby David, to another town to start afresh without him, killing Leo, and blowing up the car dealership he used to launder money, Frank returns to his solitary life of petty thievery. Like Murphy, Frank has achieved no material goals; only a more robust comprehension of himself and his personal values, a more refined sense of purpose, and the ability to lead his life exactly the way he wants to.

To emphasise the cyclical nature of this arc, *Thief*, like *The Jericho Mile*, is bookended by images that mirror one another. The film opens in an alleyway at dusk. The only illumination is provided by the headlights of a car, which creeps slowly toward the camera. The vehicle halts, and Frank walks across the foreground of the frame to step into the passenger seat. Neither Frank nor the man behind the wheel (who we later discover is getaway driver, Joe (Hal Frank)), are clearly visible; both are shrouded in shadow. The men do not exchange any pleasantries, though the ease with which they work together indicates that they are pursuing a shared goal. Without missing a beat, the car moves onward. Mann's camera tracks with it as the car rounds a bend and heads onto the main road. The camera now remains fixed on a striking one-point perspective as the car speeds into the distance. The image now becomes more heavily illuminated: two parallel rows of streetlamps stretching across the top part of the frame are reflected in the rainwater lining the road below. As Frank speeds towards the horizon, the mood expressed is one of hope for a brighter, better future within a gloomy and brutal environment. Simultaneously, however, Mann implicitly suggests the fragility of Frank's hopes. The light, after all, is the product of a man-made construct, an early symbol of the artificial nature of the suburban life which Frank mistakenly believes will provide him with genuine satisfaction.

Compare this opening sequence to the image that closes the film: Frank again moves from foreground to background across an empty road. This time, however, Frank is on foot and the streetlamps are missing – rendering the image so dark that, as Frank moves away from the camera, he becomes barely visible. This time the camera doesn't remain fixed in place. It slowly pans upwards, coming to frame Frank at a high angle as he walks. Not only is the light eradicated in this sequence, but the horizon is also no longer visible in the composition. Frank now appears to be moving along a flat stretch of grey road. All sense of optimism has been removed from the scene; all that remains is a sense of futility and dejection.

Frank's first heist is a bravura piece of filmmaking: a near-silent montage that illustrates – in painstaking detail – the vigorous physical effort involved in breaking into a jewel vault. Throughout the sequence, the three members of Frank's crew (himself, Joe and Barry (Jim Belushi)) are in separate locations but work in unison; so adept are they at assuming their professional roles that they feel no need to confer through verbal communication: Joe waits in the car, monitoring radio feeds to check for police scanners; Barry dismantles the alarm system from the roof; and Frank drills through the entrance of the metal safe. The men operate in a highly methodical manner. Each one's action is dependent on the work of the others, such that a minor slip up or delay on the part of any one of them would derail the entire operation. We learn nothing about the backgrounds of these men during this sequence; they are defined by their immediate actions and their contribution to the job at hand. To pull off the heist, these men must divorce themselves from their emotions and focus entirely on the highly specified task that each one has been given. Appropriately, Mann devotes as much attention to the equipment which enables these men to perform their jobs as to the people themselves.

The lack of friendly conversation between the men during or after the heist reinforces Frank's view of his occupation as an essentially solitary pursuit. Like the athletic sessions depicted throughout *The Jericho Mile*, the process of safe-cracking is portrayed here as an activity that one partakes in alone. While the majority of American crime films treat physical processes such as dismantling alarm systems, breaking into buildings and burning metal as secondary concerns in favour of the more intellectually-orientated matters of planning the operation, evading the authorities, and dealing with difficult team members, Mann takes the opposite approach, lavishing attention on the intense, dexterous labour that such physical processes require. There is little sense of threat throughout this scene, either from the cops (although Joe keeps watch, there are no cop cars in sight and no police signal is ever picked up on his radio feed) or from within (there is never any indication that a member of the crew is going to lose his cool or betray the others, for example). Once Frank has drilled a substantial opening through the vault door, he jolts open the tiny lock mechanism contained within. Now inside the safe, Frank searches through several wooden drawers, casually tossing aside valuable jewels and bundles of banknotes. Finally, Frank finds what he is looking for: a drawer filled with small white envelopes. A more careless thief would pocket the other valuables in the safe, but Frank is single-minded in his goal. The items contained within the envelopes (later revealed to be rare diamonds) are the most valuable items in the building, and he does not want to slow down his escape by attempting to overburden himself with other, less valuable materials.

Frank places the other drawers back in place and then utters the first piece of dialogue in the film, asking 'Are you clear?' to the other men through a transmitter attached to his collar. After receiving confirmation from Joe and Barry, Frank makes a speedy exit through the back window as Barry climbs down from the roof. Joe drives the car around to meet them. Frank and Barry do not get inside the vehicle, though. They place their equipment on the backseat and then walk away in opposite directions. Frank takes off the blue jumpsuit he had been wearing during the heist to reveal nondescript street clothes underneath. He then exits the alley and passes onto the main road, where a vacant car is waiting for him. He gets inside and drives along a circuitous route to arrive at a large warehouse. Barry and Joe have already arrived, each driving a separate vehicle and taking a different path to avoid arousing suspicion. Frank leaves the getaway car inside the warehouse as Barry closes the metal door, and the men drive away in their own vehicles. The total caution and consideration demonstrated by the men as they carry out this mission – including the multiple steps they take after the completion of the robbery to ensure that they leave behind no evidence that might connect them to the scene – establishes them as seasoned professionals, capable of devoting themselves to the high-risk job at hand without being overtaken by feelings of panic or anxiety.

What is also established during this early sequence, is the significance of Chicago as a location. After the men flee the crime scene, Mann cuts to a series of tracking shots detailing the passage of Frank's car through the city. In a retrospective interview, Mann explained that the industrial structures which dominated Chicago during his childhood years were a significant influence on the film's genesis. In his own words, Mann was always fascinated by the 'imagery of those kind of cage black bridges at night and the reflection on the black pavement of the lights even before I had any idea of storing things visually or even thinking about film directing'. Mann goes on to explain that he wanted the architecture of Chicago to be an integral part of the action, as he 'wanted Frank to be seen as a rat in the machine and the city to be seen as a three-dimensional construction that he knew his way through. The way you put a lid on the city is to shoot at night because then you've got a black lid on it and then this sense of tumult was why I was interested in having lights form that pattern, taking off from how Pissarro used perspective in painting.' (Saito, 2013) *Thief*'s cityscape is a grid of jagged lines and sharp angles, an environment composed of concrete towers, bridges, motorways, and streetlamps arranged in rigid geometric arrangements. Mann's ingenious use of architecture emphasises the increasingly obsolescent nature of Frank's lifestyle. *Thief* takes place in the industrial part of the city that is rapidly being overtaken by the gentrified malls and tower blocks operated by monolithic corporations and financial empires. Frank is drawn to the margins, to the pockets of local flavour that can still be located along the outskirts of the city. Leo, in contrast, is associated with the forces of modernity subsuming anything and everything that stands in their way. This urban landscape, it should be noted, appears relatively quaint in comparison to the sprawling metropolitan dystopias that will appear in later Mann films such as *Heat*, *Miami Vice*, and *Blackhat*. In *Thief*, there still exists the possibility of separating private and public space and disappearing into areas that have not yet been gentrified.

After finishing this first heist, Frank goes to a secluded spot to enjoy a rare moment of tranquillity. It's early morning, just before sunrise. As he walks along the boardwalk, Frank is positioned small in the frame, moving across a small concrete pathway pushed into the left third of the screen. Most of the composition is occupied by the lightly undulating surface of the ocean. In the far background is a line of skyscrapers – their presence within the frame suggests that, even though they are out of mind for the moment, Frank will inevitably have to return to the city before long. At the end of the boardwalk, Frank meets with an elderly fisherman. Frank shares a pastry with him, and the two men gaze out into the open water. Mann cuts to a wide shot framed from behind the men, allowing us to share their gaze. Frank and the fisherman are silhouetted against the sea and the sky, the early morning light producing an otherworldly purple glow. It's a striking, painterly composition; the boardwalk's edge is not visible, so it appears as if the two men are suspended over the water. 'Would you look at that?' asks Frank, in awe at the natural beauty before him. 'That's magic,' the fisherman responds.

This tranquillity is soon undercut, however, as Frank then meets with a buyer at a local diner to organise the sale of the diamonds he stole from the jewellery vault. During this meeting, Frank gets a forceful reminder that the lifestyle he's leading as an independent thief is becoming increasingly precarious. After settling on a price, the buyer tells Frank that the local mafia boss has heard of his reputation and is eager to arrange a discussion with him. 'They're stand-up guys,' the buyer tells Frank, but Frank is unconvinced: 'Why do I want to meet people? If I wanted to meet people, I'd go to a fucking country club.' Frank demonstrates here that he is attracted to the material work involved in thievery itself, as well as the sense of pride he feels after successfully pulling off a job; he does not have time for the false homosocial bonds and internal dramas that come with crime syndicates. It is vital to Frank that he decides which jobs he takes on, how he approaches each heist, and what he does with the stolen goods after the fact. Most importantly, he wishes to evade the grip of anybody who may desire to control him. Frank wants, simply, to carry out his heists with as little interference from other people or institutions as possible. This fact is emphasised when the buyer subsequently tries to convince Frank to invest the money from the diamond sale rather than saving it, promising him that he can 'double [his] money in three weeks'. Frank rebuffs this offer, not only because he wants to avoid establishing ties to the investors who will be handling his money, but also because he wholeheartedly believes in trading his physical labour for a cash value that is equal to the amount of work he put in. Although the means through which he gains his income may not be legal, he feels that the amount of effort he puts in is proportional to the amount of value he receives for his work – and this gives him a sense of pride. An investment of the kind the buyer is talking about would involve generating a greater sum of money from an existing sum of money – an abstract mode of financial creation that Frank finds no value in. Frank is, then, a man dedicated fiercely to his own personal principles, and it is this that makes him an outsider in a social environment in which individuals are increasingly being consumed by blind greed and opportunism.

But Leo will not give up his attempt to recruit Frank so easily, and he will not be satisfied until every thief in the city is under his control, helping him to expand his personal wealth. So long as Frank is operating as an independent, Leo will consider him competition. At this stage, it is preferable for Leo to enfold Frank into his organisation rather than to forcibly despatch him, so Leo keeps building the pressure exerted on him. Soon after leaving the diner, Frank gets a call from Barry, who informs him that the diamond buyer was intercepted on the way to transport the money to Frank. It turns out that the buyer owed money to Leo, and Leo instructed one of his henchmen, a man named Attaglia (Tom Signorelli), to murder him and seize the money he was carrying to cover his outstanding debts. Frank decides to take matters into his own hands and personally track down Attaglia to collect the money he is owed. After an altercation at Attaglia's workplace, Frank demands that he return the money taken from him at a designated meeting spot later that evening. However, when Frank arrives, he finds that Leo has taken Attaglia's place. Leo, we soon learn, orchestrated this entire chain of events so that he may meet Frank face-to-face and personally offer him a role in his syndicate. This crucial negotiation scene takes place at a large parking lot by Lake Michigan. As Frank arrives, a train passes directly behind Leo, associating him with the relentless drive of technological and institutional progress which is pushing men like Frank into obsolescence. Leo represents the future of crime in Chicago, while Frank represents the past, and the currents of modernity are becoming increasingly difficult to resist. Frank is characteristically hostile during the exchange. Leo asks Frank how he is, and Frank's response is curt: 'How am I? I'm Frank.' In addition to highlighting that Frank can see past the disingenuous social niceties Leo is using to lower Frank's guard, this is a significant act of self-assertion, instantly signalling to Leo that Frank has a firm grasp of his own worth and that he will not be intimated. Leo calmly hands over the money owed to Frank and explains the many benefits that he would receive if he would accept the offer of working for the syndicate: Frank can maximise his efficiency (and his profits) as he no longer needs to scope out buildings or plan routes himself; Frank will only be given assignments that Leo knows, from extensive research, are safe bets – often, Leo points out, the owners of the valuables being robbed are working with the mafia to get funds from the insurance company; if the cops apprehend Frank, Leo will provide them with a cash bribe, ensuring that Frank never suffers any legal consequences; Frank will no longer have to pull small-scale scores, Leo only deals in heists that pull in six-figures. Leo caps off this pitch by telling Frank that if he accepts he'll be 'a millionaire in four months'.

However, Frank does not give in right away, instead repeating that 'I am doing fine. I don't deal with egos.' He recognises that taking up Leo's offer would mean becoming a cog in his operation, no longer in charge of his business but a minion who is subject to the whims of a boss. Frank's apprehension is intensified by the fact that Leo refuses to tell him who his contacts in the police force are and how he managed to get so much information on the thief's previous activities: – an early indication that any potential business relationship between them will be based on a power imbalance. The scene closes on an uncertain note. Frank remains deeply distrustful of the threat to his individuality that the syndicate represents, yet is also aware that he could use such an arrangement to materialise the vision of paradise he constructed while in prison. There are clear similarities to the scene in *The Jericho Mile* where Stiles' desire for romantic companionship spurred him to make a spurious business deal despite his major reservations about the potential consequences.

There is a jarring tonal shift between this highly portentous meeting scene and the sequence which follows: Mann cuts rapidly between images of Frank speeding down the Chicago backstreets and shots of a blues band playing Tyrone Davis' 'Turning Point' at a nearby bar where Jessie is waiting for him. Close-ups of the wheels, lights and windshield are alternated with close-ups of the bass and drum set of the band, establishing a solid sense of rhythm and giving material expression to Frank's sense of momentary joy as he anticipates meeting Jessie. This sequence also provides a welcome burst of local flavour, offering a glimpse into the subculture of blues clubs, dive bars and independently owned diners that are the heart of the city but were increasingly becoming erased by the forces of gentrification and corporatisation throughout the 1980s. Considering Frank's anxieties regarding his impending obsolescence, and his desire to remain off the grid for as long as possible, it makes sense that he would be drawn to such a locale. Jessie is initially angry when Frank arrives to their date several hours late, but the tension eases when they go to a late-night diner and discuss their respective situations. This sequence, simple in terms of staging but high in emotional intensity, introduces a recurring motif in Mann's cinema of the diner being a site of genuine interpersonal bonding. Of course, the most famous example of this is the tête-à-têtes between Hanna and McCauley in *Heat*, but we see a similar dynamic play out in *Blackhat*, *The Insider*, and *Collateral*. Perhaps the diner is such an essential location in Mann's filmography because it is a site that blurs the line between private and public space, creating the illusion of a homely, intimate environment within a commercial setting. The diners may feel as though they have privacy, but they are, in fact, within the earshot of strangers. The impermanence of the meetings that take place within the diner provides the ideal spot for the fleeting connections of the type that take precedence throughout Mann's oeuvre.

In *Thief*'s diner scene, Frank reveals his tragic backstory, his vision for the future, and the importance of Jessie to the realisation of this dream. Frank explains that to cope with the stress and loneliness of life in prison, he developed a mindset of total stoicism and self-reliance. He says that, to survive on the inside, he had to reach a mental state where he 'did not care about anything. I didn't care about me; I didn't care about nothing.' Frank felt the need to suppress so many of his emotions and natural impulses while in prison, so he directed his thoughts to an idealised vision of the future. At this point, Frank shows Jessie his collage and asks her outright whether she'd be willing to accompany him in transforming this fantasy into a reality. Frank explains that he doesn't think they have time to engage in a steady, naturally evolving courtship. Although he never claims to be innocent of the crimes for which he was sentenced, he does believe that the time he spent in jail was robbed from him, and he now needs to work incredibly quickly to achieve everything he believes he is entitled to: 'I can't work fast enough to catch up. I can't run fast enough to catch up. And the only thing that catches me up is doing my magic act.' Jessie is clearly affected by Frank's story, seeing, for the first time, the internal vulnerability that lies beneath his tough exterior. Swept up in this highly emotional moment, she agrees to accompany him on his journey.

This scene kick-starts Frank and Jessie's relationship, but the flaws in their coupling are immediately apparent. Frank's language throughout the scene is controlling and condescending. Jessie tells Frank that she has painstakingly pieced her own life back together following her erratic failed marriage to a drug dealer, and is relieved to have established a routine that is 'very ordinary, which is good because it's solid.'. Frank then disregards Jessie's assessment of her current situation as if talking to a child, describing her current routine as being so devoid of excitement and spontaneity that is essentially worthless: 'You're hiding out. You're waiting for a bus that you hope never comes because you don't wanna get on it anyway because you don't wanna go anywhere'. Frank is being subtly manipulative here. By refusing to accept Jessie's decisions and casting doubt on the validity of her choices, Frank talks down to her and pressures her to feel as though she needs his guidance.

Frank acts as though he is naturally entitled to her time and devotion, implying that he does not view her as a free and independent individual but as an extension of his desires. He projects his perception of his 'dream woman' onto Jessie and does not recognise that she is, in fact, a complex and imperfect person with her feelings, hopes and beliefs, which exist independently of his own. He has decided unilaterally that Jessie is the only person who can make his fantasy come true, and he does not care whether any plans that Jessie may have for the future align with his own. The imagery of Frank's collage symbolises the misguided nature of his dream. The stubborn, all-consuming focus Frank places on this visual representation of his dream demonstrates an almost child-like yearning to create long-lasting emotional connections, yet it is pieced together from pre-existing imagery which Frank has no personal attachment to. Frank's dream is based on a clichéd, generic idea of the American dream and will not fulfil his actual needs. Frank's perception of Jessie is filtered through a lens of romanticism that no woman could possibly live up to, and the idyllic life they attempt to establish will inevitably come crashing down to reality.

Mann foreshadows the downward trajectory of their romance by cutting directly from this scene of emotional exchange to a sequence in which of Frank organises the ill-judged business partnership with Leo. Calling Leo from a payphone, he tells the mob boss that he will only assist Leo with a single, high-value score and then he wants to cut ties with the syndicate forever. Frank makes the mistake of believing that he can become involved in Leo's syndicate while still retaining a decent level of control over his profession. Frank doesn't realise that by entering any kind of deal with Leo, he has already signed away his liberty. After Frank hangs up the phone, Mann cuts to a slow pan across the exterior of a skyscraper, the traffic of the city reflected in its windows: the men are no longer on the outskirts of Chicago, but in the centre of Los Angeles, and their target is a vault worth a monumental $4 million. Frank, Leo and Barry stand on the balcony of an adjacent building, poring over an elaborate blueprint. Whereas the earlier scenes of crime featured Frank operating in by night at the margins of society, here he appears out in the open, dressed in an almost comically mundane outfit of light brown khakis and a yellow polo shirt to blend into the crowd. The scene's colour scheme of turquoise, creams and whites breaks from *Thief*'s established palette of rich browns and dark blues, visually communicating the idea that Frank is out of place within this environment. The low-level scheming that has defined Frank's work thus far is replaced by the 'legitimate' large-scale crime of Leo's crew, which works alongside, rather than in opposition to, the corporate structures which dominate the skyline.

Frank methodically constructs his suburban life while simultaneously planning out the large-scale heist for Leo. Even though Frank is finally taking practical steps to realise his dream, he appears visibly uncomfortable in these sequences, just as he does in the sequences which see him being forced to adapt his professional methods to fit Leo's process of working. When he and Jessie go to view an available property, Jessie walks excitedly around the various rooms while Frank sits motionless on the staircase. While Jessie's voice is full and animated, Frank's is quiet and muted. He mutters, with a noticeable level of uncertainty: 'You think it will do, or what? It's OK?' Frank's language here is revealing. He does not comment on whether or not he finds the place appealing; he looks for approval from others. It is clear that Frank is not buying the property for himself; he has been preoccupied with attaining a false idea of success that he's observed second-hand from popular culture. Jessie is framed with her back to a large set of French doors, a bright, flowering yard visible in the background, as she exclaims, 'Oh Frank, I love it, I think it's terrific.' In contrast, Frank is captured in a cramped composition, packed into a corner with his back against a dark brown wall. Even though Jessie doesn't hold the same idealised view of suburban life that Frank does, she can take genuine enthusiasm in the property while Frank zones out, his thoughts preoccupied with the question of whether other people will approve of the property rather than focusing on whether it genuinely feels like a potential home. After they move into the house, Barry visits Frank to discuss the upcoming score. Walking through the neatly manicured driveway, he points out the incongruity between Frank's personality and the milieu of the upper-crust neighbourhood he now resides in when he jokes: 'Who lives here? It must be a millionaire guy or something.' Frank doesn't respond, perhaps finding that the jibe cuts too close to home. This prompts Barry to ask, with the upmost sincerity, 'Are you happy?' Frank doesn't answer the question; he simply leads Barry inside the house to work on the plan.

Frank's inability to fit into this new suburban environment reaches its apex in the sequence which sees him and Jessie going to an adoption agency for a preliminary assessment. Jessie has been open about her inability to bear children since they started dating, and Frank sees the prospect of adopting a baby as an opportunity to 'save' a child from the state-run welfare system that let him down. Despite his evident enthusiasm, the interviewer treats Frank with obvious disdain from the moment he sits at her desk. She first informs him that his application contains spelling errors, then she condescendingly amends them in front of him. Throughout their meeting, she repeatedly corrects him on his pronunciation and expresses disapproval of the colloquialisms he slips into conversation. The interviewer then runs through a list of Frank's criminal convictions before reminding him, euphemistically, that the agency has 'more applicants than children'. Frank, tired of being spoken down to, unleashes his frustration in an extended tirade. Told that he is not 'desirable' as a parent, Frank sarcastically responds: 'Great, so we'll take a kid that's not so desirable. You got a black kid? You got a chink kid?' Frank's language here is shocking, but what he is voicing is not his own prejudice but his anger at the blatant classism that has been an undercurrent throughout the interview. Frank points out the irony of his official rejection to the interviewer: as a child, he was forced to live in a similar orphanage which did not adequately prepare him for life in the outside world. When he reached adulthood, he was ejected from the institution with no money, minimal education and no support system. His lack of prospects forced him into a life of crime, resulting in the criminal record, which is, ironically, now preventing him from ensuring that another child doesn't suffer the same fate. Before security personnel escort him out of the building, Frank asks the interviewer if she comes from the suburbs. When she answers in the affirmative, Frank derisively responds, 'Right, right,' as though he already knew the answer. This scene, on one level, shows that Frank's aspiration to assimilate into an affluent suburban milieu will not be as easy as he thought; on another level, it exposes that moral rot and hypocrisy which lies at the core of this supposedly 'reputable' social milieu. Frank's fantasy of upward social mobility and personal re-invention meets the brutal reality of American society; he will never truly be accepted into the fold because of his lower-class upbringing and his criminal background.

When things seem hopeless for Frank, Leo spots a chance to exploit his emotional weakness. Meeting Frank at a restaurant, Leo tells him that he heard about Frank's rejected application for adoption and reveals that he has a way of bypassing the official process to match Frank and Jessie with a child in need. Disconcertingly, Leo describes the acquisition of the baby as though he were describing a customisable consumer item: 'You state your model. Black, brown, yellow or white. Boy or girl.' It is also disturbing that Leo refuses to tell Frank exactly how he plans to get hold of the child, evasively responding to Frank's query with the answer: 'A couple of ladies have got babies to sell.' Again, Frank's emotion overwhelms his reason, and he agrees to this risky proposition. This time, Frank even goes so far as to embrace Leo gleefully, so blinded is he by his wish to become a father that he completely lets his guard down and treats Leo as though he were genuinely acting in the spirit of brotherhood and compassion.

The extent to which Leo's operation is connected to the establishment is further emphasised by the antagonistic interactions Frank has with a high-ranking police officer, Sergeant Urizzi (John Santucci), who is willing to turn a blind eye to Frank's involvement with the mafia in return for a cash bribe. Frank never gives into Urizzi's demands, though he does realise that embracing such an anti-cop stance is likely to make him a target for heavy police surveillance and intimidation in the future. Consumed by paranoia, he searches the walls of his new home for tape recorders and tests to check whether the phones have been tapped. When discussing his concerns with Jessie, he runs the kitchen tap to drown out their voices, out of fear that somebody in a high-ranking position may be listening to their private conversations. The suburban home, supposed to be a space of safety and security, instead becomes a breeding ground for suspicion, where nefarious outside forces may intrude at any moment.

Like the opening scene, the central heist in Los Angeles plays out as a nearly dialogue-free montage, with the viewer never invited to cast doubt on Frank's ability to do his job efficiently, despite the grander scale of the job and the extra pressures placed on him in the other areas of his life. Frank, Barry and Mitch (one of Leo's henchmen) carry out the plan, following a similar division of power to the earlier scene – albeit on a larger scale. Frank and Barry painstakingly saw a square hole in the roof of the building, which opens a path into an elevator shaft. Barry leans in and begins sorting through a dense assemblage of wires at the top of the shaft. Frank monitors the charge of the cables through a seismometer from the roof, giving Barry instructions based on his readings. Barry snips the correct wire to turn off the alarm system. Frank then makes his way down the shaft into an ornate private room and starts the lengthy process of breaking through the entrance to the vault with a thermal lance. The screen is shrouded in shadow, while luminous sparks flood the frame, abstracting the image into a pure interplay of shape and light. As Fernando F Croce notes, at this moment, an 'immersive effect takes over [...] as in a trance.' (2009) This is the most physically demanding task that Frank has ever pulled off, and he enters a transcendent, trance-like state as he works. Finally, the vault door collapses. Once inside, Barry and Mitch start filling bags with drawers of gold. Although his accomplices are rushing, Frank takes his time and savours the moment. He takes off his gloves and protective mask, looks proudly at his handiwork, and lights a cigarette. Mann does not show us the men fleeing the scene, nor does he show them trading the diamonds they have stolen for cash. What matters at this point is that Frank has reached the peak of his happiness: he has successfully carried out his job, he has secured enough capital to start an idyllic life with Jessie, and, he believes, that he will now be able to end his involvement with Leo's syndicate.

To visualise this temporary state of euphoria, Mann cuts directly from a shot of Frank's smiling face to an image of the ocean. This time, there are no artificial structures in the background of the image. Waves fill the frame, lapping on the shoreline. Gradually, the reflections of Jessie and Frank enter the frame. At first, they are abstracted by the ripples of the water, appearing as indistinguishable streaks of colour; as they walk closer, they take on identifiable forms, and we realise that they are wandering across the sand. We learn that Leo has arranged for Frank and Jessie to vacation with Barry and his wife Marie (Patti Ross) in San Diego. Leo has told them that the trip is necessary to ensure that they keep a low profile for a few weeks, and then they may go back to Chicago to receive their share of the spoils. This respite period represents the emotional high point of the film, symbolised by the imagery of Frank reaching a direct connection with the ocean rather than gazing at it from a fixed remove. It will soon be revealed that Leo has a secondary motive for keeping Frank out of town for the moment – he is using the time to invest the cash gleaned from the score, and setting up a new heist which he plans for Frank to be an integral part of. The joy experienced by Frank in this scene, therefore, is illusory and fragile. San Diego, after all, is not Frank's home – it is a spot where he may enjoy a facsimile of utopia, which disintegrates as soon as he returns, and the ramifications of his entanglement with Leo are made agonisingly clear.

When Frank goes to Leo's clubhouse to receive his cut from the heist, Leo instead gives him a sum of money that was far less than what was promised: Frank is owed $830,000, but he has only been given somewhere between $70-90,000. Leo calmly explains that, contrary to his previous promise to Frank, he doesn't conduct business by carrying out a heist and then directly giving its participants their share of the money. He pumps most of the money into other business ventures he has operating in the area. Leo tells Frank that, instead of receiving a lump sum payment, he will receive monthly payouts from these ventures, which over time, should accumulate to significant larger sum than Frank was initially promised. Frank is repulsed by this change in plan, in part because going through with it would require him to remain attached to Leo's mob for far longer than he had initially been agreed to (as Frank told Leo in an earlier exchange, he doesn't believe in 'lifetime subscriptions'), and in part, because his code of conduct does not place value in money generated by means other than through one's own physical labour. Leo wants to use the money gained by Frank during the heist to generate a greater sum of money – money generated directly from money itself and not from the production and distribution of physical goods. If Frank were to agree to Leo's terms, he would be treated like an employee, not a partner, given small sums of money every month by a man who hoards the vast bulk of wealth generated by his various ventures for himself, on the condition that he agrees to aid Leo in an unspecified number of jobs in the future that he has no control over the organisation of.

'This is payday. It is over,' Frank tells Leo, his tone much more emphatic than in his earlier conversations with him. 'I can see that my money is still in your pocket. Which is from the yield of my labour.' While Frank is given a relatively low cut, Leo takes most of the profit, which comes 'from my work, my risk, my sweat. Although Leo, at first, tries to guilt-trip Frank into compliance by asking him to show 'gratitude' for the house and the child he helped him to procure, his mask of camaraderie fully slips when it becomes clear that Frank will no longer fall for his manipulations. No longer affecting an air of professionalism or geniality, Leo dismissively tells Frank to 'join a labour union', if he has an issue with his practices. Leo runs his criminal enterprise with the logic of a large corporation, treating his 'associates' as underlings whose value lies solely in their capacity to help him increase his vast personal wealth. Frank's value system is incomprehensible to him, and his resistance to being enfolded into the syndicate renders him a threat. No longer willing to be pushed around, Frank takes command of the situation by giving Leo a clear ultimatum: 'My money. 24 hours. Or you will wear your ass for a hat.' He then gestures towards his gun to prove that his threat is serious. But, as agile a fighter as Frank may be every facet of his life has become connected to Leo's criminal network – and this gives his adversary a massive degree of power over him. So long as he resides with Jessie in the house that Leo helped him obtain, Frank will not be able to pull himself free from Leo's grasp, and the mafia boss will not allow Frank to continue this lifestyle unless he relents and gives in to his demands. Ironically, the elements that made up Frank's utopian dream are now wielded against him, as Leo attempts to use them as leverage to force Frank into submission.

The following sequence underlines Frank's lack of power at this point in the narrative. Images of Frank driving across town are intercut with shots of Leo's men arriving at the dealership, tackling Barry, and taking him hostage in Frank's office. Leo's men wait in there silently as Frank arrives at the lot. Frank strolls across the sales area with no inkling of the threat which awaits him, as Mann repeatedly cuts to shots of Leo's henchmen, getting ready to pounce. Frank, who is usually highly perceptive and alert to potential danger in his surroundings now appears to be completely out of his depth. As Frank approaches the door to his office, one of Leo's men throws Barry into his path, disorientating him. As Frank fumbles with his gun, another henchman jumps out of a door behind him and knocks Frank out with the butt of a firearm. Frank lies comatose on the floor as a wounded Barry struggles to escape. Barry's path is cut short, however, as one of Leo's men shoots him multiple times in the chest. The moment marks the first notable act of violence in a relatively bloodless film, and, as in all of Mann's work, the death is treated with an incredible sense of gravity. Mann subtly slows down the frame rate as he shows Barry being propelled across the air and hitting the side of a white van. The camera lingers on Barry as the life seeps out of his body, the bright red blood splattered on the white surface of the vehicle.

Frank wakes in an underground boiler room. The space has an otherworldly ambience: the entire room has a green tint and a thick layer of steam pervades the atmosphere. It is as though Frank is now seeing past the surface-level facade of professionalism that has characterised his interactions with Leo up until this point and now sees the true, vicious nature of the force he is dealing with. Frank lies paralysed as Leo and a crowd of his henchmen circle him like vultures. Leo bellows: 'You treat what I tried to do for you like shit. You don't want to work for me? What's wrong with you?' Leo then forcefully reminds Frank of the extent to which he controls his new life: 'You've got a home, car, businesses, family, and I own a paper on your entire fucking life.' Leo sadistically reminds Frank that all the luxuries Leo helped him to obtain (and, disturbingly, he speaks about Jessie and David as though they were commodities to be bought and sold) can be taken from him just as quickly – as Leo phrases it, everything that Frank has doesn't truly belong to him, he is only being 'loaned' them. Leo thus claims ownership over Frank's new domestic life, and threatens to have David ground down into 'wimpy burgers' and Jessie sold into prostitution. It is significant that Frank is physically unable to move during this scene: he recognises how truly powerless he has become.

After this altercation, Frank comes to the epiphany that there is no way he can continue to lead his suburban life with Jessie and remain free from Leo's grasp. And so, like Murphy, Frank realises that he cannot possibly resign himself to an existence of conformity and blind subservience to corrupt power. The only way to avoid such a fate is to regain the level of agency he held at the beginning of the narrative, even if he knows that this will entail returning to the state of isolation. This isn't an easy or painless decision, but he recognises it as the only accessible course of action. The first part of this process requires setting up Jessie and David so they may start afresh without him. Frank's abandonment of his family may come across as callous, but it is not motivated entirely by self-interest. Frank allows Jessie to escape a deeply perilous situation and ensures that she will never be tracked down by Leo (or a member of Leo's syndicate) in the future. Had he followed Leo's demands, there would also be the possibility that Leo would turn on them in the future. Frank also shows enough consideration for Jessie and David to provide them with the means to start a new life, as opposed to simply deserting them. On the other hand, Frank goes about this in a deceitful manner. Because he does not come clean to Jessie about the debt he owes to Leo, he does not allow her to make her own informed choice about how she wants to proceed. Frank expects Jessie to obey his commands without question, again underlining his inability to genuinely perceive of her as an individual with needs and desires as important as his own. Frank wakes Jessie in the middle of the night, and gives her a series of direct orders: she must accept a pay-out of $410,000, take David, and then board a train out of the city. Frank does not give any explanation for his sudden change of heart, and he fails to show a sufficient level of sympathy when Jessie, understandably, appears to be distraught. A wounded Jessie tries to appeal to Frank's emotional side, asking him if he thinks, after all they've gone through together, they can really 'just disassemble [their relationship] and put it back in a box'. Her wording here (implicitly comparing Frank's treatment of their relationship to a consumer repackaging and returning a defective item) is appropriate, considering how Frank and Leo have, throughout the narrative, treated her as though she was an object – first to be bought, and then to be used as an instrument of control against Frank. Her pleas for Frank to reconsider his decision fall on deaf ears, as he has already firmly made up his mind. After a brief back-and-forth between them, he simply refuses to communicate altogether, instead repeatedly yelling at her to 'get out'.

After Jessie has fled with David, Frank destroys the home with explosives. It's a symbolic expression of his repudiation of suburban life and the materialistic values associated with it. Frank then demolishes his car dealership, setting fire to each vehicle individually. As Frank looks back at his burning business, he removes the collage of his dream suburban life from his pocket, screws it into a ball, and tosses it into the flames. With this action, Frank demonstrates not only his acceptance that he must eradicate everything that Leo's influence has tainted, but also that the utopian vision he mapped out while in prison will be impossible for him to attain. Having abandoned this fantasy, Frank's new objective is to regain his autonomy, retain his integrity and lead a lifestyle true to his own personal value system.

There is only one thing left to do: Frank must murder Leo to ensure that he can conclusively turn his back on the entire affair and won't be targeted in the future. Just as Leo intruded into Frank's domestic sphere and imposed himself on his personal life, here, Frank turns the tables on him and breaks into Leo's abode. Dressed, once again, in the black leather jacket he wore throughout the first act of the film – a material sign that he has reverted to his old ways – Frank enters the kitchen and slams a cupboard door repeatedly into the face of Attaglia, one of the multiple henchmen stationed around the property to watch out for potential threats. Leo hears the commotion from a different part of the house and, characteristically eager to avoid physical confrontation, hides behind a closet at the other end of the building. Frank carefully inspects various rooms of the house, his movements once again agile and scrupulous.

Once Frank finally locates Leo, the final shoot-out between them is extremely brief, as Leo proves to be totally ineffectual when forced to engage in direct combat. Frank enters the room slowly to find Leo peering out from behind the cupboard, his face half-hidden. Leo steps out and attempts to aim his gun, but Frank's reflexes are too fast. Frank shoots multiple bullets into his chest before Leo can make a move. Leo's fall is clumsy; he flails his arms, crashes into a lamp, and finally lands on the floor. While on the ground, Leo makes an awkward attempt to grab his fallen gun, but an unfazed Frank shoots another load into his brain. The aftermath is a bloody mess. Broken glass, blood and fragments of wood are scattered over the room. The acts of violence Frank commits in this scene are not merely about inflicting pain upon Leo and his men but about forcefully rebuking the middle-class suburban environment; he goes out of his way to wreak havoc on home furnishings and the other material symbols of affluence. As Ari M Mattes observes, 'Thief ends with the disenchantment of its hero – and the annihilation of his dream, his vision of domestic contentment and containment,' yet 'failure to realise this dream simultaneously signifies a kind of re-enchantment, albeit via a negative potential, through his apotheosis as, once again, nomadic hero.' (Mattes: 188) Walking away from the chaos, Frank has cemented his status as an independent agent who refuses to assimilate into a broken and unsatisfactory societal system. Frank must leave behind the world of suburban entanglement and all aspirations to lead a life he truly values. This is treated as a gut-wrenching act of sacrifice and, simultaneously, an honourable affirmation of his principles and his commitment to resisting nefarious external influences.

Mysterious Object at Noon: *The Keep* (1983)

Within a body of work that primarily revolves around the subjects of American capitalism, the ethics of urban criminality, urban alienation, and the impact of technological innovation on labour practices, *The Keep* may seem to stand out as a striking anomaly. *The Keep* is the only Mann film to take place outside of America, it is his only horror film, and it is his only film that features elements of the supernatural. Perhaps because of its status as an oddity within Mann's oeuvre, it has failed to achieve the same level of critical attention as the rest of Mann's work. Although *The Keep* has its fair share of devotees among Mann fans, it was widely regarded as a disaster upon release and remains under-appreciated and under-explored. Many full-length studies of Mann's career either treat it as an unfortunate footnote, or else ignore it altogether. The common perception of *The Keep* as a dismissible misstep in the filmmaker's career has been reinforced by widely circulated stories of the difficulties that plagued the production and Mann's own claimed dissatisfaction with the final product. A combination of studio interference, budgetary constraints and bad luck made the process of shooting *The Keep* torturous. Mann had great difficulty deciding on a final design model for the primary antagonist, resulting in several key scenes having to be reshot to adapt to the filmmaker's changing vision for the character. The reshoots caused the production to be extended from the originally scheduled 13 weeks to 22 weeks. The film went so significantly over-budget as a result of this that Paramount refused to grant Mann the extra funds he requested to stage the film's grand finale, which he had envisioned as a grand duel between Radu Molasar (Michael Carter) and Glaeken Trismegistus (Scott Glenn) on top of the titular keep. This sequence was supposed to conclude with the pair ripping a hole in the space-time continuum, thus opening an inter-dimensional energy portal that would subsume both of them and the surrounding environment. Paramount's unwillingness to produce an ending on this ambitious scale forced Mann to come up with an alternate finale that would be far cheaper and quicker to film. Two weeks into the editing process, leading visual effects supervisor Wally Veevers passed away. This caused major issues for the crew, as they had to ensure that the remainder of the visual effects were produced in a way that would appear coherent with the work already completed without Veevers' guidance. As Mann explained in a 2016 retrospective interview with Bilge Ebiri, for certain sequences, the crew 'were never really quite able to figure out how he [Veevers] planned to combine all of these components that he shot, because it wasn't anything usual like green screen or blue screen. It was black velvet and all kinds of strange stuff to make smoke go backwards.' (2016). For this reason, in addition to the aforementioned budgetary problems, some of the more complex scripted special effects sequences had to be scrapped, including a scene which was supposed to feature Molasar violently dispatching a massive number of Nazi soldiers occupying the Keep (we do see the aftermath of this massacre at the end of the film, but we do not see the event itself play out).

Despite these forced omissions, the first rough cut of *The Keep* ran a staggering 210 minutes – a full hour and a half longer than the 2-hour maximum running time stipulated in Mann's contract. Under pressure from the studio, Mann agreed to edit the film down to a much shorter length. As a result, Mann was forced to exorcise important pieces of back story, character development, and narrative exposition which would have clarified many parts of the film that seem muddled and disorientating in its shorter form. After Mann's 2-hour cut received overwhelmingly negative feedback from test audiences, Paramount removed the film from Mann's control and cut it down even further to result in the final running time of 96 minutes. The extended post-production meant that the release date had to be pushed back from June to December. By the time of its release, news of *The Keep*'s troubled background had spread through the entertainment industry and influenced perceptions of the film's quality. *The Keep* made only a paltry $3,661,757 in theatres against a $6,000,000 budget, and it was savagely attacked by critics for what they perceived to be its nonsensical narrative elements, unconvincing special effects, flat performances, and unconvincing character beats. The pieces written by Vincent Canby for *The New York Times* summed up the dismissive attitude with which critics regarded *The Keep* when he wrote: 'The movie makes no sense as either melodrama or metaphysics, so that its expensive special effects go up in smoke. Literally.' (1983) F Paul Wilson, the author of the novel upon which the film is loosely based, aligned himself with the chorus of detractors, claiming that the film was 'Visually intriguing, but otherwise utterly incomprehensible.' (2011)

Before I launch into my defence of *The Keep*'s many qualities, it feels necessary to point out that the film is difficult to watch without imagining the more complete, cohesive work that could have been. *The Keep* is unquestionably a compromised movie, with many themes feeling underdeveloped, subplots ending abruptly, and characterisations seeming incomplete. There is certainly enough fascinating material in the 94-minute cut of *The Keep* to make it a worthy object of study, and it is enthralling to imagine how its exploration of collective guilt, fascism, and the nature of human evil prefigures later Mann films. Yet, one can't help but long to see how these ideas would be developed in a longer, more comprehensive cut. Unfortunately, though a dedicated subset of fans have been clamouring for an official restoration and release of the 210-minute version of *The Keep* for decades, Mann has consistently cast doubt on such a project ever reaching fruition. As Mann goes on to explain in the aforementioned interview, the rough cut is too incomplete to be released in its current form, with many of the visual effects left half-finished and some sequences containing unsatisfactory footage which would have been reshot at the time. 'Reconstructing these unfinished scenes would be nearly impossible,' Mann concludes, so the extended cut is likely to 'stay in its historical niche.' (Ebiri, 2016)

So, while it is disappointing that Mann's full vision will never see the light of day, we must grapple with the theatrical cut of *The Keep* as the unpolished and imperfect object that it is. However, as far as flawed auteur projects go, *The Keep* is a deeply interesting one. At the heart of the film lies an intriguing and ambitious conceit: the atrocities committed by the Nazis during World War II were too immense to depict directly, using the representational strategies associated with cinematic realism, so the enormity of this great moral failing must be wrestled with using genre allegory. The narrative takes place almost entirely in the remote location of the Carpathian Alps in the year 1941. Mann does not show us images of the inside of the gas chambers, the death trains, or the Jewish ghettos, though the genocide occurring off-screen is treated as a structuring absence which looms over the action (because of Mann's formal restraint in this respect, a few shots of a concentration camp exterior placed at the film's midpoint takes on particular weight as a symbol of inhumanity). Molasar is not merely an abstract supernatural being who originates on earth for unexplained reasons. It is explicated that it is the magnitude of the suffering caused by the Nazis, as well as the culpability of the nations who turned a blind eye to the rise of fascism in Europe in the years leading up to the war, is what allows the monster to materialise on Earth. Molasar is, therefore, an embodiment of all of humankind's collective wrongdoings – a figure whose power is strengthened by the avarice, self-interest and intolerance of the film's human characters. As Gaine observes, Molasar is treated as 'the ultimate manifestation of fascism, devouring all before it.' (2011: 162) Therefore, Mann's utilisation of horror and war movie tropes works as the basis for a substantial meditation on humanity's capacity for cruelty.

The Eastern European setting, the elements of the occult, the expressionistic visuals, and the incorporation of medieval imagery illustrates that *The Keep* is consciously drawing upon the vernacular of the German expressionist cinema of the 1920s and early 1930s. Furthermore, Mann's film contains several implicit references to specific films produced during this movement: the opening sequence calls to mind the early scenes of traversing a mountainous landscape to reach Orlok's castle in F W Murnau's *Nosferatu* (1922); the visual design of Molasar resembles the antagonist of Paul Wegener and Carl Boese's *Der Golem* (1920) (Mann draws attention to this connection when Eva Cuza (Alberta Watson) says that Molasar resembles 'a golem'); the architecture of the Keep echoes Fritz Lang's *Der Mude Tod* (1921). It makes sense that Mann would take visual cues from this era of German filmmaking, as these works reflect the collective feeling of anxiety and foreboding which consumed the nation in the intervening years between the end of World War 1 and the rise of the Third Reich. Siegfried Kracauer's seminal work of film scholarship *From Caligari to Hitler: A Psychological History of the German Film* investigates, in-depth, how the horror films of this era utilised elements of the supernatural and the uncanny to address the nation's slide into totalitarianism. As Kracauer observes, '[d]uring the postwar years expressionism was frequently considered a shaping of primitive sensations and experiences [...] By making the film an outward projection of psychological events, expressionist staging symbolised much more strikingly than did the device of a framing story-that general retreat into a shell which occurred in postwar Germany.' (1947: 71) In a letter written by Kracauer in the early stages of planning his study, the writer comments that, during these turbulent years, 'the unhappy, homeless soul not only drove straightaway toward the fantastic region of horrors, but also moved like a stranger through the world of normal reality [...] That free-wandering soul imagined the madmen, somnambulists, vampires and murderers who were haunting the expressionistic settings of the *Caligari* film and its like.' (Elsaesser, 2000: 72) The fever-dream quality of *The Keep* renders this link between German expressionism and political trauma explicit, drawing attention to the ideological underpinnings that formed the foundation of the expressionist style as he updates its phantasmagorical aura to a 1980s aesthetic.

The first image of *The Keep* is a glacial pan downwards from a cloudy sky, passing a dark wooded valley before coming to rest at the sight of an isolated mountain road. Three military vehicles emerge from the fog and move towards the camera. Mann cuts to a series of extreme close-ups, depicting various details of the vehicles, the men operating them, and the natural setting they are intruding upon: wheels in motion, a metal mirror, the mountaintops, the clouds slowly breaking apart overhead, the ripples of water on a lake. This sequence of images is deliberately bewildering, as it does not clarify where the vehicles are going, who the primary characters are, or what their purpose in entering this landscape is. Instead of providing concrete narrative information these images serve to plunge us into the haunting, dream-like aura which the film will sustain for the entirety of its running time.

As the vehicles enter the small Romanian village where the Keep is located, the action becomes more comprehensible – though the strange and disquieting atmosphere still remains palpable. The camera now enters the perspective of the vehicle's driver, the German Captain Klaus Woermann (Jürgen Prochnow), and we see the village just as he does: exotic, alien, and vaguely menacing. The images depicting the village as Woermann gradually makes his way through are captured in slow-motion and framed through the windshield, emphasising the disconnection between Woermann and the culture which he is intruding upon. While the German troops are visually associated with advanced technology and bureaucratic organisation, the villagers embody a simpler way of life that is self-sufficient and exists in harmony with the natural world. The emphasis on community living, respect for the land, and moderation which characterises village life, is diametrically opposed to the hostility and insatiable greed of the German troops. As a consequence, the rural environment seems as foreign to Woermann as the surface of another planet. Upon spotting the convoy, the villagers cease their activities and stop to regard it with deep suspicion.

With its otherworldly ambience and its de-familiarisation of natural environments, this opening sequence signifies the intermingling of the earthly and the metaphysical that the narrative of *The Keep* is based on. The German troops have invaded Romania to conquer the land and force the people who reside within it to submit to their will, but they will instead become the victims of a mythological conquering force that equals their strength only because it draws its power from the monumental violence that they have inflicted across Europe. The titular Keep is a liminal space in which the rational and the irrational, the transient and the eternal, the material and the spiritual converge. As Keith Uhlich observes, in *The Keep*, the viewer is not 'waiting for the monster to jump from the shadows; it's already in plain sight. And what could possibly be worse?' (Uhlich: 2011) The convoy pulls to a halt, and the soldier in Woermann's passenger seat expresses concern that the men are focused on keeping watch over a remote mountain region rather than assisting with the battle taking place in Moscow. With characteristic hubris, Woermann assures his colleague that victory over Russia is guaranteed. Woermann asserts that the Germans have already proven, through physical force, that they are the 'masters of the world', and that all other nations will soon surrender to the Nazis. The official reason why the battalion have travelled to the Keep is so that they may take control over the Dinu Mountain Pass, but we soon learn that many of the soldiers have other intentions: they have heard rumours that there are valuable metal crosses embedded within the walls of the Keep, and they plan to pry them out to exchange them for vast sums of money. This mission will entail the desecration of an ancient cultural artefact which holds great import to the people of the village, but the German troops view it as their right to claim ownership over this monument, just as they have felt entitled to exert their power over other cultures, populations and environments.

Woermann's entrance into the Keep highlights his elevated view of his own importance while also undercutting this self-perception by illustrating his insignificance and. Woermann is extremely small within the frame in a sequence of symmetrical wide shots, emphasising both the enormity and the permanence of the structure. While traversing the village within the secure space of his heavily armoured vehicle, Woermann appeared to be a figure of power and might, but within the walls of the Keep, he seems weak and fragile. He walks at a halting and unsteady pace as he enters the main floor of the Keep, constantly peering around behind him as though afraid that he is about to be accosted by an off-screen force. Woermann's sense of paranoia is amplified by the unusual angles Mann employs to capture him. The framing creates the impression that the camera is taking on the perspective of an unseen entity spying on the captain from a distant hiding place. Woermann's arrogant lack of respect for this ancient structure is revealed when he is met by Alexandru (W Morgan Sheppard), the self-described 'caretaker' of the fortress. Alexandru carries himself with a solemn, civil air, presenting a stark contrast to Woermann's impertinence. When Alexandru tries to explain to Woermann the historical significance of the keep, the German officer can only respond with sneering cynicism: 'Is that something you tell your tour customers?' Alexandru explains that the Keep has no owner and no manager; he and his sons keep watch over the Keep because it is the cause that his father devoted his life to, and he is training his sons to follow in his footsteps. He then warns Woermann that no man must stay in the Keep after dark – nobody has ever died within the walls of the Keep but that any traveller who has attempted to stay after dark has fled in terror in the middle of the night. Woermann disregards Alexandru's warning, asserting that he doesn't believe in 'demons' or 'ghosts'. Alexandru responds that what drives people out of the Keep are the 'dreams' they experience within its walls. Woermann scoffs at this, stating that 'the real nightmares man has made upon other men of this war.' Although this exchange may seem to present an opposition between Alexandru's belief in the metaphysical and Woermann's materialism, any clear-cut split between these two categories will soon be challenged as the narrative unfolds. There is not, as Woermann implies, a concrete boundary between the realm of earthly experience and the world of the imagination; the supernatural forces that will be unleashed in *The Keep* exist as reflections of real-world horrors. The actions of the invading troops summon Molasar, and he takes on an increasingly human-like form as the crimes of the characters accrue.

Woermann asks Alexandru to give him a tour of the Keep as his men enter and prepare the structure for their occupation. As they walk through a darkened passage, Alexandru becomes irate as he spots a young soldier, Private Lutz (John Vine), prying a cross off the wall with a chisel. Alexandru warns that the architectural integrity of the Keep must not be interfered with, emphasising emphasises, in particular, that the men 'must never touch the crosses.' Woermann chastises his subordinate, reminding him that all he has been ordered to do is hang up lights to illuminate the interior, not to touch the walls. Woermann then assigns Lutz to 'first watch' duty for the rest of the week before dismissing him. Woermann's outburst against Lutz may seem to demonstrate a genuine feeling of desire to preserve the Keep in decent condition, yet it is indicative of a hypocrisy that is soon revealed to be a significant part of Woermann's character and grows more pronounced as the narrative draws on. Woermann lambasts his man for his lack of respect regarding the architecture of the Keep, yet, after Lutz has fled, Woermann arrogantly disregards Alexandru's subsequent message that neither he nor his soldiers should be occupying the Keep for an extended period. Ironically, the punishment that Woermann gives Lutz leads directly to the release of Molasar and the destruction of the fortress – emphasising Woermann's ineptitude.

Later that night, Lutz breaks away from his guard duty with another officer and makes a second attempt to pry a cross from the wall. The structure is submerged in shadow, and a single cross provides the only light in the background of the image, which projects a turquoise glow. This time, the men successfully dislodge the cross, revealing a secret passage within the wall of the Keep. Lutz enters the passageway, ignoring his companion's plea for him to secure back-up from the other men in case something goes badly wrong; Lutz does not want to share any treasure they may come across, so he recklessly charges ahead on his own, his only protection being a belt tied to his foot that his companion holds onto so that he can pull him back to the main passage of the Keep. Lutz crawls through the darkened passageway and finds another cross. He pushes against it, and the block it is affixed to falls away, revealing a steep drop. Mann tracks outwards from Lutz's terrified face to reveal a vast cavernous space, organised around two parallel rows of stone pillars. The only source of illumination is Lutz's flashlight, making the exact contours of the space difficult to decipher; the lack of clarity in the image gives the illusion that it stretches into infinity. Several powerful beams of light then emerge from an unseen source in the foreground of the image to combine with the light emitting from the flashlight. Mann then cuts to Lutz's partner, still waiting at the entrance of the passageway. Noticing that the rope has become slack, he slowly pulls it back. When he reaches the end of the rope, he discovers that Lutz's body has been sliced in half. Mann does not linger on Lutz's corpse; instead, he quickly cuts back to the underground space: glowing smoke is being propelled towards an intangible form. Through a series of rapid shots, Mann then shows this smoke floating up through the passageway and consuming Lutz's partner. It is important to note that Molasar does not tempt or manipulate Lutz here; Lutz acts entirely of his own volition. The awakening of Molasar from his dormancy, then, is activated by the avarice of these soldiers, who disobey the instructions of **Alexandru and desecrate the Keep in the pursuit of wealth.** The light that comprises Molasar's form at this point merges with the beam of Lutz's torch, thus highlighting that the conjuring of Molasar is the result of human behaviour.

After the news spreads that two of Woermann's soldiers have been killed inside the Keep, an SS battalion led by the deplorable Sturmbannführer Erich Kaempffer (Gabriel Byrne) arrives to investigate the situation. The tension between the overtly sadistic Kaempffer and the Woermann, who disingenuously attempts to claim innocence, may seem to reinforce the problematic 'good Nazi' trope that blights many narrative films that dramatise the events of World War 2. This devise positions a Nazi character as being worthy of the viewer's sympathy because they are written to display a basic level of decency in contrast to more overtly insidious members of the Third Reich within the narrative. Such a storytelling technique has rightly been criticised for downplaying the depth of the atrocities committed by the Nazi party as a whole and ignoring the complicity of every individual who contributed to the perpetuation of these atrocities.

Although the dynamic between Woermann and Kaempffer may seem, at first glance, to fit into this mould, as Kaempffer is grotesquely sadistic while Woermann attempts to present himself as a reasonable, conscientious officer, morally superior to his men. I argue, however, that *The Keep* consciously draws upon and reflexively deconstructs this character type, as **Woermann is, instead, critiqued for his hypocrisy in claiming to be 'above' the other** members of the German army while, in fact, lacking the conviction to fight it actively. He claims that Hitler's speeches are 'psychotic', but he maintains his belief in the right of the German people to claim ownership over all over nations; he professes to be repulsed by Kaempffer's behaviour, but, he never breaks away from the German army or makes any serious attempt to undermine Kaempffer's authority. At one point, Woermann claims that he once considered fighting alongside the anti-Fascists in the Spanish civil war, but when asked why he never joined the resistance, he cannot give a satisfactory answer. Woermann gradually comes to claim that while he is morally repulsed by the Nazis, he is far too weak-willed to break away from them. Woermann seeks to clear his conscience by sporadically voicing his supposed objections to the wrongdoings of the German army, while still enjoying the material comforts that come with his high-ranking position in the military.

After Kaempffer threatens to have the Jewish history professor Theodore Cuza (Ian McKellen) and his daughter Eva, who have been retrieved from a concentration camp to assist in deciphering a message found on the wall of the Keep, sent back to the camp to perish unless they can complete the job within three days, Woermann pulls Eva aside and tells her that, once they have cracked the code, he will try to have them transported to safety. Eva, however, does not believe Kaempffer's hollow promise, responding not with gratitude but with the deeply sceptical retort: 'Then again you may not'. Woermann, after all, is not committing to this, and, considering that he has done nothing to stand up to the Nazi regime so far, there is no reason to believe that he would be willing – or able – to put his life on the line to pull off such a feat. The delusional Woermann did not expect such a reply, and, caught off guard, the scene descends into a lengthy, awkward silence. Unable to come up with a reasonable defence, and probably realising, on some level, that he will never make good on his offer, Woermann simply walks away. Woermann's false sense of his own worth is subverted by the very structure of the narrative, which increasingly side-lines Woermann to focus on Glaeken – ultimately, he is unceremoniously killed by Kaempffer in an act of blind rage just before the final battle begins.

The second attack by Molasar occurs when two German soldiers assault Eva in one of the Keep's passageways in the middle of the night. Molasar intercepts the act in progress, killing the men and absorbing their life force. This enables the being to take on a more recognisable form: a spectre with discernible facial features capable of communicating verbally. Molasar returns the sleeping Eva to her and Cuza's shared room. Because the pair are not morally compromised, he is unable to feed upon them. Molasar does, however, figure out a way that he can use Cuza. Molasar offers Cuza a Mephistophelian deal: if Cuza helps Molasar to strengthen his power and escape from the confines of the Keep, he will restore the ailing professor to peak physical condition (Cuza suffers from a debilitating disease which affects his immune system and leaves him confined to a wheelchair). Once released from the Keep, Molasar promises, he will use his abilities to wipe out every Nazi on earth. Cuza agrees to this deal, but he doesn't realise that the spectre does not actually represent a form of opposition to human wrongdoing; he draws upon it for sustenance and intends to inflict further pain and bloodshed upon entire whole population if he makes it out of captivity. Molasar does not kill the soldiers inside the Keep out of a sense of moral duty; he feasts upon them so that he may feed on their barbarity and heighten his own vigour. Furthermore, he did not spare Eva because he has genuine respect for her life, but because he cannot absorb the life essence of morally pure individuals. Failing to recognise the true, insidious intentions of Molasar, Cuza is drawn in by his lies and agrees to aid in his escape. Cuza may enter this alliance for valiant reasons, but his decision nearly results in apocalyptic ramifications.

However, Cuza eventually recognises the beast's true nature when Molasar asks him to commit an act of unspeakable depravity as a show of loyalty: to murder his daughter as a punishment for her attempt to impede Molasar's escape. Realising that a genuinely benevolent being, as Molasar claims to be, would not ask a father to make such a sacrifice, Cuza ends the alliance, even though this means having to go back to his weakened condition. Even in his ailing body, however, Cuza summons the strength to aid in the defeat of Molasar, disposing of the talisman that the monster requires to exit the Keep.

While Cuza ultimately proves highly important in keeping Molasar trapped within the Keep, the only character capable of returning him into the spiritual realm from which he came is Glaeken. This is because Glaeken, like Molasar, is suspended between the material and the immaterial spheres. Whereas Molasar begins as an abstract field of light and energy and takes on a more recognisably human shape as the narrative advances, Glaeken begins the film in the form of a man and increasingly takes on more supernatural qualities in tandem with Molasar's advancing form. What makes Glaeken effective in tackling Molasar is that he understands what the other characters fail to: that the evil represented by Molasar is not greater than or separate from Nazi evil but inextricably tied to it. During their first encounter, Cuza pleads with Glaeken to spare Molasar, reasoning that 'what is happening in the world is worse than anything Molasar can do.' Glaeken's response is plain and matter-of-fact: 'He is the same.' Glaeken understands that defeating Molasar shouldn't be prioritised over defeating the Nazis but that accomplishing one feat will also accomplish the other. While Molasar's transformations are intrinsically linked to the actions of the people whose wrongdoings fuel him, Glaeken's transformations occur as a direct reaction to the changing state of Molasar. Glaeken was conjured into being as a counter-force to Molasar, and his only goal is to rein him in.

The film climaxes with a showdown between these two figures, with Glaeken drawn to Molasar instinctively and now prepared to eradicate his foe, even if it means accepting his own destruction. By this point, Glaeken has evolved into an otherworldly form that resembles Molasar's, and he wields a staff that emits a powerful beam of light, calling to mind the beams of energy that Molasar discharges to drain the life essence from his victims. Glaeken successfully eradicates Molasar, but he must also enter the same vortex that Molasar is dragged into. If Molasar is not present in this world, then Glaeken cannot be either.

Unfortunately, Glaeken's arc feels under-developed in the theatrical cut of *The Keep*. In the small amount of screen time Glaeken is afforded, we get glimpses of his struggle to reconcile his earthly desires with his grand spiritual mission. This is seen most clearly in the highly sexually charged relationship he begins with Eva after voyaging to the Romanian village. As they make love, Glaeken speaks of his desire to 'touch, as mortal men do', and his susceptibility to human lust seems to distract him from his mission momentarily. Sadly, the relationship between Glaeken and Eva is dropped from the narrative until the very final scene, when Glaeken stands at the edge of the portal, taking one last glance at the woman he must leave behind to ensure that Molasar's reign is suppressed. He is clearly filled with emotional pain as he gazes at the material world for the final time before entering the void, and the film briefly hints that Glaeken has experienced an intense internal struggle before committing to his destined purpose. Conceptually, Glaeken's arc has much in common with the journey undertaken by other Mann protagonists: an isolated figure who lives according to a strictly defined professional code which comes with a heavy emotional price. However, the fatalistic romantic sub-plot in *The Keep* is so thinly sketched that its inevitable dissolution carries little gravity. Unlike most Mann protagonists, Glaeken's mission is unambiguously heroic, which removes much of the ambiguity that makes other protagonists more fascinating to observe. Considering that Glaeken serves as the embodiment of the all the noble aspects of humankind, there is little room for the deep and multifaceted characterisation Mann is usually capable of achieving. According to multiple interviews conducted with Mann, Glaeken's emotional arc, particularly his romance with Eva, took a more central role in the original 210-minute cut of the film but was largely exorcised by the studio to focus on the events that occur within the Keep. But this is one of the unavoidable issues that come with applying critical analysis to a compromised work of art such as *The Keep*: we may never know to what degree the extra material may have deepened Glaeken's character.

After shooting **Woermann** dead, Kaempffer flees the scene to discover that his entire troop of men has been massacred by Molasar, who then arranged the burned bodies into giant piles. The inner walls of the fortress have collapsed, and the ground has become engulfed by a thick fog. As Rayner perceptively argues, the expressionistic hellscape created by Molasar resembles a 'historically allusive landscape of man-made horrors', with the mass of burned corpses and the vision-obscuring fog conjuring images of 'the war's end in the atomic bombings' and 'the fires of the concentration camps.' (2003: 136) Kaempffer wanders through this ruinous site completely petrified, registering, for the first time, that the monolithic evil contained within the Keep represents a mirror image of his own genocidal fantasies and psychopathic lust for power. Molasar makes this explicit when a hysterical Kaempffer, coming face-to-face with the entity, asks where he comes from, and Molasar responds: 'I am from you.' He then absorbs the evil contained within Kaempffer, and tosses him to the ground, rendering him a victim of the very type of mass-destruction event he has dedicated his life to perpetrating.

Because anybody who is morally compromised is rendered powerless in his presence, it is up to Cuza and Glaeken to obliterate Molasar. Following the murders of Kaempffer and Woermann, Mann intercuts between two actions occurring simultaneously; Cuza searches through the rubble to locate the crucial talisman that will release Molasar from the Keep, while Glaeken climbs out of the pit into which he was thrown by a group of SS guards and makes his way towards the entrance of the structure. While Glaeken has always been aware of Molasar's true nature, Cuza has to snap out of his trance and see through Molasar's seductive but empty words. Requested to murder his daughter to ensure that Molasar may escape from the Keep without obstruction, Cuza questions why a truly compassionate being would ask him to commit an act of violence against an innocent to prove his devotion: 'Who are you,' Cuza asks, 'that I have to prove myself to you by killing my child?' Cuza will not allow himself to become an agent of violence and will no longer follow Molasar's commands, even if the supernatural being tries to convince him that the life of a single innocent individual is insignificant weighed against all the people they can save if they work in collaboration outside the Keep. Cuza resists Molasar's insistence that he commits an act which conflicts with his moral values and accuses Molasar of using him as a pawn to fulfil his own ambitions, just as Kaempffer and Woermann did when they brought Cuza and Eva to the fortress in the first place. Cuza then disposes of the talisman, trapping Cuza within the boundaries of the Keep. Enraged that Cuza has broken free of their partnership, Molasar exerts his supernatural power and condemns him to live out the rest of his days in his illness-stricken body as one final malicious gesture before being dragged into the portal opened by Glaeken.

At the end of *The Keep*, the supernatural entities representing eternal evil and eternal virtue respectively disappear, leaving humanity to grapple with the aftermath of the atrocities. Lest anybody accuse Mann of ending his film about the most horrendous events of the 20th century on a simplistic, restorative note, however, it should be noted that the final image is not one of jubilance, and Mann does not provide the viewer with any false sense of closure. Instead, the haunting image emphasises the wounds that have been inflicted of mankind as a result of these horrendous deeds. This trauma cannot be easily overcome – the road to recovery will be long and painful. Eva and Cuza are left bruised and exhausted on the steps of the spot upon which the Keep once stood – the evil has been vanquished but the scars remain. The villagers rush around them to offer support, carrying the weakened Cuza to safety. An unsettling wind sweeps through the scene as Eva stands isolated in the foreground of the frame, staring at the site in which she witnessed the absolute worst of humanity. Her face is not one of relief but of profound uncertainty – she is unsure how to move forward from this trauma, unsure whether she can ever place faith in humanity, and unsure as to whether she will ever truly feel safe. Although *The Keep* is an undeniably imperfect and uneven project, this final shot is one of the most heart-wrenching images in Mann's entire filmography.

In the Mouth of Madness:
Manhunter (1986)

Although both films have gained cult followings over the decades that followed their initial release, both *Thief* and *The Keep* failed to launch Mann's theatrical career to the extent that he had hoped for. *Thief* received a modestly positive critical reception but failed to make a splash at the box office, and *The Keep* was treated – almost unanimously – as a colossal failure, critically and commercially. Disillusioned by his experience making the latter film, in particular, and having difficulty securing funding for a new theatrical venture, Mann returned to broadcast television. At this time, Anthony Yerkovich, a television writer who played a significant role in the creation of the hit crime series *Hill Street Blues* (1981-1987), was in the early stages of discussion with NBC's Entertainment Division to helm his own show. NBC president Brandon Tartikoff had approached Yerkovich with a broad idea for a series that would revitalise the staid genre of the police procedural through extensive use of pop music, fashionable clothes, and high-tech gadgetry. Reportedly, Tartikoff sold the concept to Yerkovich with a two-word pitch: 'MTV cops' (Dyess-Nurgent, 2014). With continuous input from Tartikoff, Yerkovich fleshed out the idea into a two-hour pilot script about a cop duo tackling the illegal drug running trade that was increasingly expanding across the coast of Miami. Initially titled *Golden Coast*, the project was soon renamed *Miami Vice*.

The artistic palette of *Miami Vice* (1984-1989) draws on the Art Deco revival prominent in 1970/80s painting and architecture, distinguished by geometric shapes, primary colour palettes, and an intentional lack of pictorial depth. Art Deco flourished in the 1920s, a period of mass economic growth, technological development, and increased consumer spending. Art Deco gave material expression to the feelings of optimism that dominated this era, combining the striking colours of Fauvism with the rigid forms of Cubism to articulate a feeling of exuberance, glamour and faith in industrial progress. These properties of the style were prominent during its comeback in the Reagan era, as financialisation and the expansion of the free market system was vastly increasing the wealth of the upper and middle classes, and there was a cultural emphasis placed on material greed and copious consumption. The influence of Art Deco is all over *Miami Vice*, a series composed with a pastel colour scheme dominated by blinding whites, pinks and aqua blues. The aesthetic scheme draws on the language of music videos and advertisements just as much as it does on the language of episodic television, capturing the action with fast cuts, MTV-like montages timed in rhythm to hit songs, and lavishing attention on luxury commodities, flashy architecture, and toned bodies.

Yerkovich and Tartikoff's quest to update the procedural genre for a new generation paid off magnificently: *Miami Vice* was an instant cultural phenomenon, rapidly becoming one of the network's highest-rated shows and earning a record-breaking number of Emmy nominations in its first few seasons. So popular was *Miami Vice*, in fact, that its impact spread far beyond the sphere of television. The aesthetic design of the show had an indelible influence on men's clothing, advertisements, home furnishings, and car design. The main characters, especially series lead James 'Sonny' Crockett (Don Johnson), soon became icons of the 'yuppie' craze that came to define a generation of well-off, image-conscious young professionals during the 1980s. Many high-end clothing companies sought to capitalise on the popularity of *Miami Vice* by offering to have their products featured on the show, in an attempt to reach out to the young viewers eager to emulate the glamorous lifestyles depicted on the show through the acquisition of luxury consumer products. The massive popularity of the Giorgio Armani fashion brand throughout the 1980s has often been tied to the frequent use of its pastel suits in *Miami Vice*, illustrating just how deeply the series became perceived as a lifestyle brand (Gallagher, 2018).

It is difficult, of course, to discuss the issue of authorship when dealing with a medium as inherently collaborative as '80s network television serials, which tended to be organised such that an established creative team would oversee the overarching production process, but each episode would be written by a different writer and directed by a different filmmaker every week. Mann was hired as an executive producer early into the production of the pilot, a position he would continue to hold over *Miami Vice*'s entire 6-season run. Although Mann is frequently described as being an integral participant in establishing the tone and visual style of the series, he isn't credited with directing a single episode, and he is only credited with writing one: season one's 'Golden Triangle: Part 2', which he co-wrote with Maurice Hurley. It is easy to spot the echoes of themes which Mann had been developing in his feature work (and would go on to develop in the future) in *Miami Vice*: the difficulty of maintaining a healthy balance between professional and personal life; the Sisyphean nature of police work; racial tensions; the evolving architecture of drug trafficking networks, aided by advanced technology. But the television series *Miami Vice* is significantly different from Mann's solo work in terms of tone and formal style. Unlike in *The Jericho Mile*, *Thief* and *The Keep*, the darker and more aspects of the subject matter touched upon in *Miami Vice* tend to be hidden under its r its sleek, surface-level pleasures – the yachts, the expensive suits, the cocktails, and the Lamborghinis. Lawrence Grossberg's description of *Miami Vice* hits the nail on the head: 'The cops put on a fashion show (not only of clothes and urban spaces, but of their own 'cool attitudes') to a top-40 soundtrack [...] It undermines the difference between narrative cinema, video clip, and advertisement.) Young people spend their lives not so much patrolling Miami as cruising it, only to rediscover the narrative as an afterthought in the last few minutes.' (Grossberg, 1988: 140).

In its first season, *Miami Vice* at least made an attempt to point to the more troubling undercurrents, though it nearly always came up short. In the later seasons, however, the show leaned further and further into its consumerist appeal, and *Miami Vice* rapidly became a symbol of the very materialism, greed, and superficiality that Mann critiques so effectively in his solo projects. Indeed, as I will explore later in this book, Mann's reimagining of *Miami Vice* in the 2006 film reboot of the same name is radically different from the original series in terms of texture, tenor and subject matter, as though Mann was actively seeking to repudiate the values that had come to be associated with the television series.

The reason why I chose to begin this chapter with a lengthy discussion of Mann's involvement in *Miami Vice* and the status it occupied in '80s pop culture is not only that the popularity of the series enabled Mann to take another shot at directing a theatrical feature, but also because it is deeply interesting to consider these two projects in relation to one another. On paper, *Manhunter* may seem to bear many similarities to *Miami Vice*: it follows a young, affluent male detective as he tracks down a dangerous criminal; it displays ultra-modern architecture, clothes, vehicles and technologies; and it is scored to a pulsating electronic soundtrack. In terms of its overall affect, however, *Manhunter* could not be more different. *Miami Vice* is gaudy, energetic and jubilant, while *Manhunter* is sombre, subdued and detached. Crockett and Tubbs (Philip Michael Thomas) are charming, witty, and self-assured alpha males strolling through a landscape in which they are regarded with admiration; it is clear why so many viewers came to view them as aspirational figures. *Manhunter*'s Graham, in contrast, is deliberately portrayed as awkward, insecure and alienated – by those around him and the urban centre in which he works. The protagonists of *Miami Vice* are always presented as being the show's moral centre, dutifully restoring the status quo when abject criminal elements threaten to destabilise it, and therefore ensuring the safety and security of the city's population. On the other hand, Graham is a disturbingly ambiguous and morally compromised character, a man who has a preternatural ability to enter the minds of vicious killers and understand their sadistic fantasies. The ending of *Manhunter* is not restorative but uncertain – Graham may return to the domestic space after successfully apprehending the Tooth Fairy Killer, but he remains deeply troubled by everything he has done to reach this point: he has plunged into the darkest recesses of the human mind, recklessly endangered his family, and demonstrated his capacity to identify with heinous psychopaths. We are not left with the impression that the security of the domestic sphere has been restored through his actions; we instead see a profoundly uncomfortable and unsuitable patriarch attempting, in vain, to patch things up with a family that he still feels fundamentally alienated from – and Mann hints that he is likely to be drawn towards the darker side of his psyche, once again, in the future, and next time he may be lost entirely.

The sleek, ultra-modern surfaces which dominate the mise-en-scène do not make the urban spaces of *Manhunter* look appealing; on the contrary, they appear monolithic and inhuman, threatening to engulf everyone who passes through them. While Crockett and Tubbs are always in control of their surroundings, Graham drifts through a succession of urban spaces in a tentative and apprehensive manner. After the first meeting between Graham and Hannibal Lecktor (Brian Cox), Graham flees the cell and sprints through the vast, serpentine space of the mental institution. The building appears eerily antiseptic, the blinding white corridors seeming as though they could stretch on into infinity. When Mann cuts to a high angle shot of Graham frightfully running towards the exit, he is framed very small against a great expanse of blank space, like a rat running helplessly through a maze. During a later scene, Graham has a conversation with his son in the middle of a supermarket aisle. Although this space is ostensibly one of consumer leisure, it is framed in a similar manner to the mental institution: an enormous, soulless, sterile space that seems frighteningly indifferent to human life. Pat

Graham's 2005 *Chicago Reader* review perceptively describes the film's tone: 'Simultaneously hypnotic and enervating, meditative and empty, like a white-noise background or a field of electronic snow on the tube.' (2005). Indeed, the atmosphere of *Manhunter* is deliberately icy and clinical; it invites the viewer to share the lens of affective disconnect through which Graham regards his environment and share in his feeling of alienation.

In *Manhunter*, then, Mann transposes the existential themes and piercing societal critique of *The Jericho Mile* and *Thief* to a culture of hyper-modern, consumerist gloss. As a character, Graham has much more in common with *Thief*'s Frank than with the protagonists of *Miami Vice*. Consider Graham's character arc in comparison to Frank's. Both Graham and Frank are isolated introverts, struggle to maintain close familial relationships, fail to assimilate into the domestic sphere, and are highly skilled at their chosen profession. However, Frank begins the film as an isolated individual who briefly enters mainstream society and establishes social bonds before cutting himself free of these bonds so that he is alone, once again – and he accepts this solitude as a necessary condition of retaining complete control over his work. Graham, on the other hand, begins the film enmeshed in a nuclear family unit (though he does not feel a sense of genuine fulfilment from his domestic life he derives no genuine fulfilment), is removed from the domestic sphere to pursue his work and then returns to the family at the film's denouement. This plot description may make *Manhunter* sound like the optimistic flipside to *Thief*, but, as this chapter will argue, this ending is far more inconclusive and unsettling than it might seem at first; Graham may catch the killer, but his internal battles and contradictions central to his character have not been sufficiently reconciled, and it seems inevitable that Graham will lapse back into his destructive patterns of behaviour at another point in the future, and when this happens, his family will be placed at risk, once again. Frank realises that he is destined to lead a solitary lifestyle and removes himself from all social ties, but Graham remains in a state of denial, returning to his family and immersing himself in the illusion that the domestic sphere can cure his malaise and contain his destructive impulses – though it is clear to the viewer that this is a false solution.

The opening sequence of *Manhunter* depicts a break-in at a suburban home. The camera assumes the first-person perspective of the intruder: we see a stairway being climbed, a corridor being entered, and a bedroom being peered into. It is night, and the only source of illumination is a torch carried by the POV character. As such, our view of the scene is somewhat hazy and unclear. Finally, the camera comes to focus on the intruder's target: an attractive blonde woman sleeping in the master bedroom next to her husband. The intruder shines the torch onto her face, and she slowly stirs from her slumber. She looks around for a few beats, groggy and confused, before she notices the intruder and looks directly at the camera. Before we see the intruder inflict violence on the couple, Mann abruptly cuts to black.

It is only later into the narrative that the viewer learns that these images were recorded by serial killer Francis Dollarhyde (nicknamed 'The Tooth Fairy') during his brutal murder of the entire Leeds family: the couple in the bed as well as their young child. Because we are not aware of the context of the images at first, it is only in retrospect that we realise our perspective was aligned with that of a murderous predator. In watching the opening sequence and anticipating what would happen next, then, the viewer is unwittingly placed in the position of identifying with a sadistic criminal. The opening sequence, then, immediately establishes the complex relationship with identification and voyeurism that will be developed over the course of the *Manhunter*. Mann's decision to withhold the climactic act of violence also feeds into these themes. We only witness the lead up to the murder and then, later, its aftermath in the form of photographic evidence and the blood-covered bedroom. This ellipsis puts us in a similar position to Graham, denied the ability to see the act of carnage itself and, therefore, encouraged to visualise the murder in our own minds; how the individual spectator may mentally visualise this moment will likely reveal something uncomfortable to them about their own capacity to imagine the unimaginable. As Kendall Phillips observes, it is clear from the opening moments of the film that 'The act of looking is not entirely innocent.' It is because Graham makes concerted attempts to 'see' the world through the eyes of his target that he 'risks being absorbed into the murderous gaze he seeks to understand.' (2003: 11). The idea that voyeuristic looking as being an act of violence in itself is emphasised throughout the film: Dollarhyde has a ritual of filming his victims before, during, and after the murders and gets a sadistic thrill from watching the tapes; Graham clearly gleans some degree of voyeuristic satisfaction from watching Dollarhyde's tapes (which the film treats as a violation of privacy comparable to Dollarhyde's intrusions into domestic spaces); and when Graham is attempting to enter the mind of the killer, he places particular emphasis on their visual experience.

What is immediately surprising about the structure of *Manhunter* is that it begins with Graham having (seemingly) achieved the utopian lifestyle that many of Mann's protagonists long for but never have the opportunity to actualise. In the first act, we see Graham living in an elegant beach house with his wife Molly (Kim Greist) and his step-son Kevin (David Seaman) after retiring from the FBI. In most Mann films, the protagonist is denied the opportunity to build a family life away from the pressures of their work (either through their own actions or through the efforts of external forces), but here Graham has (seemingly) achieved this goal. Yet, it soon becomes clear that this situation does not bring Graham true happiness. Graham is still troubled by the psychological wounds he sustained while tracking down Lecktor, a cannibalistic serial killer and he feels, on some level, a continued commitment to the profession he tried to leave behind. While hunting Lecktor, , Graham used emotionally draining identification techniques to enter the headspace of his target, visualising his fantasies and desires in the hopes of better understanding what motivated him to kill. Graham suffered a mental breakdown as a result of these exercises and, after receiving professional psychiatric treatment, made the decision to permanently retire from law enforcement. Graham clearly hoped that if he left his work behind, he could rid himself of the troubling aspects of his psyche and embark on a life of domestic bliss.

But, like Frank, Graham is ill-equipped to handle a life in the domestic sphere, and Mann draws the viewer's attention to the cracks in this façade from the outset. After the opening title card, Mann cuts to an image of the clear blue sky before slowly panning downwards to capture the point where the sky meets the surface of the ocean. This shot may initially suggest tranquillity and liberation, luring the viewer into a false sense of security following the disorientating opening sequence, but the camera continues panning down, finally coming to rest on two figures perched on either side of a large, twisted log which sits in the middle of the sand: Graham and Jack Crawford (Dennis Farina), Graham's former superior officer at the FBI. The log now dominates the foreground of the image, creating a visual barrier between the viewer and the ocean. If, in Mann's visual scheme, the act of gazing out into the water symbolises hope and liberation, then the fact that Graham sits with his back to the water further emphasises that he is not truly free. He may be placed within a natural environment, but he is not entirely 'present' within this setting. Crawford tells Graham about two horrific incidents that occurred in Birmingham and Atlanta within the past few months; in both cases, a killer entered a suburban home and slaughtered the entire family within. The Atlanta police nicknamed him 'The Tooth Fairy' due to his penchant for biting his victims. Crawford urges Graham to return to the force, as nobody can understand the inner workings of serial killers' minds as intricately as he can. To further emphasise the necessity of Graham returning to the force, Crawford stresses that the killer seems to strike every full moon, so he must be apprehended within the next three weeks before he will attempt to strike again. Graham is initially reluctant, but Crawford has full confidence that he will cooperate. Molly and Kevin enter the movie unceremoniously, framed small in the background behind Crawford's shoulder as he hands Graham a set of photos of Dollarhyde's victims. The fact that Graham's former colleague takes prominence over his family in the composition foreshadows Graham's later choice to privilege his professional role over familial obligations. Like Frank, Graham naively believed that familial affection and material comfort were all he needed to provide him with satisfaction, but he is left with an unshakeable sense of emptiness. Even though the pressures of his work cause him intense anxiety, he feels, deep down, an irrepressible need to return to the lifestyle of the solitary crusader (and, though Graham is an employee of the FBI, almost all scenes of him applying his professional gifts involve him working on his own -- watching the killer's self-recorded videos, visiting the homes of the victims, and engaging in elaborate psychological exercises to perceive the world through the perspective of the murderer).

'What do you think?' Graham asks Molly later that night. But Molly knows that her husband isn't truly interested in hearing her opinion 'I think you already know', she replies,' and you're not really asking.' She makes a desperate plea for him to 'stay home with [me].' Graham doesn't respond, but it is clear that he has already made up his mind, and he expects unwavering cooperation from his domestic partner. The two make love, but it is not an act of genuine connection between them. Mann captures the action not in wide shots that would show both of their bodies intertwined within the same frame, but in isolating close-ups that emphasise the gulf between them. As Graham nuzzles her neck, Molly's expression is one of concern; Mann lingers on a close-up of her face as she gazes away from him and out of the window, anticipating the danger that lies ahead. Molly knows that Graham will be unable to resist the call of his work and that their family will be placed under extreme pressure as a result.

Graham's sense of professional duty places a gulf between himself and his family, not only emotionally but also geographically: he is uprooted and sent to a series of different urban spaces, heightening the distance between himself and his family and making it more effortless for him to shut them out from his work. After Graham has taken on the case, he completely shuts Molly out, never discussing the investigation with her, nor being open about the mental toll the work is taking on him. The fact that Graham is unwilling to let Molly share in the most important part of his life illustrates that he does not see her as an equal partner but an idealised symbol of domestic joy; like Frank, he fails to take into consideration the independence and emotional life of his wife, he only sees her as an extension of his own desires.

Mann cuts directly from this scene to a shot of a FBI vehicle transporting Graham to the home of the murdered Leeds family. This transition takes us from a fractured domestic space, destabilised by an unbalanced patriarch, to a domestic space where an appalling tragedy has taken place – suggesting a disturbing parallel between them. Graham carefully traverses the house's interior, inspecting the layout of the building and attempting to envision the path that the killer took through it. Graham tries to recreate the conditions of that night as precisely as possible, so he navigates the home at night, using only a small torch to illuminate his passage. Graham silently passes a series of bloodied bedrooms before arriving at the master bedroom. At this point, Graham, standing in the same position, it is implied that Dollarhyde must have stood, speaks into a tape recorder: 'The intruder entered through the kitchen sliding door. Used a glass cutter anchored to a suction cup. His entry was skilful. All the prints are smooth gloves. [...] It was hot out last night, so inside the house must have felt cool to him.' As he speaks, Graham transitions fluidly from a matter-of-fact recounting of objective facts (the instruments used by Dollarhyde, the physical evidence left behind in the rooms) to a vicarious assumption of the sensations and emotions that the killer must have felt while breaking into the space and hunting his prey. This communicates the complex fluctuations between internal and external experience that Graham has to navigate when contemplating the killer's actions. After describing the killer's thoughts into his tape recorder for a while, Graham becomes anxious that he is being *too* absorbed in the mental processes of the murderer. Taking a break to gather his composure, Graham enters the bathroom, takes an unidentified pill and splashes some cold water on his face. He gazes at his reflection in the mirror, as if to remind himself of who he truly is, to reassert a sense of self he was at risk of letting slip away. He is jolted by the sound of the phone ringing, which is followed by a generic answerphone message delivered in the voice of Mrs Leeds. The answering machine message blurs the line between past and present, creating the illusion that the deceased woman is in the room with Graham. This further immerses Graham in the mindset of the killer, as he briefly feels as though he is in the same space with the late Mrs Leeds, just as Dollarhyde had been.

Later, Graham sits in a grubby hotel suite, obsessively watching home movies of the Leeds family. At first, he takes notes impassionately, making general observations regarding the relationships within the family and the design of the domestic space. As though fearing the possibility that he is becoming overly absorbed in the images, he makes a phone call to Molly. Molly is woken up by the phone call and is, disconcertingly, unable to recognise Graham's voice at first. She asks him, 'Will, is that you?' ironically underlining his uncertain sense of identity at this moment even further. The phone call was intended to re-affirm Will's sense of identity by reconnecting him with his family and his home, but it instead has the opposite effect, reminding him of how distant he truly is from his wife. Realising that conversing with Molly with bring him no comfort, Graham urges Molly to go back to sleep and he returns his attention back to the television set, focusing intently on an image of Mrs Leeds. Graham stares into the screen while musing, 'What are you thinking?' It is unclear whether he is directing this rhetorical question at the killer or the victim, but it is obvious that he feels drawn to the images in a way that extends beyond professionalism. His voice grows faster and his demeanour more heated as he continues: 'God, she's lovely, isn't she? It was maddening having to touch her with rubber gloves on wasn't it?' As Graham obsessively observes this family without their knowledge, fantasising over touching Mrs Leeds, he appears deeply unsettling. It appears as though Graham is perceptually violating the private, domestic space, just as Dollarhyde literally intruded into the Leeds family home in the opening sequence. By making videos of families and watching them repeatedly without their consent, Dollarhyde flattens individuals into filmed images that he can fantasise about in any way that he wishes. At this moment, Graham is inflicting upon Mrs Leeds the same de-humanising gaze, with his focus on her physical beauty adding an unsettling element of sexual desire – even if Graham is assuming the imagined perspective of the killer. Like Dollarhyde, he projects motivations and feelings onto a family that is unaware of his presence. The merging of Graham and Dollarhyde's perspectives in this scene problematises our identification with Graham, creating a queasy parallel between the two men and undermining the viewer's ability to place their trust in the film's protagonist as an upholder of moral order.

The second extended sequence of Graham working alone sees him surveying the garden of the Jacobi house. Rather than entering the home where the murders took place, Graham thinks in a more literal manner, searching through the vast outdoor space, attempting to locate the spot where the killer must have sat as he recorded the videos. The theme of voyeurism again comes back into play as Graham searches out several potential locations, and determines which one would have been the most effective vantage point for spying on the family. The camera repeatedly enters Graham's POV as he looks through the home's windows, creating a clear visual link between this scene and the one in which Graham vicariously spied on the Jacobi family through the videotapes in his hotel room. Here, as in that scene, Graham truly comes alive, appearing genuinely zealous and invested in his work, in contrast to the disinterest he expresses during his scenes in the FBI headquarters. Graham, entering the mind of the predatory voyeur, climbs up a tree perched opposite the window of the main bedroom and surmises that this would be the idle spot for Dollarhyde to sit – the marks on the bark confirm his suspicion. He again speaks to himself, offering rhetorical questions to the killer in an imagined verbal exchange: 'When night comes, you saw them pass by their bright windows, you watched the shades go down. And you saw the lights go out one by one. And after a while, you climbed down and you went into them, didn't you, you son of a bitch? You watched them all goddamn day long! That's why houses with big yards.'

As the narrative goes on, more connections will be drawn between Graham and Dollarhyde, underlining the shared thrill both men take in voyeurism and suggesting that Graham poses a similar threat to the domestic space. As he deems it necessary to spend extended periods of time alone, dwelling over the evidence and attempting to enter the killer's perspective, Graham is increasingly drawn away from the social ties of his family and his colleagues and into the realm of these psychopaths. Graham's descent into mental instability is visualised in a dream sequence that occurs when he falls asleep during a plane journey. He dreams of Florida: we see a calm ocean surface, a clear sky, and a boat engine. It's a quintessentially Mannian image of an out-of-reach utopia. The warm hues and nature imagery may initially appear to code this dream as an idealised fantasy of domestic reverie, but the atmosphere is far from euphoric. Mann cuts to a wide shot of Molly walking towards the foreground of the image. She is framed in shallow focus and at a distance from the camera's gaze. Next, Mann cuts to a reverse shot of Graham, doing manual work on the boat. The scene cuts to a reverse angle on Molly; she is still walking towards the foreground of the image but her gaze suddenly breaks away from Graham's as she directs her attention to an off-screen element. Then, an extreme close-up of Graham, now looking directly into the camera lens, his facial expression inscrutable. Graham's gaze upon Molly is ambiguous: is he looking at her with resentment, is he trying to discern what has grabbed her attention, is he filled with sorrow that he must leave her to fulfil his professional calling?

Throughout the film, Graham justifies his actions by claiming that he is working towards the goal of saving other families who may potentially fall victim to the Tooth Fairy. However, he doesn't recognise that he is placing his own family at risk by doing so. This danger takes two forms: the external threat represented by Dollarhyde and Lecktor *and* the internal threat posed by Graham's disintegrating mental state. This sense of doubling is made explicit in Graham's first visit to Lecktor in the mental institution. Lecktor's cell is painted pure white – not only the walls, the ceiling and the floor but also the furniture and the bars separating him from his visitors. Although Graham is the 'free' man interrogating a convicted felon, Lecktor quickly turns the tables on him and takes control of the conversation. And what Lecktor proposes to Graham is a proposition he very much doesn't want to think about: that the reason Graham is so skilled at hunting down murderers is that, on some level, he feels a deep kinship with them. At the end of the interaction, Lecktor hammers this point home: 'You know how you caught me, Will? Because we're just alike. If you want the scent, smell yourself.' As Lecktor says this, a disturbed Graham dashes to the exit. Finding the cell door locked, Graham pounds on the glass anxiously until a security guard allows him to leave. Once out of the building, Graham has a panic attic. His view of the outside world appears distorted, as indicated by an abstracted, shallow-focus shot of the grass outside the facility. Graham takes a moment to regain his composure, loosening his tie and taking a deep breath. When he looks again at the yard, the grass is in clear focus. This brief panic attack is comparable to the temporary breakdown of mental faculties he experienced while inspecting the Leeds house. In both instances, he comes close to losing control when he dwells on the psychology of a killer for an extended period. The pressure builds to the point that Graham can no longer bear it, and he must take a respite from his work to re-stabilise his sense of identity.

Though he is ostensibly on the side of moral order, Graham is constantly on the precipice of lapsing into his darkest impulses. In Graham's later scenes with Lecktor, the cannibal underlines the parallels between Graham and the killers he hunts with even greater force. He accuses Graham of having both a predatory instinct and an insatiable bloodlust, which he exercises through his work with the FBI. Graham, Lecktor suggests, did not become involved in the homicide department because he has a genuine desire to save others, but because he wanted to be in close proximity to bloodshed. Lecktor focuses on a case from Graham's past which resulted in Graham fatally shooting the serial murderer Garret Jacob Hobbs. Lecktor claims that Graham got a magnificent rush from the act of taking another man's life, and only a false sense of righteousness separates him from Dollarhyde. Devoting his career to tracking down killers enables Graham to get a vicarious thrill from witnessing the violence inflicted on others, Lecktor reasons, and he secretly longs for another chance to commit a 'justice killing'. Graham is drawn to his profession, Lecktor reasons, because it allows him to indulge his sadistic impulses in a manner that is considered socially acceptable – and the intense anxiety that Graham feels when confronted by Lecktor indicates that he realises there is some truth to his claim. As Jason Holt argues, Graham's behaviour throughout the narrative shows that he is drawn to police work by a desire to 'indulge at great risk his own sociopathic tendencies.' (Holt, 2006: 31). These impulses render Graham incapable of connecting with others and maintaining a healthy domestic life, and he will always be pulled back towards the darkness no matter how vehemently he tries to escape it. Graham's fear of descending into insanity when placed in contact with vicious killers is rooted in his fear that he may one day lose his grip on reality and fully embrace his worst instincts.

Graham's interactions with Lecktor directly places his family in jeopardy when Lecktor obtains Graham's home address and phone number through a fraudulent call to the University of Chicago's Department of Psychiatry. When Crawford discovers this, he arranges for Molly and Kevin to be relocated for their own protection. Mann stages the scene in which Graham's family hears of this news in a similar manner to the staging of the opening home invasion, again pointing to a fundamental similarity between the protagonist and Dollarhyde and emphasising the sense of fear and uncertainty that Molly and Kevin are burdened with as a direct result of Graham's work. Kevin wakes Molly in the middle of the night, telling her that he heard strange noises outside. Molly inspects the house tentatively, the building bathed in blue light, which recalls the colour scheme of the opening break-in. When Molly reaches the kitchen, she spots a mysterious shadow looming on the ceiling, making its way towards the front door. Molly slowly makes her way towards the doorknob before rapidly thrusting it open. The tension is released when she sees an officer standing at the door, who asks her, 'Ma'am are you all right?' Though Molly and Kevin have escaped physical danger in this instance, the sequence is indicative of Graham's inability to ensure their safety. Graham is not even present to comfort them following this scare – the officer who brings Molly and Kevin to their new safe house is a total stranger to them. Following the move, Kevin is reluctant to leave Molly alone with Graham, suggesting that he can intuit there is something wrong with his step-father and he feels the need to provide the protection for Molly that he can't. When Graham asks Kevin to give he and his mother some privacy, Kevin instead hovers around the other side of the room, calling back to his mother that he'll be staying close by. Graham comments that he seems 'afraid' to leave them together without supervision. Like in *Thief*, the protagonist's home becomes a space of intense tension and threat, not a peaceful respite from the demands of work. As Graham exits the building, the camera pans to a landscape painting of the sea mounted upon the wall, cementing the idea that the illusion of familial warmth and stability glimpsed in the opening Florida scenes was just that – an illusion.

As they sit at the end of a wooden walkway, Molly begs Graham to give up the investigation and return to his retirement. He admits that the investigation is making little progress, confessing that 'everything we've tried is either a dead end or it's backfired. Crawford is already prepping the next crime scene so we can get it fresh.' Yet, when Molly asks him, 'Can you quit?' Graham responds with a simple 'no', providing no further explanation. At this point, Graham is offered an opportunity to cast aside the professional role that is causing him such mental turmoil and devote his attention, instead, to the restoration of his shattered family. Not only does Graham fail to seize upon this opportunity, he doubles down on his commitment to the case by telling Molly that he must cut contact with her and Kevin entirely if he is to apprehend the killer before he strikes again. Graham tells Molly that he will reside in Atlanta without calls or visits from them until the investigation is solved – that way, he can focus without being distracted by the demands of domestic life. Recalling the final act of *Thief*, Graham cuts himself off from his family completely so that he may focus on the completion of his professional task. This time, however, Graham vows to return to her once his professional objective has been completed. Molly voices her shock and anger at Graham's decision, but Graham cannot be swayed. Graham has made up his mind, and she can say nothing to dissuade him. She storms back inside the house, and Graham does not follow. Like Frank, he is incapable of consoling those closest to him during times of emotional distress.

Graham's inability to reconcile the competing halves of his personality is a constant source of internal torment. It is no accident that the vague title *Manhunter* could conceivably refer to Dollarhyde – who hunts down murder victims – or Graham – who hunts down wanted criminals to bring to justice. Ironically, the task of appending Dollarhyde requires Graham to spend so much time engaging in the very activities that Dollarhyde derives intense pleasure from: viewing footage of strangers, stalking families and forcibly inserting himself into domestic spaces.

Another troubling parallel between the two men is that Dollarhyde, like Graham, demonstrates a desire to alleviate his loneliness by forming a nuclear family unit – and he is similarly incapable of sustaining a romantic relationship for any substantial period of time. This desire – and his inability to fulfil it – is the primary motivating force that drives Dollarhyde's murders. Dollarhyde's longing to foster a family is illustrated by his short-lived relationship with Reba McClane (Joan Allen), a colleague from the photographic laboratory where the killer works. McClane's warmth and emotional generosity temporarily seems to offer Dollarhyde an escape from his solitude, but his internal demons get the better of him and he ends up sabotaging the relationship in spectacular fashion. During this subplot, Dollarhyde appears surprisingly vulnerable and childlike. He is socially awkward, insecure about his physical appearance and emotionally naked, clearly desperate to make his relationship with McClane work out yet also held back by his internal trauma. He even performs little gestures of compassion such as making McClane a drink and taking her to experience the sensation of stroking a sedated tiger at a vet's office. After they make love for the first time, Dollarhyde weeps as McClane affectionately cradles him. The romance that blossoms between them represents the first time Dollarhyde has tried to pursue a reciprocal and two-sided relationship. Unfortunately, even though McClane is reliable and supportive, and Dollarhyde makes a concerted effort to be conscientious, his myriad insecurities split the couple apart. Although Dollarhyde's relationship with McClane increases his ability to connect with others to a certain extent, he cannot give himself fully over to McClane. During their courtship, Dollarhyde experiences a tension between his sadistic impulses and his desire to become a caring and empathetic partner – ultimately, however, the former side of his personality overcomes the latter. As Gaine observes, the depiction of Dollarhyde's courtship with his co-worker draws the viewer's attention to a 'contrast between his human and monstrous impulses' that he ultimately fails to resolve [2012: 81].

Dollarhyde's inability to resolve his conflicting impulses during this sequence is evidenced when he and McClane make out on his couch. Dollarhyde has filmed images of his next victims playing constantly on his home projector, and his gaze alternates between McClane and the family on the screen. Because McClane is visually impaired, she cannot tell what images are playing in the background, and Dollarhyde lies to her about the nature of the films he's watching. Mann crosscuts between Dollarhyde's voyeuristic video footage and the pair caressing one another, suggesting that Dollarhyde is becoming sexually aroused by both elements simultaneously. Furthermore, the following morning, Dollarhyde acts in a possessive manner towards McClane. He wakes to find her standing at the end of his yard. She tells him that she wants to go back inside to make coffee, but he physically prevents her from re-entering the house, even after learning that she left her purse inside. He tells her that he wants her to remain in that precise spot, because she 'looks so good in the sun'. McClane is not bothered by this request, but as the viewer is aware of Dollarhyde's tendency to manipulate his victims to fit his fantasies in a similar manner, it registers as deeply menacing behaviour.

Dollarhyde is both 'inside' and 'outside' of the relationship simultaneously he is appreciative of McClane's affection and wishes to return it, yet he is incapable of dealing with the fact that she is not fully controllable like the images in his one-sided voyeuristic fantasies. Dollarhyde projects his self-hatred onto McClane, falsely believing that she is cheating on him with their mutual co-worker Ralph Dandridge (Bill Cwikowski). A suspicious Dollarhyde follows the pair after Dandridge offers to give McClane a ride home from work one night. The scene enters Dollarhyde's POV as he imagines the two of them kissing in front of her front door – though, in reality, he was only taking a piece of dirt out of her hair. Watching through the lens of Dollarhyde's paranoid fantasy, we see McClane and Dandridge backlit by an otherworldly white glow – the same glow seen omitting from the eyes of Mrs Leeds in one of Graham's imagined recreations of the night of the break-in. The visual connection Mann draws between the two women emphasises that Dollarhyde's murderous impulse is bound to his desperation to be loved and his fear of rejection. This imagined act of betrayal by McClane is what pushes Dollarhyde over the edge. He murders Dandridge outside of the house and then kidnaps McClane, announcing to her that 'Francis is gone. Francis is gone, forever'. This experience of (perceived) betrayal convinces Dollarhyde that there is no point in trying to establish a close interpersonal relationship with anybody else; he now fully abandons any attempt at maintaining social relations and embraces his fantasy life. By killing McClane, Dollarhyde intends to render her a passive and fully controllable object, like his other victims.

As Graham digs deeper into Dollarhyde's history, he finds himself better able to sympathise with him: Dollarhyde was subjected to horrific, unbearable abuse when he was a child. It was this abuse that has shaped his disorder in the present day. His longing to create the ideal nuclear family expresses his anger over the fact that he was denied a real childhood; his desires are perfectly natural – love, acceptance, admiration – but because he was never properly socialised, he has no blueprint for seeking out healthy connections. Graham is the only one in the bureau who can feel sympathy for Dollarhyde, perhaps because he can connect to the killer's struggle to assimilate into mainstream society: 'This all started from an abused kid, a battered infant [...] My heart bleeds for him as a child. Someone took a kid and manufactured a monster. At the same time, as an adult, he's irredeemable. He butchers whole families to pursue trivial fantasies.' That Graham is able to sympathise with Dollarhyde from a human perspective makes him more adept at tracking him down than his colleagues, who are incapable of viewing him as anything other than a deranged monster. Yet this awareness comes with a discomforting realisation: if Dollarhyde was once a young ball of potential who was warped by his surroundings into a beast, then, perhaps, Graham may have grown into a comparably perverse figure if he had the misfortune of being brought up in less favourable conditions.

Indeed, though Graham is very talented at his work, he appears awkward in the sterile FBI office and does not cooperate effectively with his co-workers. This is evidenced in an early scene. While the head of the department briefs the staff on the Tooth Fairy Killer case, Graham stands at the back of the room, rather than sitting amongst the rest of the agents, and wears a black suit while the others wear white or light grey. The crowd disperses and Graham is cornered by his colleagues. In contrast to their upright, confident body language, Graham's posture is meek and self-effacing. He hunches over, leaning against a desk, and his voice is soft as he timidly interjects: 'It's in his dreams. His motive. His act fuels his fantasy.' Graham cannot form friendships with his co-workers, just as he cannot properly connect with his family members. As the subject turns to previous murder cases, the reason for Graham's insecurity within this work environment becomes clear. Graham's success in taking down prolific killers has earned him much admiration from his colleagues, but his methods are controversial. While his colleagues privilege concrete evidence which may supply a motive, Graham believes that the most effective way to hunt the killer is to think the way that he does. Graham's tendency to slip into anti-social behaviour becomes even apparent in the following sequence when Graham is pestered by local journalist Freddy Lounds (Stephen Lang). Lounds, we gather, previously published unflattering information regarding Graham during the previous two cases and is eager to force information about him to spin into a smear piece. After putting up with his teasing for a few moments, Graham throws the journalist onto a car, smashing its windshield. Graham then grabs Lounds by the throat and seems on the verge of inflicting greater damage, before Crawford forcibly pulls him away and calms him down. This sudden outburst of violence comes as a shock to the viewer, considering that Graham demeanour is typically restrained and self-effacing. This is an ominous sign of Graham's potential to lose grip on his self-control when under pressure. In another unnerving parallel between the two men, Dollarhyde will later subject Lounds to torture as a form of vengeance after discovering that he has printed fraudulent information about him in the same newspaper. It is an illustration of just how fragile Dollarhyde's ego is that he deems it necessary to commit this murder in retaliation for a newspaper article that he believes casts him in a negative light.

Mann's decision to reveal the killer's identity halfway through the narrative shifts the viewer's focus away from wondering who is responsible for the crimes and toward studying Dollarhyde's character and the parallels between his own behaviour and that of the protagonist. The scene that introduces Dollarhyde is arguably the most disturbing in the film: our POV is aligned with Lounds, who is tied up in Dollarhyde's mansion and subjected to intense torture. Lounds is totally powerless, physically restrained and ignorant of his situation. As Lounds sits strapped to a chair, Dollarhyde forces him to observe a series of snapshots: first of the Leeds family during the break-in, in the moments leading up to their murder, and then of the family that Dollarhyde is currently stalking. With each photo transition, Dollarhyde emphatically asks, 'Do you see?' The importance of visual pleasure to the realisation of Dollarhyde's fantasies is demonstrated here, as it becomes clear that Dollarhyde believes the act of looking grants him immense power. 'It is not fear you owe me,' he tells Lounds, 'you owe me awe.' When Lounds then shuts his eyes to avoid meeting Dollarhyde's gaze, the killer aggressively commands him to 'Open your eyes!' The repeated emphasis on sensory input here is significant, as tapping into Dollarhyde's desire to be visually regarded with total, all-consuming admiration by his victims is what ultimately leads Graham to track him down.

Rewatching the home movies of both murdered families, Graham reaches the epiphany that Dollarhyde must also have seen their home movies – this is how he developed his infatuation with them, gathered information on them and worked out how to break into their homes. And Graham also realises that he must record these acts of violence on camera so that he can relive them again and again: 'Everything with you is seeing, isn't it? Your primary sensory intake, which makes your dream live is seeing. Reflections, mirrors, images. You've seen these films, haven't you, my man?' This explains the unusual arrangement of the bodies at the scene of the crimes – Dollarhyde positions them to be meeting his gaze and the camera lens, as though they were looking at him with love and admiration. He also organises the mirrors around the rooms so that they seem to be multiplying the gazes of the corpses. Graham's realisation inspires him to track down background information on the development of the films. Discovering that the home movies of both families were processed at the same film lab in St Louis, Graham and Crawford contact the site and gather information on all the employees who have handled the negatives.

Graham's climactic revelation only occurs after his final phone call with Lecktor, who Graham shockingly continues to contact for guidance, even after his actions have traumatised his family. To kill is the ultimate act of power, Lecktor explains, because it aligns the murderer with God. God is the supreme power because the lives of all people depend on them, and he can take away anybody's life if he wishes. God forces those beneath him to worship and obey him, in large part because he holds – and regularly exercises – the power to take life. To feel a sense of total domination over another person (to experience their devotion, their admiration, and their fear) and then to abuse this power, to use it to crush the person who is giving themselves over to you – this, Lecktor explains to Graham, is the rush of murder. 'And if one does as God does enough times,' Lecktor concludes, 'one will become what God is.' With this sentiment in mind, Graham returns to the Leeds house for a second time, now with the intention of physically repeating the killer's invasion of the space. He no longer carries a voice recorder, notepad, or any other official police equipment. Upon entering the bedroom, Graham stands at a vantage point in the room where he assumes the killer must have stood, gazing upon the deceased bodies with their lifeless eyes directed straight at him), here Graham acts out the murder as if possessed. Graham now speaks through the events of the murder entirely in the first person, addressing his observations to the late Mrs Leeds: 'I move to the door. I step into the room. I see you there. And I see me desired by you, accepted and loved. In the silver mirrors of your eyes.' This time, Mann depicts Graham's fantastical imagining of the event, as he believes the killer must have experienced it: Mrs Leeds sits up in bed, her eyes replaced by two glowing silver orbs. The distance between Graham's perspective and that of the killer has fully collapsed, as the detective now surveys the crime scene with the same objectifying, predatory gaze with which Dollarhyde perceived it on the night of the murder. Tony Williams recognises the significance of this moment: 'When Graham finally achieves his dark epiphany of identifying with Dollarhyde, he sees a vision of the slaughtered Mrs Leeds looking at him with mirrors in her eyes and mouth. He identifies with the demon inside of him, a demon from the dark world occupied by a serial killer fascinated by family home movies.' (2007). Although I agree with Williams' description of the significance of this movement in Graham's character arc, I disagree his subsequent argument that Graham then goes on to 'overcome his demonic dragon' by murdering Dollarhyde – the final act, I argue, is far more ambiguous and unsettling.

Dollarhyde's compulsion to feel a God-like control over life and death, as described by Lecktor, is evidenced by his malicious toying with McClane in the moments preceding his attempted murder of her. McClane is free to walk around the space of Dollarhyde's locked living room, but her senses are confused by the unusual arrangement of the furniture and the blaring of rock music at full volume. To heighten her disorientation, Dollarhyde moves around the room erratically, lightly touching her in different places every now and then so she cannot firmly grasp where he is in relation to her. Having obtained information on the developers of the home movies of the slaughtered families, Graham and Crawford track down Dollarhyde's location and travel together to the outside of his home. Crawford advises Graham to wait outside to allow for the SWAT team to take the killer out, but Graham disregards this request, instead loading a gun and running towards the house on his own. It is vital to Graham that he must confront and eliminate Dollarhyde personally because this case is about more to him than bringing a criminal to justice – it is a quest to dispose of his perverse double and, he believes, to therefore eradicate the perverse side of his own personality. Graham longs to eliminate the part of himself that is drawn to bloodshed, gets a thrill from voyeurism, routinely places his family in peril, and holds the potential to become a perpetrator of violence against innocent people. Graham enters Dollarhyde's home by smashing violently through the window, and throughout the fight, Mann repeatedly cuts to images of glass and other reflective surfaces shattering. Considering the centrality of reflected doubles in the visual scheme of *Manhunter*, this symbolically reflects Graham's need to defeat the unsavoury part of himself.

Graham successfully kills Dollarhyde, sets McClane free, and returns to Florida with Molly and Kevin, yet the ending does not carry any true sense of closure. The composition of *Manhunter*'s final sequence creates a sense of circularity. First, Graham and Crawford are shown staring out into the water in a static wide shot that immediately calls to mind the scene which saw Crawford convince Graham to give up his retirement so that he may work on the Dollarhyde case. Then we see Graham and Kevin on the beach, monitoring the enclosure they constructed to protect a nest of turtles at the start of the narrative. In the earlier sequence, Graham assured Kevin that, though assorted sea creatures may try to attack the newborn turtles, the enclosure will ensure that 'they're all going to make it.'. However, when Molly brings up his earlier promise to the family by asking how many of the turtles actually 'made it', Graham supplies the unsatisfactory answer: 'most of them'. The revelation that not *all* the turtles survived undermines Graham's authority in this scene, and calls into question his capacity to ensure true stability. If we interpret Graham's comment to also be referring to his now-closed investigation, it is unclear what exactly he means when he implies that some of 'them' did, in fact, *not* make it. 'He could either be referring to the victims of Dollarhyde that he was, tragically, too late to save, or, more disturbingly, he could be suggesting that he himself was not able to make it through the case without suffering serious mental damage. Although the family are reunited, the final scene on the beach is far from idyllic. Graham and Molly remain distant and unable to properly communicate. Molly tells Graham that she considered leaving him while the investigation was in process, before breaking down in tears. Graham does not address this confession, he simply hugs her, and then they both fall silent as they gaze into the ocean. Once again, Graham turns a blind eye to his marital problems instead of addressing them, and it is uncertain whether the relationship will survive this rocky period. Over the course of the narrative, Graham has recklessly endangered his own family and forced others to become the victim of his own objectifying gaze while taking a vicarious thrill in spying. He has once again driven himself close to madness to capture a criminal, just as he did in the Lecktor case that preceded his earlier retirement. There is ultimately no indication that Graham is in a more sound metal state now than he was at the beginning of the narrative, and it seems certain that if he received a similar invitation to return to the FBI he would accept it once again. Because the internal tensions and contradictions that lie at the core of Graham's personality remain unreconciled. It seems inevitable that he will once again feel the need to return to his line of work and be consumed, once more, by his demons – and perhaps next time his family will lose him definitively.

Intruder in the Dust:
The Last of the Mohicans (1992)

Following a decade of moderate successes, *The Last of the Mohicans* was the film that definitively cemented Mann's status as one of modern American cinema's most visionary auteurs. Although it took Mann until the early 1990s to produce this adaptation, Mann's history with the source material – both the 1826 novel by James Fenimore Cooper and the 1936 film version directed by George B Seitz – dates back much further. In a career retrospective interview, Mann revealed that one of the seminal movie-going experiences of his childhood was when his parents took him to see Seitz's *The Last of the Mohicans* in the theatre at the age of three. According to Mann, he soon forgot the exact elements of the plot, but specific stray details stuck in his mind. In particular, he was fascinated by the costuming and the contrast between the dress of the European settlers and the Native Americans: 'If you track the geology of an idea that may become a motion picture, what sparked it was something that took you over emotionally – it's rarely logical. In one instance, it was an image I had of American Indians with very strange haircuts, in conjunction with European military people, the 18th century, in uniforms. I was used to Westerns and there were a plethora of Westerns in the 1950s. So why were these people who had seemed to be coming out of an opera with people who were Iroquois? [...] Literally every single week in my entire life I had been thinking about *Last of the Mohicans*. I saw it when I was three and it was just rattling around in there.' (Appelo, 2014).

The process of producing a new adaptation of Cooper's novel was a more ambitious undertaking than anything Mann had attempted at this point in his career: the budget was $40million, more than double the budget of *Manhunter*; it was based on a universally beloved work of classic literature, which meant that expectations were extremely high (though Mann had directed films based on books before, they were recent bestsellers and not considered canonical masterworks of the art form); and the production required a more extensive cast and more expansive range of natural locations than any production Mann had worked on before. The risk paid off, and *The Last of the Mohicans* became the first unequivocal commercial and critical hit of Mann's directorial career, nearly quadrupling its budget at the box office and receiving several major awards (the most notable being the Academy Award for 'Best Sound Design', as well as the BAFTAs for 'Best Cinematography' and 'Best Make-Up'). The film's overwhelming success on every conceivable level allowed for Mann to continue expanding his artistic scope across the decades that followed. From the '90s onwards, Mann would devote himself to films that were epic in scale and hugely ambitious in terms of thematic content.

The Last of the Mohicans is a crucial text in Mann's body of work because it casts an eye back to the origins of American society, thus allowing us to see the roots of so many issues that Mann critiques in his later films. At the core of *The Last of the Mohicans* is the tension between the lofty abstract ideals that the nation was supposedly built upon and the unspeakable atrocities which the European settlers committed in the process of establishing a new settlement on Native American land. This issue is explored through the complex interactions that occur between three social groups: the Munros, a family of British settlers; the Mohicans, the three remaining members of a Native tribe that the Europeans have nearly wiped out; and the Huron, a rival tribe presided over by Magua (Wes Studi), a war chief who is motivated by a desire to exact vengeance on the Munro family as retaliation for the murder of his children at the hands of a British squadron lead by the Munro patriarch, Colonel Edmund Munro (Maurice Roëves).

Hawkeye (Daniel Day-Lewis) is defined by his hybrid and multifaceted identity. He is British by birth but was adopted by the Mohican tribe after his parents were murdered in an ambush by the Natives. During his upbringing, Hawkeye developed a respect for the landscape, a connection to nature, a disinterest in material riches and an adeptness at hunting and gathering, which aligns him with Native culture. However, he was also given an education at a school run by the European settlers, from which he learned British values and customs. Hawkeye's dual identity is exemplified by the multiple names he's referred to throughout the film. Although he is mainly referred to by his adopted Native name Hawkeye, he is also called by his birth name, Nathaniel, by several characters. As such, Hawkeye doesn't fully belong to any single faction: he is repulsed by the violence and greed which runs rampant amongst the European population, but he feels an ingrained need to provide some degree of guidance to them because of his familial lineage; he chooses to immerse himself in Native culture, but the fact that he does not share a bloodline with the Native population means that he will never truly be considered one of them (the very title of the film highlights the painful fact that Hawkeye is biologically incapable of continuing the Mohican bloodline, even though he is committed to passing down their traditions and values to the next generation). As one of the few multilingual characters, Hawkeye serves as an envoy between the Native myriad cultural groups present in the narrative. He rejects the notions of European exceptionalism, patriotism, and blind allegiance to authority that drive the British. Because he has received a first-hand glimpse into the lives of the Mohicans, he has a clear understanding of the violence inflicted upon the Natives at the hands of the settlers. While the British characters in the film rationalise their heinous actions as being part of a process of 'taming' the land and civilising those who live on it, Hawkeye recognises the atrocities they've committed as being wrapped up in an insatiable lust for power and wealth.

The romance that develops between Hawkeye and Cora Munro (Madeleine Stowe) takes place against the backdrop of a power struggle between the British and French factions vying for control of the environment. The land rightfully belongs to the Native Americans, but their rights are not recognised by the Europeans, who treat them either as barbaric threats that need to be eradicated or as pawns that may be manipulated to further their aims in the territorial struggle. As Mann explains, it was essential for him to intertwine the intimate with the expansive, so that the romance between Hawkeye and Cora becomes the lens through which broader socio-political tensions are explored: 'I wanted to have the scale of a geopolitical conflict – the ethnic and religious conflicts, the struggle of white imperialism on a grassroots level, the conditions of the struggle for survival of the colonial population, and the struggle between the Euro-American and European powers and the American Indian population [...] at the same time, I wanted an emotional intensity that came from the stories of Hawkeye, his father and brother, from each of their points of view, and from the Munro daughters and the obvious central love story.' (Smith, 1992: 10).

Hawkeye's refusal to bow down to the demands of the British, to be indoctrinated into their warped view of themselves and their distorted sense of duty, makes him interesting to consider as an anti-authoritarian Mannian protagonist in the mould of *Thief*'s Frank and *The Jericho Mile*'s Murphy. Frank's resistance to taking on a position of subordination in a crime syndicate and Murphy's refusal to betray his true values so that he may appease the whims of the Olympic committee chime with Hawkeye's resistance to joining the British militia, despite the generals' repeated attempts to enlist him. While the British troops are characterised by an attitude of unwavering servitude to the state, the monarchy, and dubious figures of authority, Hawkeye prides himself on his ability to remain autonomous and make his own decisions. He can challenge orders, think beyond the boundaries of what is deemed socially 'acceptable' behaviour, and reject laws that he considers unjust. Hawkeye's commitment to his own ethical code enables him to resist the pressures of public judgement and institutional demands. Hawkeye's emphasis on personal independence and self-determination is diametrically opposed to the slavish obedience to British authority exhibited by Major Duncan Heyward (Steven Waddington). Heyward feels a sense of obligation to carry out whatever commands are handed down to him without thinking about whether they are morally justifiable or not. Therefore, he becomes a conduit through which the imperialist crimes of the past are perpetuated in the present.

Many Hollywood films that dramatise the European colonisation of the Americas depict a Native American character becoming edified through their interaction with the invading forces. Settler-Native romance films such as Eric Goldberg and Mike Gabriel's *Pocahontas* (1995), Roger Corman's *Apache Woman* (1955) and Lew Landers' *Burning Arrows* (1953) downplay the magnitude of the atrocities committed by crafting narratives in which the lives of the Natives are enriched by their encounter with the 'enlightened' attitudes, advanced tools and material goods brought to them by the Europeans. In such a narrative framework, the Native tribes are suspicious of the foreign invaders at first, but once they are exposed to their traditions and ideals, they gradually develop a respect for European customs and make a conscious choice to adapt to the way of life they represent. *The Last of The Mohicans* doesn't just stray from this formula; it directly inverts it. Mann's film does not depict its Native characters becoming more civilised, educated, or morally upright through their interactions with the Europeans – a plot trajectory which would imply that indoctrination into the European value system transformed his life for the better, thus reinforcing an exceptionalist view of Western culture. Instead, *The Last of the Mohicans* celebrates characters who are able to break away from European tradition and embrace the characteristics of the Natives. Hawkeye has already achieved this at the beginning of the narrative, and his romance with Cora sees him encourage her to become cognisant of the collective sins of British society and, as a result, gravitate toward Native culture. Cora's character arc, which sees her distance herself from Heyward – a close friend of her family who proposes to her in the film's first act – and become closer to Hawkeye, illustrates her capacity to come to terms with the true history and ambitions of the culture into which she was born and, therefore, to make positive steps towards genuine progress in the future.

The closing image of *The Last of the Mohicans* depicts Hawkeye, Hawkeye's adoptive father Chingachgook (Russell Means) and Cora grouped together as a newly formed family unit. Cora has definitively broken away from the oppressive rule of the British and embraced the ethos of Native American culture. *The Last of Mohicans* may be an elegy for a vanquished way of life that can never be recaptured, but it's not a totally hopeless film. At the end of the narrative, the only remaining Mohican stands in unity with Hawkeye and Cora. Because of Chingachgook's advanced age, and the death of his biological son Uncas (Eric Schweig) in the final battle, we know that the Mohican bloodline will end with him. The Mohicans may be a vanishing people, but the incorporation of Cora into their fold represents the continuation of their beliefs and practices amongst younger generations. Both Hawkeye and Cora are adopted into the Mohican community; they represent a progressive union of Native and settler culture, tradition and modernity.

Mann's film opens three years into the Anglo-French war. Villages on the frontier have already been built and inhabited by Europeans, and a considerable amount of the Native population has already been wiped out. The Mohicans represent a tribe that has almost been completely destroyed by the colonialist invaders but who honourably hold to their traditions and customs. Echoing the opening sequence of *The Keep*, *The Last of the Mohicans* begins with a series of images of the natural landscape – though here we see the environment through the eyes of those who are in tune with it, rather than the invaders. The tone is far more tranquil. The sound of indigenous American drums fills the soundtrack, immediately rooting the film in the viewpoint of the Natives. Mann captures Hawkeye's motion through a clearing in a beautiful mountainous region with a serene tracking shot. He is soon joined by the two remaining members of the Mohicans, Chingachgook and Uncas. They cross a small river then climb up an elevated mount. The camera ceases its motion and becomes fixed in place as Hawkeye pulls out a rifle and aims it, carefully, at a stag swerving between trees in the distance. Hawkeye aims and fires with remarkable precision, resulting in the stag's swift, painless death. Hawkeye's hybrid identity is immediately highlighted through his fusion of Native hunting techniques and advanced European technology. Hawkeye's utilisation of the modern technological instrument is integrated into the traditional practices of the Natives; it doesn't supplant them. The three men then perform a vigil over the stag's deceased body. Chingachgook, the senior member of the group, offers a lament for the deceased animal: 'We're sorry to kill you, brother. We do honour to your courage and speed, your strength.' This scene immediately establishes a central tenet of Mohican culture: they have a fundamental reverence for the sanctity of life. They only kill animals that they intend to feed on for crucial sustenance, and they do so in a way that minimises their suffering. In contrast to the bloodthirst of the European settlers who commit acts of violence to assert their dominance over those they consider to be inherently 'inferior', the Mohicans treat the animals they hunt as being on an equal footing with themselves. This is supported by the later scene in which Chingachgook and Hawkeye pay tribute to the deceased Uncas in a similar manner, demonstrating that they view an animal's life as being just as important and worthy of respect as the life of a family member.

After their hunting session, the Mohicans visit the Camerons, a family of British descent who live in a cosy rural cottage in a village on the frontier. The Mohicans and the Camerons initially treat each other with mutual kindness and courtesy, creating an atmosphere of peaceful co-existence between the Natives and the Europeans, which will rapidly disintegrate. The overtly, almost paradoxically, halcyon visual design of the space suggests that it is not intended to depict an accurate snapshot of the period but to set up a fantasy of racial and cultural unity of the kind that never truly existed. The interior is a warm, golden haven, bathed in a hazy amber glow. This makes the entire scene radiate an unreal, dream-like quality. Both families share dinner together, but fissures in this sentimentalised vision are soon revealed as they engage in conversation. Alexandra (Tracey Ellis), the youngest member of the Camerons, comments that Uncas has reached the age where he should have already settled down with a wife and had children. This isn't an intentionally malicious comment, but it demonstrates the Cameron family's inability to see the world in a way that doesn't conform to their deeply ingrained European perspective – Alexandra attempts to impose her European bourgeois expectations onto a character raised in a culture that does not have the same values and expectations. The discussion turns to war. The Mohicans are told that the two armies are heading to the area. The county is recruiting militiamen to support the British military in the area, and the Camerons are planning to join the British militia. The next time the Mohicans visit the Cameron home, it will be under tragic conditions: they pass by following an ambush on the village by the French army to find that the Cameron house has been set on fire and the family brutally slaughtered.

In the scene that follows the dinner sequence, a British soldier rides into the local village on horseback, and the briefly present sense of solidarity quickly dissipates, revealing that it was only a fragile illusion. The village inhabitants are called upon to leave their homes defenceless so that they may form a militia to travel to Fort William Henry. Although some of the crowd appear apprehensive about leaving the village, the British lieutenants appeal to a sense of national pride and allegiance to the crown to encourage the villagers to submit to their demands. Hawkeye, interested in observing how the situation plays out but feeling no obligation to participate, watches the recruitment drive from a distance. Hawkeye advises the villagers to resist the call, foreseeing that if the village is dragged into a territorial conflict, it will likely descend into irreversible devastation and hardship. Hawkeye emphasises independence and liberty of thought as higher values than subservience to the authority and patriotism, as emphasised by his line 'I do not call myself subject to much at all.' The lieutenant tells the villagers not to pay attention to Hawkeye's warnings, issuing the disingenuous promise that the British military will guarantee the security of the villagers' homes in their absence. Hawkeye, however, can see past this false promise to recognise that the military officers don't truly have any interest in protecting the well-being of their subjects; they only see them as tools they may use to further their territorial ambitions. The lieutenants tell the villagers that they have achieved freedom by settling in America and that it is sometimes necessary to engage in combat to protect this freedom – but, Hawkeye reasons, if they are coerced into joining a war through lies told to them by dubious authority figures, the villagers cannot truly consider themselves to be free. As a result of Hawkeye's protests, the lieutenant agrees to allow the men to return to protect their homes if they hear that French troops are approaching the village. Hawkeye remains sceptical, but the villagers do not heed his warnings and accept the call. The emphasis that the British officers place on formal tradition, ownership, and the exertion of power extends into their personal lives as well. Following the recruitment drive, Heyward offers a marriage proposal to Cora in a way that is extremely formal and stiff, resembling a business proposition more than a romantic gesture. Heyward is a high-ranking officer of extreme wealth and noble background. He is also a close friend of Cora's father, and knows that he would be General Munro's ideal choice of a life partner for his daughter. Heyward dispassionately reminds Cora of this fact during the proposal, asserting that she has an obligation to honour her father's wishes: 'Respect and friendship, isn't that a reasonable basis for a man and woman to be married? All else may grow in time.' In stark contrast to the sensuality and intense emotion she experiences in her romance with Hawkeye, the proposed union between her and Heyward is treated like a financial and social transaction. As Heyward tells her with characteristic coldness, their parents have decided that they would make an appropriate pairing, and to disobey would be a sign of disrespect towards both of their families. Heyward is a mirror image of Cora's father – a slave to authority who actively desires to act as an instrument of British imperialism. By rejecting the proposal, Cora demonstrates a rebellious nature and a concerted interest in determining her own path in life. She refuses to be treated like property by Heyward and would rather fail on her own terms than lead a life that has been shaped for her by others. Her assertion that she must live according to her 'own judgement' sounds like it could have been voiced by any number of Mann protagonists, such as Frank, Murphy and Hawkeye himself. However, although signs of dissent are already evident in Cora's behaviour, she is yet not as strong-willed or independent as she will grow to be later in the narrative. So, although she rebuffs Heyward's offer of marriage, she does so politely, telling him that she needs more time to come to a firm decision. She is still tied to the conservative attitudes and demure behaviours instilled in her by her upper-class British upbringing. Her relationship with Hawkeye, however, will encourage her to break free from these beliefs and express her own thoughts and feelings.

The British militia, which includes Heyward, Cora and Cora's sister Alice (Jodhi May), is escorted towards Fort William Henry by Magua, along with a few other members of the Huron tribe. Hawkeye, accompanied by Chingachgook and Uncas, watches the participants from a distance – he is not part of the militia but he casts a protective eye over both the British men and the Huron tribe. It is indicative of the exceptionalism and the ignorance of the British army that they accept Magua's offer of help at face value – they are seemingly unaware of the grave injustice committed against Magua's family by the British military and of the tenets of Huron law, which dictate that every act of unjust violence must be met with an act of restorative violence of equal intensity.

Not long into their journey, Magua turns against the militia and wrestles a rifle from one of the soldiers. Magua proves to be adept at wielding the weapon, just as Hawkeye is, revealing a point of connection between the two men: Magua is similarly a hybrid figure who merges characteristics of the settlers with elements of indigenous culture, but Magua takes on the worst, most mendacious qualities of the settlers despite being born as a Native, whereas Hawkeye was born an Englishman but chooses to adopt the positive values of the Natives. The fact that the rifle – used recurringly in the film as a symbol of the new technologies brought to the Native land by the settlers – is the primary instrument used in this ambush emphasises that the violence directed towards the British at this moment is a result of the violence they introduced to a once peaceful land. The camera initially follows the motion of the militia through a clearing with a smooth tracking shot, but it abruptly becomes shaky and unstable as the Huron tribe strikes the British soldiers. While the suddenness of the assault blindsides the British soldiers, leaving them incapable of responding effectively, the alert and cautious Hawkeye successfully intervenes. Hawkeye angles his rifle with the same dexterity he exhibited during the opening sequence, this time firing it from afar to skim the fingers of a Huron who is about to slice Cora's throat. Hawkeye does not kill the attackers, and he does not cause unnecessary harm. He then fires a second shot, this time aiming towards the air to alert the rest of the Huron to his presence, and they quickly flee the scene. Hawkeye does not wish to commit harm to the Huron people; he has a driving impulse to safeguard *all* life, and, here he recognises that all he needs to do to end this moment of conflict is make the Huron aware that he is positioned in a vantage point. Hawkeye does not express disapproval of the Huron when he discusses the incident with Heyward afterwards. Heyward comments that the British army never should have trusted a Native tribe to protect them. Heyward indicates that he views the Natives as being inherently feral, and driven by unmotivated hatred.

The more compassionate and clear-eyed Hawkeye counters this perspective and expresses his deep familiarity with the nuances of Huron law when he informs Heyward that Magua must have been attempting to kill for either 'vengeance or reparations'. Heyward articulates a fundamental inability to recognise the British Empire's crimes and see other races as being on the same level as the Europeans. Duncan cloaks these ugly aspects of his personality under a thin veneer of civility – this is the worldview that has been instilled in him by his cultural background, and he has never once thought to question it. Although Hawkeye was taught to this belief system during his years at a British-controlled school, he has the power to challenge the settler mentality. Hawkeye offers to take Magua's place and to provide the troops secure guidance to the fort, but he emphasises that he is not, and never will be, an ally of the British army. Indignant at Heyward's habit of referring to him as 'scout', Hawkeye forcefully retorts, 'I ain't your scout, and I sure ain't in no damn militia.' Duncan believes he holds power here because it has been bestowed upon him by British generals, but Hawkeye is confident that he is the one who truly controls the situation. Hawkeye has disdain for the territorial war, and he loathes the British forces that have so inflicted so much oppression and suffering upon this environment. The reason he aids the militia in their journey is that he knows that the villagers have been manipulated into fighting against their own interests and he wants to see them return safely – he doesn't believe this is possible under the incompetent and opportunistic leadership of the British generals. Because Hawkeye remains separate from the British and French armies, because he is not driven by culturally conditioned attitudes of national pride and cultural exceptionalism, he can acknowledge the humanity of all parties involved in the war and is therefore capable of standing up to all forms of injustice.

As the militia gather around a campfire after a day of travelling, Hawkeye tells Cora about his background and explains that his exposure to both Native and European culture emancipated him from the strict values imposed on students by the British school system. As such, Hawkeye has developed a thorough understanding of both cultures and can now make informed decisions about where to stand in relation to both of them. By informing Cora of other worldviews that break away from the perspective of the British, Hawkeye educates her in the same way that Chingachgook educated him. Cora realises that she was raised to view the Natives as being lesser than the British, and has never talked to anybody who has encouraged her to understand the process of colonisation from their perspective. Just as Hawkeye was taught about the ways of Mohican life by Chingachgook, here he teaches Cora about the cruel realities of European imperialism, thus continuing the cycle of emancipation through pedagogy. With Hawkeye's guidance, Cora is able to address the limitations of her myopic worldview and, therefore, listen to and learn from the experiences of others. As Gaine perceptively observes, Cora's character arc throughout the narrative demonstrates that 'European decorum and superiority are [...] replaced with the freedom and vivacity of the frontier.' (2011: 171). While Heyward remains unmoveable in his steadfast quest to force all foreign peoples and cultures to conform to British values, Cora is increasingly drawn to the lifestyle of the Natives and seeks to distance herself from the culture she was born into.

The militia reaches Fort William Henry to find that a siege by the French military and their Huron allies is already in progress. They are greeted by Cora's father and brought into the fort's headquarters. In this scene, we witness a significant ideological conflict between the film's two most prominent symbolic father figures: Munro and Chingachgook. Munro is a symbol of unreliable patriarchal, imperialist and military authority, and he fails to ensure the safety of his daughters. Chingachgook, on the other hand, is caring and nurturing, providing the protection of his sons while still proudly allowing them to determine their own paths (as evidenced by his decision to send Hawkeye to a British school, therefore giving him the option to align himself more heavily with British culture if he thought it was right). Munro escalates unnecessary violence while Chingachgook seeks to quell it; Chingachgook is attentive while Munro is absent; Chingachgook respects the agency of his sons, while Munro tries to manipulate his daughters into doing whatever he wants of them. The portrayal of Munro as destructive, domineering, and self-centered establishes an explicit connection between colonial authority and ruinous fatherhood. The condescending paternal language used by Munro to address his daughters is similar to the language used by the British generals when addressing their soldiers. This further cements the impression that the British authority figures disingenuously use a rhetoric of national debt, duty and patriotism as a means to manipulate others into committing to decisions against their better judgement – whether this is a case of encouraging men to risk their lives in territorial war or encouraging their daughters to marry against their wishes. The sense of chauvinism expressed by Munro – and inherited by

Heyward – is connected to his sense of racial supremacy. He dismisses the advice of the Mohicans and his daughters while placing unwavering trust in Heyward.

Munro informs Heyward that he sent a courier to inform them that a siege was underway and that they should not travel to the fort without heavy reinforcements. This failure forces the British to discuss potential strategies to regain control of the fort. Munro calls for the men to remain at the fort to ward off the French army and draw on families living at the frontier to get extra support. Hawkeye, fulfilling a role similar to the one he performed during the formation of the militia, is present to offer helpful guidance while essentially retaining his independence from the troops. He warns Munro that if he goes through with his plan, the French army will form a war party on the frontier, and more families like the Camerons will be murdered. Munro does not take kindly to Hawkeye's insubordinate behaviour, threatening to imprison him and anybody else who raises doubts regarding the effectiveness of his plan. He then tells the men that if any of them leave the fort to see to their families, they will be charged with sedition. In spite of this warning, Hawkeye encourages the troops that the risk is worth it if it means they can ensure their families safeties, and several of the men take his advice. Watching the soldiers gradually desert the British military in the middle of the night, Cora warns Hawkeye that he must too leave, lest he suffer the consequences. But Hawkeye does not recognise the authority of European law and therefore refuses to flee the fort – he knows that his services are still needed there, and if he were to leave now the remaining men would be subject to the manipulations of their nefarious superior officers. To the astonishment of Heyward, both Cora and Alice support Hawkeye in this decision and reject the tyranny of their father. Cora offers Heyward the opportunity to join them in opposing Munro's ruling, but his devotion blinds him to his superior officer. Finally breaking free of the shackles of British tradition, she goes as far as to tell Heyward that she'd prefer to be thrown in jail than to obey laws that she knows to be unjust: 'If it is sedition, then I am guilty of sedition too'.

By directly positioning herself in opposition to figures of British cultural tradition, and voicing her lack of faith in the rule of law, Cora makes a giant leap in her journey towards self-actualisation. Her acknowledgement that British law does not provide a reliable moral framework for determining the righteousness of one's actions, but, instead, is a man-made system was created by the aristocracy to protect their wealth and authority, echoes a discussion in which Hawkeye convinces the militia volunteers that they must adopt a sceptical attitude towards the law because it is the ultimate tool wielded by those in power to hold on to their control. Many men are afraid to leave the militia to protect their families, not only because of the risk of being thrown in prison but also because the law forms the backbone of their sense of right and wrong. Hawkeye pleads with them to develop a more nuanced and critical ethical code: 'I believe that they set aside their law as and when they wish. Their law no longer has rightful authority over us. All they have other us, then, is tyranny. And I will not live under that yoke.' Under Hawkeye's guidance, these men no longer see the British commanders as noble figures but as mendacious authoritarians driven by self-interest. This awareness is necessary to break the chain of violence and domination passed down throughout generations of British rule. Many of the volunteers follow this advice and leave to check on their homes and families; Hawkeye and Cora make the risky decision not to run, despite knowing that they risk capture and execution because they view it as their place to protect those who have been misled into joining the territorial war.

By laying her freedom on the line to stand up for the men and fight the demands of their reckless commanders, Cora reveals a protective instinct akin to that of the Mohicans, further aligning her with Hawkeye. The attraction which builds between them is rooted in emotional, intellectual, and physical respect and reciprocity, making it one of the few relationships in Mann's oeuvre which can be sustained in the long term. This is because, unlike Frank and Graham, Hawkeye is open and honest with Cora; he tells her about his commitment to his belief system from the moment they meet and tells her frankly about the level of personal sacrifice which results from his commitment to this perspective. Cora, then, can make an educated decision to accompany him on his quest, and this is why this is one of the few romances in Mann's filmography that can survive in the long-term. As Gaine observes, 'The romance between Hawkeye is intertwined with her abandonment of oppressive British values and their shared solicitude.' (2011: 172). The morning after they make love for the first time, their compartment is stormed by British guards and Hawkeye is apprehended and sentenced to death . Despite Cora's protestations, Munro and Heyward remain unmoved; they perceive Hawkeye as a threat to the smooth running of the military operation, and he must be made a sacrifice to quell any potential insurrection amongst the soldiers. There is also the added incentive of forcibly separating Cora from the supposedly 'corrosive' influence of Hawkeye, and therefore contain Munro's 'transgressive' desire. It is not until Hawkeye and Cora cut ties with the British establishment entirely and embark on a new existence in the heart of nature that their relationship can flourish.

Coming to the gradual realisation that the British army is unlikely to hold on to control of the fort, even with the help of reinforcements, Munro reluctantly accepts French commander General Louis-Joseph de Montcalm's (Patrice Chéreau) offer to meet to discuss the possibility of setting up a conditional surrender. Ironically, the men who previously offered false promises to the villagers on the frontier to manipulate them into joining the war now become the victims of a similar ruse. Montcalm gives Munro his word that he will leave the fort untouched and spare the lives of the British commanders if they flee the site immediately. If the British choose to stay, however, the French army will show them no mercy and seize the fort by any means necessary. Munro, illustrating his lack of judgement, agrees to Montcalm's deal, unaware that the French general has already made a pact with Magua to deliver Munro and his daughters into the hands of the Huron. In exchange, Magua promises that the Huron will become collaborators with the French army in the territorial war.

Montcalm and Magua meet at a secret rendezvous spot in the forest to discuss the arrangement. During this meeting, Magua delivers a powerful monologue about the horrific violence his people suffered at the hands of the British. *The Last of the Mohicans* has received criticism in some circles for its depiction of Magua, with detractors of Mann's film arguing that the characterisation reinforces negative stereotypes about indigenous Americans. For these critics, the portrayal of Magua as vengeful and bloodthirsty supports the insidious figure of the animalistic, irrational Native, which has been perpetuated in American media for centuries to demonise the indigenous people and rationalise the genocide of Natives by white colonisers. Often, such a stereotype has been used to create a divide between Natives that were willing to assimilate without protest into white European culture (portrayed as being noble and virtuous) and Natives that resisted European rule and held on to their own customs (portrayed as bestial primitives unjustly hostile to settler forces). Ian K Steele, for example, argues that: 'To serve the modern taste for gratuitous violence [...] Mann has perpetuated an ancient lie about Indian savagery at Fort William Henry, a lie used to rationalise brutal policies toward Indians.' [sic] Steele concludes that Mann's decision to portray Magua in this light renders ineffective the film's 'Real and fanciful efforts [...] to convey Indian values and perspectives sympathetically.' (1993: 1181). However, Magua's extended monologue in this scene makes it clear that, in contrast to Heyward and the other European antagonists who commit acts of violence for the purpose of imperialist expansion, Magua's motivation in inflicting violence is vengeance for the grave acts of injustice perpetrated against his loved ones. As General Munro was directly responsible for the murder of his children, he believes that he must now murder the Munro daughters in retaliation, wiping Munro's legacy from the earth just as his own lineage has been destroyed. The violence inflicted upon the British in the final act is, therefore, explicitly treated as a consequence of the sadistic actions the army committed against Natives in the past. Again, when the British soldiers fail to keep Cora safe, Hawkeye must step in to shield her from harm. The French commanders lead the British troops out of the fort through a clearing, and, when they sense that their guard are down, they signal for Magua, along with several other members of the Huron, to emerge from the surrounding trees and stage their ambush. Hawkeye is positioned in the centre of the assembly, his wrists restrained and his movements heavily monitored by the military commanders. The tribe first attack slowly, taking out a few members of the British military at the front and back of the line. A close-up on Hawkeye's face as he quickly realises that the British troops been set up by the French, indicates that only he is capable of responding to this threat – though his shackles prevent him from acting as swiftly as he did during the earlier ambush by the Huron. The military commanders, in contrast, are paralysed by fear. After a moment of uncertainty, a large group of Huron fighters appear from the foliage and charge on the crowd. Magua mortally wounds Munro, telling him as the life seeps out of his body that he will go on to murder his daughters so that his family line is forever wiped from the face of the earth. He then ritualistically cuts out his heart and lifts it skywards to show the other Huron. Hawkeye shakes himself free of his shackles as the British guards are engaged in combat. He then tracks down Cora in the carnage and rescues her just as she is about to have her throat slit.

Cora and Alice are kidnapped and taken to the top of a mountain by the Huron to be sacrificed by Magua under the watchful gaze of a high council of elder Huron. At this stage, Hawkeye intervenes and makes a fervent appeal to the council, urging them to spare the lives of the Munro daughters. This scene has drawn heavy criticism from detractors of the film, with some believing that Hawkeye's emotional testimony places him firmly on the side of the Europeans, decrying the 'savagery' of the Natives, represented by Magua. These critics have supported this reading by highlighting Magua's accusation that, because of his familial lineage and close proximity to the Europeans, Hawkeye is not – and has never – truly between part of indigenous culture, and he, therefore, has no right to criticise any aspect of it. Magua disparagingly calls Hawkeye a man who 'speaks two tongues', implying that his tendency to cross back and forth between the two communities has means that he does not truly belong to either community – and, therefore, Hawkeye cannot possibly represented the values of the Natives. I contend, however, that a closer analysis of this scene reveals that Hawkeye holds a more nuanced and multifaceted ethical stance than this. Hawkeye never claims that Munro is innocent or Magua's rage is unfounded. Hawkeye's speech attacks Magua on the grounds that he has become warped by the selfishness and vindictiveness of the invading Europeans – and that the indigenous people must resist the noxious influence of the Europeans if they want to avoid perpetuating the same sins as the invading forces. The Colonel was responsible for the injustice committed against Magua, Hawkeye reasons, and since he has been killed, the case should be satisfied. It is an important tenet of Huron law that restorative justice must be brought about without passion or emotion to ensure that the one pursuing justice does not descend to the same level of cruelty as the ones they are seeking vengeance against. Magua, on the other hand, allows himself to be overwhelmed by anger as he hunts down the Munro family. Because of this, Magua ends up killing numerous people who are not directly connected to those who slaughtered his family – a *violation* of Huron law. Furthermore, because Magua views all members of the settler community as being perpetuators of imperialist violence incapable of change, he does not consider the fact that the two Munro daughters have rejected the ideology of the colonial European invaders. Magua's rash and destructive actions throughout the film, then, demonstrate that he does not genuinely respect for Huron law – and, indeed, an older Huron leader chastises the war chief at one point for breaking away from the traditional scripture of the tribe. Magua's lack of interest in preserving indigenous culture is also evidenced by his decision to make a pact with the French army to help them consolidate their ownership over the land (while Hawkeye acts to guard the lives of several British-born individuals, he never assists the army in their imperialist ambitions; in fact, he actively convinces the soldiers to reject the commands of their military commanders). Hawkeye voices his opposition to the imperatives of the Europeans *and* Magua simultaneously when he says: 'Would the Hurons make their Algonquin brothers foolish with brandy and steal their lands to sell them for gold to the white man? [...] Would the Huron kill every man, woman and child of their enemy? Those are the ways of the Yengees and Les Francais traders, their masters in Europe infected with the sickness of greed.' As Hawkeye accurately observes, Magua has been consumed by the ideology of capitalist avarice and lust for power two characteristics that are fundamentally opposed to the traditional values of Native culture. Magua, then, is not treated as the villain of the film *because* he represents the supposed 'barbarity' of the Europeans; on the contrary, he is treated as the villain because he has turned his back on Native culture and taken on many negative traits of the

Recognising that the Huron crowd sees the truth in Hawkeye's speech, Magua announces that he will set the captured British men free on the terms of unconditional surrender. However, he still intends to publicly slaughter Alice and Cora as an act of retaliation against the murder of his own family. Magua's decision is supported by the Sachem (Mike Phillips), the leader of the Huron elders and a patriarchal figure of wisdom. Although Sachem concurs with certain parts of Hawkeye's condemnation of Magua, he believes that the Huron law of restorative violence should be respected and that the execution of Alice and Cora can be reasonably justified according to the conditions of Huron law. At this point, however, an unexpected development occurs: Heyward offers to atone for his own sins and the sins of white patriarchal authority in general, by offering himself in sacrifice in place of Cora and Alice. He argues to the council that, although he is not a blood relation of the Colonel, he is a high-ranking military officer, and his loss would be an equivalent blow to the British. After some discussion, the council agree that this proposition would be in keeping with Huron law, and Heyward is burned alive at the stake. Heyward's self-sacrifice is an act of enormous moral courage, which indicates that he has finally developed an awareness of the enormity of the crimes committed by his countrymen and, he now feels an ethical imperative to make amends for them. Unlike Hawkeye and Cora, though, Heyward knows that he is incapable of breaking out of his learned patterns of behaviour he inherited from the British authority figures. So, the only way that Heyward can make a positive change is by sacrificing himself so that Huron law may be satisfied while the more open and adaptable characters escape to set out a more positive vision of America's future. Hawkeye, who has demonstrated disdain for Heyward throughout the entire narrative, now expresses a newfound admiration for him, acknowledging the magnitude of this gesture and the change in attitude it signifies. Hawkeye is powerless to stop the Mohicans from murdering Heyward, but he shows a remarkable display of compassion when he shoots Heyward from a distance as he escorts Cora to safety. The bullet strikes Heyward and instantly ends his agony.

Again demonstrating his duplicity and lack of respect for Huron customs, Magua overrides the council's decision and still attempts to slaughter Alice and Cora. As the Huron council has already committed to sparing these women, Magua's attempt to override this decision and kill them anyway is the most egregious display of the war chief's disregard for Huron law. All three Mohicans intervene to prevent a potentially endless cycle of violence, and Magua responds by fatally stabbing Uncas multiple times. This is an unspeakable atrocity, as it ensures that the Mohican bloodline will die with Chingachgook. When targeting the Munros, Magua's anger could be justified as he was acting as a victim lashing out against the family of the man who deeply wronged him. But here, Magua commits an act of atrocious and unmotivated violence against a fellow Native – and, as a consequence, has contributed to the extinction of an indigenous tribe.

Standing on the edge of the mountaintop, Chingachgook, Hawkeye and Cora grieve the death of Uncas and reflect upon the fading of the Mohican lifestyle. Hawkeye and Cora may represent the Mohican spirit, but only Chingachgook is a blood descendent, and after he has gone, the Mohicans will be no more. Hawkeye and Cora will hold on to the respect for nature, egalitarian ideals and belief in the importance of resisting corrupt figures of authority associated with the indigenous population. The fact that the film ends on a hybrid family articulates the belief that the positive values of the Natives may be constructively integrated into post-Revolutionary life. This is, to a certain degree, an idealistic ending, but it should not be interpreted as a simplistic expression of America's fundamental purity and virtue. Indeed, *The Last of the Mohicans* does not shy away from depicting the bloodshed and racism that the nation was founded upon. Mann, however, offers a positive vision of what American society should aspire to be. Hawkeye and Cora's unification at the end of the narrative represents a positive vision of how the individual in American society may stand up to injustice and corruption. Although the critical representation of American institutions in later Mann films suggest that, although the materialism, avarice, prejudice and inequality perpetuated by the powerful in *The Last of the Mohicans* continue to be dominant features in contemporary American society the resilient anti-authoritarian spirit represented by Hawkeye and Cora has also endured within certain individuals who heroically refuse to submit to tyranny.

Road to Nowhere:
Heat (1995)

Mann's deeply ambitious, panoramic crime epic *Heat* begins in darkness: the fades slowly from a black screen to a shot of an elevated metro platform at night. Several electrical towers cut across the frame vertically, creating a barrier in the middle of the composition. The lights of the city can be seen faintly in the distance. A thick stream of smoke is emitted from the left side of the screen, obscuring our view of a train cart as it powers toward the foreground. Mann cuts across the 180-line to show us the station, a symmetrical grid of chrome silver that stands out against the otherwise darkened backdrop. The carriage passes from the foreground to the background of this composition before pulling to a stop. Following these two extreme wide shots, Mann abruptly cuts to a close-up. We focus on McCauley's face as he exits the carriage, slowly, eyes darting around as if instinctively checking the spot for suspicious behaviour, and then makes his way toward the exit. McCauley smoothly steps onto an escalator and drifts down into the main foyer of the station, his visage obscured by poles and beams in the foreground, as if becoming subsumed by the cityscape that will soon become his resting place.

Heat also ends in a location associated with mass transit: the final chase sequence takes place on the tarmac of Los Angeles International Airport, the lights of the city again visible in the far distance as the life drains out of a mortally wounded McCauley, shot by LAPD officer Hanna on the way to board a plane that would take him out of the city. Mann's choice to bookend the film with images of McCauley's arrival into and (thwarted) escape from Los Angeles is fitting for a film that is as much a city symphony as it is a heist film and a character study. As Dzeis observes, the film takes as its central subject the 'the interplay between the intimate and the panoramic.' (2002). Spaces of ephemerality abound: business discussions take place in diners and public walkways; there are frequent interstitial images of motorways, bridges, and subway platforms; private spaces are designed to resemble public ones. No character has a fixed domestic space: McCauley rents a thread-bare apartment that he deliberately keeps free of possessions so he can quickly move on to a new residence if the cops track his location; Vincent Hanna initially lives with his wife in a house she won from her ex-husband during their divorce, but he relocates to a hotel room after discovering her infidelity; the living situation of McCauley's colleague Chris Shiherlis (Val Kilmer) and his wife Charlene (Ashley Judd) is split apart when, first, he moves into McCauley's dwelling after an explosive argument, and, then, she is transported to a safe house by the LAPD.

In *Manhunter*, Mann portrays the modern American city as a dehumanising wasteland that fosters feelings of alienation and loneliness in those who drift through it; in *Heat*, this theme is elaborated upon further, becoming the film's central subject. As Rybin notes, the representation of the cityscape in *Heat* is intrinsically intertwined with the feelings of alienation, transience and isolation experienced by its characters: 'richly realised city images figure as an overarching metaphor for postmodern contingency.' (2005: 176). The Los Angeles of *Heat* is a vast, man-made dystopia in which the lost souls which populate the narrative can find no solid footing. The urban landscape is dominated by monolithic, dwarfing architectural structures – from the skyscrapers which dot the skyline to the giant concrete car parks to the sprawling road which connect it all together – which overwhelm and ensnare their inhabitants. Within indoor settings windows, doorframes and stairways dominate the compositions, blurring the line between interior and exterior.

Hanna attempts to maintain a stable family life, but the ultra-modern urban environment is hostile to the maintenance of healthy emotional bonds. McCauley, on the flipside, prides himself on his ability to survive without establishing any substantial connections to others. As he explains to Hanna during their discussion at the diner: 'Don't let yourself get attached to anything you are not willing to walk out on in 30 seconds flat if you feel the heat around the corner.' McCauley deliberately organises his lifestyle so that it may be uprooted at any moment; he lives for his work and believes that anything that may provide him with a degree of stability would only impede his ability to pursue his work. McCauley's commitment to his criminal profession may bring him a sense of purpose, but it does not truly make him feel fulfilled. There is an essential sense of emptiness, of longing, at the core of McCauley's character, which he does not acknowledge – and, perhaps, cannot consciously comprehend – until he meets and becomes infatuated with Eady. Eady shares McCauley's feelings of isolation and detachment within the vast urban environment, confiding in him that she placed a distance between herself and her family when she moved to the city and has found it imposssible to make new friends since arriving. McCauley's guarded and suspicious reaction when she innocently asks him a question about the book he's reading during their first meeting in an all-night diner ('Lady, why are you so interested in what I read or what I do?') is indicative of the lack of communication between the citizens of Los Angeles. The fact that the two manage to form a genuine bond over the course of their night together is something of a miracle, and McCauley feels the need to maintain it, despite knowing that keeping in contact with her goes against his code of professional conduct.

Yet, despite the clear attraction between McCauley and Eady, their romance is destined to fail, as does every other relationship depicted in the film. The families of Hanna and Shiherlis are torn apart by the end of the narrative due to each character's inability to reconcile the demands of their work with the obligations of familial life. McCauley dreams of escaping the city and eloping to New Zealand with Eady, but, at the last minute, he falls victim to self-sabotage, feeling compelled to make a detour on their way to the airport so that he may exact revenge against Waingro (Kevin Gage), a former associate whose betrayal caused the failure of a major heist. This decision to ultimately privilege the professional over the personal is what directly causes the destruction of the relationship, as McCauley makes the impulsive decision to flee the scene without Eady after the cops arrive at the parking lot where she is waiting for him to return. Waingro himself is beset by the very same solitude and desperation for affection that haunts the other characters. However, he allows his feelings of alienation to twist him into a monstrous figure. Incapable of achieving genuine intimacy with another person, Waingro hires prostitutes to speak sweet nothings to him in a perverse simulacrum of affection. Then, infuriated by the lack of satisfaction he gets from these encounters, he murders them. Hanna's adolescent step-daughter Lauren (Natalie Portman) is so overwhelmed by the hollowness of city life and the resulting estrangement from the various members of her own family that she attempts to take her own life. To commit the act, she goes to the impersonal site of Hanna's hotel room, then slits her wrists in the bathtub while her step-father is absent. The homosocial relations formed between the men in the professional sphere fare no better. McCauley's gang is split apart from the inside, as Waingro's decision to inform the police of an upcoming heist leads to all the other gang members being murdered, incarcerated or forced to cut ties with the other men and flee the city.

Heat is, therefore, a richer and more expansive exploration of the themes Mann touched upon in *The Jericho Mile*, *Thief* and *Manhunter*. Like these films, *Heat* is preoccupied with interpersonal alienation, the complex relationship between cop and criminal, the dehumanising nature of post-industrial urban life, and the pressure of retaining one's agency in American society, and it filters these lofty themes through a genre framework which combines elements of the police procedural, the heist genre and the crime film. However, unlike these films, *Heat* does not focus solely on a single protagonist but a vast network of interweaving loners. And though the cityscape provided a significant backdrop to the action in *Thief* and *Manhunter*, in *Heat* it is integrated into the textural fabric of the film in a more sophisticated way.

Both McCauley and Hanna follow in a lineage of Mann protagonists such as Murphy, Frank and Graham; they are consummate professionals whose overwhelming dedication to their respective crafts renders them incapable of functioning in any area of life outside of their work. They both live according to rigid behavioural codes but struggle to recognise the extent to which their all-consuming commitment to these codes impedes their chance at experiencing real happiness. Both are unable to assimilate into mainstream society (the suburban normality that McCauley derisively refers to as 'barbeques and ball games'). Both are also incapable of establishing healthy long-term relationships and shun material possessions. The intense pride that McCauley takes in carrying out heists is matched by the pride that Hanna takes in carrying out police work. Moreover, McCauley devotes much of his time to imagining the experience of the legal professional so that he may predetermine their actions; similarly, Hanna devotes a significant portion of his working life to entering the mindset of the pursued criminal so that he may understand their motivations and the strategies they implement to evade police capture.

The intense similarities between McCauley and Hanna take precedence in the film over their superficial differences (in regards to profession and social standing). Despite being pitted against one another, over the course of the narrative they gradually come to view each other with a reciprocal sense of admiration. In this sense, *Heat* offers a variation on a central theme of *Manhunter*: as in that film, the line that divides criminals from law enforcers is thin and porous. The earlier film is told from the perspective of the cop, and the criminal is positioned as the distant and abnormal 'Other' in the narrative; *Heat*, in contrast, devotes equal attention to both the cop and the criminal, granting them both equal weight in the story. Although the main parallel between these men is their all-consuming devotion to their profession, ironically, the specific nature of these professions keeps them at an essential distance. As Hanna tells McCauley at the end of their conservation in the diner: 'If I'm there and I've got to put you away, I won't like it. But I'll tell you, if it's between you and some poor bastard whose wife you're about to turn into a widow, then brother, you are going down.' McCauley respectfully absorbs this warning and then retorts: 'There's a flip side to that coin. What if you do got me boxed in, and I've got to put you down? Because no matter what, you will not get in my way. We've been face to face, yeah. But I will not hesitate, not for a second.' When Hanna makes good on his promise and guns McCauley down in the film's final scene, he kills the only character in the movie he feels a genuine bond with. McCauley responds to the blow with the simple statement, delivered calmly, 'I told you I'm never going back.' He then reaches out his hand for Hanna to hold as he passes out of existence. Hanna retorts with an empathetic 'yeah' and comforts McCauley in his final moment on Earth. There is no anger in McCauley's voice, just an acknowledgement that Hanna has followed his professional instinct to its logical conclusion; the only way this pursuit was going to end was with one of them killing the other, and McCauley can't fault Hanna for doing the same thing that he would do if the roles were reversed.

Heat is also populated with supporting characters afflicted with the same malaise. *Thief*'s Jessie and *Manhunter*'s Molly are innocents who fall victim to the corrosive behaviour of the men they attach themselves to. These films are certainly critical of the condescending attitudes and selfish conduct of the men at their centre, but these female characters are not fully fleshed out; they seem to exist primarily to respond to the destructive decisions made by their romantic partners. On the other hand, the women in *Heat* demonstrate agency, and the film handles their emotional pain with sensitivity and nuance. Justine, for instance, is the one who ultimately ends her marriage to Hanna, realising that he will never be the nurturing husband she needs him to be, but also that it would be wrong of her to force him to change his true nature. Whereas in Mann's earlier films (with the exception of *The Last of the Mohicans*), it is entirely up to the male figures to decide when to form and when to dissolve romantic relationships, here Justine takes on this active role and makes this difficult, but necessary, choice.

The opening section of *Heat* is dedicated to illustrating the act of carrying out a heist in meticulous detail, in the process introducing each member of McCauley's team as they play a specific, vital part in the operation. First, Shiherlis buys equipment from a construction site, providing false information so that it cannot be traced back to him. Michael Cheritto (Tom Sizemore) collects Waingro in a truck and then confirms the pick-up to McCauley and Trejo (Danny Trejo) through a radio transmitter, each in separate vehicles; McCauley keeps watch near the entrance of an extensive used car lot, monitoring the movements of his crew. When Trejo, who is tracking the motion of the targeted armoured car, informs Shiherlis that it is only 300 yards away, McCauley gives the signal for the men to don white hockey masks to conceal their identities. Cheritto positions the truck so that it is on the far side of the road, opposite the lot. Shiherlis, who now drives an ambulance, turns on the siren and slowly reverses the vehicle so that it obstructs the path of the armoured car. The armoured car halts, and the truck slams into it from the side, forcing it into the used car lot. The collision causes the vehicle to turn over sideways. McCauley monitors a call made to the police regarding the crash sets a stopwatch for three minutes. An explosive is triggered to shatter the windshield glass of the other cars in the lot, creating an explosion that temporarily deafens the guards so they cannot hear McCauley's men converse with one another. A spike strip is laid across the alternate entrance to the lot. Shiherlis enters the armoured car, searches purposefully for the gang's target – bearer bonds worth $1.6million. Waingro threatens the guards occupying the lot and holds them hostage in front of the vehicle. The rest of the men are strategically stationed at various vantage points in the yard to watch out for suspicious activity.

Like Frank's team in *Thief*, then, McCauley's men appear as astute, cool-headed professionals who can work perfectly in sync with one another. In *Heat*, however, the team unknowingly has a wildcard amongst their ranks, and it is this rogue element that will set them on a course toward catastrophe. Waingro is clearly differentiated from the rest of the group from the moment he first appears on screen. Unlike the other men, who demonstrate silent concentration during the build-up to the robbery, Waingro is fidgety and excessively talkative. As they drive, Waingro asks Cheritto questions about the gang and at one point expresses his excitement over being part of such a 'tight-knit crew' – implying that he's never been part of a group operation before. Cheritto curtly asks him to keep quite so that they can focus on the score, and, in response, a clearly offended Waingro removes his sunglasses and gazes at him with resentment – a clear case of him allowing emotion to overwhelm the senses in a manner that is diametrically opposed to the way in which Mann's criminals choose to conduct their work. When the heist begins, it becomes clear that Waingro gleans a sadistic thrill from exerting control over others, as evidenced by the joy he takes in brutally beating a guard when he doesn't immediately follow one of his verbal commands. Shiherlis locates an envelope containing the bearer bonds, exclaims 'got it' and then exits the vehicle, signalling the other men to follow suit. Despite the robbery being complete, Waingro spitefully shoots dead a guard he believes to be showing him disrespect. This action sparks a spiral of violence, as the other guards instinctively reach for their weapons and start firing wildly. The men are now guilty of murder and the stakes have been raised, so McCauley makes the ruthless decision to shoot the remaining guards. McCauley's gang climb into the van and make a swift escape, unscathed but still outraged at Waingro's erratic behaviour. A fleet of police vehicles arrive at the scene and attempt to trail the gang, but the strip of spikes punctures their tires, and they are left stranded in the middle of the car lot. After driving several blocks, McCauley's men remove their masks, climb into different vehicles, and trigger an explosion which destroys the ambulance behind them.

While McCauley is introduced in a professional context, Hanna is presented in the domestic sphere. The fact that Hanna and Justine are first introduced while making love may seem to suggest that the relationship between them will be one of warmth and intimacy. But the way the scene is framed dispels any sense of intimacy between them. The scene opens with both parties obscured by a large white pillow in the foreground. Justine's face is blocked, and only Hanna's is visible, immediately creating the impression that, at this moment, Hanna is not entirely 'present' in this moment; he is wrapped up in his own thoughts rather than engaging with his wife. The rest of the segment has a fragmented, stuttering rhythm. Throughout, Hanna avoids meeting Justine's gaze straight on – instead of looking directly at her, he either closes his eyes or turns his head to the side. At the end of the sequence, Justine grabs Hanna's head and pulls it close to hers, as if imploring him to look at her. The moment of climax is then omitted, as Mann cuts straight to an image of Hanna in the shower, alone, appearing dissatisfied and dispirited.

The tensions in their marriage become more explicit in the scene which follows. Justine is framed in the foreground, reclining on the bed and smoking, while Hanna is in the background, out of focus. Justine asks him if he is taking her to breakfast. Hanna responds that he doesn't have time to eat with the family as he must leave immediately to be on time for an early meeting. Immediately, the gulf between them is tied to his commitment to work over family. Lauren then bursts into the bedroom, emphasising the distance between them even further by referring to Hanna by his first name but to Justine as 'mom'. Lauren is frantic because she cannot find her barrettes and wants to wear them when she meets her biological father for lunch. After she leaves, Hanna expresses resentment towards Lauren's stepfather, commenting derisively on his repeated failure to turn up to his arranged meetings with his daughter. Justine ignores this remark, and instead offers to make her husband a cup of coffee. Hanna reiterates that he's in a rush and leaves for work. After Hanna leaves the house, Lauren suffers an anxiety attack, collapsing in her mother's arms. The fact that Hanna is not present to comfort his step-daughter in this moment of emotional need is an early indication of his inability to recognise the depth of her emotional issues and provide the family with emotional support and stability – later into the narrative, Hanna's casual disregard for his step-daughter will later turn out to have devastating repercussions.

Justine challenges Hanna's hypocrisy on this matter when he arrives home very late that night. Hanna finds Justine waiting up for him. She tells Hanna that Lauren's father showed up, and Hanna claims to be enraged by the betrayal – however, Justine is disturbed by his use of language: 'Does this guy have any idea what's going on with his kid?' Hanna's wording here unconsciously places a distance between himself and Lauren ('his kid'). This suggests that he views Justine as a burden, as though it is the sole responsibility of Lauren's biological father to 'fix' his daughter's problems. Justine undercuts Hanna's sense of superiority by reminding him that he, too, hasn't been present for his wife or stepdaughter. Justine tells Hanna that she has 'been in her room all day, so no, she's not OK. Neither am I.' She reveals that she made dinner for them hours ago and has been waiting for him to join her. She feels unable to maintain a healthy routine for the two of them because Hanna is so often absent and consistently fails to include her in his plans. The way she sees it, Hanna is so consumed by his work that he has no energy to put into his familial life, and she feels that she is not a priority for him. For Hanna, the sensitive nature of his work means that he must pursue it on his own, and to share details of it with others – even those he is supposed to be closest with – would risk jeopardising the safety of the other party and his commitment to the investigation. This excuse is somewhat self-serving, though, as it is clear that he takes a great deal of pride in his professional ability, and he retreats into the sphere of work as a way to avoid confronting the significant problems which plague his personal relationships.

For both Hanna and McCauley, insurmountable tensions arise in their romantic relationships due to their inability to openly communicate. Hanna refuses to discuss his profession with Justine, thus locking her out of the aspect of his life he devotes most of his time and attention to. Justine, therefore, does not feel as though she fully 'knows' her husband, and that she is not treated as an equal in the marriage. Because of the emotional disconnect between Hanna and Justine, and because Hanna stubbornly refuses to acknowledge the depth of this distance between them, she feels the need to take solace in the arms of another man. McCauley similarly refuses to honestly talk to Eady about what he does for a living, in this case going so far as to lie to her about what line of work he is in. McCauley, too, rationalises this lapse of reciprocal communication by telling himself that he is shielding Eady from becoming dragged into the Los Angeles crime scene, but his inability to be open with her is what ultimately drives the couple apart. McCauley's effort to keep his profession hidden from Eady backfires when she catches footage of his failed bank robbery on the televised news and feels betrayed that he lied to her about what he does for a living. The breakdown in trust between the couple almost drives them apart at this moment, but McCauley makes a last-ditch attempt able to repair the damage by suggesting that they escape the corruption of the city together and embark on a new life abroad.

But despite his promise that he has changed his ways, McCauley is still incapable of being honest with Eady and thwarts their attempt to flee Los Angeles. On their way to the airport, McCauley feels a compulsion to track down and murder Waingro as a matter of professional honour. If he explained the importance of this to Eady, it is possible that she may have seen things from his perspectives, but, instead, he just tells her that he 'has to take care of something', but he's confident that they have time for him to complete his errand and still make it to their flight. For both men, an opportunity to reconcile with their lovers arises, and they are given a clear-cut decision to either commit to their professional endeavour or enter the domestic sphere; however, in both cases, they opt for the latter. The sense of purpose that drives these two men is so overwhelming that they cannot be shaken from the path they laid out for themselves by their profession – even if this profession leaves them with an inescapable sense of emptiness. McCauley's belief that he can alleviate his loneliness by marrying Eady is naïve. The deeply unsatisfying relationship between Hanna and Justine illustrates that entering a marriage doesn't alleviate the emotional issues of a man like McCauley – it is possible that, even if he had successfully eloped with Eady, he may have felt an insatiable urge to return to a life of crime and sabotaged his familial life at a later date, much like Graham proved to be incapable of staying away from his job at the FBI after his retirement.

When Hanna makes it to the scene of the armoured car heist, he immediately demonstrates his incredible grasp of his profession, and his preternatural ability to enter the headspace of criminals. As in *Manhunter*, law enforcement practice here involves establishing an empathetic mental link with the pursued criminal. Hanna is highly animated as he surveys the scene, physically retracing the steps of the perpetrators while providing a verbal running commentary. Based on small clues, he accurately deduces that the men burned their vehicles so they couldn't be traced, kept hockey masks on for the duration of the robbery so no eye-witnesses would be able to identify them, paid attention to the response time of the police and made sure they made a rapid escape by only focusing on the most valuable bearer bonds and ignoring the loose cash contained in the car. Hanna closes his analysis with a sincere compliment, stating that the handiwork of these thieves proves that 'these weren't gangbangers working the local seven eleven,' before adding 'the MO is that they're good.' Hanna can instinctively tell that he's dealing with a criminal that operates on the same high level of professional brilliance as he does. As he leaves, Hanna tells one of his men to take his hand out of a dead guard's pocket as if looking for a wallet. This act of callous greed emphasises that there is no easy distinction between morally pure and corrupt in the film and that the police also indulge in predatory acts of money accumulation- the dog-eat-dog nature of life in the city fosters a lack of empathy and a desire to collect material wealth at all costs.

Although McCauley does not hesitate to resort to violence if he deems it absolutely necessary for his own self-preservation, he gleans no joy from inflicting pain upon others. This is what differentiates him from a man like Waingro. While McCauley gains satisfaction from the act of carrying out an intricate, carefully planned heist, Waingro is driven takes perverse pleasure in inflicting suffering upon others. For this reason, McCauley regards Waingro with extreme contempt, and his outburst at the diner in which the crew meet after fleeing the scene of the heist is motivated by more than mere frustration that he caused the robbery to veer off course. As the crew sit silently around a diner table, Mann captures them in a series of shallow-focus one-shots. They appear simultaneously part of a group and isolated from one another, each man consumed in their own thoughts and personal space. When McCauley arrives, he sits, wordlessly, next to Waingro. Waingro, sensing the tension in the booth, makes a pitiful attempt to explain his actions: 'I had to get it on man, he was making a move.' McCauley is so disgusted that he slams Waingro's head down on the table, a rare moment in which anger cuts through McCauley's ordinarily stoic demeanour, and he lets his emotion overwhelm his better judgement – as illustrated by the shock and attention that this act draws from on-lookers. To avoid making a scene, McCauley takes Waingro out into the privacy of the parking lot. He punches Waingro repeatedly in the stomach until he collapses on the ground. Just as McCauley retrieves his gun with the intention of killing Waingro out right then and there, but he gets distracted when a cop car pulls into the lot and Waingro crawls away undetected. McCauley returns to his apartment. It is introduced as an abstract grid of blue and black, with the reflecting top of his kitchen counter stretching across the centre of the screen, backdropped by wall-sized windows. Through the windows, the ocean is visible, stretching into the horizon. A silhouetted hand enters the frame from above, in the foreground, and places a gun on the counter. He then walks into the distance, still bathed in darkness, stops at the window and gazes out into the sea. Mann cuts to a close-up, framing McCauley so that the bottom side of his face fills the right of the frame, and the view drifts into shallow focus. Mann pans up slightly to align the viewer with McCauley's eye-line while simultaneously shifting focus so that the seascape appears in vivid detail. The sound of waves undulating softly briefly overwhelms the soundtrack as McCauley takes a necessary respite from the relentless forward motion that characterises his working life. But this doesn't last long. After a few seconds, McCauley walks away from the window, and Mann cuts back to a wide shot of the apartment, this time at a low angle, making the bars of the windows look like the bars of a prison cell. As Jean-Baptiste

Thoret states, 'For Mann, the sea is the canonical image of impossible journeys, those that everyone dreams about but no one is able to take.' (2000). If Hanna's home is a source of perpetual discomfort and distress, then McCauley's apartment is a perpetual reminder of the impermanent and hollow nature of his existence. It is spare and austere, with no decorations and only a few pieces of furniture. Like Murphy's cell in *The Jericho Mile*, it is not a true home but simply a space where McCauley can go to fulfil his essential bodily functions. He has no interest in filling the space with objects that hold ties to personal relationships or past experiences. McCauley's discomfort with domestic arrangements is further emphasised after he first sleeps with Eady. Unable to sleep, he gets out of her bed in the middle of the night, gets dressed, and places a glass of water by her bedside before leaving. It appears as though even sharing a roof with a romantic partner for one night would be an act of intimacy too close to a domestic familial situation for him to be comfortable with.

While McCauley returns to solitude, Shiherlis returns to his dysfunctional relationship with Charlene. Upon entering the house, he shows her his $8,000 cut of the spoils. Charlene makes it clear that she is unhappy with the size of his portion and that the gains are not worth the enormity of the risk. Like Hanna, he doesn't address her concerns directly; he walks away from her, avoiding a serious discussion. She tells him that there is no point in talking to him, as her concerns fall on deaf ears: 'We are not making forward progress like adults living our lives, because I'm married to a gambling junkie who won't listen.' He loses his temper at the insult and storms out of the house, breaking multiple household items as he goes.

McCauley's problematic view of women is illustrated in his attitude towards Shiherlis and Charlene's marital problems. After storming out of his home, Shiherlis stays at McCauley's apartment for several days. McCauley phones Charlene, hoping to glean more information on the situation, but all she tells him is that they're dealing with 'marriage stuff', before hanging up. McCauley's first response is to ask Shiherlis whether he is genuinely committed to the marriage, reminding Shiherlis of his belief that a professional thief should avoid establishing personal attachments, as they may be forced to cut ties with them at any moment. McCauley tells Shiherlis that he would be better off cutting ties with Charlene to devote himself completely to his work. However, Shiherlis remains firm in his commitment, telling McCauley that: 'For me, the sun rises and sets with her.' Shiherlis' loyalty to Charlene, despite their hardships, seems to have a profound effect on McCauley, convincing him first to attempt to repair their marriage and then, later, to pursue a similar union with Eady. However, in his attempt to meddle with Shiherlis and Charlene's marriage, McCauley demonstrates his naive perspective of relationships and overly controlling tendencies. Passing through the street on which the Shiherlis live, McCauley spots Charlene discretely escorting a stranger out of their front door. A furious McCauley barges into the house and corners Charlene. She denies having done anything wrong, but McCauley will not listen to her. Refusing to consider the depth and complexity of the issues plaguing their marriage, McCauley demands that Charlene call off her affair and give Shiherlis a second chance. He addresses Charlene in a cool-headed yet authoritative manner as if giving his crew instructions before a heist: 'Here's the deal. You give Chris one last shot. After that, he fucks up, I will finance setting you up on my own. Anywhere you want. Dominick [the Shiherlis' son] will go with you. And my word counts. But right now, you will give him a chance.' A visibly frightened Charlene agrees to comply with McCauley's demands, perhaps for no other reason than to get him out of her house. Although McCauley believes that he is acting in the best interest of Shiherlis and helping to repair the relationship, his behaviour is invasive and burdensome. He has gone behind Shiherlis' back, spied on his wife, and forced her to re-enter the relationship without her proper consent. This is, of course, a rocky foundation for the rekindling of their marriage to be rebuilt on, and, sure enough, as soon as the pair gets back together, the very same problems arise once again. In the end, Shiherlis, like Hanna and McCauley, prioritises his work over his family: first, he chooses to participate in the final, dangerous heist despite Charlene's objections (paying no thought to the potentially disastrous consequences the entire family may suffer as a result), and then he relinquishes ties to Charlene and Dominick after he discovers that the police are waiting for him at their residence.

McCauley is a man of contradiction. He lives his life according to a rigid, self-determined code of behaviour in which he places a high degree of value. At the same time, this code leaves him feeling unfulfilled and alienated. He grows dissatisfied with the lifestyle he has crafted for himself, and so he searches for a way to transcend the very isolation that is the by-product of his professional life. He exemplifies the self-defeating internal tension that Thoret identifies as being central to most of Mann's protagonists: they 'spend days dreaming of the world' outside of the hyper-modern, dehumanising 'aquarium'-like space they are trapped within, but are simultaneously aware that 'coming out of the water would be fatal.' (2000). Like Thief's Frank, McCauley places an enormous amount of importance on maintaining independence and autonomy over his working life, and therefore avoids being embroiled in any institutional or interpersonal ties that he believes will impede his control over his work, yet he paradoxically believes that he can cure his malaise by establishing a romantic relationship. When McCauley meets Eady they are both involved in activities related to their work: McCauley browses an aisle at the bookshop where Eady works, looking for books on melting metal which may provide practical guidance for later scores. Eady walks behind him and steals a quick glance, unnoticed. Like Jessie and Frank, the moment of initial connection between the pair happens at a diner – a space that combines the private and the public, creating a false sense of intimacy within a bustling setting. Eady recognises him from the bookstore, though she is shy and seems apprehensive to start a conversation. After the waitress, by chance, sits McCauley next to her at the counter, she timidly leans over and asks him what his book is about. McCauley is taciturn and acts with closed body language, as though he is expecting to be attacked. Unused to genuine gestures towards affability from a stranger, he snaps at her: 'Lady, why are you so interested in what I read and what I do?' She apologises for bothering him and then turns away. McCauley, recognising that she is not a threat, introduces himself. In a film where characters are primarily defined by their immediate actions and try to keep personal information at a minimum, this is a rare scene in which the characters feel comfortable discussing their personal backgrounds. Eady is completely open with McCauley: She tells him that she graduated from college the following year and moved to Los Angeles to build a career in graphic design, but, as she has had little luck in that field, she was forced to take an unfulfilling day job as a bookseller. Although McCauley is uncharacteristically candid with Eady about his feelings, he remains somewhat guarded and evasive. He mostly gives brief, vague answers to her questions, sometimes overtly withholding information and sometimes outright lying (when asked about his living arrangements, he simply replies, 'I live with people,' with no further elaboration). Nevertheless, this is the closest the reticent thief has come to expressing affection towards another person in the film thus far. As the conversation draws on, he scoots across his seat to get physically nearer to her.

Despite this, the pair feel a connection and go to Eady's apartment. Mann cuts to a slow, smooth pan of the view of the city as seen from Eady's yard, a spectacular wash of glistening gold and blue-tinted lights. It is nighttime, and the contours of the buildings below are obscured by darkness; all we can see are the artificial lights, which form an abstract arrangement like a pointillist painting. The camera comes to rest on McCauley and Eady standing in the foreground of the image, centred, their backs to the viewer. McCauley poetically describes the view with marine imagery: 'In Fiji, they have these iridescent alga, they come out once a year in the water. That's what it looks like out there.' The comparison McCauley draws between the panorama of LA and a Fiji seascape recalls the earlier scene in which he became lost in thought while viewing the ocean out of his apartment window. If the sea represents McCauley's unconscious desire to escape the dehumanising effects of the city and retreat into the freedom of the natural world, then the 'ocean' of lights signifies that he is moving closer to the achievement of that dream, even though he is far from its complete realisation. The lights, after all, are artificial constructs, and the effect they produce is a simulacrum of a landscape, not the real thing. Already, Mann is signalling that the vision of a dream life McCauley builds with Eady is illusory and bound to fall apart.

McCauley confides to Eady, the depth of his estrangement from his family when he tells her, 'my mother died a long time ago, my father, I don't know where he is. I have a brother somewhere.' McCauley has become hardened by life-long isolation; he has developed internal mechanisms which help to prevent him from experiencing the pain directly. 'I am alone,' he continues, 'I am not lonely.' Contrary to this, Eady comes from a tight-knit family, and her sense of loneliness only began after she moved to the city. When McCauley asks her, in turn, 'Are you lonely?', and her response is a simple 'Yeah.' It is her ability to straightforwardly express her emotional state that attracts McCauley to Eady at this moment, and they embrace. Like in the earlier sex scene between Hanna and Justine, Mann chooses not to show the moment of climax, following the scene of the pair kissing on the balcony with an overhead shot of them in bed, post-coitus. Eady is asleep, McCauley is wide awake. He realises that he has lapsed from his philosophy of life and now sees it as a necessity to leave as soon as possible lest he develops stronger feelings. To fall in love with her would be to establish one of the 'unnecessary' ties that he believes he must avoid if he is to continue his success in the world of crime.

But McCauley soon regrets this action and gets back into contact with Eady. This shift in McCauley's motivation arises during a scene at a busy restaurant. McCauley sits at the head of a large table, around which several members of his crew are accompanied by their romantic partners. The soundscape is consumed by ambient noise, drowning out the conversation, as McCauley looks forlornly at the couples: Chiherlis and Charlene, Cheritto and Elaine (Susan Traylor), Trejo and Anna. Mann alternates between two-shots of these pairs, seemingly happy, and one-shots of McCauley on his own. Ironically, McCauley does not realise that none of these relationships is harmonious; they are all plagued by severe problems, and these romantic entanglements do not alleviate the loneliness of his crew members. Achieving a healthy equilibrium between work and personal/domestic life is impossible for all these figures, but McCauley is too preoccupied with his own loneliness to acknowledge the cracks in these other relationships. McCauley impulsively excuses himself from the table to find a payphone. Eady tells him that after he'd left that night, she was afraid that he was only interested in a one-night stand. McCauley lies, telling her that he had always intended to call her a few days later. Like Frank, McCauley knows that he needs a substantial amount of funds to set up his retirement, and so he decides to embark on one final heist with an exceptionally high financial reward.

As this is happening, Hanna leads a team of LAPD officers who watch through surveillance cameras as McCauley and his crew members exit the restaurant. Mann now switches from the perspective of the criminals to the perspective of the cops, who look down at the action from a high angle. As Hanna narrates the information they have on each member, based on their past convictions, the camera focuses on each man, one by one. However, Hanna is captivated by McCauley, the only member that he does not recognise from existing police files. Zeroing in on McCauley's face, Hanna asks, 'Who's the loner?' Another cop replies, 'First time I'm seeing him, we're not on him yet.' Hanna can intuitively tell that McCauley must be a 'big player', and orders his team to dig up whatever information on his they can find. As if he can instinctively tell that Hanna has set his sights on him, McCauley gazes up directly into the path of Hanna's viewfinder. Mann alternates between a frontal one-shot of Hanna and a frontal one-shot of McCauley, whose face is filtered through a thermal vision monitor. This is the first time in the film when the two characters appear in the same visual space, though they do not directly interact. Alternating between the image of McCauley on the monitor and Hanna surveying his movements creates an effect of paradoxical distance and intimacy; the two men are physically separated, and McCauley does not even know who is looking at him, but they appear as though they are gazing at one another.

The callous attitude towards women expressed by McCauley and Hanna is taken to a grotesque extreme by Waingro. Assuming Waingro's perspective, Mann opens the scene with a sexualised shot of a young female prostitute in lingerie putting on a grey jacket by a bedroom wall. Leaving the coat unbuttoned, she turns towards the camera lens and says, 'Hey baby, it's time to go.' Desperate to feel a greater sense of intimacy with the prostitute, Waingro remains on the bed and implores her to compliment his love-making ability. She dutifully obliges, responding, in an unconvincing tone of voice, 'Oh yeah. You fly. You cool.' Despite her considerable patience, Waingro is frustrated by the lack of emotion she puts into her performance. He leans forward and says, 'You're lying to me. I can always tell when people lie to me.' He continues to ignore her requests for him to vacate the room so that she may entertain her next client, and then delivers the deeply unsettling threat: 'You don't know what this is. The grim reaper is visiting with you.' Waingro slowly approaches her, a deranged smirk forming on his face. He grabs her by the hair and drags it violently backwards. Mann cuts directly to an image of Waingro calmly drinking at a bar, appearing to be completely unphased by the act of violence he just committed. The earlier disregard for human life exhibited by Waingro during the armoured car robbery, therefore, carries over into his personal life. This is not an isolated incident; we later learn that Waingro routinely murders prostitutes as a perverse way to express his despair and simultaneously achieve sexual satisfaction. Although the extent of his sociopathy renders Waingro a far more a horrific character than any of the other characters in the film, the ailments that drive him are fostered by the pressures of city life – a debilitating sense of emotional detachment, an inability to form long-lasting personal relationships, and a frustrated longing for genuine connection.

The news of the murder directly drives a wedge between Hanna and Justine. The couple are show enjoying an evening together at a local bar. They are unusually physically affectionate here, slow dancing and kissing. 'I can't take my hands off you,' Hanna tells Justine, to which she responds 'I feel so wonderful about you.' However, as in their earlier sex scene, this moment is abruptly cut short. Hanna gets a call informing him that a body has been found at a nearby motel, and the murder seems to be part of a series of killings that his department has been investigating. Hanna leaves Justine to explore the crime scene, giving no indication of how long he's going to be or what the nature of the crime is. When he returns to the bar, Hanna carries the weight of his professional disappointment with him – Hanna was informed that the murder was likely conducted by a serial killer targeting young girls in the area that Hanna has personally been attempting to track for months. He knows that, if he had been more successful in his investigation, it is likely that the young woman would still be alive. It is unclear how long Hanna has been gone for, but the venue is now nearly deserted and Justine sits alone. She is clearly frustrated, but is open to hearing about Hanna's experience, so she asks him what was so urgent that it required him to leave for so long, but Hanna is characteristically evasive, simply telling her: 'You don't want to know.' Irritated by her attitude, Hanna reminds Justine that before they were married, he made it clear to her that she was 'going to have to share [him] with all the bad people and all the ugly events on this planet.' Justine tells him that she knowingly accepted this as a condition of their marriage, but she thought that he would be willing to share more with her and, therefore, she could do more to help to relieve his burdens. Justine clarifies that she respects the importance of his work and is fully willing to support him as he devotes so much of his life to the pursuit of criminals, but he is shutting her out of his experiences.

Hanna, again, talks down to Justine, assuming that she would be unable to handle the stress if he did open up about his daily encounters on the force: 'So what I should do is come home and say "Hey honey, guess what, I walked into this house today where this junkie asshole just fried his baby in a microwave because it was crying too loud, so let me share that with you?" And in sharing it, we'll somehow cathartically expel all that heinous shit?' After ridiculing her concerns, Hanna offers a brief summation of his professional philosophy, has a notable similarity to McCauley's 'heat' mantra. He explains that he must 'hold onto his angst' in order to retain his intense focus and stamina. 'I preserve it because I need it. It keeps me sharp, on the edge, where I've gotta be.' Justine is unimpressed, however, perceiving his speech not as the expression of a genuine and fully developed philosophy of life but as merely a rationalisation of his shortcomings as a partner and a father figure. She tells him that he is preoccupied with his work to such an extent that his familial life has become a 'mess you leave as you pass through.' The behavioural code that Hanna perceives as a noble code is flipped around by Justine as she points out how much damage his commitment to this lifestyle inflicts on those closest to him.

When communication between Hanna and Justine reaches a low point, he finds some degree of solace by seeking out his double, a man who, Hanna intuits, will emphasise with his situation. Hanna meets with McCauley at this point not to apprehend him (as Hanna makes explicit in an earlier scene, he needs to catch McCauley when he is in the process of carrying out a large heist to ensure that he gets locked away for a substantial amount of time), but to finally come face-to-face with the man he has been tracking and that he feels an unshakable connection to. The conversation the two men share at a diner functions as *Heat*'s emotional centrepiece. Occurring approximately halfway into the film, it is the only scene, aside from the finale, in which Hanna and McCauley directly interact. In this lengthy sequence, both characters break away from their professional roles and address each other as individuals. Hanna and McCauley momentarily form a bond as these maladjusted men discover a large amount of common ground. They express a mutual, empathetic comprehension of each another's loneliness, a loneliness which is fostered by the nature of the city they reside in and by their commitment to their respective professions. They both recognise that they share an aversion to what they term 'a regular type life', which McCauley sardonically describes as being filled with 'barbeques and ball games'. McCauley explains to Hanna that his lifestyle is dependent on maintaining an emotional distance with everybody and everything around him so that he may leave them at the drop of a hat to escape the authorities. McCauley refers to the careful maintenance of his lifestyle as his 'discipline', and Hanna seems to sympathise with his perspective. Hanna leads his life according to a similar 'discipline' in the sense that he deliberately keeps Justine and Lauren at an emotional remove, ostensibly to prevent them from having to cope with the horrendous situations he encounters in his work on a regular basis, but, in actuality, because he feels that connecting his work to his domestic life will impede his ability to perform his professional role effectively.

This extended dialogue over shared obsessions, fears and predilections creates a bond between the two men which is more deeply felt than any other relationship depicted in the film. Each man is so relieved to find somebody else who can empathise with their emotional experience within the inhuman landscape of modern LA that they briefly shed their respective roles of 'cop' and 'robber' and simply talk as two individuals. McCauley expresses his weariness of the transitory nature of his lifestyle, telling Hanna that he has a romantic partner – although Hanna recognises that this romantic attachment is a contradiction of McCauley's own, self-defined 'discipline'. Hanna is ultimately proven to be correct on this point, as McCauley's adherence to his internal 'discipline' will later lead him to desert Eady so he can pursue vengeance against Waingro. Hanna, in turn, reveals the depth of his alienation from his familial life: 'My life is a disaster zone. I got a stepdaughter so fucked up because her real father is this large-type asshole. I got a wife. We're passing each other on the down slope of a marriage, my third, because I spend all my time chasing guys like you round the block. That's my life.' Upon hearing this, McCauley recognises that Hanna is beset by the same internal contradiction that he is, and that Hanna's dedication to his profession also makes it difficult for him to maintain a healthy personal life. Hanna then describes the anxiety he feels from his awareness of all the victims he has let down. This anxiety is poetically symbolised in the recurring dream in which Hanna is 'sitting at this big banquet table and all the victims of all the murders I ever worked are sitting at this table and they're staring at me with these black eyeballs because they got 8-ball haemorrhages from the head wounds.' The corpses are still and silent, and although they 'don't have anything to say', Hanna seems to intuit that they hold him responsible for their grisly deaths. This imagery reflects the heavy emotional burden placed on Hanna by his knowledge of all the atrocities he's encountered and all the people he was unable to rescue – he cannot safeguard the lives of everybody in the city and his knowledge of all the violent crimes he was unable to prevent weighs down heavily on him. Despite the sense of despair Hanna expresses, McCauley can infer that Hanna is committed to his line of work and that nothing could persuade him to quit. 'I do what I do best,' McCauley says, 'take down scores', before adding: 'You do what you do best. Try to take down guys like me.' Indeed, the scene ends with both men reaffirming their commitment to their work, which takes precedence over all their personal relationships – including the fleeting bond established between them in the coffee shop. The pair share an acknowledgement that, because of the different occupational paths they have chosen, they will likely be pitted against one another at some point in the future. During this sequence, both Hanna and McCauley are at their most candid and emotionally naked, which makes it especially heart-wrenching that it ends with both men stating that they would not hesitate to kill the other if they stood in the way of the achievement of their professional objectives. Furthermore, each man readily accepts that the other must follow this path of action if placed in a similar situation.

The botched bank robbery that takes place shortly after this meeting is the focus of the film's final act and is the event that pits Hanna and McCauley against each other. McCauley, Shiherlis and Cheritto enter the lobby of the Far East National Bank in the plain light of day. They position themselves at various strategic points around the main floor, keeping a close watch on the customers. After a few moments, all three put on balaclavas. Shiherlis blindsides a security guard and tackles him to the ground. While the crowd is distracted, McCauley pulls out a gun and forces the customers to get down on the floor. In line with Mann's other criminal protagonists, McCauley does not see ordinary citizens as the target of his crimes; instead, he wages war on large financial institutions. As he enters the bank in the opening sequence, McCauley reassures customers waiting in line: 'We're here for the bank's money, you're not going to lose a dime. Think of your families. Don't risk your life. Don't try to be a hero.' The three men make it out of the building with several million stashed in large black bags. But, in a parallel to the opening heist, Waingro introduces an element of chaos into an otherwise smooth operation – despite not being physically present at the scene. Waingro forced Trejo to give him information about the robbery through physical torture and then gave the information to the LAPD. As a consequence, Hanna and his team are aware of the heist far in advance and arrive at the scene just as McCauley's men are entering their getaway vehicle. Noticing the presence of the police, Shiherlis fires several shots behind them as they make a swift escape. In a counter-attack, the cops fatally injure the getaway driver, Donald, and McCauley takes over the vehicle. McCauley avoids the bullets, but Shiherlis is hit. Cheritto runs away but is trailed by Hanna on foot. In a wretched act of cowardice, Cheritto picks up a young girl who has become separated from her mother and uses her as a human shield as he sprints through a crowded street. The camera switches perspective from Cheritto to Hanna, as the law enforcer pursues him while being careful to avoid harming the girl. The sequence concludes with Hanna taking a risky decision to shoot at Cheritto as he turns – he successfully hits his target, knocking Cheritto down with a single blow, but he only narrowly misses the young girl. Although Hanna comes out on top here, it is troubling that the circumstances forced him to take the risky decision of firing a deadly weapon with a child nearby. If his aim had been slightly off, or if his timing had been too slow, then he would have hit the child. Hanna comes out on top in this scene, but only by endangering a young child's life – indicating his instability in the domestic sphere.

The botched heist makes national news, and the faces of McCauley's men are plastered all over the city. From this point onwards, *Heat* charts the dissolution of each main character's familial relationships as a consequence of their involvement in the robbery. As Rayner observes, 'After the bank robbery, the deliberate decision to compromise the domestic sphere [...] is marked by the actions of each member of the crew.' (2013: 73). Notably, this happens in tandem with the definitive disintegration of Hanna and Justine's marriage, further underlining the similarity between the central cop and the members of McCauley's gang. After losing track of McCauley, Hanna returns to the house early to find Justine cooking food for another man, who sits in the living room watching the television. The fact that Hanna walks in to see Justine preparing food for another man is significant, as Justine previously criticised Hanna for failing to arrive home in time for them to share a family dinner to his erratic work schedule and lack of communication. And yet Hanna still refuses to face these issues directly, instead choosing to affect a cavalier attitude. Addressing the stranger in the house, Hanna says, 'You can ball my wife, if she wants you to. You can lounge around here on her sofa. In her ex-husband's dead-tech post-modernistic bullshit house, if you want to. But you do not get to watch my fucking television set.' Hanna's behaviour here is intended to infuriate Justine: he addresses the third party, rather than his wife; he speaks with a heavy layer of irony; and he claims to be more upset at the violation of his property than his wife's infidelity. The fact that Hanna seizes upon this opportunity to take a swipe at the house itself indicates that not only has he given up on his relationship with Justine, but that he feels disdain for the domestic space itself and, by extension, the architecture of the whole city. Hanna unplugs the television set and moves toward the exit, only to be intercepted by Justine. Justine reveals to him, explicitly, what should have been obvious to an attentive husband: that she embarked on her affair in a conscious attempt to shock Hanna into finally confronting the vast gulf that has opened between them. But, once more, this plea for open and reciprocal dialogue is brushed aside by Hanna, who silently storms out of the house to stay in a hotel suite for the foreseeable future. Significantly, the only item that Hanna brings with him to his new residence is not a photo album or a family heirloom, but the television set – which he later uses to monitor the news for updates about the botched robbery, transforming it into an instrument of his work. Once he has moved into a hotel room, Hanna's lifestyle becomes even closer to McCauley's, as he too occupies a stripped-back, impermanent living space with few possessions of his own. Not long after Hanna moves out of the house he shares with Lauren, he arrives back at the suite to find Lauren unconscious in the bathtub. This scene is the most graphic in the entire film, as Mann frames Lauren in a wide overhead shot, lying in a pool of her own blood. As in the earlier scene in which Hanna was called to the site of the murdered prostitute, thus forcing him to directly acknowledge his inability to apprehend the murderer before he could commit such a heinous act, Hanna feels that he has fallen short in his duty as a protector. He has consistently failed as a father figure to Lauren, and now he has failed to prevent her from harming herself, only arriving to witness the aftermath. Hanna lifts her out of the tub and wraps towels around her arms. Although his professional training has prepared him to deal with such a situation, merging his professional duties with his personal life overwhelms him. He appears panicked and clumsy while tending to Justine's wounds. The attempted suicide of his stepdaughter is a stark sign of just how severe her emotional scars are, and this forces him to consider the devastating effect that his wilful emotional detachment has on those around him. Lauren's decision to go to Hanna's hotel room, rather than Justine's, demonstrates an impulse to forcibly make Hanna aware of his inadequacy as a nurturing father figure.

When Hanna meets Justine in the hospital waiting room, the situation between them calms down significantly – but this is only because they both come to the mutual acceptance that their marriage is broken beyond repair, and they need to call it off lest they keep making the exact same mistakes over and over again. Justine asks him whether he thinks there is 'any way that it could work out between us?', and, for once, Hanna is honest with her: 'I wish I could say yes but, in the end, it's like you said, all I am is what I'm going after. I'm not what you want, Justine.' The combined shock of Justine's infidelity and Lauren's suicide attempt forces Hanna out of his stupor – he recognises now that there are very real problems in his familial life, and that things cannot continue the way they have been. Hanna will always be defined by his work, he can do nothing to change that, and he recognises that it is unfair to expect Justine and Laurent to suffer as a result. When Hanna gets a beeper notification informing him that McCauley is heading toward the airport, he initially tells her that he is willing to stay with her in the waiting room. Justine, however, makes a selfless gesture, urging Hanna to go forth and pursue his professional objective: 'Well, go on if you have to.' This moment is bittersweet. Hanna embraces his true nature and is now liberated from the constraints of the domestic life that caused him so much stress, and Justine has given up on her futile attempts to change him. Though the act of separation is painful, it will benefit the lives of Hanna, Justine and Lauren in the long term. Like Charlene, Justine has the inner strength to make this difficult decision. So Hanna leaves the hospital to track down his double and finish the case, with no intention of returning to Justine and Lauren.

In contrast, McCauley's decision to leave Eady is sudden and one-sided. As McCauley journeys towards the airport with Eady, they seem to be on the path to a blissful life together. There are no external obstacles standing in between them and their flight, and McCauley could have made an effortless escape if he had stuck to their plan. But when Mann cuts to individual one-shots of the characters, there is a clear disconnect between them: Eady is ecstatic, gazing upwards towards the sky, but McCauley appears solemn and lost in his own thoughts. His attention turns to an intersection to their left. Eady is startled when McCauley makes an abrupt turn, vaguely telling her that he has 'to take care of something'. Despite Eady's apprehension, Hanna pushes on ahead, driven by a compulsion to enact revenge against Waingro and, hence, tie up all lose ends from the failed heist. McCauley lives by a carefully cultivated, self-determined code of conduct that he expects all his associates to follow as well, and he is disgusted by Waingro's blatant disregard for these professional standards. McCauley feels an ingrained need to exact revenge on Waingro for the dishonourable way he treated the gang, and he won't feel comfortable until he knows for certain that his adversary is out of the picture.

McCauley tracks down Waingro to his suite at a hotel near LAX, but doesn't realise, that two police officers are stationed in the room next to his, monitoring the entire building with surveillance cameras. Because Waingro had fed information to the cops, they are alert to the possibility that McCauley may pursue vengeance against him in retaliation. They therefore have organised for several officers to stick close to Waingro at all times, so that they may apprehend McCauley if he draws near. McCauley is usually highly calculating and careful in his professional life, but here he allows his personal feelings of betrayal and anger to overwhelm him, and he embarks on his reckless vengeance quest without properly planning his course of action. Instead, McCauley acts on impulse. He enters through a back entrance and locates Waingro's room number by pretending to be a concierge and calling a manager for assistance. He quickly changes into a staff uniform he finds hanging near the back door and then enters the main foyer. McCauley then takes the elevator to Waingro's floor and pulls the fire alarm to clear the crowd. While the other guests flock towards the exit, Waingro remains in his room, accurately speculating that McCauley was responsible for the stunt. One of the cops heads to the reception desk to ask whether there is a genuine emergency in the hotel, while the other remains in the surveillance room to study Waingro's curiously subdued reaction.

Waingro hears a knock at the door and a voice telling him that security has arrived to evacuate the building. Waingro does not fall for this ruse; he cocks a pistol and inspects the spy hole to determine McCauley's exact location in relation to his own. When McCauley briefly turns his back, Waingro swiftly opens the door, hoping to catch him by surprise. However, McCauley's reflexes are too fast, and he effortlessly slams the door into Waingro's face, knocking him to the ground. McCauley picks Waingro up, beats him on the nose with the butt of his gun, and then shoots him multiple times in the head. Although McCauley may seem to be in charge of the situation, there is a variable that he did not account for: the LAPD officer in the next room sees the entire incident through the surveillance feed and calls for reinforcements. Mann cross-cuts between the action occurring within the hotel and images of Eady, waiting in the car park outside. At first, Eady is visibly concerned as she sees streams of clients flee the hotel. She then appears mortified when a swarm of police cars arrive at the scene. The successful carrying out of McCauley's revenge, which we may expect to be treated as a moment of personal triumph and honour, is instead framed as the point at which he seals his own fate. The viewer's attention is drawn to the damage inflicted upon Eady as a result of McCauley's actions, not to any sense of satisfaction that McCauley may feel from eliminating his adversary. McCauley indulgently takes a moment to watch over Waingro's body, unaware of the commotion he has caused outside. When McCauley leaves the room, he is immediately accosted by a cop who points a gun at the back of his head and orders him to drop his weapon. McCauley, at first, pretends to play ball, raising his hands and methodically stepping in the guided direction. He then catches the cop off guard, grabbing his torch and using it to beat him until he collapses on the ground. As McCauley makes his way out of the building through a back entrance, which is becoming increasingly filled with heavily armed officers, Mann cuts to reaction shots of Hanna watching the events unfold from the overhead perspective of a police helicopter. McCauley escapes into the parking lot and briefly locks eyes with a distressed Eady. As they gaze at one another, McCauley appears to be weighing the different options in his mind and struggling, momentarily, to decide on the right course of action. Yet, like Hanna and Shiherlis, he ultimately acts in the interest of his own self-preservation. Without exchanging a single word with his romantic partner, McCauley turns away from her and disappears into the crowd.

So, in a notable parallel to the end of *Thief*, *Heat* concludes with McCauley cutting himself off from all his personal commitments, firmly rejecting the domestic sphere, and marching into an indefinite future. This time, however, he is not by himself: he is chased by Hanna, an equally alienated man who has cut ties with his own family to facilitate the pursuit of his professional objective. The two men run into the docking bay of the airport; a setting rendered so uncanny by Mann's camera it resembles the surface of an alien planet. Per Wildermuth says that the airport tarmac is a setting where machines take precedence over anybody who may stray into their path: 'Human beings have no place here, there is no space for them.' (2005: 148). A liminal space that individuals move through to either enter or exit LA, the airport tarmac encapsulates the evanescent nature of life in the city. There are no other signs of life as the two men run across the tarmac, weaving through a multitude of large red-and-yellow cubes. The space is underlit, with the primary source of illumination being the lights of passing aircraft as they temporarily cross overhead. As a result, the tarmac constantly dips into and out of darkness, obscuring the men's view of one another.

Eventually, McCauley hides behind one of these geometric structures, poised with his gun. Hanna takes a few tentative steps forward before ducking behind an adjacent cube. The two men are at a standstill, each one unsure of the exact whereabouts of their target. When a plane flies low overhead, McCauley's shadow becomes visible, and Hanna can determine the thief's position. Hanna immediately turns and fires, first hitting McCauley in the arm to knock the gun out of his hand, and then twice in the chest to finish him off. As with the death of Cheritto, Mann follows the moment of impact with an extreme close-up of Hanna's face as he lowers his weapon, visibly disturbed by the act of violence he's just committed. Hanna experiences no pleasure while taking somebody's life, even if he is doing it to fulfil a professional obligation. McCauley slowly slips out of consciousness, and Hanna is overcome by a feeling of intense dissatisfaction. Hanna has caused the death of the only individual in the film who could truly identify with his searing emotional pain and he knows that he'll soon throw himself into a new investigation. His work as a law enforcer will never be complete: there will always be a new crime to investigate, a new outlaw to hunt, and a new victim to console. And, what's worse, there will always be criminals that slip through Hanna's fingers, crimes that he fails to solve, and people he cannot save.

Despite being at the receiving end of Hanna's bullet, McCauley expresses no sense of anger or contempt toward him, as he did towards Waingro. This is because Waingro was dishonest and unprincipled; he pretended to be an ally to McCauley's crew, only to turn the tables on them when it became personally advantageous for him to do so. Conversely, Hanna has never deviated from his own, personally-determined behavioural code, which is comparable to McCauley's, and now he has followed it to its conclusion. As established in the diner sequence, McCauley embarked on the bank robbery knowing this would be the outcome if he and Hanna crossed paths, and he now accepts the outcome. *Heat* closes with an immaculately composed symmetrical wide shot. Hanna and McCauley hold hands in the centre of the composition, framed small against the vast open space that surrounds them on either side. On frame left, an overhead power line stretches into the distance, appearing as though it reaches into infinity. On frame right, the artificial lights of the city are visible, providing a faint spot of illumination in the darkness. As Gaine observes, the wide composition 'emphasise[s] the empty space in the frame around them, separated and isolated, just as the planes and passengers around them are transient.' (2011: 106). Hanna and McCauley are locked in a physical expression of intimacy, a rare sign of mutual compassion and respect between two individuals within the dehumanising environment of this vast metropolis. Because of their mutual commitment to their respective professional roles, these men must sever their emotional bond. At the end of the film, McCauley is dead and Hanna faces a bleak future: the investigation has ended, he has alienated himself from his family, and he has murdered the only other individual who could fully understand and identify with his situation.

Band of Outsiders:
The Insider (1999)

Building on the themes of *Heat*, *The Insider* focuses on the relationship between two men who struggle to fulfil their promise within an oppressive and dehumanising society. At first glance, CBS reporter Lowell Bergman and scientific researcher Jeffery Wigand may appear to be more mundane and everyday figures than the criminals, warriors and master athletes who typically populate Mann's work. But, under closer inspection, they embody many qualities that distinguish characters like Frank, McCauley, Murphy and Hawkeye: unquenchable idealism, self-determination, belief in personal liberty, and dedication to their chosen line of work. As with these earlier Mann protagonists, these characteristics render both Bergman and Wigand outcasts within their respective communities (mainstream broadcast journalism in Bregman's case, corporate scientific research in Wigand's). Nevertheless, these protagonists refuse to compromise their ideals, no matter how overwhelming the external pressure on them to acquiesce becomes.

The film is structured as a dual character study, tracking the emotional journeys that Bergman and Wigand undergo as they each risk their financial security, social standing, and family's well-being in their quest to reveal the corruption at the centre of the tobacco industry. Each man's pursuit of this goal creates friction between them and the industry in which they have developed a distinguished, high-profile career: Wigand, a researcher for the Big Tobacco company Brown & Williamson, signed a non-disclosure agreement as a condition of employment, and spreading the truth about the company's manipulation of data will be a breach of the conditions of this contract; Bergman, a journalist for the CBS-produced current affairs show *60 Minutes*, is warned that, if this non-disclosure agreement is breached, the company could be implicated in the legal proceedings which follow, – potentially forcing CBS to pay a fortune in damages and jeopardising their reputation in the public arena. Like *Manhunter* and *Heat*, the narrative is structured to emphasise the parallels between its two lead characters and their respective professional quests. In those earlier films, however, the professional objectives of the two central figures are fundamentally opposed to one another, which ultimately results in one eradicating their double. In *The Insider*, both men work in partnership to pursue a shared goal: to resist the overwhelming institutional power of the tobacco industry and make the truth about the health risks of nicotine available to the broader public. Wigand and Bergman recognise the similarities between their personalities early on, and they quickly develop a mutual sense of respect that remains strong throughout the entire narrative (even if there are a few points where they clash over certain decisions regarding how they approach this shared objective).

Although Wigand isolates himself from his family, and Bergman cuts ties with his peers, their motivations are never portrayed as being self-serving or narcissistic. They are driven, first and foremost, by a belief in the honour of their work and the potential for that work to bring about substantial socio-political change. Therefore, they must fight the cynical pragmatists within their respective professional spheres who care only about material comfort. In committing to this difficult journey, each character is forcibly made aware that the professional sphere they occupy is not truly as benevolent as they once believed: Wigand realises that Brown & Williamson hired him to conduct scientific research not so he may help them to produce a healthier product but, but to aid them in concealing the hazardous nature of their cigarettes from consumers; Bergman discovers that, despite the company's stated commitment to 'honesty and integrity', CBS News has strong financial and institutional ties to corporations which influence the nature of the content it airs.

Although it is difficult to call the ending of *The Insider* an unambiguously jubilant one (after all, the Big Tobacco industry still remains strong and mainstream American news stations are still connected to toxic corporate entities), both Bergman and Wigand are granted a more favourable fate than the typical Mann protagonist. Wigand may lose his family and his luxury upper-middle-class lifestyle, but his testimony against Brown & Williamson is broadcast to the world, and he finds satisfaction in his new career as a high school teacher. Bergman may cut ties with his colleagues, but he reconnects with his intellectual roots and pursues a form of journalism that is more radical and hard-hitting than anything he is permitted to carry out at CBS. Thus, while both men end up socially disconnected, to a certain extent, at the end of the narrative, they have both fulfilled their goal of bringing major social injustice to the public's attention. In doing so, they both break away from the control of monolithic corporations which wish to force them into submission, and seek out new, fulfilling professional opportunities. The personal cost for each man is heavy, but, regardless of this, they both take great pride in what they are able to achieve, and – unusually for a Mann film – the prevailing atmosphere at the end of the feature is one of victory. As Mann explains, he and co-writer Eric Roth always intended for *The Insider* to be about more than the tobacco industry specifically. The film's scathing observations regarding the connection between the media, the corporate sphere and the political arena may apply to many different areas of modern American society: 'What this film is about is corporate power and malfeasance. And huge businesses that are highly profitable, that are really in a drug trade. From their point of view, they have a wonderful business — they have a market addicted to their product.' (Sragow, 1999).

In its portrayal of individuals pitted against vast corporate machines that systematically conceal the truth and socially condition the broader public to accept an unjust societal order, *The Insider* consciously recalls of the American conspiracy thrillers of the 1970s. Jean-Baptiste Thoret makes this link when he writes that 'With *The Insider*, Mann undertook a very personal and disenchanted re-reading of the film canon of the 1970s, delivering to its passing a melancholic and politically sublime work on the contemporary illusion of counter-politics.' (2000). Films such as *Winter Kills* (1979), *The Conversation* (1974) and *Blow Out* (1974) reflect the widespread dissolution with government power and distrust in mainstream information channels which characterised American society in the years immediately following the Vietnam War, the Watergate scandal and the intensification of mass surveillance under the Nixon administration. These films depict an America in which deeply corrupt organisations wield immense power, and any attempt by an individual to reveal the misconduct at the core of these organisations is a tremendous struggle likely to bring about personal ruin. Evil is not personified in the form of a single person or even a single group: political organisations, the court system, the police, and the media are all interrelated, and they all work in conjunction with one another to exert a frightening level of control over the population. The hero of the conspiracy thriller is a truth-seeker, a lone agent who launches a crusade against the system to break through the layers of deceit and refuses to back down despite facing an intense degree of pressure to conform and accept the dominance of the prevailing orthodoxy.

1970s conspiracy thrillers were steeped in a melancholic tone, a sense that the radicalism of the 1960s had given way to the crushing authoritarianism of the Nixon era, that the interconnected institutions which governed American life were overwhelmingly determined to prevent positive sweeping social change. *The Insider* was released in 1999, many decades after the high point of the genre's popularity had passed. The socio-political landscape of the period was markedly different from that of the 1970s. The United States was riding the wave of economic success and liberal reforms under the Clinton administration, the collapse of the Berlin Wall which ostensibly ended the cold war lead many theorists to proclaim that Western democratic capitalism represented the end point of societal development, and declaring that the 1960s' utopian dream for a complete overhaul of the political system seemed to be a remnant of the past. Certainly, films were produced during this period that portrayed dominant American institutions in a sceptical light and explicitly undermined the dominant cultural narrative of societal progress (including, as we have seen, Mann's own work), but the prevailing mood in American cinema at this point was a far cry from the disillusionment and distrust which dominated the conspiracy thrillers of the 1970s. Mann's decision to revisit this genre model within such a socio-political landscape is indicative of his continued scepticism towards institutional power in America and his unwavering commitment to left-wing politics. Indeed, if we are to interpret the character trajectory of Bergman (a radical journalist who studied under Herbert Marcuse and worked for a number of alternative newspapers before landing his position at CBS) as a reflection of the absorption of the counter-cultural impulses of the 1960s into the neoliberal mainstream, then Bergman's gradual disillusionment with his professional milieu and his ultimate decision to get back to his journalist roots, may be read as Mann's message to the American public that the work of history as never truly 'finished' and it is vital to continue to continue recognising and resisting social injustice in its contemporary manifestations. It is notable that Mann's next film, *Ali*, will directly look to the 1960s to draw parallels between the inequality and oppression of that era and still prevalent in American society at the turn of the millennium.

In *The Insider*, Mann connects these themes to his longstanding concern with the tension between personal and professional life. When he poses a challenge to the power of Brown & Williamson, Wigand is threatened with financial ruin, his family is hounded, and he is smeared in the press, all in an attempt to coerce him into complying with their demands. Although Wigand is strong enough to withstand the personal attacks, he finds it difficult to cope with the company's actions' effect on the well-being of his family. Wigand's choice to act as a whistle-blower is motivated by his strong moral compass and his belief in the integrity of scientific research, but his commitment is tested by the warning that his large severance package – which includes healthcare services for his daughters (one of whom has severe asthma) – will be withheld from him if he does not fulfil his contractual obligation to conceal all information regarding the company's illicit health and safety practices. The comfort and stability of the Wigand family are therefore reliant on Wigand's silence, but Wigand knows that blowing the whistle on Big Tobacco is likely to have a positive impact on the habits of many consumers who are unaware of his former company's shady business practices. Wigand's decision to place the wellbeing of his family on the line, while concealing the severity of the threat they face from his wife Liane (Diane Venora), creates a tension between himself and his loved ones that ultimately results in the collapse of the family unit. If Wigand were to resign himself to passive compliance, as his fellow researchers in the tobacco industry have, he would continue to enjoy his lifestyle of material luxury and remain with his family, but he would also have to compromise his ideals and allow himself to be used as a pawn by a noxious corporation for the rest of his working life.

Although Wigand's intentions are noble, he repeatedly makes impulsive choices that place his family under extreme duress, and he makes these choices without consulting Liane (Diane Venora). When Wigand's refusal to obey his bosses' orders at Brown & Williamson results in his dismissal, he leaves the company without fully taking into account the extent to which his suburban familial life was reliant on the steady funds and benefits he received from the company – the medical care of their children, the mortgage payments on their home, and the financial instalments on their car need to be covered, and Wigand has no clear plan to handle their fragile financial situation.

Similarly, Bergman's career and his reputation are threatened by the bosses of CBS when his desire to broadcast the truth about Brown & Williamson threatens to derail a merger between the two companies that will bring the company CEOs millions of dollars in revenue. As he finds his position as producer for *60 Minutes* is in jeopardy, Bergman reflects on just how deeply his reputation relies on his affiliation with his comfort. At a low point, He tells his wife: 'Lowell Bergman of *60 Minutes*. You take the *60 Minutes* out of that, and nobody returns your phone call.' Like Wigand, Bergman is let down by colleagues who are too apathetic to challenge the corrupt structures of power and control – represented in the film by journalist Mike Wallace (Christopher Plummer) and programme director

Don Hewitt (Philip Baker Hall), both of whom are willing to cut Wigand's testimony from the broadcast of *60 Minutes*, in accordance with the demands of Brown & Williamson. Bergman and Wigand are brilliant men, who are adept at their respective professions, but they are both expected to be at the whim of opportunistic, unfeeling plutocrats who expect them to function as cogs in the systems they preside over. The central secret that Bergman holds regarding the practice of cigarette manufacturing company Brown & Williamson is divulged at the mid-point of the narrative; following the taping of Wigand's interview, there are no more shocking revelations, or further additions, to Wigand's account; the film becomes concerned wholly with the issue of how Wigand's testimony may make it to air without being manipulated or censored by competing interest groups. To simply know the secrets of the tobacco industry is not sufficient, Wigand learns – what matters just as much is holding the ability to access widely circulated information channels so that this message may be spread to a large audience without it being manipulated or censored. And what is intended to shock the viewer of *The Insider* more than the specific practices of Brown & Williamson is the mechanisms they employ to keep these practices concealed from the population. Such is the extent of the company's influence over various branches of American society – including the courts and the media – that the exact nature of their corrupt working methods may be systematically kept from the public, and anybody who threatens to challenge this power will be targeted with an aggressive campaign designed to force them into silence.

In contrast to the heroes of earlier conspiracy thrillers, the ambitions of Bergman and Wigand are comparatively small scale; they are both under no illusion that they have the power to topple the entire tobacco industry or put an end to nefarious practices in cigarette manufacturing. In the face of overwhelming corporate pressure, what becomes important to them is committing a relatively minor act of dissent: broadcasting a relatively short interview within a segment of a one-hour current affairs programme. Proliferating Wigand's testimony widely, he and Bergman believe, will lead to the emancipation of the consumer by making them aware of the business operations of the companies they purchase commodities from. Therefore, they wish to make the everyday citizen truly conscious of the exploitative practices of monolithic corporations. Both men take immense pride in their work and are unprepared to blindly follow the rules imposed on them by their exploitative bosses. The shared values and drives of Wigand and Bergman bind them together when nobody is willing to back them up within their respective professional communities.

The Insider begins with a bewildering, quasi-abstract opening credits scene. The first image we see is an obscure shot of beige fabric undulating violently. Mann holds on this shot for nearly a full minute, and it is almost impossible to tell what exactly it is we're looking at. The next few images give us more visual information, though the exact nature of the situation unfolding in these opening moments remains uncertain. A man is shown driving a vehicle, in which a passenger sits at the back with a thick blindfold obstructing his vision. We come to understand that the first shot was filtered through the passenger's perspective. Mann then cuts to close-ups of the sack, the windshield, the wheels, and the dashboard. As the journey continues, we gradually pick up on more details. A sign reveals that the car is entering Beirut, and the suspicious expressions of the locals indicate that the vehicle contains a foreign and potentially malignant influence. Mann repeatedly cuts to close-up shots of the passenger's blindfolded eyes and POV shots from his perspective – emphasising his position of powerlessness, as he seems to be subject to the whims of whoever is transporting him. The vehicle comes to a halt outside of a building that is heavily patrolled by armed guards, and the driver leads the passenger inside, still with the sack on his head. As we still cannot see the face of the passenger, we do not know what his emotional state is; the lack of context we are given leads us to assume that we are watching a kidnapping or hostage situation. The unusual structure of this opening sequence, which first unmoors the viewer and then feeds them vital contextual information piece-by-piece, immediately establishes a central theme of the film: the ability of audio-visual to obscure and manipulate information to warp the spectator's perception. As Dzenis observes, this bizarre opening 'introduces a key metaphor about blindness and concealment in a film where so much is hidden and so much remains unclear.' (2002). The viewer is thrown into the film in media res and has to actively think *through* and *about* the images on screen to make sense of the narrative. This, therefore, immediately stresses the importance of active, critical spectatorship – a profoundly significant theme in a film that problematises our perception of the filmed image as a straightforward record of truth and highlights the capacity of audio-visual media to strategically manipulate and distort data.

Our expectations are soon upended. Guards sit down the passenger and remove the sack from his head (though Bergman remains blindfolded). Opposite him is Sheikh Fadlallah (Clifford Curtis), the leader of Hezbollah. He introduces himself as Lowell Bergman, explains his professional background, and then explains why he believes that broadcasting an interview with Fadlallah on the show could be mutually beneficial for them. During the first sequence, Bergman appeared to be in grave danger, and he seemed to be at the mercy of the driver and the guards. We learn now, however, that Bergman was, in fact, the one who set up the meeting. An episode dedicated to Hezbollah, Bergman promises, will allow the group to have its perspective aired on American television, and therefore give them an opportunity to counteract the unfair representation of them prevalent in

Western media – as such, it may aid them in establishing themselves as a legitimate political organisation. The abrupt re-positioning of Bergman from a helpless victim to an active agent who is in full control of the situation immediately establishes his ability to exercise intellectual agility and calmness in adverse circumstances and work productively within the parameters of a power structure in which he is seemingly at a disadvantage. Moreover, his willingness to meet with Fadlallah indicates his ideological opposition to the normative currents in American media, and his eagerness to take on subject matter that strays outside what is typically considered to be 'acceptable' within the realm of broadcast programming in the US. The Sheikh is understandably hesitant to collaborate with a mainstream American television network, fearing that they will twist his words to portray Hezbollah in an overwhelmingly negative light. Bergman attempts to break down the Sheikh's resistance, however, with a skilful piece of rhetoric: 'You've seen *60 Minutes*, and Mike Wallace, so you know our reputation for integrity and objectivity. You also know we are the highest-rated, most respected TV magazine news show in America.' Bergman's self-assuredness, communication skills and intelligence are clearly on display here, yet his promise regarding the integrity of CBS unconvincing. It seems unlikely that Bergman can make good on his promise to ensure Hezbollah will receive fair and impartial treatment on *60 Minutes*. Bergman demonstrates an idealistic belief in the power of American journalism that does not match the reality of how the field actually functions. The fact that he points to the presence of Mike Wallace as a symbol of the excellence of CBS news comes across as particularly ironic, as Wallace is one of *60 Minutes* reporters who will later fold when CBS is placed under pressure by Big Tobacco to omit their interview with Wigand. The veracity and authority of CBS news, passionately espoused by Bergman at this early stage, is gradually revealed to be an illusion, as big capital later governs what the network is willing and is *not* willing to put on the air. When the pressure mounts, Bergman is the only journalist working for the network who is not willing to let the interests of lobbyists impede his journey to uncover injustice and deception. Although he boasts of the virtues of CBS, he will later find that he is the only employee willing to stick his neck out to fight for these very principles he claims are central to the organisation. Bergman evidently has a great deal of talent in his line of work and has built a substantial reputation over the decades, but he suffers from a hubristic belief in the integrity of his network which will later prove to be his downfall.

In contrast, Wigand is aware of the toxic nature of the tobacco industry from the beginning of the narrative, and when we first see him, he is clearing out his desk after being fired for insubordination. Wigand has spent much of his professional life sleepwalking through his days at Brown & Williamson, a company that took him for granted. The corporation disregarded his scientific excellence and his potential contribution to the field of human knowledge, instead expecting him to obey orders and refrain from voicing any opinions that go against the grain of the views held by the company's board of CEOs. An insignificant cog in a well-oiled machine, Wigand's brilliant scientific mind has been exploited for the financial benefit of Big Tobacco, but they can expel him the moment that he becomes an inconvenience to them – as a later scene reveals, the only official reason given for Wigand's dismissal was 'poor communication skills'. When they first meet, Wigand is amused by Bergman's career trajectory, asking him incredulously: 'How did a radical journalist from *Ramparts* magazine end up working for CBS?' For Wigand, the idea of channelling radical socio-political impulses into a current affairs programme produced by one of the most profitable companies in the country is absurd, despite Bergman's insistence that he still tackles the 'tough stories'.' While Bergman believes that CBS provides him with vital support in pursuing his noble journalistic goals, Wigand recognises that his noble professional ambitions are at odds with the objectives of the company that employs him. In contrast to the pride in CBS expressed by Bergman during this opening act, Wigand appears eager to get out of the building as fast as possible; he slips past his colleagues wordlessly and then slinks out of the front door.

Wigand is not only disconnected from his working environment, he also feels deeply alienated within the domestic space. Wigand enters the house silently, Mann's camera tracking him from the side in a slow-motion, side-on tracking shot as he slips past multiple opulent rooms. He passes a large set of French doors, through which Liane is visible, sitting out on the patio, but neither character acknowledges the other. Instead, Wigand walks through to the kitchen, where he pours a glass of brandy for himself. Despite the material splendour of the suburban home, it does not provide him with any true sense of joy. All the luxury commodities have been paid for with the dirty money he earned from morally questionable scientific practices, and so the house serves as a constant reminder of the extent to which he has abandoned his principles for the sake of material comfort. Wigand, however, springs into action when Deborah (Renee Olstead), the youngest daughter, suffers an intense asthma attack. After hearing the sound of her wheezing, Wigand sprints up the stairs and passes her an inhaler. To ease her nerves, he gives her an in-depth explanation of what's happening inside her body: 'It was dusty in there, sweetheart. It was duty, and you breathed it in. So what's happening to you now is that cells called mast cells, told your lungs "don't breathe any more of that dust in". There are airwaves in your lungs, like branches. And when these branches close up, you get an asthma attack. But I've given you medicine, and you'll get better. OK?' Deborah stops panicking, and her breathing returns to a healthy rhythm. Wigand and Liane hold hands, both relieved to see their daughter calm down. Wigand is in his element at this moment, drawing upon his scientific knowledge to guide his daughter through a frightening experience. When he can combine his paternal instincts with his love of science, he functions effectively as the head of the family.

However, Wigand's inadequacies as a husband and a father become apparent in the following scene. Wigand leaves the dinner table early under the pretext of going to the store to buy more soy sauce. Liane goes out to speak to him and spots boxes containing Wigand's office supplies in the back of his car. Wigand is forced to reveal that he lost his job that morning. That Wigand has to be forced to tell Liane demonstrates the lack of intimacy and open communication in their marriage. Wigand makes a half-hearted attempt to quell her concerns by dispassionately telling her that he has been offered a decent severance package that includes regular cash payments and some continued healthcare benefits. Liane is clearly distraught at hearing this news, but Wigand gets into the car and starts the engine rather than staying to console her. As he pulls out of the driveway, Liane calls after him, but he refuses to acknowledge her plea for help. While helping Deborah through her asthma attack, Wigand proved to be caring, decisive and helpful. When he has to deal with practical, material considerations such as paying essential bills and keeping on top of mortgage payments, however, he seems uncomfortable and evasive. Wigand delays telling his family the bad news for as long as possible and then proves insufficient at providing Liane with the emotional support she longs for after hearing of their change in financial circumstances. In typical Mannian fashion, Wigand is so committed to his area of professional expertise – advanced scientific research – that he neglects to pay sufficient attention to all the other areas of his life. There is an essential tension, then, between Wigand's professional values and the practical demands placed on him in his domestic life.

Mann draws a connection between his dual protagonists by showing Bergman in his own home environment immediately after this sequence. Bergman also appears to be disconnected from his domestic space, but in a considerably different way. Wigand disengages from the domestic sphere because his work constantly occupies his thoughts; Bergman has firmly merged his domestic space with his professional space, carrying out essential work duties within the home. In the first glimpse we see of Bergman's house, he sits in bed taking a vital work call. His wife, Sharon (Lindsay Crouse), enters the room and places his mail on the bedside cabinet, as though acting as his secretary. When Bergman's son, Jake, enters the room, Bergman barely notices him. He shakes his hand as an obligatory sign of recognition, but he then averts his gaze and returns to his call. A second phone starts ringing on the other side of the room, and Sharon answers it, reinforcing the impression that the bedroom is akin to a second office for Bergman. Whereas Wigand keeps his professional and familial life separate to the point of neglecting the latter, Bergman merges the two to the point that they become indistinguishable; his family members resemble assistants keeping track of his professional duties. Although Bergman's home environment is less overtly chaotic than Wigand's, it also demonstrates a fundamental inability for Bergman to 'switch off' from his work.

Bergman receives a dossier filled with scientific papers related to the health effects of nicotine – research for an upcoming *60 Minutes* episode on the dangers of smoking. The information is dense, and Bergman decides that he must hire an expert on the subject to help him decipher the research. When Bergman phones the Wigand house, Liane answers and, knowing the trouble that will befall the family if Wigand breaks the terms of his confidentiality agreement, she initially rebuffs Bergman's offer. Wigand, however, disregards Liane's concerns and secretly sends Bergman a fax to arrange a meeting. Flicking through the dossier, Wigand tells Bergman that he can write up a summary of the documents, but he can provide no further information about the inner workings tobacco industry. The fact that Wigand adds this clarification without Bergman pushing him first signals that, despite his claim to the contrary, Wigand has already considered the possibility of revealing scandalous details about the company that mistreated him for so many years. Bergman is intrigued, and delves into the subject further, though he knows that he cannot *force* Wigand to testify. After hearing Wigand assert that the summary of the dossier is 'as far as I go,' Bergman retorts, 'As far as you go where?' Wigand's response whets Bergman's appetite: 'All this in here is a drop in the bucket. But I can't talk to you about anything else.' Wigand explains if he were to delve deeper into this subject, he would risk breaching his agreement with the company. Bergman retorts that confidentially agreements can always be worked around and that the demands imposed on him by a corrupt company shouldn't prevent him from revealing truths that may prove beneficial to a large percentage of the public. Wigand leaves the meeting without giving Bergman any more details, but he can tell instinctively that Wigand is being drawn toward the option of blowing the whistle.

Bergman is the first individual Wigand encounters who truly believes that the confidential information Wigand holds about Brown & Williamson could potentially bring about a substantial change in the broader public's attitude towards the tobacco industry if made widely available. Unlike the other research scientists at the company, Bergman places greater importance on shedding light on injustice than on ensuring his material comfort and stability. As will become clear over the course of the narrative, Wigand finds Bergman's idealism a refreshing change from the opportunism and greed of his former colleagues. However, Bergman's idealism registers as being somewhat naïve here, just as it did in the opening sequence – his intentions are good, but his casual claim that non-disclosure agreements are not important registers as being flippant in light of the extreme obstacles that Wigand will later face while seeking to air his testimony. If Bergman was more honest with Wigand about the difficulties that lay ahead, Wigand could have better prepared himself and his family for the fight, rather than being blindsided by the immense opposition he faces from the television network, advertisers and Brown & Williamson.

Wigand's definitive decision to break the terms of his employment contract is preceded by an excruciating meeting he has with Brown & Williamson CEO Thomas Sandefur (Michael Gambon). During this meeting, Sandefur reiterates the conditions of Wigand's confidentiality agreement and emphasises the horrendous consequences he will face if he fails to comply. Throughout the session, two lawyers sit at the back of the room; they are mostly silent but their presence adds an aura of intimidation to the proceedings. When Wigand confesses that he feels uncomfortable being back in the building, Sandefur is openly hostile towards him. Sandefur tells his lawyers that Wigand 'says exactly what's on his mind. Most people consider what they're saying, social skills, but Jeffery just charges right ahead.' After this insult, Sandefur talks about the absolute necessity of Wigand abiding by the terms of the non-disclosure agreement. He first reminds Wigand of everything he stands to lose if his severance package is taken away, and then tells him that the primary personal quality that enabled him to get to his position of authority is his ability to 'never break a promise I couldn't keep.' He then adds: 'I knew that if I ever broke a promise, I'd suffer the consequences.' Sensing the presumptuous tone of Sandefur's speech, Wigand emphatically gives his boss his reassurance that he will not breach the terms of the contract he signed. 'I don't believe that you can maintain corporate integrity without confidentiality agreements. The health and welfare benefits are good. The severance package is fair. I have no intention of violating my confidentiality agreement and disclosing that which I said I wouldn't.' Wigand's behaviour here is uncharacteristically firm and decisive, but Sandefur continues to treat him with blatant disrespect. Sandefur refuses to look Wigand in the eye – instead, he shoots glances at his lawyers, swivels in his chair, looks at the ceiling, and flicks through the papers on his desk. Finally, he tells Wigand: 'I appreciate all that, Jeff, but upon reflection, we've decided to expand our zone of comfort with you. So we've drafted a supplement to your agreement. It broadly defines and expands in more detail what is "confidential". Nobody will be able to say, "Well, hell's bells, Margaret, I didn't know that was a secret …".' Essentially, the company is expanding the non-disclosure agreement terms to forbid Wigand from discussing *any* detail of his employment with Brown & Williamson, placing even more strident constraints on his freedom of speech. It will now be entirely within the purview of the company directors to determine what is and isn't libellous at their own discretion – even information that may seem, to Wigand to be completely uncontroversial. One of the lawyers enters the conversation to clarify that, if Wigand says anything about the company which may be interpreted to cast it in a negative light, the benefits received by his family will be cut immediately: 'If we "arrive" at the conclusion you're acting in bad faith? We would terminate, right now, payouts under your severance package. You and your family's medical benefits' This is a severe affront to Wigand's freedom of speech, essentially granting the company the power to claim that *anything* that Wigand says about them is libellous.

The typically restrained Wigand responds with an unexpected display of aggression. Wigand accuses Sandefur of calling his integrity into question: 'It never crossed my mind not to honour my agreement. But I will tell you Mr Sandefur – and Brown & Williamson too – fuck me? Fuck you.' Mann holds on a lengthy close-up of Wigand as he castigates his former employer, unloading years of pent-up anger. Mann here reworks the earlier scene in which Wigand left the company building, signalling a significant shift in his character. Wigand will no longer allow his behaviour to be dictated by the demands of Brown & Williamson; he will develop an actively antagonistic relationship to the company.

Yet, in his pursuit of justice, Wigand does indeed place his family at risk, as nefarious forces increasingly intrude into the domestic sphere and threaten those close to the whistle-blower. While testing his skills at a driving range, Wigand becomes suspicious of another player. The sequence takes place at night, the range shrouded in an inky blackness only illuminated by breams of turquoise-tinged spotlights. Wigand's thoughts become overwhelmed by paranoia as he gets the sensation that the other man is watching him. As Mann alternates between the two characters, the second player's gaze lingers upon Wigand, although he remains silent. The scene climaxes as the player picks up his golf club, straightens his tie, and then stands up straight, all the while gazing directly at Wigand. The lights illuminating the range turn out, one by one. Wigand returns to his car to find that the mysterious figure is leaving the range at the same time, and his car is parked next to Wigand's in the otherwise empty lot. Wigand finally snaps when he spots the player blatantly staring at him from the adjacent vehicle. Wigand exits his vehicle, club in hand, and follows the car as the player pulls away, repeatedly yelling at him to 'stay away from me'. Mann keeps the scene fairly ambiguous, with the intentions of the second player left uncertain. We do not know exactly who he was working for, nor do we know how long he had been trailing Wigand for. This keeps the viewer in the same state of paranoia that consumes Wigand, constantly unsure of the precise level of surveillance he has been placed under.

Tensions within the Wigand family are accelerated when Wigand takes up a new job as a high school chemistry teacher. Following his experience with Brown & Williamson, Wigand believes that he is in dire need of a career change, and he seeks out a professional environment that isn't tainted by corporate greed. However, the consequence of this is a significant loss of income, and so the family must downgrade from their luxurious home to a more modest property. The pleasant atmosphere of Wigand's preliminary interview with a local high school principal is undercut when Mann cuts to an image of Liane, framed from behind, gazing at a blank white wall, upon which the spots where family photos once hung are still visible. Mann then cuts to a side-view tracking shot as Liane walks through the hallway, tearful at the sight of her now-empty home; the decorations have been removed, all the belongings now sit in cardboard boxes. She gazes through the French doors at the empty patio area outside. The shot is the inverse of the image in which Wigand first entered the home at the film's beginning: in the first sequence, Wigand felt alienated and unfulfilled within the domestic space, with the material surroundings serving as a reminder of the soulless work he was forced into to afford this lifestyle; In this later sequence, it is Liane who feels despondent and empty, forced to give up the space she called home for the past three years. At first glance, this sequence may seem to paint Liane as a superficial character overly invested in material goods, but it must be considered that Liane views the house as a material embodiment of cherished family memories. She tears up looking at the backyard, reminiscing to Wigand: 'Debbie took her first steps, right there on the grass.' She then starts crying, and Wigand's brief attempts to make her feel better are characteristically ineffectual. Wigand feels no reservations about leaving the house behind because he only associates it with the corruption of the tobacco industry. However, he does not consider that, for Liane, the house has different and far more positive connotations. Wigand thought that moving house would bring stability to the family unit, but the new property soon becomes a site of intense anxiety and paranoia, intensifying the rift between himself and Liane. Shortly after moving in, Deborah wakes Wigand in the middle of the night to tell him that she thought she heard a stranger in the backyard. Wigand panics, taking Deborah to the basement and instructing her to remain there until he gets back. Wigand then fetches his gun and skulks around the yard, inspecting the bushes for signs of movement. Startled by the sound of a racoon, Wigand directs his weapon and the creature and only stops himself from pulling the trigger at the very last minute. 'You almost got your damn head blown off,' he mutters. Mann cross-cuts between this action and a series of shots of the furnace flaring up in the basement, shocking Deborah; this visual rhyme foreshadows the extent to which his family will come under pressure by outside forces as a result of Wigand's crusade. As in *Manhunter*, the protagonist's actions place the domestic space under threat and fracture the family unit from within. The violence inflicted upon the domestic sphere does not dissuade Wigand from following this course of action but, instead, strengthens his resolve to fulfil his professional goal and bring those responsible for this abuse to justice.

As a research scientist, Wigand isn't used to being placed under scrutiny by forces as powerful as Brown & Williamson. Bergman, however, is used to working in a high-pressure environment, and, is in a good position to offer Wigand helpful advice on how to maintain his composure. Bergman tells Wigand that, due to the sensitive nature of the information Wigand intends to expose, he will be placed under scrutiny from the company and from various parts of the media (he does not foresee any pushback from CBS at this early stage, though). Wigand reveals that he has a history of alcoholism, was once prone to temper tantrums, and was once charged with shoplifting (though never served time). Wigand stops halfway through, as this line of discussion makes him realise that several other factors will shape the public's opinion of him, whether he is speaking honestly or not. Wigand questions the extent to which Bergman's own journalistic practice is entwined with these corporate powers: 'I'm just a commodity to you, right?' Wigand asks. 'Anything worth putting on between commercials.' Bergman responds, 'To a network you're probably a commodity. Probably we're all commodities. To me you're not a commodity, that's what's important.' Bergman asserts that *60 Minutes* is devoted to transparency and will never bow down to external pressure. Bergman naively tells Wigand that his testimony will be broadcast to three million people and that, when it is aired, judgement will be handed 'to the court of public opinion'. Wigand, who is becoming increasingly sceptical of CBS's motivations, asks Bergman: 'You believe that simply getting information out to people is enough to make change happen? [...] Maybe that's just what you've been telling yourself all these years to justify having a good job and status. Maybe for the audience, it's just voyeurism, something to do on a Sunday night. And maybe it won't change a fucking thing.' Wigand, whose experience within the tobacco industry forced him to abandon his principles, has an inkling that there is something delusional about Bergman's all-consuming confidence in his company is somewhat delusional, but Bergman is skilled enough at persuasive rhetoric that he is able to assuage Wigand's fears. An outraged Bergman retorts: 'Don't evade a choice you've got to make by questioning my reputation, or *60 Minutes*, with this cheap scepticism.' Despite the reservations expressed here, Wigand quickly becomes convinced by Bergman's rhetoric and agrees to conduct the interview.

The rising tension in the Wigand house reaches a disturbing peak when Liane is interrupted while preparing a family meal by the sound of an email alert coming from the basement computer. Liane leaves the kitchen to check the source and sees the horrifying message displayed on a blood-red screen: 'WE WILL KILL YOU. WE WILL KILL ALL OF YOU. SHUT THE FUCK UP.' Tellingly, Wigand is not in the house when this happens and is therefore unable to provide guidance or support. Mann cuts between images of Liane fleeing the basement and Wigand pulling his car into the driveway, placidly unaware of the panic occurring inside. He stops to check the mail while Liane carries Deborah and Barbara (Hallie Kate Eisenberg) out of the house. A wide shot from Liane's perspective depicts the street in deep focus, the composition accentuating the distance between Wigand and the home, making him appear powerless and insignificant within the frame.

The arrival of the cops also provides no relief. The agents ask probing, invasive questions to Wigand, implying that he may have staged the events. Overhearing this aggressive line of questioning, Deborah, who is standing at the back of the room, begins to cry and is carried into another room by Liane. Wigand makes a feeble attempt to hold the hostile police officers back as they storm into the house to search the premises. Despite Liane's objections, the cops seize the family computer as evidence. Liane calls Wigand to retrieve the machine, but as soon as he leaves the house in pursuit of the officer, he slips over and lies helpless on the lawn. The security of the living space is forcefully undermined here, and Wigand's rapidly disintegrating control over his domestic situation is made painfully apparent. If Wigand's refusal to be cowed by these intimidation tactics is admirable, his consistent refusal to be open with his family about choices that will inevitably affect them is less so.

Wigand's interview for CBS is composed so that the screen is split into two parts: on the left side, we see Wigand's face, in close-up, on a television monitor tinted blue. In the background of the composition, on the right side, we see Wigand sitting on a soundstage, his visage obscured by Mann's use of shallow focus. This framing implies that Wigand is being transformed into a media image that will be removed from reality; not an accurate depiction of Wigand as he truly is, but a piece of media to be distorted, edited, and misconstrued by the network. It is not until this scene that we finally learn the most scandalous secret that Wigand holds about his former employers: through a process termed 'impact boosting', the company artificially intensifies the addictive properties of nicotine in each cigarette through the addition of chemical elements like ammonia. This results in more rapid absorption of nicotine in the lungs and causes a direct effect on the brain and nervous system. Wigand explains that, while he complied with the demands of his bosses for several years, he knew he could no longer be a part of this practice when the company incorporated a compound named 'coumarin'; Wigand wanted to make his research on this topic freely available to the public, but his findings were suppressed by the CEOs. At the time, Wigand sent Sandefur a memo detailing the hazardous nature of this compound and explaining that he could not, in good conscience, work on any product that contains it. Sandefur did not recall the product, and he did not speak to Wigand about his concerns directly; he simply sent him a written notification that his contract was being forcibly ended. At the end of the interview, Wallace asks Wigand whether he has any regrets over his decision to blow the whistle, considering the heavy price he's had to pay. Wigand pauses for a moment to think and then confesses that there are moments when he wishes he had taken another path, but, weighing up the benefits, he is confident that speaking out was, indeed, 'worth it'.

When Wigand returns to Kentucky, he finds a crowd of strangers in the house. Wigand is suspicious at first, but then Bergman arrives to explain that they are security agents sent over by CBS to watch over the family in the lead up to the broadcasting of the interview. Liane previously held a degree of sympathy for Wigand, but this sympathy quickly fades after the incident in New York. The rift between the couple rapidly intensifies until, one night, Liane enters the basement while Wigand is working to tell him that she can no longer to support him throughout his ordeal. 'I want to stand by my husband, I really do, Jeffery,' she tells him, before adding, 'but I don't think I can do this anymore.' As he has done in every other potentially tricky conversation with Liane, Wigand dances around the subject rather than addressing her fears. He asks if they can discuss her concerns at an unspecified later date, as he is preparing to give a deposition in Mississippi – Bergman has arranged for Wigand to travel to the state to speak at a hearing in support of a lawsuit being filed on behalf of the state to get reimbursed medical expenses for the citizens with nicotine-related illnesses. There is no sense of anger or grief in her voice. She has already made up her mind and is determined to remain firm in her conviction. Liane goes upstairs, leaving Wigand to return to his research. This is the last scene they share in the film; when Wigand returns to the house after speaking in Mississippi, he finds that Liane has vacated the house and taken their daughters with her. As with many Mann protagonists, Wigand is incapable of balancing his professional role and his personal life; He ultimately chooses to embrace his identity as a man of science over his familial responsibilities. Liane recognises that this is an unacceptable situation, so she cuts Wigand loose.

When Wigand arrives in Mississippi, he is served with a gag order issued by the attorneys of Brown & Williamson informing him that if he testifies in court, he will be in breach of his confidentiality agreement and he may face jail time when he returns to his home s. Wigand is shocked by this news, and his first thought is of the possible impact that his incarceration on his children's ability to access their vital medical care. 'I have no medical. *They* have no medical,' he tells Richard Scruggs (Colm Feore), the attorney representing the state of Mississippi against the tobacco companies. Scruggs expresses his sympathy and tells Wigand that he will not be forced to testify if he feels too uncomfortable about the potential consequences: 'I know that you're facing jail. And I think I know what you're thinking. [...] You feel you're whole family's future is compromised, held hostage. I do know how it is.' Before testifying, Wigand takes a moment to reflect on the situation. Bergman, aware of the gagging order, tells Wigand that he is free to pull out, as 'things have changed.' Wigand, however, does not back down, instead committing even more fervently to broadcasting the truth. 'What's changed?' Wigand retorts. 'Since this morning?' Bergman replies, misunderstanding the question. Wigand corrects him: 'No. I mean, since whenever.' Wigand goes to court, now fully committed to tackling Big Tobacco and willing to take on anybody who may attempt to hold him back.

While Wigand is aware of the opportunism and exploitation at the heart of his company from the beginning of the narrative, Bergman only discovers the corruption at the core of CBS gradually. Previously, Wigand had expressed his anxiety about being transformed into a 'commodity' by the network – his image manipulated and his testimony reworked to suit their corporate agenda, but Bergman empathetically promised him that this wouldn't be the case. The events that transpire over the second half of the film, however, reveal that Wigand's early worries were well-founded. When word spreads amongst the mediasphere of just how scathing Wigand's testimony is, he is subjected to a mass smear campaign by the mainstream media, with various newspapers and magazines selectively digging up details from Wigand's past in an attempt to paint him as an untrustworthy source. The smears against Wigand accelerate beyond Bergman's control because Wigand was not completely transparent about every incident in his past, which may potentially be used against him. A private investigator hired by Brown & Williamson discovers that Wigand has a child from a previous marriage, and there was a legal conflict between them and his ex-wife at the time over child support payments. Bergman is furious that Wigand did not tell him about an incident of this magnitude that the press may use to discredit his testimony, but Wigand stresses to him that an incident like that shouldn't matter. For Wigand, all of this is irrelevant to the veracity of his testimony: 'Whose life, if you look at it under a microscope, doesn't have any flaws?.' Bergman, who is more familiar with the workings of the American media, puts it succinctly: 'Their strategy: discredit this guy, ruin his reputation in the *Wall Street Journal*, and then nobody will ever listen to anything he's got to say about tobacco.' The relentless hounding of Wigand by the media becomes a second source of intense pressure which compounds the campaign launched against him by the tobacco industry.

Upon discovering that a gagging order was placed on Wigand during his time in Mississippi, CBS CEO Don Hewitt tells Bergman his misgivings about airing the testimony as the journalist is at work in the editing room. Hewitt observes a section of the episode that would be particularly damaging to the public image of Brown & Williamson: footage of Sandefur explicitly claiming that nicotine does not produce any addictive reactions in the human body is directly juxtaposed with a segment of Wigand's interview in which he asserts that the board of CEOs were not only *aware* of the addictive properties of nicotine, they made a conscious effort to *amplify* the addictive properties of their cigarettes to get customers hooked. This is followed by a shot of cigarettes being mass-produced in a factory. Bergman looks over at Hewitt with pride, but the CEO is visibly apprehensive about putting such a scathing indictment of Brown & Williamson on broadcast television.

Shortly after this, Bergman is called into a meeting with Eric Kluster (Stephen Tobolowsky), the head of CBS News, and corporate lawyer Helen Caperelli (Gina Gershon). Caperelli explains to Bergman that if Wigand is taken to court for his breach of the non-confidentiality agreement, then CBS may be implicated in the crime as the third party who provided a platform for his testimony. This could result in CBS being sued for damages. Bergman is unperturbed by this prospect, telling her that serious journalism must always run the risk of offending specific individuals and groups, but they can't allow that to determine which information they deem fit or unfit to air. The only factor which should determine whether an episode is suitable for broadcast, Hanna asserts, is the accuracy of the content. Caperelli directly challenges Bergman's rose-tinted view of the network by presenting him with a bizarre legal paradox: because Brown & Williamson legally own the information that Wigand is divulging in his interview, the 'truer it is, the greater the damage to them'. In other words, Caperelli believes that if Wigand's testimony is true, that makes it more damaging more CBS: they are not concerned that Wigand is fabricating information about Brown & Williamson, they are only concerned about the fact that CBS do not have legal ownership over that information. This line of reasoning challenges Bergman's faith in the journalistic nobility of CBS news, and, shocked at this information, he responds with the sarcastic quip: 'is this Alice in Wonderland?' For Bergman, this refusal to air Wigand's interview represents an amalgamation between the corporate branch of CBS and the news branch of CBS – two departments that should be fundamentally separate. Bergman soon discovers that there is an additional reason why CBS are protecting Brown & Williamson: a merger is soon going to take place between CBS and Westinghouse Corporation. If CBS is threatened with a multi-million-dollar lawsuit in the middle of this merger, Westinghouse could choose to pull out of the arrangement. If carried out successfully, however, this merger will prove highly profitable to several members of the upper management team of CBS, including Caperelli and Kluster.

Unlike these characters, Bergman is willing to risk the company's stability and his own professional standing to serve a higher journalistic calling. As he tells his apathetic team: 'Jeffery Wigand who's out on a limb … does he go on television and tell the truth? Yes. Is it newsworthy? Yes. Are we going to air it? Of course not. Why? Because he's not telling the truth? No. Because he *is* telling the truth. That's why we're not going to air it.' Bergman here draws a direct parallel between himself and Wigand. In the first half of the film, Wigand was inspired by Bergman to consent to the interview; now, Bergman is inspired by Wigand's fearless crusade to challenge the pressure placed upon him by the upper management of CBS. Wigand risked his mental and financial well-being to record the testimony and give his disposition in court. Now Bergman sees it as his duty to put his career and reputation on the line to ensure that the interview is broadcast in full. This quest does not prove to be easy, however. The controversy surrounding Wigand's testimony eventually builds to the point that Kluster demands the entire interview be removed from the episode. When Bergman refuses to re-edit the show, Kluster threatens to take the show off his hands and have another team produce the new cut. 'Since when,' Bergman asks, 'has the paragon of investigative journalism allowed lawyers to determine the news content of *60 Minutes*?' A disempowered Bergman turns to Hewitt and Wallace for support but finds that they have acquiesced to managerial pressure. 'I don't think that being cautious is so damn unreasonable,' Hewitt argues, fearing for his job. Wigand was willing to alienate himself from his family and former colleagues as a result of his all-consuming commitment to revealing the shocking secrets of Big Tobacco; now, Bergman finds himself alienated from his professional community as he becomes the only one willing to fight to broadcast the episode in its original form. The producers and journalists who Bergman formerly saw as his allies let him down, as they, like the research scientists at Brown & Williamson, place greater importance on protecting their careers than on serving the greater good.

Yet, because of the lack of support from his colleagues, CBS management take it upon themselves to air the redacted version of the 60 Minutes episode. Feeling as though his efforts, though valiant, have ultimately proven to be futile, Bergman has the unenviable task of informing Wigand that he was not successful in convincing the CEOs to air the interview. When Bergman makes the phone call, Wigand is already at a low ebb. Wigand reveals to him that Liane has filed for divorce, the girls have gone with her, and he is now living in a hotel room. Wigand hangs up the phone and silently stares at the ground. He is forced to confront the possibility that he has abandoned his family and subjected himself to months of emotional torment for nothing. The story of the censored testimony is covered in the national news, and the *60 Minutes* staff watch the broadcast in the offices of CBS. The news programme includes several talking head interview clips with different CBS employees, each one voicing their own perspective on the decision undertaken by the network's board of CEOs. First, Hewitt is shown providing a clear and concise defence of the censorship decision; then the programme cuts to a very short clip of Wallace, who just says a few words that vaguely seem to support the choice. Wallace recognises immediately that his interview has been cut down significantly and that he has been made to appear as a mere 'yes man'. An enraged Wallace turns to Kluster and demands to know why his interview was cut short without his permission, an act which, in his words, 'cut the guts out of what I said'. Witnessing his own image be manipulated to serve the corporate interests of CBS, Wallace now develops a greater understanding of Wigand's ordeal, and his perception of his bosses shifts to be more closely aligned with Hanna's. Wallace directs his anger primarily at Caperelli, accusing her and her team of prioritising monetary interests over the honour of the most respected show on the network.

Though Bergman now has Wallace on his side, the two are powerless to change the network's decision at this point. The redacted version of the *60 Minutes* episode airs, with Wigand's testimony replaced with a black screen and an explanation of the legal reasoning behind the company's decision to cut the testimony. As the episode airs, Mann cuts to reaction shots from Wallace, Bergman and Wigand, all visibly crestfallen. Both Bergman and Wigand watch from an impermanent, transitory residence. Wigand has been forced out of the family home and into a hotel room; Bergman is staying in a beach hut after Hewitt has placed him on mandatory leave from CBS. In both cases, typical Mann symbols of freedom and contentment are warped into portentous images: in Wigand's room, there is a large painting of a forest scene, a simulacrum of freedom which only emphasises the claustrophobic nature of the small room; Bergman walks across a dark and stormy beach, the heavy rain interfering with his cell phone reception to the point that he is forced to walk into the ocean to hear the other speaker clearly.

Wigand appears despondent as he sits in his hotel room, staring silently into space after the broadcast has ended. He refuses to answer the phone despite several attempts by Bergman to reach him. Instead, he gazes into the painting of the forest, imagining it mutate into an idyllic family scene: a sunlit suburban garden in which his daughters play merrily. Notably, the fantasy depicted is not based on a memory of any real moment he shared with his daughters at any specific point in time. As Rayner observes, 'The apparent interaction between Wigand and his daughters in the dream appears more imagined and desired than recalled.' (2013: 122). This indicates that Wigand's fantasy is based on an idealised vision of his familial life that does not resemble his domestic situation as it ever actually existed. He imagines an alternate timeline in which he did not breach his non-disclosure agreement and remained on good terms with Liane and his daughters.

Wigand may hold a romanticised view of what his life might be like if he had made different decisions, but it has already been made clear to the viewer that he would not feel content if he had continued to live under the thumb of Big Tobacco. Bergman reminds him of this fact during their subsequent phone conversation. At first, Wigand takes out his anger on Bergman, accusing him of using deception and manipulation techniques to trick him into agreeing to act against his own interests, without adequately warning Wigand of the possibility that nothing might come of his sacrifice. Wigand accuses Bergman of manipulating him as part of an exercise in building his brand as a tough-as-nails reporter who can convince any source to get on board. Bergman chastises him for refusing to acknowledge the role he played in his own downfall, asserting that he did not *force* Wigand to do anything; he merely offered Wigand a platform to broadcast his testimony if he decided to pursue that path. Bergman emphasises that Wigand repeatedly sought him out, acting on his desire to release the secrets of the tobacco industry to the public. Despite the heated beginning of this exchange, the two men stop blaming each other for their respective problems and they reaffirm their mutual sense of admiration. 'I'm running out of heroes, man,' Bergman says, demonstrating his disappointment in his colleagues. 'Guys like you are in short supply.' Bergman responds: 'Guys like you, too.'

Though he briefly considers giving up the fight against Brown & Williamson as a lost cause, Bergman regains his enthusiasm and resolve when he receives a message from Scruggs telling him that the governor of Mississippi has threatened to obstruct the lawsuit being filed against Big Tobacco by the state's residents. The collective citizens of the state stand a better chance of success, Scruggs explains, if Wigand's testimony is broadcast in full. Galvanised by Scrugg's support, and reminded of the monumental positive change that may result from the public's exposure to the truth, Bergman takes matters into his own hands, pursuing a path of righteous action without the aid of CBS. He contacts the editors of *The New York Times* and relates the entire story to them – the bravery of Wigand, the cowardice of the CBS upper management, the shamelessness of the character assassination launched by Brown & Williamson against Wigand to discredit his testimony, and the depth of the link between the corporate and the news departments of CBS. Robert van Es argues that this act further cements the similarities between Bergman and Wigand: 'Both men made inside information public. Wigand is blowing the whistle on B&W on television; Bergman is leaking information about CBS to *The New York Times*.' Thus, each man becomes 'the whistleblower in his own corporate world' (2003: 92). Like Wigand's rebellion against his former employers, Bergman's actions deliberately place the public standing of his company into jeopardy – and implicate many of his former co-workers. As such, he risks destroying his career by dedicating himself to this crusade. Before passing over the information regarding CBS' handling of the Brown & Williamson case, Bergman receives a similar warning to the one given to Wigand by Scruggs during the lead-up to his deposition: 'Are you sure you want to do this? Hey, if this doesn't work, you burn your bridges, man.' Bergman, like Wigand, is not deterred by the potential repercussions and passes on the information he knows to be accurate. When later confronted by a furious Hewitt, Bergman explains to him that he has never abandoned or misled a source in his entire career and he won't be forced to betray his principles to support the financial imperatives of CBS managers: 'When I came into this job, I came with my rules intact. And I'm going to leave with my rules intact.' Although Wallace had expressed a higher level of sympathy toward Bergman in the scenes leading up to this moment, he now abandons him at the final hurdle, egotistically prioritising his own legacy over public well-being. This act of ending a friendship and a creative partnership that has lasted 14 years has a heavy emotional impact on Bergman, and this is a sacrifice comparable to the heavy personal losses that Wigand endures throughout the narrative.

The Insider climaxes with a sequence that inverts the earlier scene in which various characters watched the broadcast of the bowdlerised *60 Minutes* episode. This time, Mann intercuts between shots of Bergman, Wigand and Scruggs watching from different locations as the full interview makes it to the airwaves. Hewitt has ultimately come to the decision that, in light of the heavy criticism directed against CBS by multiple media sources in the wake of *The New York Times* report, the only way for the network to repair its reputation would be to air the original episode in full. *The New York Times* described the attacks on Wigand launched by rival newspapers as 'the lowest form of character assassination' and associated their lack of integrity with the pusillanimity demonstrated by CBS when they censored Wigand's interview. The U-turn made by the network CEOs does not, then, indicate that the company has changed for the better – they are airing the testimony not because they feel a newfound sense of responsibility to inform the population, but because they feel a desperate need to engage in damage control to protect the company's public image.

Thus, this accomplishment is only a fleeting one. Brown & Williamson is still operational and employing unethical practices, CBS continues to work in tandem with corporate lobbyists to produce biased news coverage, and aggressive smear campaigns are still regularly employed to silence whistleblowers and dissidents who pose a threat to corporate power. Bergman and Wigand have completed the task they set for themselves and can both feel a sense of personal achievement, but the degree of societal change they have directly brought about is minimal. Although he pressured the network to compromise on this one occasion, Bergman realises that he's unlikely to replicate this favourable result, and his faith in CBS has been irreparably shaken. The final scene of *The Insider* mirrors the earlier sequence in which Wigand left the offices of Brown & Williamson: as in that scene, the character is shown leaving his former workplace for the final time glass revolving doors, his movements captured in slow-motion. This visual parallel implies that Bergman is beginning a journey akin to the one that Wigand embarked upon at the start of the film: he is now aware of his former employers' ties to nefarious corporate influences, he must find a way to pursue his journalistic goals within a new setting which will not stifle him. But whereas the earlier shot was locked tight into a close-up of Wigand as the camera tracked his insecure and self-effacing motion, here Bergman is captured in a wide shot, marching forward with his sense of integrity intact and a genuine sense of hope for the future. Although Bergman faces significant challenges ahead, the ordeal he has gone through and survived has been hugely informative in teaching him to overcome the challenges of corporate intimidation and manipulation. Wigand and Bergman have both been put the ringer, and they have both been forced to make intense personal sacrifices, but, in the end, they feel satisfied with what they've accomplished, and they are both now ready to enter into new professional ventures with a much higher degree of knowledge, conviction and autonomy.

World in My Corner:
Ali (2001)

Michael Mann's first feature of the new millennium is also his first foray into the genre of the 'sports film' since his debut feature, *The Jericho Mile* and it is interesting to compare and contrast these two works to study what remained constant in Mann's filmmaking style over this period as well as what changed. Like *The Jericho Mile*, *Ali* is a character study of a great athlete who resolutely resists the grasp of various authority figures and institutions that wish to manipulate him to further their own material interests. As in the earlier film, the protagonist's resistance to conformity is treated as being more significant than any specific sporting achievement, and so, in remaining true to their self-determined values, both lead characters willingly reject and/or sabotage professional opportunities and partnerships which would require them to compromise their integrity. Furthermore, in both narratives, the protagonist consciously positions himself in an antagonistic relationship to the US government, and the government, in turn, exerts a great deal of pressure on them to submit to authority.

The most substantial difference between *Ali* and *The Jericho Mile* – and this difference reflects Mann's growing ambition as a filmmaker – is that *Ali* deals with a protagonist who has a far more comprehensive socio-political awareness than Murphy. While Murphy is preoccupied solely with maintaining his individualist lifestyle without interference from any external force, Muhammad Ali (Will Smith) is motivated by a strong ethical code rooted in his interactions with many seminal civil rights thinkers and activists of the 1960s. Whereas Murphy pays attention to his own immediate experience and expresses little interest in the world beyond the prison walls, Ali has a profound desire to make the truth of systemic racism known to the public and, therefore, inspire concrete social change. Unlike *The Jericho Mile*, in which Murphy exists in a self-contained environment cut off from the wider world, *Ali* focuses on a protagonist whose professional journey towards athletic accomplishment plays out against a wider backdrop of epochal social transformation. While Murphy feels no sense of obligation to anybody or anything other than himself, Ali feels a need to use his platform to give a voice to the marginalised and, therefore, galvanise wider support for these causes – Rayner perceptively describes the process through which *Ali* consciously constructs a politically engaged public persona as 'politicised 1960s self-fashioning.' (2013: 140).

While Murphy's athletic victories can only be experienced in private, Ali becomes a hero to millions of fans all across the globe. Therefore, his ultimate triumph against George Foreman is celebrated as a collective victory for the international civil rights movement. Unlike most Mann protagonists, Ali can fulfil his ambitions without giving up his position of prominence within his professional field *and* remaining a popular icon within the cultural mainstream (although there is a substantial period when he is banned from boxing as a punishment for his refusal to comply with the call for conscription into the Vietnam war, he manages to make his way back to the top). Ali exercises his higher moral purpose without sacrificing his material needs, and holds on to his autonomy within his field of work while still maintaining constructive relationships with others. However, this feat is not easy to achieve, and, in the process, Ali repeatedly faces the prospect of professional, familial, and financial ruin.

Because of his open support for these radical activist causes, Ali becomes the target of intense surveillance from the government. His wealth, celebrity status, and commitment to his chosen sport become instruments of control leveraged by a state that desires to force him into a state of passive subservience. The assassinations of the revolutionary racial activists Malcolm X (Mario Van Peebles) and Martin Luther King Jr (LeVar Burton) in the narrative serve as forceful reminders of the monumental threat he faces by daring to speak out against the systematic inequality and discrimination prevalent in 1960s America. In this sense, Ali builds upon the exploration of mass surveillance and coerced compliance in *The Insider*, and Ali becomes consumed by paranoia as it increasingly seems to him that anybody in his vicinity could be a potential suspect and a hostile force could be tapping into any conversation he has. Writing for *Senses of Cinema*, Dzenis nicely summarises Mann's approach: 'In the complex world of *Ali*, Michael Mann privileges the poetic courage of belief and resistance, of hope and resurrection. It transcends biography. It is an impressionistic odyssey interweaving the heart and mind of the great Muhammad Ali.' (2002).

Ali is motivated by a desire to live according to his own, self-determined moral code, but he also feels immense pressure to appeal to the broader public. Whereas Mann's characters typically lead solitary lifestyles on the margins of society, Ali exists the forefront of mainstream culture and is surrounded by people in almost every scene. He is hounded by photographers constantly, he has a group of friends and colleagues who flit in and out of his life, and details of his private affairs quickly become public knowledge. In *The Insider*, Wigand and, to a lesser extent, Bergman become objects of media scrutiny over the course of events, but they remain, essentially, everyday citizens who can escape from the limelight when they need some time for private introspection. On the other hand, Ali is one of the most famous men in the world, and this extreme level of public prominence makes him feel a high level of responsibility to his fans.

Unlike other Mann lead characters, then, Ali is acutely aware that the general public will closely watch his actions and therefore, his choices hold the potential to encourage others to commit to worthy political and social causes with the same intensity that he has. In his mind, his ethical quest is only valuable if it can influence a large amount of people, which is why he sinks into despair during the latter half of the film when he is suspended from fighting in a public arena. While so many Mann characters fail to reconcile the different aspects of their personality (for example, McCauley's failure to reconcile his desire for romantic companionship with his need to maintain agency over his work), Ali is remarkably adept at finding a point of reconciliation between these his private and public life, managing to hold onto his values, excel in his professional sphere and maintain strong friendships. This reaches its apex in the climactic Rumble in the Jungle sequence. Ali fights the most important match of his life in Zaire, Africa, and Ali is able to witness first-hand that his open resistance to American racism and imperialism has made him a heroic figure to marginalised communities across the entire world.

Ali opens with the ambient sound of a busy nightclub playing over a black screen. An announcer introduces the Chicago-based soul singer Sam Cooke (David Elliott). As Cooke addresses the crowd, Mann cuts to a disconnected shot of Ali (still named Cassius Clay at this point) jogging along an empty suburban street at night. A rough, handheld tracking shot frames Ali from the shoulders-up as he jogs, his face barely visible in a grey hoodie against a backdrop of nondescript buildings. Mann then cuts to an image of Cooke in the nightclub, from behind, a silhouette against a powerful turquoise spotlight. As Cooke breaks into song, we see more images of Ali exercising – a figure positioned small in the frame against a murky and overcast night. Considering that Ali is such a larger-than-life figure, it is interesting that these introductory images seem deliberately un-romantic. As Ignatiy Vishnevetsky argues, Will Smith's performance as Ali in this sequence appears as 'the opposite of James Caan in *Thief*. Smith talks like he's just grown into his voice; Caan speaks like a man who's tired of hearing himself.' (2009). At this point, Ali has not yet come into himself; he's still young and inexperienced, he's in the process of forming his political perspective. This opening sequence, furthermore, establishes the competing aspects of Ali's personality: the hard-working individual who knows that he must rely on himself and himself alone to achieve his goals (Ali embarking on a routine jog); and the consummate showman (represented by Cooke), the entertainer who feels a compulsive need to perform to the public.

The next moment illustrates the atmosphere of racial discrimination and intimidation that surrounds Ali. Over the soundtrack, Cooke's singing becomes overwhelmed by the sound of a police siren. A cop car slows down as it passes Ali, and a white officer asks, completely unprovoked, 'What are you running from, son?' Ali has seemingly become accustomed to this type of taunting, as he simply casts his head downwards and continues to run along his set path. Cooke's music then swells up again, as Mann crosscuts between images of Ali training in a private gym and a series of formative events from his childhood, presented in a non-linear order. As a young boy, Ali observes his father, Cassius Clay Sr (Giancarlo Esposito), as he paints a mural of a blond, blue-eyed, white-skinned Jesus on the wall of a church. Mann cuts to a close-up of the young Ali looking at the image with uncertainty, but it is clear that the young Ali does not feel confident enough to speak up against his father. It seems that he does not yet have the education necessary to articulate why the mural seems wrong to him, but, it is clear that he, on some level, is uncomfortable with the idea of revering a light-skinned divinity. In the following sequence, the young Ali is taken by the hand to the segregated area of a passenger bus – an overhead sign announces that this small, over-crowded section is for 'Coloreds Only'. As they enter, Ali sees the front page of a newspaper being read by one of the passengers, which carries the headline 'Nation Shocked At Lynching of Chicago Youth'. The accompanying image is a graphic image of Emmett Till, a young African American fatally beaten by a mob because he committed the 'transgression' of flirting with a white woman. In the photograph, Till's face appears, battered nearly beyond recognition. The passenger, an older black man, spots Ali staring at the newspaper cover, and he thrusts it towards the child's face, as if warning him of the horrors of American society. The young Ali jumps back, and, in a reverse shot, Mann cuts in tighter on the newspaper image. These two events were clearly crucial to shaping Ali's understanding of systemic racism, as he refers back to them in two later scenes. During a heated argument with his father, he lambasts him for painting Jesus in a physical form that has been influenced by a white colonial viewpoint; at another point, he comments to Malcolm X that, as a child, the image of Emmet Till imprinted itself so strongly onto his psyche that he found it, cut it out and kept it under his bed. This is a clear-cut example of a case of extreme violence inflicted upon the African American community – the type of atrocity that abounds within an environment where racial hatred is tolerated by white patriarchal authority figures (the fact that the police officers in this scene address Ali in such a casually bigoted way is a sign of just how deeply racial prejudice is ingrained in American institutions).

The next scene shows Ali, now in late adolescence, standing at the back of at the Masjid Al-Ansar Mosque, listening to a speech delivered by Malcolm X. Malcolm X tells the crowd that the days of submission in the African American community must come to an end. Substantive social progress will never happen without the community collectively committing to an active struggle against racial injustice in all its forms. Malcolm X tells the crowd that they cannot be satisfied with any small concessions that may given to them by the government. Malcolm X implores the community that they mustn't back down from forceful action until they achieve true emancipation, as any sign of weakness will be used by the state to keep them in a perpetual position of subservience: 'Those of you who think you came here to hear us tell you to turn the other cheek to the brutality of the white man and this system of injustice that's in place right here in America. You think you're gonna come here and hear us tell you to go out there and beg for a place at their lunch counter again? I say you came to the wrong place.' Malcolm X asserts that any act of violence must be met with an equally forceful reaction – this is the only way that they may resist the power of the state. Ali is framed in middle-ground, staring straight ahead, his image slightly obscured by soft-focus faces in the foreground. This composition resembles the earlier sequence in which a young Ali gazes at the mural of a white-skinned Jesus. Though he is absorbing Malcolm X's message here, his body language suggests self-doubt rather than conviction. He is gaining an awareness of the injustices of American society, yet he doesn't yet have the confidence to carry over the principles that Malcolm X espouses into his own life. This outstanding opening montage contextualises Ali's early boxing career within a wider landscape of systematic racism – as well as varied forms of resistance to governmental oppression. Although these flashes from Ali's youth depict him as being somewhat submissive to authority, his political consciousness is clearly being sharpened by these seminal experiences. He will later form a close relationship with Malcolm X when he becomes a more outspoken activist for progressive social causes.

In the present timeline, Ali continues to train while being spotted by his trainer Angelo Dundee (Ron Silver) and his cornerman Drew 'Bundini' Brown (Jamie Foxx). Mann zooms in on Bundini's face, swelling with pride, and then cuts back to the first meeting between the two men. As Ali reclines on a chair in his backyard, Bundini slides out from behind a wall in slow motion. After introducing himself, explaining his professional background, Bundini tells Ali that he has been watching his work in the gym and, impressed by his skills, wants to 'be in your corner'. This short segment establishes another significant aspect of Ali's life: the close network of trainers and assistants who provide Ali with emotional and professional support. Interpersonal connections between friends and colleagues in *Ali* take precedence to a degree that is uncommon in Mann's filmography, in which protagonists tend to work alone. As Sam Cooke swells into the chorus of 'Bring It On Home To Me', Mann cuts to images of Ali in the immediate run-up to his fight with Liston. Ali, Bundini, Dundee, and Ali's personal photographer Howard Bingham (Jeffery Wright). Ali is silent and lost in thought, engaged in a moment of meditation necessary for him to perform successfully in the ring. A shot from Ali's perspective pans around the car's interior, showing the three members of Ali's team smile at him, encouragingly. Although these men are well-meaning, the intense focus they place on him creates an overwhelming sense of pressure. Bingham takes a photograph of Ali – demonstrating that Ali is unable to escape the omnipresent eye of the camera, even during moments that should be private.

Mann immerses the viewer into Ali's psyche during this sequence, highlighting the societal factors and public figures that influenced his intellectual and moral development. In the next scene, Mann introduces Ali's bombastic public persona. Ali bursts into the convention centre where the weigh-in is being held. An energetic Ali works the ground of reporters with the same charisma and charm with which Cooke worked the nightclub audience during the opening scene, taunting Liston with a stream of creative insults and delivering his catchphrase, 'Float like a butterfly, sting like a bee' in unison with his entourage. This verbose display is somewhat jarring, coming immediately after the montage which depicted the young Ali as a quiet, rather self-effacing presence. This suggests that, at this early point in the film, there is a split between the private and public versions of 'Ali' at this point. As Trevor McCrisken and Andrew Pepper observe, the film, at first, presents us with the 'contemplative "private" Ali and the loquacious, brash "public" Ali,' but the character's emotional arc finds the two modes gradually merging together until there is only one single, unified Ali who feels confident in expressing his opinions without giving up his desire to engage in displays of showmanship. (2005: 178).

The verbal match with Liston is an impressive yet ultimately insubstantial display of bravado. It's a pantomime for the press, the sort of playful linguistic gymnastics that made Ali such a well-liked admire figure outside of the ring. But the jubilant atmosphere is undercut when a journalist asks him, with a hostile tone, whether there is any truth to the rumours that he has become a 'black Muslim'. Ali ignores the reporter while Angelo, apparently prepared for this line of questioning, steps in to snap back with an insistence on keeping Ali's faith private. 'A man's religion is his own business,' says Angelo, as the room becomes silent. 'What kind of question is that?' This question, however, is followed by another accusatory question from a reporter at the back of the room, who enquires about Ali's relationship with Malcolm X. The reporter states that he heard a rumour that Malcolm X had been in town, but he left before the match, then asking that if Ali made sure he left before he had a chance to 'embarrass; him. Mann cuts to a close-up of Ali, who again ignores the reporter while Angelo rebuffs the aggressive line of questioning. At this point, Ali does not deny his involvement with radical political groups, but he also does not yet have the conviction to actively advocate for these causes within a public forum. He prefers to keep his private life and his professional persona separate, as evidenced when Ali immediately jumps back into action when ABC sports reporter Howard Cosell (John Voight) directs the discussion back to the upcoming fight between Ali and Liston, thus giving Ali another chance to wax lyrical about his own ability in the ring.

The match between Ali and Liston is a bravura 20-minute set-piece, establishing, in exhilarating detail, the protagonist's skill, dexterity and ability to think on his feet in a similar manner to the extended first-act depictions of Mann's lead characters at work in *The Jericho Mile*, *Thief*, and *Heat*. As in those sequences, Mann composes the event from the lead character's perspective and emphasises the intense physical labour involved in their work. The camera remains tethered to Ali's affective experience throughout this scene. As Ali navigates the confined space of the ring, is movements are captured in a series of fluid, agile handheld shots. When a blow is landed against Ali, Mann formally articulates a sensation of shock and confusion, either by cutting in close to the point of impact or by briefly lapsing into slow-motion. At one point, Ali gets hit in the face by Sonny, and the image drifts in and out of focus to mimic his temporally impaired vision. What differentiates Ali from earlier Mann films in regards to its portrayal of physical labour is that, here, the protagonist has an audience observing the character at work. Although Mann connects his camera closely to Ali's experience, emphasising the fact that, as Ali tells a journalist later into the narrative, he's 'the only one in the ring', the soundscape is filled with the ambient sound of the crowd, yelling, gasping, cheering, and wincing in response to the action. Mann captures most of the match with a high-aperture lens, so Ali and Liston appear in crisp focus while rendering the crowd a blur of indistinct shapes. Although Mann avoids cutting to reactions from individual reactions from the crowd until the end of the match, there are frequent insert shots of Bingham taking snapshots and Cosell narrating events from the side-lines, serving as a constant reminder that Ali's actions are being viewed by a wide network of fans. Even as Ali is engaged in intense physical labour, a task that requires unyielding concentration, he is conscious of the fact that millions are watching him.

After Liston falls and Ali is declared the winner, the athlete instantly lapses back into the loquacious popular persona he adopted during the weigh-in. Various reporters and members of Ali's team ecstatically storm into the ring, turning it into a site of bustling celebration. Ali now directly addresses the crowd, leaning over the side of the ropes while repeatedly chanting 'eat your words!' Mann cuts to an image of Ali's victory being broadcast on a small black-and-white television, emphasising that this moment is not only being experienced by the crowd within the stadium, but also by a broader international audience. As Cosell climbs through the crowd to get an interview with the victorious Ali, the boxer responds with performative bravado: 'I'm only 22 years old. I ain't got a mark on my face. I must be the greatest.' Here, Ali is clearly playing up to the popular perception of him as a young, audacious, cocky performer; his silent concentration within the ring transitions into a public display of bravado. This conflict between personal belief and public expectation is one that Ali struggles to balance over the course of the narrative, but he is ultimately able to overcome this struggle in the film's final act.

This tension is foregrounded in the next series of scenes, as Ali, newly emboldened by his status as heavyweight champion of the world, begins to feel more comfortable about vocalising his radical leanings. Walking down a public street with Malcolm X, Ali becomes surrounded by a crowd of adoring fans. Spotting the commotion, a journalist approaches to question him about what he intends to do with his elevated platform now that he has a new title. Unlike in the weigh-in scene, Ali is not self-effacing about his involvement with revolutionary currents here; he is open about his relationship with Malcolm X. Addressed as Mr Clay, Ali asserts that he no longer wants to be addressed by a surname inherited from the family of plantation owners who claimed ownership over his ancestors. He instead insists on being addressed as 'Cassius X'. Afterwards, in the privacy of Ali's apartment, Malcolm X asks him in confidence whether he had ever arrived at the point where he thought he'd 'lose it. Like, really lose it'. Ali instinctively knows the feeling that Malcolm X is describing. In response, Ali thinks back to the formative moment of his childhood in which he saw the newspaper cover featuring an image of the beaten Till. After he kept a copy of the image, Ali explains that he could never 'take [his] eyes to it', but nor could he 'throw it away'. That Ali is aware of the severity of racial oppression in the United States, represented by the photograph, yet also unable to confront it head-on encapsulates his conflicted attitude towards tackling systematic injustice at this point in the narrative. He is aware of the horrifying extent of systematic discrimination in the US, yet he is only gradually building up the confidence to openly confront it – in large part because of the pressure placed upon him by the media to conform to a more sanitised, inoffensive model of African American celebrity.

When Cassius Sr discovers that his son has approached Elijah Muhammad (Albert Hall), head of the Nation of Islam, to legally change his name to Muhammad Ali, Cassius Sr does not recognise Clay as a 'slave name', as Ali phrases it, but as the name has been attached to the family for generations. He, therefore, views Ali's name change as a rejection of his familial heritage and a personal insult to the people who raised him. Cassius Sr views Ali's choice to adopt a new name as a personal sleight – as if Elijah had taken over the patriarchal role model that he previously held. In the argument that ensues, Ali confronts his father over his possessive attitude towards him. Ali asserts his independence from his parents, telling Cassius Sr that, as a fully grown man, he has the right to construct his own identity, and that nobody can claim that they were responsible for his meteoric rise other than himself. His father tells him that 'We made you boy, and no bow tie-wearing, Arab talking nigger going to change that.' Ali, in response, forcefully asserts his individual, self-defined identity: 'I know who I ain't. I ain't drinking, I ain't going back on my wife, and I sure ain't praying to no blond-haired, blue-eyed Jesus.' This is a notable step forward in Ali's ideological becoming. His attack on his father's obedience to authority is comparable to the emancipation of the Munro daughters from their parents in *The Last of the Mohicans*. But Ali defines himself here in terms of what he isn't, as opposed to what he *is*; he is still a site of potentiality, an individual in the process of forming his own distinct identity.

Cassius Sr takes offence to Ali's comment regarding his former profession painting murals of Jesus, retorting that he simply did whatever he needed to do to keep the family finances stable and ensure that his son grew up to be a robust and healthy specimen *capable* of fighting in the ring. Despite his anger, Cassius Sr defends his former career on practical grounds rather than moral ones – he has no regrets about his work because it was necessary to provide for his family's material needs. This reflects the mechanisms of control through which the American state oppresses the black population. By making compliance to white orthodoxy a necessary condition for many careers, the state coerces marginalised peoples to become complicit in their own subjugation. To put it in the terms used by Malcolm X in his earlier speech, Ali's parents have accepted this as the natural order of American life and 'turn the other cheek to the brutality of the white man'; Ali rejects his parents' willingness to go along with this system, and instead makes a pledge to stand up against all forms of injustice, even if he knows he will risk losing his revenue stream and his lofty social standing as a result.

Malcolm X invites Ali to accompany him to Nigeria, where he has been invited to give a lecture. Ali agrees, but Elijah later forbids him from meeting with Malcolm X, who has distanced himself from the Church of Islam after they ruled his speeches to be unnecessarily incendiary. Ali does take the trip to Nigeria, but he is accompanied by Elijah's son, Herbert (Barry Shabaka Henley), instead. Ali is used to being approached by fans on the street, but in Nigeria he truly receives a hero's welcome. He is transported through the streets in a convertible, waving to the streets of cheering spectators as though he were riding a parade float. Ali appreciates the warm reception, but he is visibly overwhelmed by the sheer amount of enthusiasm directed towards him; he realises that his iconicity transcends geographical boundaries and feels immense pressure to live up to the lofty image of him held by his international fan base.

Reaching the American embassy, Ali runs into Malcolm X by chance. They first exchange a friendly greeting, but then Ali feels obligated to align himself with the demands of the Muhammad family and distance himself from his former mentor. He cuts the meeting short and tells Malcolm X that he should not have angered Elijah, walking away abruptly before Malcolm X has the chance to reply. Ali later regrets this choice, however, after hearing of Malcolm X's assassination, which occurs before they have a chance to make amends. Ali nobly stood up to his father in an earlier scene, but here he blindly follows the demands given to him by Elijah and Herbert Muhammad. Later, Ali will arrive at the realisation that he may live in accordance with the teachings of Islam without obeying the orders of these men motivated, in large part, by mercenary incentives. As they speak, Ali and Malcolm are positioned on the right side of the frame. Gradually, these two figures go out of focus as the camera focuses on a high window in the hotel building behind them. Mann cuts to an interior shot to reveal two suspicious, sharply dressed men, watching Ali and Malcolm X intently. In a later scene, these same agents are shown discussing the recent actions of Malcolm X and Martin Luther King Jr. As the agents look through a series of photographs they've taken, they reveal that they know much about Malcolm X's recent movements, and the intricacies of his dispute with Elijah. 'We got Malcolm travelling all over the world,' one of the agents says, and then expresses anxiety about Malcolm's recent meetings with revolutionary Algerian socialist Ahmed Ben Bella and anti-imperialist Egyptian politician Gamal Abdel Nasser. The scene ends on a menacing note, as the agent then turns to a photo of Ali and tells his colleague, 'We gotta talk about this guy, too.' The recurrence of these agents throughout the film serves as an ominous reminder of the pervasive influence of the American state and the unquenchable nature of its quest to force revolutionary black activists into submission – by violent force if necessary. Like Wigand in *The Insider*, Ali finds himself placed under increased surveillance after he begins to associate with figures and movements thought to hold the potential to destabilise existing power relations.

The assassination of Malcolm X is depicted in a sequence which visually parallels the earlier scene in which a young Ali watches him deliver a lecture at the Masjid Al-Ansar Mosque. As in that scene, Mann alternates between images of Malcolm X framed from behind as he speaks to a large crowd, and a corresponding reverse angle, framing Malcolm X in the centre of a wide shot as he faces towards the camera. However, this time, a commotion erupts in the audience as an unspecified member yells, 'Get your hand out of my pocket.' Malcolm X tries to calm the crowd as it rapidly erupts into a panic. But the rowdy audience member is revealed to be a gunman, who stands up and fires at the podium. Mann then interrupts the visual language of the earlier scene, cutting to a birds-eye shot of the stage as Malcolm X falls backwards, covered in blood. This horrific event is intercut with images of Ali calmly driving through a tunnel. Suddenly, Ali becomes surrounded by pedestrians running around the streets frantically. One of them sprints directly in front of his car, forcing Ali to swerve abruptly. The man hysterically yells, 'They shot Malcolm! They shot Malcolm!' Ali turns on the radio for verification. He finds a news broadcast that reveals more information. Mann lingers at length on Ali's pain-stricken face from behind the windshield. Tears well in his eyes as he listens to the report, then he aggressively punches the steering wheel in a gesture of sheer despair. This is intercut with several shots of other citizens responding to the news outside the vehicle. Some weep, some embrace, some break down in hysterics. Ali's anguish is connected visually to a collective act of mourning, though he also remains separated from the other civilians within the frame – this interplay been connectivity and distance communicates the cultural position Ali occupies as being simultaneously embedded within a wider community while also separated from the general public through his immense fame

The assassination intensifies Ali's oppositional stance towards the American government even further, as evidenced by his subsequent decision to publicly denounce the Vietnam War. Ali discovers that he has been specifically called upon to enlist through a report in a broadsheet newspaper. He correctly assumes that he has been personally targeted because of his involvement with the Black Muslims. At a USAF station in Huston, Ali is warned of the consequences he will face if he refuses to enlist: 'Refusal to accept a lawful induction order constitutes a felony punishable by up to five years' imprisonment and a five-thousand-dollar fine. Do you understand?' Ali responds in the affirmative but refuses to budge. He knows that he will lose his fortune, boxing licence, and even freedom, but consciously takes this risk to avoid becoming embroiled in an imperialist war. When he is subsequently arrested, he obliges without physical struggle. He was aware of the legal punishment he would face when he decided to resist the draft and he is willing to fight the legal system in the public arena to bring attention to the injustice of the military action.

After Ali is released on bail, he voices his moral opposition to the war more explicitly. Surrounded by the press, Ali emphasises his lack of faith in the United States government and draws a parallel between the plight of African Americans domestically and the suffering inflicted by the United States on the people of Vietnam: 'I ain't got no quarrel with the Vietcong, ain't no Vietcong ever call me nigger.' A reporter warns Ali that he will face extreme repercussions if he continues to publicly call the legitimacy of the war into question. Ali thinks about this for a moment and then emphatically retorts: 'So what? I don't got to be what anybody else what me to be, and I'm not afraid to be what I want to be, think what I want to think.' Taken before the Boxing Commission, Ali is told that he may be able to escape some of the negative legal consequences if he is willing to give a public apology for his 'unpatriotic' remarks about the war. The commission makes a hollow attempt to shame Ali by accusing him of letting down his supporters by refusing to back down, but Ali knows that to truly serve his fans, he must speak and act in a completely unfiltered manner. This is a significant step forward in Ali's self-actualisation, as he realises that he cannot conform to any pre-judged idea of what the public want him to be like – he must decide, on his own terms, how he wants to act, and allow the people to either reject or accept his choices.

Ali is later summoned back into the courtroom, where he receives the maximum sentence for his evasion of the draft: five years in prison. He is later informed that his legal team will launch an appeal, but while the request is being processed, Ali will have his boxing licence and his passport revoked, and he will have the title of 'heavyweight champion of the world' removed. Reeling from the news, Ali is shown walking, dejected, through the streets at dusk, captured in a tracking shot which frames him from the waist up – it's a mirror image of the shot which introduced him at the beginning of the film, but, this time, he does not appear a fresh-faced young athlete making his name in the field. He is at his lowest ebb, appearing uncharacteristically defeated and on the verge of hopelessness. This section of the film depicts a despondent Ali watching searing images of protests and political marches on television but feeling powerless to intervene. The fact that these images are transmitted through the lens of a television screen (as opposed to being depicted directly) illustrates how alienated Ali feels from the very civil rights struggles which used to be at the centre of his life. In a considerable difference to *The Jericho Mile*'s Murphy, Ali does not gain pleasure from participating in athletic activity for its own sake. The craft of boxing is undoubtedly important to him, but even more important is using the elevated platform his professional status affords him to shed light on injustice. Just as Ali is forced to watch civil rights demonstrations in mediated form through televised broadcasts, he is also reduced to a spectator of boxing. Ali spends much of his spare time watching inferior athletes in the ring, loudly commenting on their mistakes and inadequacies – he is clearly frustrated being relegated to the role of an observer to the sport he loves *and* to larger world events.

Desperate to return to the ring, Ali asks his lawyer Chauncey Eskridge (Joe Morton) if there is any way that he could work around the boxing ban, and says that he would even be willing to fight 'in a phone booth' or 'the middle of Times Square'. Eskridge knows that any of these options would be in breach of the law, but articulates his anger at the injustice – he points out that there are several convicted rapists and murderers in New York who are still legally licensed to fight, but Ali has been targeted specifically because his ideological message is considered to be too subversive and the state wishes to suppress such an outspoken critic. Eskridge tells him that, rather than thinking of how he may be able to fight again, Ali needs to focus on the practical matter of how to practically support himself. He goes on to tell Ali that a successful restaurant company that has expressed interest in launching a chain of boxing themed restaurants and are interested in a sponsorship from Ali. They have proposed the names 'Muhammad Malts', and 'A Fistful of Fries' for their new venture. Tragically, the man who previously pledged to use his celebrity to fight for the rights of marginalised peoples and cultures is now faced with the prospect of turning his image into a commodity to sell fast food. Eventually, Ali receives a call from Eskridge, informing him that they could potentially restore his boxing licence if they argue that Ali could not fight on religious grounds – that the tenets of Islam are incompatible with the demands of warfare, and so Ali could not participate in the Vietnam War without betraying his religious beliefs. Ali is initially reluctant, but he is reminded that this may be the only way to convince the court that his refusal to comply with the draft was within the boundaries of the law, and if they fail, Ali may never be allowed to box again.

During this period of his life, Ali marries a new bride, the young Muslim baker Belinda Boyd (Nona Gaye). Although their marriage eventually breaks down due to Ali's inability to commit to a single woman, their relationship is closer and more harmonious than Ali's earlier romance with the former playboy bunny Sonji Roi (Jada Pinkett Smith), who resents being forced to live according to the teachings of Islam. Belinda begs him not to allow himself to be led astray by greedy and opportunistic people if his career is successfully revived. Belinda was raised within the faith, and warns her husband that Elijah and Herbert do not truly represent the spirit of Islam, nor do they have Ali's best interests at heart: They used him when he had a public platform and could generate a healthy stream of revenue for them, but they ditched him as soon as his luck turned and he could no longer turn a profit for them. Ali doesn't want to hear this at first, but the tension between him and the Muhammad family soon intensifies. After seeing Ali make a spectacle of himself during a phone-in appearance on Cosell's show, Elijah demands his suspension from the Nation of Islam: he may no longer go to temple, pray or lecture, and the organisation will generally place a distance between themselves and the fallen boxer. The Muhammad family do not demonstrate any admiration for Ali's principled stance against the war, they simply recognise that his public image has been damaged, and they do not want to risk jeopardising their own reputation through association with him. The news is relayed to Ali in a phone call from Herbert. Ali can tell from the tone of his voice that Herbert was not in charge of this decision, but he is deeply disappointed that Herbert has made no significant effort to convince his who, though not in charge of the decision, makes no attempt to convince his father otherwise. This abandonment by an organisation he previously invested so much of his energy in represents Ali at his most discouraged – but he soon recognises how far he's drifted from his chosen path and takes active, positive steps to pull himself out of his depression (this represents a striking contrast to other Mann protagonists such as Frank, Graham and McCauley, who descend into an emotional abyss and never manage to pull themselves out of it). Ali visits Cosell to enlist his help in organising a fight against himself and Joe Frazier (James Toney); a match which will enable Ali to regain his former title of Heavyweight Champion. Cosell tells him that, as his friend, he would do anything to help him out – but the content of his show is ultimately determined by network executives, and they may be reluctant to put Ali on air out of fear of alienating their advertisers.

In response, Ali promises Cosell that any fight that he participates in will be a major ratings winner for whichever network dares to broadcast it. In an energetic, passionate monologue, he describes how a hypothetical fight between himself and Frazier might play out. Ali's ambition is to make such a scenario sound so appealing that there would be overwhelming demand placed upon the network to make the fight a reality. As Ali speaks, Mann cuts to images of his speech on various television sets, signalling that Ali is, once again, successfully reaching out to an appreciative audience. Ali cannily ends the speech with the deflating statement: 'Don't wait for that fight. It ain't gonna happen. The only thing you can do is wonder and imagine.' Immediately, the network offices are inundated with calls requesting that the fight be put on the air. Like in *The Insider*, the protagonist ultimately finds a way to work around the constrictions of network and utilises its potential to draw attention to mass-scale injustice. Therefore, the very mechanisms which oppress him become the means of his emancipation. Ali's appearance on Cosell's show is magnetic.

Ali also negotiates a meeting with Frazier, arguing that until they fight one-on-one nobody will know for sure who the best boxer in the league truly is. He goes on to tell Frazier that it's unbelievable there are two undefeated heavyweight champions, and they haven't taken on one another. Ali then appeals to Frazier's sense of sportsmanship and proposes a plan: Ali will take on Jerry Quarry (Robert Sale) in a fight in Atlanta (where Ali can legally fight as there is no state boxing commission there), and then Frazier will announce that he will give Ali a shot to reclaim his title. Frazier questions why he should do this favour for Ali. After all, Frazier already holds the title, so he has everything to lose and nothing to gain. Ali tells Frazier that, unless the two men fight head-to-head, the public will always wonder whether Frazier only won the title of Heavyweight Champion because the rightful champ was disqualified. A match between them would determine, once and for all, that Frazier truly is the greatest fighter – adding that, if Frazier had any confidence in his own ability, he shouldn't shy away from proving this fact to the world. Frazier has enough integrity to agree to Ali's proposal – though he ends the meeting with the threat that he is not motivated by compassion; he wants to prove, in a fair contest, that he has genuinely surpassed the former champion. The set-up of this fight coincides with Ali receiving the news that the Supreme Court has approved his appeal on religious grounds, and he returns to the personal gym for further training. When Ali is told the good news, he is having a large dinner with several family members and his colleagues – including Cassius Sr and Bundini.

Mann's protagonists tend to live in solitude. So, it is notable that when Ali is told that he will once again be allowed to fight, it is when he is having dinner with a large crowd of family and friends. Ali is pulled away from the table to receive a call from Cosell, and afterwards, he sits back down at the table to inform the others, who join him in his celebration. Ali, therefore, emerges from this low point more self-assured and assertive than ever before, and is more capable of forging his own identity away from manipulative authority figures. He becomes the rare Mann protagonist who can excel in his professional field without compromising his ideological principles, and who can fulfil his sense of ethical duty without having to surrender his relationships with others (although marriage to Belinda eventually break down, he maintains many close friendships and keeps his strong positive connection with his adoring fans in tact).

Ali's warm-up match against Quarry – a relatively low-level boxer – is short and relaxed. Ali achieves an easy knock-out, and Quarry immediately gets up to express his admiration for Ali, happy just to be in the ring with a legend, regardless of the outcome. The two men hug, and the crowd bursts into applause, a sign that the public still support Ali enthusiastically, in spite of the multiple media attacks against him and his lengthy absence from the ring. Herbert goes to see Ali after his victory and tells him that his father has decided to lift the suspension in light of the court's recent decision. In response, Ali asks Herbert whether that means he is permitted 'to be a Muslim again'. Herbert enthusiastically answers in the affirmative, but it is too late for him to win back Ali's favour: 'I've never stopped being a Muslim, just as I've never stopped being a champ.' Ali realises that his identity does not rely on the approval of others, and especially not on those who opportunistically latch onto his fame and fortune to further their own interests, only to abandon him. Ali says that he loves Herbert's father, and loves the Nation, but Elijah does not own him and has no right to say whether or not he is a 'true' Muslim. Ali realises in this moment that it is not up to the Muhammad family to decide whether or not he is properly practising his faith, just as it is not up to the American legal system to decide whether his actions are permissible or not.

Ali is not successful in his match against Frazier, but Foreman's later victory over Frazier gives Ali an opportunity to reclaim the title of Heavyweight Champion. This paves the way for the film's climactic set-piece: the match between Ali and Foreman in Kinshasa, the capital of Zaire, Africa. The fight at once gives Ali the chance to regain the Heavyweight Champion of the World and grants him a monumental opportunity to speak out against global oppression. The setting of the climactic 'Rumble in the Jungle' fight is deeply significant. In Africa, Ali no longer trains in luxury private gyms, but in open, collective spaces. In what is perhaps the film's most moving passage, Ali jogs through several paths in central Kinshasa. As he runs, Native Zaire children gradually join him, yelling 'Ali, boma ye!' ('Ali, kill him!'). As he approaches the end of his route, Ali encounters several pieces of wall art which portray him in a heroic light. In one of them, he is depicted punching an American fighter jet which is dropping shells over Vietnam. Ali gazes at the mural for a lengthy period of time, gradually realising just how significant his stand against American imperialism has been to the people of Zaire, and how much it would mean for them to see him emerge victorious in the ring.

With this awareness comes intense pressure, however, as Ali feels the need to live up to the iconic status that has been bestowed upon him by the people of Zaire. The final match takes on monumental significance, then, as Ali feels that if he loses to Foreman he will also let down the international community that has stood in solidarity with him for so long. Ali's intense sense of purpose as he prepares for the Rumble in the Jungle causes tension between him and Belinda. Mann cuts directly from the image of an awestruck Ali gazing at his visage on a mural to the opulent hotel room where he and Belinda are staying. Mann here makes the point that the imperatives of the Rumble in the Jungle's producers are crassly commercial and that the chief organiser Don King (Mykelti Williamson) is only interested in exploiting Ali's fame for monetary benefit. As Belinda asserts, King doesn't genuinely care about Africa and he would have never chosen Zaire as the location for the fight if the nation's President hadn't offered a hefty financial investment to the American company responsible for organising the match. Belinda comments that it is of no concern to King whether Ali 'lives or dies' fighting Foreman, and accuses Ali of, therefore, allowing himself to be manipulated to work against his own interests.

Belinda's criticism of the Rumble in the Jungle is justified, but she is wrong in one respect: she fundamentally misunderstands Ali's relationship with King and his attitude towards the climactic fight. Ali is not ignorant to the questionable motivations of King, but he harbours a genuine belief in his power to work against the commercialism of the event's organisers to deliver a powerful message of utopian possibility to viewers. Just as Wigand invested in the potential for *60 Minutes* to reach a vast audience of receptive listeners, despite the commercial nature of the network, Ali has faith that the Rumble in the Jungle will be a cultural event of great magnitude and his victory in the ring will enable him to broadcast a powerful anti-imperialist message. As such, the symbolic value of the fight will transcend the avaricious intentions of its financial backers. Ali takes Belinda's comment as an unforgivable attack on his ability to think for himself and recognise when he is being exploited. In response, Ali refuses to look at his wife and retreats into a corner. When Belinda asks him if he thinks it would be a good idea for her to move back to Chicago, he blurts out a simple, 'sure'. Stunned by Ali's inability to engage, even during this heated moment, Belinda parts with the derisive comment, 'Maybe I'll be back before the fight. If that's alright, my husband,' placing hard emphasis on the term 'my husband', as if feeling to need to remind him that he has familial duties that exist concurrently with his professional ones. Belinda does not recognise the profound significance of this fight to Ali, nor does she recognise that he is using it as a platform to further a genuinely progressive ideological agenda. Instead, she believes that Ali's participation in the spectacle is a sign that her husband is becoming a complicit participant in the very corporate system that he publicly rails against. For Ali, this is a sign that a considerable gulf has opened between them, and it becomes clear at this point that the relationship cannot be repaired.

When Ali enters the stadium for the climactic fight, he framed from the shoulders-up in a wide shot which emphasises the magnitude of the space and the huge volume of spectators that have travelled to see Ali succeed. The camera performs a full 180-degree rotation, positioning Ali as the central focal point for the tens of thousands of screaming supporters. While, in his first fight against Liston, the audience members were captured in shallow focus, they are now crystal clear; this formal choice signifies that Ali has achieved a newfound connection with the broader public, and now has the ability to synthesise his skill in the ring with his desire to advocate for concrete socio-political change. Without having to compromise his principles, Ali is now able to reach a multitude of individuals on a collective level and involve them directly in his ideological mission. Foreman is a daunting physical force, and Ali is required to change his fighting style to deal with such an opponent. During this match, Ali no longer darts around the ring, misleading his opponent and landing fast shots, he instead spends most of the fight standing stationary with his back against the side of the ropes in a defensive position, waiting for Foreman to become so exhausted that Ali can knock him out with a few strategic blows.

The intense physical beating Ali takes from Foreman emphasises the nobility of his physical struggle in a more intense way than in the earlier fights. The connected emotional and physical turmoil is underlined when Ali's passage of thought is narrated through voice-over: 'You want the title? You want to wear the heavyweight crown? Nose broke, jaw smashed, face busted in? You ready for that? Because you're facing a man who would die to achieve that.' Although this piece of narration is structured as a series of questions running through Ali's mind as he is battered, the viewer does not get the impression that Ali is seriously doubting his abilities or considering throwing in the towel. Instead, he is psyching himself up, reminding himself of the intensity of the struggle ahead to build up the mental strength necessary to withstand the immediate physical pain. As this narration finishes, Mann cuts to an image of Ali standing up in slow-motion, the camera fixed on the side of his face, his eyes cast downward, and two blinding white lights in the background. The staging of this scene makes it appear as though Ali is definitively reaching transcendence, rising above the physical pressures of the moment and finally achieving his status as a legend. Ali fully fuses his political and athletic ambitions here, and he does so in a way that communicates directly to a massive and highly receptive crowd. His knowledge of this gives him the resolve he requires to withstand an agonising level of bodily torment.

By the eighth round, Foreman starts to falter. He breathes heavily as he struggles to regain his composure. Although Foreman has the advantage of being physically larger than Ali, his lack of stamina ultimately results in his failure against the unstoppable determination of his opponent. Foreman is so tired that he physically collapses onto Ali, and Ali must push him away to get Foreman standing upright once again. Spotting an opportunity, Ali jumps up and delivers a sharp series of blows to Foreman's torso and chin. As Foreman's body hits the ground, Mann cuts to a series of shots of the ecstatic crowd and images of Bundini and Bingham. As in the scene in which Ali discovered that his court appeal was successful, his final success is enjoyed collectively; friends and colleagues praise Ali, and his supporters across the globe are ecstatic to see their idol pull off such a spectacular feat.

Ali stands with his gloves in the air, striking a self-consciously iconic pose as if cognisant that he is passing into the realm of myth. In the crowd surrounding the ring, thousands of spectators ecstatically wave the Zaire flag. Kegan Doyle points out that, while the imagery of an elated crowd is a fairly common one in the climaxes of American biopics, what is distinctive about Ali is that 'this crowd is not American: it is African and almost entirely black; to this degree, *Ali* is subversive of the genre. It could be read to imply that America is too conservative to contain or recognise the radical Ali.' (2006: 392). Indeed, Ali has found a wide audience who find value in his message, but he is never fully embraced on American soil. He is still treated with hostility by the American authorities and viewed with suspicion by large sections of the press, but he no longer lets this concern him. What matters is that his success in the ring serves as a public display of dissent against American imperialism, white supremacy and cultural hegemony.

Ali pushes past the rabble of congratulators within the ring, including photographers and reporters scrambling to get his attention, instead choosing to stand against the ropes with his fists lofted skywards, facing the audience. The final image is a tableau: On the left side of the screen is the massive arena filled with cheering spectators; on the right of the screen, Ali is elevated above the ring, his gloves pointed in the air, surrounded by his team. This striking composition emphasises Ali's legendary stature. This contrasts greatly with the opening shot. At the beginning of the film, Ali was merely a man, jogging along a nondescript street, but here he is truly framed as an icon. If the opening montage of *Ali* established two sides of the protagonist's personality through its focus on the figures of Malcolm X (representing Ali's radical racial politics and confrontational personality) and Sam Cooke (representing his showmanship and popularity within mainstream pop culture), then in this final sequence, Ali definitively fuses these two modes and, in doing so, becomes a cultural legend.

Los Angeles Plays Itself: *Collateral* (2004)

Like *Heat*, *Collateral* is a nocturnal crime film about wandering souls struggling to form substantial interpersonal relationships within the dehumanising environment of late capitalist Los Angeles. As in that earlier opus, *Collateral* is based on a structure of parallelism, centred on dual protagonists who initially appear to be diametric opposites (the self-assured, ruthless assassin Vincent and the soft-spoken, insecure cab driver Max), but gradually form a sense of kinship based on their shared sense of alienation. *Collateral*, too, symbolically begins in a space of public transit – in this case, an airport – as the film's central antihero Vincent makes a smooth entrance into the city that will soon consume him. However, while the first image of *Heat* is a wide shot of LA – the subway track bisecting the image and guiding the viewer's eye towards the vast expanse of the city – *Collateral* opens with a flat, planimetric shot: Vincent has already arrived at the terminal and is framed in a frontal close-up against a plain grey wall, strolling directly towards the camera. The surrounding commuters are obscured by the shallow depth-of-field into hazy blurs of colour and motion, unacknowledged by Vincent, who moves past them effortlessly.

The differences between these two opening images point to significant points of divergence between the two projects: *Heat* is a sprawling, epically-scaled work that weaves together many characters and subplots into a rich tapestry of city life; in contrast, *Collateral* is a lean, hyper-focused film that unfolds over a single night, restricts much of its action to the interior of a taxi cab, and never diverges from its primary narrative strand. This is not to suggest, however, that *Collateral* is a comparatively minor work. In its own way, it is just as nuanced and emotionally impactful as *Heat* in its melancholic exploration of the nature of work, ethics, and isolation in post-industrial America.

At first glance, Vincent may seem to be more comfortable with his situation than McCauley is. McCauley's deep sense of dissatisfaction and yearning to embark upon a more rewarding lifestyle are clear from the outset – evidenced by the lonely evenings he spends in his sparsely decorated apartment and his ill-fated courtship with Eady which leads him to break several tenets of his self-determined behavioural code. Vincent, on the other hand, expresses no interest in pursuing a romantic relationship and demonstrates no serious desire to break away from the shackles of his professional code (in contrast to the longing expressed by many Mann protagonists to retire or elope – even if they ultimately sabotage their own attempt to leave their profession). Unlike most Mann professionals, Vincent has no end goal in mind, and he lacks even the meagre material possessions that other Mann protagonists have (McCauley may be a drifter, but he occupies a series of temporary residences; Vincent is never shown within any private space, and it's left completely unclear how he spends his time between jobs). While other Mann protagonists demonstrate some kind of rapport with the individuals they work with, even if their bonds are too insubstantial to be called friendships, Vincent works entirely on his own: he is sent a 'kill list' from a source he does not directly interact with, carries out the job, and then sends back the message that his task has been completed. Notably, the only individual associated with Vincent's work that we see in the feature is the drug kingpin Felix Reyes-Torrena (Javier Bardem), who Vincent has never met in person – indeed, the distance between Vincent and Felix is so great that he does not suspect anything is untoward when Max poses as the hitman in his presence.

Even though he remains an enigma, Vincent is verbose in a way that few other characters in Mann's oeuvre are. Whereas McCauley treats his isolated and transitory lifestyle with weary resignation, acknowledging that the emotional distance he maintains from those around him is a difficult but necessary sacrifice he must make to maintain autonomy over his work, Vincent enthusiastically espouses his individualist beliefs to Max over the course of the night. Vincent rationalises his disinterest in the lives of others by describing the world as being essentially insignificant when considered within a larger cosmological framework. When considered in relation to the grand expanse of the universe, Vincent repeatedly argues, human life is inconsequential, relationships are superficial, and the notion of 'community' is nothing but an illusion meant to distract humankind from the daunting indifference of the world around them. The disdain that Vincent expresses toward other people – and the cityscape itself – is expressed by the anecdote he tells Max, soon after they meet, of a man who died while riding the subway and whose corpse wasn't discovered until six hours later. The other passengers were so absorbed in their own activities that they didn't notice they were riding in the same carriage as a dead body. In Vincent's eyes, everybody is motivated by self-interest, and he is simply more honest about the true condition of humankind than those who 'pretend' to care about other people. After murdering a police officer, Vincent says to Max: 'Indifferent. Get with it. Millions of galaxies of hundreds of millions of stars, in a speck of one in a blink. That's us, lost in space. The cop, you, me, who notices?' As the narrative goes on, however, Vincent becomes increasingly incapable of maintaining his aura of studied insouciance as the flaws and inconsistencies of his worldview are revealed and the true extent of his inner torment begins to surface.

In contrast, Max begins the narrative as a weak-willed, indolent, frustrated character incapable of making any forward progress. Unusually for a Mann protagonist, he feels no commitment to his work. He initially took on a job as a taxi driver as a way to make ends meet until he could get pursue his dream of starting his own limo rental company, but, because he lacks the courage to embark on this business venture, he is still working as a cabbie, 12 years later. Furthermore, Max has no autonomy over his work at all. While working, he is entirely at the whim of the customers, and the cab he operates does not even belong to him – it is owned by the mercenary operators of the taxi company, who view Max as an insignificant middleman who can easily be replaced if he causes them any trouble. Although there is obvious chemistry between him and Annie (Jada Pinkett Smith), the young lawyer he transports to the airport in the film's first act, he lacks the confidence to ask her on a date, and it is up to her to give him her contact details as she is leaving the vehicle. Max's dissatisfaction with his life is made clear through the symbol of the postcard of a tropical island he keeps taped to the visor in his cab. Max explains to Annie that he gazes at it longingly whenever he needs a moment to mentally escape the tedium and frustration of his daily routine: 'I just go there, and I concentrate on absolutely nothing.' Like many leading men in Mann's cinema, Max knows that his life in the city is suffocating him; yet, while the majority of Mann's protagonists take active steps to embark on the life they long for (even if their escape is thwarted), Max lacks the conviction to make any forward progress at all.

The relationship between Max and Vincent is complex and multifaceted. It is only through his encounter with Vincent's mentality of self-interest and impulsive action that Max summons the willpower to break out of his inertia and, ultimately, begins to construct a more rewarding life. However, before Max reaches this point in the final act, he allows himself to become a complicit participant in Vincent's heinous acts, and, at certain points, even demonstrates a disturbing aptitude for performing criminal tasks. Although Max never shares Vincent's sociopathic lack of concern for other people's lives, he does repeatedly express a vicarious thrill when he acts as an accomplice to Vincent's crimes. Furthermore, though the men are eventually pitted against one another, they also develop some degree of affection for one another which belies both Vincent's insistence on remaining detached from all other individuals and the sense of disgust Max expresses towards Vincent's violent actions.

One of the first lines of dialogue delivered in the film, spoken by a mysterious, unnamed businessman (Jason Statham) to Vincent following their swift briefcase handover, is 'enjoy LA'. As this would indicate, despite the condensed nature of its setting, *Collateral* is just as much a city symphony as *Heat*. The conversations between Max and Vincent are intercut with stunning and evocative images of LA nightlife, and the sense of ennui experienced by both men is explicitly framed as being a natural condition of city life. The film's formal design treats the cityscape as monolithic and all-engulfing; its imposing buildings overwhelm the characters, even in moments of ostensibly private reflection. Indeed, the taxi itself is a symbol of the fragile line between private and public space in LA. Max refers to the cab as his own, but it is legally owned by the taxi company he works for, which set up strict parameters regarding how he may and may not conduct his business within it – the extent of the restrictions placed on Max is made clear when Max initially rejects Vincent's offer to give him $600 if he is willing to transport him to the locations of his six targets, because it is 'against regulations' for one passenger to hire the car for the night. Max indulges in leisure activities within the vehicle, such as eating and reading, but the cab is always sited on the public space of the freeway, the clear windows rendering his every move visible to passers-by. And, of course, the nature of Max's work facilitates only fleeting and insubstantial meetings; Max's cab is always open to the use of any passenger who wants a ride, but any connection that may form between him and his passenger is severed as soon as the they reach their destination and the meter stops running.

The airport handover scene is followed by a series of quick shots which establishes the space of the taxi company's holding bay: an ad for Bacardi Silver sitting on the top of a cab; a Farsi newspaper; glistening windshields; a meter being activated; headlights passing; surveillance footage of a motorway on a monitor; a mechanic working at a car's engine; Max completes a crossword in *The New York Times*. Max does not receive a heroic entrance; he appears as just another fragment in this flux of audio-visual information. Max's visage is overwhelmed by the images of machinery and glossy surfaces that dominate the rest of the montage. It is only when Vincent enters the cab and closes the door – drowning out the ambient noise – that he becomes the focus of the composition. The camera rests on Max's face in close-up as he enjoys a brief moment of silent contemplation. But this moment soon passes; Max he places his driver's license in its holder above the steering wheel, signalling that he is about to throw himself into his professional role. And, when he is occupying this professional role, Max is expected to be a silent observer, not an active participant. We see brief snippets of Max's routine: a young couple in the back seat argue about an unspecified event, while Max listens in, a bemused smile on his face; Max's cab cruises the freeway, in search of the next customer; Max gives a pedestrian directions to the airport. This sequence is edited in a way that is simultaneously fast-paced and cyclical. There is a strong propulsive energy throughout this scene, emphasised by the rapid edits and the constant motion of vehicles, but no real sense of forward progression is communicated. The snapshots of Max's daily tasks are intercut with temporally and spatially abstracted images of the car in motion. To emphasise the lack of linear progression, Mann varies the direction in which the vehicle is moving, alternately moving from screen right to screen left, screen left to screen right, and the bottom of the screen to the top.

Annie is introduced from behind, framed from the waist-up, speaking on a cell phone. She is just a figure on the sidewalk, with little to distinguish her from the crowd of pedestrians who surround her. Max pulls up by the side of the road opposite. Annie enters the back of the car while still talking on her cell, not even thinking to acknowledge Max. It is only when Annie is inside the cab that the film's pace slows down, and Max is able to pull himself out of the relentless pace of his workday. The conversation between Max and Annie is, at first, composed in the same manner as the earlier scene in which Max eavesdropped on the fighting couple: Max is in the foreground, occupying frame right, while Annie is in the middle-ground, pushed to frame left. Between them is the rear window looking out onto the streets of the city. In this case, however, Mann does not hold on this composition for the entirety of the dialogue. As their conversation develops, he instead frames both characters in complementary close-ups so that the sheet of glass longer creates a split between them within the frame, and a sense of reciprocity is established. This collapsing of visual planes within the composition expresses the rapid formation of an emotional connection the connection between them. For once, Max has found a customer who treats him as an individual and not merely as an instrument to transport them from point A to point B.

After disagreeing over which is the fastest route to take to the airport, Max offers not to charge Annie for the trip if he is incorrect in his prediction that taking a detour through the 105 east and then up the 110 turns out to be a faster way to reach downtown than following the more congested Le Brea route. From a mercenary viewpoint, this is a deal that Max cannot win: if he is wrong and the journey turns out to be longer than scheduled, he loses the fare; and if he is correct, then he will make a smaller fare than he would have received if he had simply taken the direct route. Annie expresses her admiration for Max's selflessness in making the bet when she asks him, 'How many cabbies get you into an argument to save you money?' While Annie and Max have, up until this point, been defined solely by their work (Annie, speaking into her cell phone, tells her assistant that she'll need to stay up all night to finish prepping a case for the following day, an indication of the extent to which her professional life has crossed over into her leisure time), as the ride goes on, they bond over their respective passions, backstories, and dreams for the future. Annie reveals that she once had a passion for music while in high school, but since graduating, she has switched her viola for her 'different instrument', referring to her cell phone. Central characters in Mann's films typically take a deep level of pride and honour in their work, even if the pressure of this work ultimately takes a heavy toll on their well-being, but here both Max and Annie express their dissatisfaction with their current occupations. Max confides in Annie that he still views cab driving as being a stopgap while he raises the funds necessary to start a limousine rental business that will double as a 'club experience'. As Max explains, he envisions a limo ride so enjoyable that the customers won't want to leave the vehicle when they arrive at their destination. Evidently, Max is tired of existing in an interstitial state, perceived as a tool to move clients from one point to the next. Annie, in turn, expresses her anxiety regarding the immense stress and extended hours she is expected to deal with by her bosses, who view her instrumentally, just as Max's clients do. She describes the physical symptoms of anxiety she always suffers on the night before she enters a courtroom: 'I always get this clenched-up thing the night before the first day [...] I think I'm gonna lose. I think I suck. I think my case sucks. I haven't prepared enough.' However, she clarifies that she always gets over this anxiety attack and ultimately summons the courage to: 'get it together. Rewrite my opening statement. Work the exhibits.' As Annie explains, these panic attacks happen so regularly that she has come to accept them as an inevitable part of 'the routine'. Annie has become so accustomed to the demands of her profession that she no longer views such periods of intense stress as being unhealthy or unnatural.

When Max comments that 'you need a vacation', Annie's response: 'I just had a vacation, on the harbour freeway,' should only be read as half-ironic. Although the notion that a short cab ride gives Annie a break within her workday substantial enough to qualify as a 'vacation' may sound ridiculous, there is some truth to the idea that the space established by Max and Annie should be perceived as a respite from the de-humanising pressure of urban life. As Nick Pinkerton notes, 'Pinkett-Smith and Foxx's easy interplay catches the discreet sexiness in those little pockets of intimacy and connection – say, a warm taxicab interior – that pop up in the big, dark, empty city.' (2004). But when Annie leaves the vehicle, a hesitant Max cannot bring himself to ask her for a date or exchange contact details. The pair would probably never see one another again, if Annie did not make the spontaneous decision to run back to the vehicle and offer Max her business card.

Max is elated, but this moment of personal triumph is interrupted by Vincent, who knocks impatiently at the passenger door. When Max fails to acknowledge his presence after the first knock, Vincent swiftly moves on to the cab lined up next in the queue, prompting Max to panic and call over to the stranger. Although Max does not know yet what Vincent's reason for being in the city is, it is notable that Max actively invites Vincent to enter his cab, rather than Vincent entering without permission – this is an early indication of the extent to which Max will attach himself to the hitman and become complicit in his actions over the course of the night. As much as Max may wish to view himself as a victim of circumstance, sucked into a dangerous situation against his will, there are two points at which he is given the opportunity to cut ties with Vincent but chooses not to: first, when Vincent is preparing to move on to the next driver; secondly, when Vincent makes Max the offer for $600 to accompany him for the entire night, an offer which Max actively accepts despite knowing that the deal is illicit. Mann could have easily portrayed Vincent forcing himself into Max's vehicle and forcing him to comply with his demands at gunpoint, thereby genuinely rendering Max a victim of circumstance, but instead he makes it clear that Max is, to a certain degree, choosing to be part of Vincent's odyssey. Indeed, Max is initially drawn to Vincent despite sporadically expressing his moral outrage at his violent tendencies. Perhaps this push-pull is, in part, due to the difference between the two men's constitutions. While Max is defined by stasis and hesitancy, unable to move forward personally or professionally, Vincent is presented as a man of productive action. Vincent has been given a list of five targets and a deadline for the following morning – this single, clearly delineated goal is his sole driving force over the course of the narrative, and he never asks questions such as 'why?' or 'what next?' While Max can't seem to commit to a single action without getting distracted or side-tracked, Vincent focuses on nothing but the completion of this professional task, and he operates according to a strict, self-defined professional code, rather than following the rules given to him by others. He will not let anything stand in his way: not any moral qualms, not Max's stated objections, not even the moment when Max disposes of the briefcase that contains the list of his targets. For Max, a man who has spent his entire life rigidly following the rules and expectations of others, there is a transgressive thrill in attaching himself to somebody who so brazenly (and unrepentantly) breaks the law. The very decision to accept Vincent's deal represents a breach of the regulations enforced by the taxi company, and Max clearly takes joy in this act of rebellion.

But Max eventually realises that there is an essential vacuity at the core of Vincent's lifestyle. His ideology is fundamentally vacuous and self-defeating. He claims to be disgusted with the impersonal nature of the modern city ('sprawling, disconnected', as he phrases it), but in so aggressively divorcing himself from any sense of duty to the rest of humanity, he has come to embody the aspects of city life he claims to despise. As Gaine acutely observes: 'Vincent's lack of concern makes him the personification of the city's indifference, as he moves easily between one target and another.' (2009: 6). Vincent views his actions as being both a symptom *of* and a response *to* the daunting inhumanity of the environment he has been thrust into, but he does not consider the possibility that anybody may transcend the de-humanising aspects of the city or transform the world for the better. His total lack of concern for human life, coupled with his absolute belief that it is impossible for things to improve, ultimately leads Vincent to self-destruct. As Rybin acknowledges, 'ultimately the film critiques Vincent's empty mannerism implicitly in its own employment of an expressive mise-en-scène and Max's ability to discover a greater degree of agency as the film progresses.' (2013: 177). What, then, differentiates Vincent from the other criminal protagonists in Mann's work, such as Frank, McCauley, Murphy and Hathaway? Like them, Vincent has constructed his own strict personal philosophy that he is determined to live his life by. However, unlike these characters, Vincent's philosophy lacks a crucial moral dimension. The grotesque nature of Vincent's worldview is evidenced by his chosen profession of assassin – a role that requires robbing other individuals of their lives for material reward. This profession is not shared by any other protagonist throughout Mann's filmography, and, in fact, Mann's other outlaw lead characters pride themselves on their commitment to avoiding violence -unless they deem it to be an absolutely necessary last resort.

Vincent is extremely proficient at his work and takes pride in having total agency over his profession. As a contract killer, he has no fixed superiors, leaving him free to take on whatever assignments he deems worthy of his skillset and carry them out in whatever way he sees fit. At one point, he mocks Max for thinking about the wishes of his bosses who, in Vincent's words, 'don't even pay him sick leave.' Over the first two acts, Vincent demonstrates his determination and skilled manipulation of others in an undeniably impressive manner. During his first kill, Vincent glides up the stairwell of a high-rise apartment complex, scoping his environment and passing open windows without drawing attention to himself. Mann intercuts Vincent's pursuit of his target with images of Max sitting stagnant in the limo, flicking through a limousine catalogue. Vincent's complete command of the situation is ironically contrasted with Max's lack of knowledge about what is happening in his vicinity, with Max's ignorance reaching an apex when throws the body of his deceased target from a high window and it lands on the cab's windshield. While Vincent's demeanour remains calm and collected, Max instantly descends into hysteria. The cabbie exclaims, 'Oh no!', while struggling to remove the book of flyers from his lap and fumbling while attempting to open the door. Mann rapidly alternates between three images: a close-up of Max, an image of the cracked windshield, and a medium-wide of the car interior. This barrage of imagery destabilises the viewer's spatial awareness, immersing us in Max's hysteria. After collapsing onto the street and dragging himself across to the other side of the alley, Max jumps to his feet and, still in a daze, is only capable of repeatedly yelling 'What the hell?' and 'Shit' while stumbling around the crime scene. When Vincent enters the scene, visibly unaffected by the sight of the fall, Max does not connect him to the murder at first. Max describes the confusion and chaos of what just happened to him breathlessly, only to be cut short by Vincent's sarcastic comment: 'Good guess.'

The decision not to show the murder of Vincent's first target may seem an odd choice on Mann's part, but considered within the broader structure of *Collateral* this decision serves a clear thematic purpose. By withholding the sight of Vincent killing a man in cold blood, Mann keeps the viewer at a distance from the true extent of Vincent's toxicity at this early point in the film, and therefore ensures that they are more likely to comprehend Max's decision to continue to accompany him. As Max is the figure who offers the focalising perspective through which we view the action, choices like this encourage the viewer to emphasise with him as he becomes pulled further and further into Vincent's criminal activity. This decision also emphasises Vincent's detachment from the horrors he inflicts upon others. 'I didn't kill him,' Vincent tells Max. 'The bullets and the fall killed him.' After they flee the scene, Max assists Vincent in placing the body in the trunk of the cab and washing down the windshield. Although he makes a small, minor attempt to break free from Vincent's command – promising that he will remain silent if Vincent takes the cab to fulfil the remainder of his assignment alone -Max ultimately buckles under pressure when Vincent refuses to take his word that he will not tell another soul about what has transpired.

Although Max and Vince, at first, seem to view one another only in terms of what they can do for each other, the distance between them is bridged as the night goes on, as the two form a tentative bond over their shared experiences. As the two men flee the crime scene, Max tries, in vain, to convince Vincent to show remorse for the murder. But Vincent refuses to do so; instead, he attempts calm Max's nerves by insisting that it is futile to dwell on the past. They can only think about the immediate moment, he reasons: a man died and now they must adapt to the situation they are both now embroiled in, rather than argue over what could have been done differently. 'I didn't throw him,' Vincent insists. 'He fell.' Vincent distances himself from any sense of personal guilt by refusing to learn anything about his targets before killing them. He responds to Max's query of 'What did he do to you?' by calmly retorting that he never met the target before that night and that his job is made easier by the fact that he has no concrete personal ties with his victims. If he knew them or any details about their lives, then it would be harder to view them as abstracted targets. As such, to form any kind of emotional connection with them at all (even this is just a matter of finding out who their family is or what they do for a living) would be to allow his own emotions to jeopardise the perfect efficiency of the kill.

Although this verbal exchange may seem to set up a clear contrast between the moral constitutions of these two men, the interaction which follows creates an uncomfortable synchronicity between them. Max is pulled over to the side of the road by two police officers dismayed by the large crack on the windshield. At first, Max responds to them honestly and obediently, answering their questions in a collected manner and willingly handing over his licence for inspection. However, when one of the cops notices blood on the window, Max nonchalantly slips into 'criminal' mode, quickly fabricating the convincing story that he hit a deer on his route. Max could, at this point, break away from Vincent and turn himself in to the police. Doing so would mean that he would potentially suffer consequences for the role he played in the disposal of a dead body, but he would put an immediate end to the crime spree and ensure that the remaining targets on Vincent's list would not suffer the same fate. Max ultimately chooses not to do so, and it thus becomes more difficult to see him as being merely a hapless victim being led astray by Vincent. And in lying to the police in such a convincing manner, Max demonstrates his aptitude for criminal activities – a skill which will be demonstrated more overtly in later sequences – as well as his strong instinct for self-preservation. This instinct drives him to become more complicit in Vincent's wrongdoing than he would have thought possible at the start of the narrative.

Max has lied to protect Vincent's freedom, and immediately afterwards, a grateful Vincent returns the favour. On his way to track down his second target, Vincent overhears Max's line manager Lenny (Michael Waxman) angrily berate him. Lenny was informed by the cops that Max had been driving with a cracked windshield, and he now threatens to make Max cover the cost of repair. Sickened less by the abuse being dealt out by Lenny than by Max's passive acceptance of this verbal barrage, Vincent orders Max to stand up to his boss and feeds him lines to deliver into the speaker. At first, Max complies, albeit with visible discomfort, as Vincent tells him to make it clear that the crash was an accident and should therefore be covered by the company's insurance, not his own salary. But when Vincent demands that Max tell Lenny 'to stick his cab up his fat ass,' Max refuses, fearing the professional consequences he may face if he were to use such explicit language. After tiring of Max's repeated refusals, Vincent takes over the intercom, assuming the fabricated identity of an assistant US attorney who overheard the argument and felt the need to intervene. Vincent threatens to report the taxi company to the DMV if Lenny persists in treating his employee in a manner that does not comply with official labour regulations. A humiliated Lenny apologises profusely to Vincent while meekly attempting to justify his inexcusable behaviour. Sensing Lenny's weakened demeanour and submissive behaviour when faced with a man he believes is higher than him on the social pecking order, Vincent again asserts that Max should tell him to 'stick his cab up his fat ass.' A newly empowered Max obliges, and Vincent hangs up the intercom before they have a chance to hear Lenny's response. If, in the previous scene, we observed Max pick up several of Vincent's worst qualities (his duplicity, his lack of scruples, his adherence to self-preservation, no matter the cost), then here we see the genuinely positive character traits that Max is picking up from his companion; by following Vincent's lead in his confrontation with his boss, Max manages to evade paying an unjust fine, and this encounter is likely to make Lenny think twice about exploiting his employees in the future. Max is beginning to exercise agency and stand up to the poor treatment he receives daily; however, he can only achieve this through the direct guidance of Vincent at this point.

The fact that Max is dependent on Vincent's advice to carry out more active, resourceful behaviour explains, in part, why he is reluctant to cut ties with his passenger. The growing bond between Max and Vincent is intensified when Max is threatened at gunpoint by a group of young thugs who are passing the cab. Vincent is out of the vehicle, and Max has been left in the driver's seat with his hands tied to the steering wheel. The men take several items from the vehicle, including Vincent's briefcase, as Max sits, unable to move. To maximise Max's humiliation, the gang leader mockingly mimes shooting him as he makes a swift and effortless escape. Mann cuts to a point-of-view angle from Max's perspective as he gazes through the windshield at the thieves walking away. The camera remains static as the men recede into the distance for an uncomfortable length of time, visually communicating Max's sense of frustration at his inability to intervene. At this point, Vincent walks out into the street and confronts the thieves without missing a beat. Unperturbed by the gun being waved in his face, Vincent calmly shoots this low-level criminal and takes back the stolen items. The two men are left lying unconscious in the middle of the alleyway. Once again, Max relies on Vincent's prowess and lack of trepidation to help him escape a difficult situation in which another individual was attempting to take advantage of him. Notably, Vincent takes back Max's belongings as well as his own briefcase; this is an act of selflessness which belies Vincent's stated belief that all interpersonal relationships are worthless, and it helps to strengthen the bond between the hitman and his driver. This section of the film sees the relationship between the two lead characters transform from one of antagonism to one of camaraderie, culminating in Vincent promising to buy Max a beer once they reach their next destination – a jazz club owned by Vincent's third target, a talented musician named Daniel Baker.

Collateral also represents a significant step forward in Mann's incorporation of digital technology into his craft. After experimenting with the format during a few sequences of *Ali* (most notably, the first images of *Ali* jogging through pedestrian streets and alleys in low-lighting conditions), Mann used high-definition digital cameras far more extensively during the production of *Collateral*. The use of the technology provided both practical and artistic advantages. The handheld Thomson Grass Valley Viper Film Stream and Sony CineAlta cameras allowed for Mann to shoot at close proximity to perilous and high-octane action and capture a great variety of coverage within tightly confined interiors. Furthermore, the intense light-capturing ability of these cameras allowed for on-location shooting with a high degree of spontaneity. To point to one salient example, late into the shoot, Mann and the crew spotted a coyote wandering around the streets of LA at night. Whereas a classical photochemical film shoot would have required extensive lighting set-up to capture the coyote in high quality, the nature of the lightweight digital cameras enabled Mann to spontaneously gather several pick-up shots of the animal, tracking its unpredictable movements without the need to change lenses. The footage was then integrated into the sequence which follows Max and Vincent as they approach the Fever nightclub.

Mann's use of digital video in *Collateral* is simultaneously hyper-realistic and expressionistic. The small, lightweight design of the cameras allowed Mann to shoot footage in real locations, with less mediation from artificial lighting and other studio elements than would have been possible in a classical film shoot. On the other hand, the extensive depth-of-field and the powerful light-capturing abilities also allowed Mann to craft images with an intense density of detail that appears qualitatively different from images of the city produced with photo-chemical film. The way LA is captured in *Collateral* appears truly new and radical, unlike any cityscape that has ever graced the silver screen before it. As Mann explains: 'My reason for choosing

DV [digital video] wasn't economy but was to do with the fact that the entire movie takes place in one city, on one night, and you can't see the city at night on motion picture film the way you can on digital video. And I like the truth-telling feeling I receive when there's very little light on the actors' faces.' (Olsen, 2004: 81). In particular, the neon lights of the bustling streets and the fluorescent bulbs lining the highways appear as unnaturally vibrant, centres of illumination which bathe the city in an otherworldly glow. Whereas the LA of *Heat* is dominated by a muted colour scheme of chrome and silver, *Collateral* positively radiates with the primary colour lights of the urban space, a landscaped awash in oranges and greens and dark blues augmented by Mann's use of digital equipment.

The scene in the jazz club encapsulates the increasingly close and complex relationship between Max and Vincent. Instead of keeping Max in the car, as he did when conducting his earlier hits, Vincent brings him into the club with him; the two men sit at a table and watch Daniel perform, as though they were just a pair of ordinary friends enjoying an evening on the town. The opening to this sequence marks a rare moment of genuine respite for the two men. The film's tight and tense visual language breaks down into a more spontaneous and free-wheeling montage of leisurely activity. Mann cuts rapidly between the musical instruments, the crowd's rapt faces, and the ambient space of the club. For a few blissful moments, Vincent and Max drop their professional roles and talk as two individuals appreciating the moment. Vincent leans over and describes the excitement of the night to Max; he says that most men in the city are trapped in a staid, repetitive routine (with the implicit implication that Max was, too) – but, ever since Vincent entered his life, Max has no idea where he'll be or what he'll be doing from moment to moment. Combined with the exuberant atmosphere of the club, this monologue is intoxicating, and articulates to the viewer the strange feeling of elation that Max feels when he's around Vincent. Although Max morally objects to Vincent's actions, he undoubtedly gets a rush from being in such close proximity to this figure and the criminal underbelly of the city. After the band has finished performing, Vincent offers the waitress a generous tip to convince Daniel to join their table for a drink. While Vincent usually tries to remain as detached from his targets as possible to make it easier to view them as distractions and therefore remove himself from the guilt of his crimes, here he listens diligently as Daniel speaks at length about his background and love of music – in particular, Daniel relishes in telling the men an anecdote about the night he had a jam session with Miles Davis. So jovial is that atmosphere that it comes as a shock when Vincent slips back into the hardened persona of professional killer. Vincent stops the conversation in its tracks when he hints at the real reason why he is visiting the bar, responding to Daniel's story with the ominous comment that he'll have to 'tell the people in Culiacan and Cartagena that story.'

When he hears these words, Daniel's smile drops instantly. We never learn exactly the relationship between Daniel and Felix's gang is, but it is clear that after hearing these words, Daniel knows exactly what's coming next. He and Vincent stare at one another for an extended period as a portentous atmosphere fills the establishment. Vincent genuinely enjoyed the dialogue he shared with Daniel, and, for the first time in the narrative, the assassin seems to express a degree of uncertainty over whether or not to go through with the hit.

But, ultimately, Vincent allows his sense of professional duty to overwhelm any sense of camaraderie. Daniel tries to dissuade Vincent from making the hit, telling him that he thought he was a 'cool guy', Vincent replies stoically: 'I am a cool guy. With a job I've got to do.' The use of language here illustrates that Vincent prioritises his profession over all else – his commitment to making sure that the 'job' gets done effectively supersedes his desire to be perceived as a 'cool' guy by Daniel or anybody else. Max limply attempts to hold Vincent back, but his efforts are ineffectual. Vincent overpowers Max with a single insult, and he remains quiet for the remainder of the exchange. Although Max has demonstrated a capacity to stand up for himself against others with Vincent's help in the previous scenes, he still clams up when it comes to challenging the hitman himself. Vincent grants Daniel a proposition: if he can correctly answer a single question about Miles Davis – Daniel's self-proclaimed subject of expertise – he will allow him to remain alive and flee town to evade Felix's grasp.

Vincent's choice of question is significant here. Vincent is a man who admires professionalism above all else; he devotes himself 100% to his job and expects others to do the same. Although Daniel appears affable and a skilled musician, Vincent takes issue with the fact that he failed to get back into contact with Davis following the single jam session they shared when Daniel was a young man. Pressing him on the subject, Daniel simply says that life got in the way for him: 'I got drafted. And into some other things.' To further test Daniel's commitment to his work, Vincent challenges his knowledge of the area he claims to know about inside and out. After Daniel accepts Vincent's offer, he asks Daniel the seemingly simple question: 'Where did Miles learn music?' Daniel responds confidently with the answer: 'His father sent Miles to Juilliard School of Music, New York, 1945.' Without hesitation, Vincent pulls his gun out from under the table and shoots Daniel twice in the forehead. Gazing at Daniel's deceased body, Vincent corrects his response: 'Dropped out of Julliard after less than a year, tracked down Charlie Parker on 52nd Street who mentored him for the next three years.' The insufficient answer given by Daniel immediately convinces Vincent that this admiration was misplaced; Daniel lacks the conviction that Vincent looks for in others, he is only half-hearted in his commitment to his chosen field. Therefore, for Vincent, Daniel is disposable. As Daniel bleeds out, Vincent holds his head and lays it carefully on the top of the table, his voice becoming muted and fragile. Vincent appears to be crestfallen as his belief in the musician's devotion is shaken. It seems as though he was truly hoping that Daniel would provide him with the correct answer. Yet, Vincent felt let down by the musician, and, therefore, he felt no need to stray from his established professional code.

Perhaps it is because of the sadness Vincent felt, on some level, while committing this assassination that the next scene sees him further develop his relationship with Max. Vincent's decision to accompany Max to visit his mother in the hospital may be motivated by self-preservation at first (it may look suspicious if Max failed to attend his scheduled visit), but when they arrive, Vincent expresses an active interest in Max's relationship with his family. First, Vincent urges Max to bring a bouquet of flowers to his mother, Ida (Irma P Hall), to show respect and appreciation for the woman who 'carried [him] in her womb for nine months.' Then, when they arrive in Ida's room, Vincent pretends to be an acquaintance of Max's, and makes lively conversation with his mother, discussing Max's childhood, ambitions, and familial history. Vincent carries the conversation effortlessly as Max stands in the corner, fidgeting and anxious to leave. Max's relationship with Ida is filled with friction; she scolds him for wasting money on the flowers and then thoughtlessly reveals details of his personal life to Vincent which he had hoped to keep private. Ida fills in some information about Max's early life that elucidates his current disposition: Max grew up with few friends, and spent much of his leisure time alone in his room; he has remained sensitive and ill-equipped to handle social situations over his adult life; and he has lied to his mother about the nature of his work, pretending that he owns the luxury limousine company that, in actuality, is only a distant fantasy. Max interrupts their conversation when his mother delves into these sensitive details, asking Ida to refrain from discussing him as though he's not the room. This gives an indication of the way he was treated when he was growing up, hinting that his parents were not attuned to his needs and sensitivities. The humiliation of being berated by a parent, coupled with the uncomfortable intrusion of Vincent into his most private affairs, spurs Max to commit a brazen act of rebellion against the hitman . While Vincent is distracted, Max snatches his briefcase and runs out of the hospital exit. Followed on foot by Vincent, Max makes it onto a bridge suspended above a freeway and tosses the case into the path of incoming traffic. The briefcase hits the front of a truck, resulting in its contents being scattered across the road; these contents (a laptop and sheets of paper) are then run over by several vehicles, damaging them beyond repair.

Vincent tackles Max to the ground, but decides to spare his life – a surprising choice considering that he previously shot two men dead for attempting to steal the case from the back of the cab. Vincent briefly chastises Max, but instead of cutting ties with him, he demonstrates a certain degree of admiration at Max's ability to take charge of that situation. Impressed by Max's skills, he cryptically tells the cabbie, 'Let's see what else you can do,' as they lie on the ground. Frome one perspective, this may seem to demonstrate some level of affection for Max on Vincent's part. Yet, this is complicated by the fact that Vincent, in this moment, primarily views Max in terms of his instrumentality; as he is interested in determining what Max can do to aid his own mission, his bond to Max is intrinsically intertwined with his desire to effectively carry out his job. Vincent is so thoroughly committed to his professional task that he only develops a degree of fondness towards a man who is assisting him in the completion of his job. Despite the small gestures of kindness that Vincent shows towards Max, he never considers straying from the task at hand, and it difficult to tell whether Vincent genuinely cares for Max as an individual or whether simply looks out with him because he knows that keeping Max safe will further his own objectives. Either way, it is clear that Vincent views Max's value as being intertwined with his role as a transporter helping him to track down his targets.

Ironically, Max's impulsive attempt to escape from Vincent brings the two men even closer together. Vincent fears the horrific consequences he may suffer if he tells Felix that he has lost the vital information contained within the briefcase, and so he persuades Max to assume his identity for a face-to-face meeting; so impersonal is the structure of Felix's chain-of-command that he and Vincent have never met directly, so he is unable to tell the difference between the two men. Pressed by Max for more information that may help him better understand the situation, Vincent can only tell Max that Felix is 'connected to the guys who hired me.' Vincent knows very little about Felix, aside from his name and where he can be found in the event of an emergency. Unlike McCauley, Vincent has no regular crew of associates who assist him in his work; he longs to remain as distant from the network of criminals as he possibly can. As Vincent phrases it, he prefers to maintain 'ultimate anonymity' to ensure his self-preservation in the criminal world, thus taking the isolationist ethos of characters like McCauley and Frank to an extreme logical endpoint. A vital part of remaining anonymous is ensuring that he does not have his real face captured by the surveillance cameras that Felix has placed all over his regular meeting spots, which is part of the reason why Vincent is so desperate for Max to take his place in his meeting with the drug kingpin. Although Max is initially reluctant, he slips into the role of Vincent with surprising ease once he makes it to the entrance of the club. Unperturbed by the security guards' insistence that there is nobody by the name of Felix in the building, Max emphatically tells them that he's sure Felix will be eager to meet him if he knows that his name is 'Vincent'.

There is a clear point during the meeting in which Max visibly switches from tentatively performing an adequate impersonation of Vincent to fully committing to a convincing criminal persona. Sitting opposite Max, Felix can barely conceal his rage upon hearing the news about the missing case. He asks Max to imagine if their positions were reversed: how angry would he be if he found out that a carefully compiled list of targets (created through the use of extremely valuable counter-intelligence technology) was simply lost by the assassin hired to take these targets out? Max is framed in shadow as he sits at a booth table in the club's private room. After being furiously reprimanded, Max looks at the ground for a moment. The viewer is lead to believe that Max is experiencing a deep sense of guilt and shame here, and is perhaps even at risk of breaking the charade. But, instead, Max summons up his courage and immerses himself further into Vincent's persona. He meets Felix's gaze directly and sternly responds: 'I think you should tell that guy behind me to put that gun down.' Mann cuts to a reverse angle, framed behind Max's head, with Felix sitting in the middle ground of the frame, as a shocked Felix retorts: 'What did you say?' Felix drifts out of focus as Max turns around, so his face becomes fully bathed in darkness, and he snarls, 'I said you should tell that guy to put his gun down before I beat his bitch-ass to death with it.' The fact that Max's face lapses in and out of shadow throughout their dialogue underlines the porous boundary between the persona of hardened outlaw and the persona of law-abiding citizen. Max can effortlessly slip between the two modes and convince those around him that he is a seasoned hitman.

Max stuns Felix with his hardened demeanour as he effortlessly takes control of the situation. Max first lies to Felix about how the list went missing, claiming that he was forced to ditch the document quickly or else he – and Felix's entire operation were going to get rumbled. He then re-appropriates a speech given to him by Vincent earlier in the narrative about the importance of contingency and flexibility. 'Shit happens. You've gotta roll with it. Adapt,' says Max, with total self-assurance. Earlier, Max managed to stand up to others by repeating the words fed to him by Vincent; here, Max and Vincent seem to have merged into one, with Max adopting a performative role built from his observations of Vincent's beliefs and mannerisms. Although Max's intense confidence in this scene is largely the result of him adopting the persona of somebody more assertive than he is, he also demonstrates remarkable self-assertion and quick-thinking in his own right- and he does so without Vincent directly giving him instructions.

Tensions come to a head at the Fever nightclub, the site of Vincent's third hit and the feature's central action set-piece. Mann signals the significance of this incident through the cross-cutting of Max and Vincent in the cab and a group of LAPD officers lead by Detective Ray Fanning (Mark Ruffalo), all heading toward the same location. The LAPD have, up until this point, been several steps behind Vincent, always arriving at crime scenes after his targets have already been killed and tasked with to piecing together events in retrospect. Here, for the first time, Mann shows us Fanning's progress at the same time as he shows us the actions of Vincent and Max, and, for once, the viewer is lead to believe that Vincent may be stopped before he has a chance to go through with the murder. Ironically, the definitive piece of evidence linking the taxi to the series of assassinations is the surveillance footage obtained by the LAPD from the surveillance cameras positioned outside of Felix's club. Because of this, they have gotten Max and Vincent's identities confused, mistakenly believing that Max is the murderer and Vincent is a mere accomplice. Only Fanning, acting on sheer intuition, has an inkling that Max is not actually the driving force behind the string of crimes.

The resulting shoot-out at Fever marks the film's most erratic and disorientating sequence of violence. In stark contrast to the experience of watching the smooth, brisk murders of Vincent's earlier targets, it is difficult to keep track of the central players as they wade through the bustling dance floor, each driven by a different motivation: Fanning is trying to apprehend Vincent and escort Max out of the club safely; the other members of the LAPD are, conversely, trying to capture Max, dead or alive; Vincent is trying to take out his mark, evade Felix's henchmen, and fight off the cops; and Felix's henchmen are trying to kill Vincent, Max and the cops. The darkened interior, the loud music, the mass of indistinct swaying bodies that fill every frame, and the multitude of digital video monitors around the club, purposefully confuse our sense of time and space. Identities, motivations and allegiances are blurred as the dance floor descends into violent chaos. Within this disorientating environment, only Fanning and Vincent are able to retain some degree of rational control over their actions. While Max, the cops and the various henchmen of Felix's stumble around helplessly, Fanning makes a beeline towards the cab driver, calmly explaining to him that he believes he has suffered from a case of mistaken identity, before leading him toward the exit. The more agile and combat-ready Vincent manages to evade the multiple individuals attempting to take him out, clear the floor to the point that he can get a clear view of his third victim, and then shoot the mark twice in the centre of his forehead. After completing this swift and effortless kill, Vincent turns his attention to Max. Spotting Fanning escorting Max off the premises, Vincent mistakenly believes he is being arrested and is in need of rescuing. Vincent and Fanning appear in this sequence as equal but opposite forces, both vying for control of the pliable Max. And Vincent becomes the victor. Immediately after Fanning and Max leave the club, Vincent fatally wounds Fanning, leaving Max shocked and distraught. That Vincent chooses not to shoot Max too shows the extent to which he has developed a feeling of attachment to the taxi driver. After all, from a practical perspective, it would have made sense for Vincent to kill

Max as well as Fanning. The cops are clearly aware that Max is in some way connected to the previous murders, and, so they have, in all likelihood, already linked the licence plate of the taxi to the crime spree. The sense of closeness that Vincent is starting to feel toward Max is also evidenced by his faith that Max wasn't the one who informed the police of their whereabouts – he doesn't even question Max about this, he just instinctively believes that the cabbie wouldn't betray him.

Unfortunately for Vincent, however, this is the point at which Max begins to pry himself away from the hitman's influence and exert control over the situation himself. As they flee the scene, Vincent, riding in the backseat of the cab, expresses his disappointment in Max's supposed lack of appreciation: 'You're alive. I saved you. Do I get any thanks?' It seems that seeing a decent man like Fanning murdered in a senseless, spur-of-the-moment decision is the final straw for Max. As Max points out, the after-effects of the murder are likely to extend far beyond Fanning himself; he probably has 'family, kids that are going to grow up without him.' Vincent's murder of him was so offhand and so thoughtless he doesn't even recall the cop's name. When Vincent, in response, tells Max that 'We're both in this together', Max truly realises that he has become a willing participant in the hitman's repulsive actions. This abrupt shift in Max's attitude is also, in part, due to his awareness that the LAPD will be powerless in stopping Vincent's wave of destruction. If Fanning is positioned, in the Fever nightclub sequence, as the closest figure in the film to a traditional hero, then his sudden and unceremonious murder at the hands of Vincent results in the removal of any clear moral centre for the action. It becomes Max's duty to fill this void and become a force of moral order.

During this sequence, Max also recognises the fundamental lack of consistency in Vincent's philosophy of life. As Max says to Vincent, if life is fundamentally meaningless, then 'there is no good reason, there's no bad reason, to live or to die [...] The cop, you, me. Who notices?' Yet, if Vincent truly believes this, then it makes no sense that he would choose not to murder Max at the same time that he murdered Fanning. Max deduces that Vincent has, in fact, broken his own code of professional conduct by developing feelings of affection toward his driver (even though, as mentioned earlier in this chapter, this affection is rooted in self-interest to a certain extent, it still suggests that Vincent longs for human connection on some level). To test his hypothesis, Max puts both of their lives in danger, ramping up the acceleration and recklessly speeding through the streets of the city. Mockingly telling Vincent that if nothing has any value, he should be able to do anything without fear of consequence, Max steers randomly from side to side, powers through red lights, and repeatedly places the vehicle in the path of upcoming traffic. Seeing that his life is in danger, Vincent's composed demeanour collapses, and he begs Max to slow down.

Vincent is clearly in fear of dying in the back of the cab, yet he still cannot bring himself to harm Max. Even after he brandishes his gun and performatively aims it toward the back of his driver's head, Vincent cannot summon the strength to pull the trigger. The fear that Vincent expresses her, coupled with his continued reluctance to kill Max, even though doing so would easily assuage this fear, contradicts his stated belief that he places no value on his own life or on the lives of anybody around him. Seeing this, Max accurately deduces that Max's claim that all human life is insignificant is, first and foremost, his way of avoiding having to feel guilt for the atrocities he commits. As Max comes to this realisation, he no longer views Vincent as a figure of authority and he gains the willpower necessary to resist the hitman's demands.

Max, sensing that Vincent is thoroughly disempowered at this moment, juts the steering wheel far to the right. The vehicle crashes and turns over on the side of the road. While Vincent calmly slips out of the passenger window and runs into the night, Max is left standing by the wrecked vehicle; disorientated and barely coherent. He is unable to defend himself when a cop arrives at the scene and spots the corpse in Max's trunk. This results in yet another case of mistaken identity, as Max's impulsive action to prevent further loss of life leads him to be falsely blamed for Vincent's murders. And, at first, Max is willing to submit to the whims of the cop, obediently following his orders to kneel on the ground and place his hands behind his head. But when Max spots Annie's photo inside the cab, labelled as Vincent's fifth target, he summons the courage to break away from the officer. The LAPD have failed time and time again; it is now up to Max to take matters into his own hands and provide protection for the innocent that they are clearly incapable of providing. Max forcibly overpowers the cop, wrestles him to the ground, handcuffs him to the vehicle and, finally, steals his weapon. Whereas, in the club scene, Max was subservient to Fanning, , a figure who proved tragically insufficient in stopping Vincent, here he recognises the officer's shortcomings and takes charge of the situation himself.

Notably, Max undertakes the journey to rescue Annie on foot, abandoning the taxicab that has long served to insulate him from the perils of the city and, thus, from direct engagement with the outside world. Max makes it to the exterior of Annie's office block and spots her through the 16th floor window. Max attempts to call her, but she is too engrossed in paperwork to acknowledge her phone ringing. This leaves her a sitting duck as Vincent swiftly walks past security and up the elevator. After a few attempts to get through to her, Annie finally answers her cell, and Max attempts to warn her of the encroaching danger. At first, Max tries to move Annie out of the line of fire by giving her directions, watching her through a plane of glass. Max has spent his entire adult life viewing world through a layer of disconnect, symbolised by the windows which place a physical barrier between himself and the external world when he's driving his cab and by the transparent screen which separates him from his customers. When Max notices that Vincent is on the floor below and Annie seems to be trapped, Max must physically cross this barrier and take control of events. Max no longer appears to be subordinate to Vincent; the two men are positioned as forces on an equal footing.

Although Max and Vincent become equal opponents in this final sequence, it must be noted that Max is only capable of protecting Annie using the skills he has picked up from his time with Vincent – wielding a firearm to break through the building's security doors, scoping out the facility to determine where Annie and Vincent are in relation to one another, etc. Thus, Max has transformed from a passive observer to an active hero, and though Vincent has provided him with valuable advice on how to make this change, Max is driven by an antithetical motivation to his – to safeguard life rather than to snuff it out. This character transformation is the culmination of a long and challenging process. The self-assertion exhibited by Max when he insulted his boss and bested Felix in a battle of wits was only possible because he was directly role-playing as Vincent. However, here he draws upon the assassin's admirable qualities while using them to prevent him from carrying out his professional mission. In the office building, Max shoots Vincent to prevent him from attacking Annie – the wound he inflicts is not fatal, but it is the first act of violence committed by Max in the film, signalling that he is now willing to overcome his aversion to conflict and commit to resolute action.

Collateral's finale serves as an ironic call-back to Vincent's anecdote about the deceased commuter who circled the city by train for hours before any other of the travellers noticed that he wasn't breathing. Vincent follows Max into a carriage of an above-ground passenger train, where he is fatally shot by his former driver. With a note of amusement in his voice, Vincent reminds Max of the story he regaled to him when they first met: 'Hey Max. Guy gets on the MTA here in LA, and dies.' But, then, the amusement fades from his voice as he asks Max, with a sense of genuine fear, 'Think anybody will notice?' The question reveals not only Vincent's feeling of dread as he passes out of existence but also the lack of confidence Vincent truly has in the nihilistic philosophy he espouses. He previously used the anecdote as evidence of the lack of interest that all inhabitants of the city take in the lives of others. Like McCauley, he has followed his professional path to his bitter end, and can take some degree of pride in his steadfast refusal to become acquiescent to anybody else. Yet, as he faces the prospect of eternal emptiness, he is scared of the possibility that nobody on earth will remember him. Despite the immorality of Vincent's earlier behaviour, and despite all the torment that he has put Max through, Max has enough empathy to sit down in the seat opposite and offer him a degree of comfort as he fades out of consciousness. Telling Vincent that they're 'almost at the next stop', Max fulfils Vincent's need for companionship in his final minutes on earth. As with Hanna's murder of McCauley, there is no sense of joy or catharsis when Vincent is killed. As Luis M Garcia-Mainar notes, Mann's framing of the events leaves the viewer feeling the same sensation of sorrow that Max does: '[Vincent's] punishment is not completely welcomed by viewers because Max's transformation, which makes that cultural pleasure possible at the end, is presented as the result of a process for which we actually consider Vincent responsible. Vincent's presence is thus too visible at the end for the viewer not to regret, at the same time as cheer, his death.' (2008).

Max demonstrates an awareness that the rhythms of the city will continue as usual, unaltered by the absence of Vincent. As Robert Arnett argues, at the end of *Collateral*, the 'heroes do not win their confrontations with the modern urban spaces, non-place triumphs over place […], they do not effect any change and only preserve the hegemony of non-place and supermodernity.' (2009: 52). However, Max's final gesture of tenderness illustrates the importance of seeking out emotional connections with others within these spaces, even if these connections are only fleeting. The ending of *Collateral* is, therefore, bittersweet. Vincent dies while locking eyes with the one person who will lament his passing, and, despite his acknowledgement that Vincent's project is immoral, Max genuinely appears to be saddened by the loss of a man he has shared such a singular experience with. Yet, this moment of mourning must, by necessity, be short-lived. Max knows that he must swiftly flee the scene and move onwards. And so he leads Annie off the train at the next station, wrapping her in his coat. Yet, instead of focusing on Max's victory, Mann's camera is drawn back to Vincent. As Max and Annie walk away into the labyrinthine streets of LA, Mann cuts back to the deceased hitman, drifting through the cityscape on the train carriage. He is framed in the background of a wide shot, several rows of seats obscuring him from our view. As he sits, lifeless and propped up against the back of his seat, we view him as any passing passenger would: small, distant, virtually indistinguishable from any other commuter Mann then cuts to a wide view of the train running along a bend in the track, bordered by power lines. The cart will circle endlessly, a permanent component of the lifeblood of Los Angeles, just as the electrical current is. The hyper-accelerated pace of the city will not slow down in response to this loss of life – only Max, the one individual Vincent has left an indelible mark on, will feel the true weight of his absence.

Ashes of Time:
Miami Vice (2006)

Mann opens *Miami Vice*, his 2006 reboot of the crime procedural series, with a black screen, over which the opening bars of Jay Z and Linkin Park's 'Numb/Encore' plays; then, as the beat drops, the film smash cuts to an image of a lithe female dancer moving against an abstract field of digital noise. The dancer, wearing a full-body suit, appears as a silhouette. The composition is dominated by computer-generated explosions of magenta and cobalt, expanding and decompressing, rapidly changing shape and hue, like an action painting in motion. The next shot helps to clarify what we're seeing: a handheld camera pans slowly down the dancer's body, revealing the edge of the LED screen which displays the digital light show before coming to rest (briefly) on a DJ platform stationed underneath – the source of the scene's diegetic music. A wide shot follows: the dancer is now positioned in the middle ground of the image, surrounded by a small crowd of bodies swaying to the music. In the foreground are Miami Dade officers Ricardo Tubbs and Sonny Crockett, framed from the back and the neck-up, their attention directed toward something that lies off-screen. The camera rotates around them to reveal fellow cop Trudy Joplin (Naomie Harris), also on the lookout, who comes to be framed in profile close-up. Mann then cuts to a frontal, close-up, two-shot of Joplin and Crockett, their faces obscured by the motion of an out-of-focus element in the foreground. Next, an off-kilter two-shot of Crockett and Tubbs. Tubbs is in the extreme foreground, pushed to the right of the screen, and Crockett is framed behind him, just to the left of centre. Finally, Mann gives us a point-of-view shot from the perspective of the lead characters, but it obfuscates more than it clarifies: adopting Crockett's sightline, the camera whip-pans across the entire length of the club, filling the screen with the bodies of the swaying bodies of the dancers. There is no indication of what Crockett – and, by extension, the viewer – is supposed to be looking for.

This disorientating sequence plunges the viewer into the deep end of Mann's vision, establishing a propulsive sense of rhythm that the rest of the feature will not let up on. The rapid and fragmented editing unmoors the viewer of any clear point of identification, and it is difficult to piece together what we're witnessing in narrative terms. Like the deliberately disorientating Fever nightclub scene from *Collateral*, Mann rapidly alternates between several points of action happening concurrently: Crockett, Tubbs and Joplin watch over the dance floor; Detective Zito (Justin Theroux) monitors a bedroom in the back of the club through a surveillance feed; Detective Calabrese (Elizabeth Rodriguez) blends into the crowd on the main floor, stationed closer to the entrance; Detective Switek (Domenick Lombardozzi) negotiates the procurement of escorts from the Haitian pimp Neptune (Isaach De Bankolé). This is not explained through dialogue or conventionally constructed dramatic scenes. The various officers are first shown operating in different parts of the club, focused on their own individual activities. The viewer must actively piece together these fragments to gather that all of these characters are working in tandem as part of a sting operation, with the collective aim of gathering information on a vast, transitional sex trafficking network. The pulsating soundtrack – which transitions mid-scene to a remix of Nina Simone's 'Sinnerman' – drowns out much of the speech, the dim lighting obscures several points of action, and the continuous fluctuations of the electronic displays disorientate our sense of space.

In marked contrast to the tone of the original show, the officers in *Miami Vice* take little pleasure in their work; even though they are skilled at and committed to their chosen profession, the Sisyphean nature of police work constantly leaves them feeling frustrated and disappointed. Even when they complete a case, there is no real sense of satisfaction; they know that the criminal sphere of Miami is so expansive that it can never be brought down entirely. The serialised structure of the show *Miami Vice* hints at the repetitious nature of police work, but at the end of each episode (and each case), Crockett and Tubbs are allowed to feel a sense of catharsis; on the other hand, in the film, the cops are constantly troubled by a sensation of hopelessness. When Tubbs' wife Joplin lies in a coma, he voices his anger over the possibility that she will lose her life over what he describes as 'this bullshit line of work.' In Tubbs' view, the work is 'bullshit' because it is never-ending; the criminal underworld will keep recruiting members, developing their methods, and adapting to the new technological and strategic advances made by the police. As Ignatiy Vishnevetsky observes, Mann's film paints an unromantic portrait of police work in which 'characters exist within an endless cycle of informants and moles, takedowns and retributions, seizures and countermeasures.' (2013). Not every citizen of Miami can be safeguarded, and the sense of devastation they feel over those they fail to save will always take precedence over their sense of satisfaction over those they can protect.

The first act of *Miami Vice*, in fact, sees the central pair repeatedly fail to prevent catastrophe. The first instance of this is Tubbs' aborted effort to rescue one of the women embroiled in Neptune's sex trafficking ring. The woman, referred to only as No 3, appears to be in distress when Neptune brings her, along with two other escorts, into the club. Switek picks up on this, asking Neptune 'What's wrong with No 3?' To which Neptune responds disingenuously: 'She's sick, man.' Switek leads the other two women towards a backroom, and Neptune glares at No 3 with rage in his eyes before asking his bodyguard to force her out of the club. Despite expressing his anxiety over the young woman's fate, Tubbs is not allowed to chase Neptune out of the space. To leave the club interior would be to compromise the pre-organised sting operation and, as Crockett explains when he catches up with his partner, taking down a single pimp will, in the grand scheme, be less valuable to the team than extracting information about the entire trafficking ring from the women in the backroom. As this opening indicates, the portrayal of police work in *Miami Vice* is far from idyllic; Tubbs must abandon his quest to save somebody in obvious mental and emotional turmoil because the bureaucratic nature of the police force demands that he must work within particular, strictly delineated boundaries. While Tubbs may have been motivated to join the organisation by a genuine desire to help the vulnerable, the practical demands of the job force him to let a violent abuser walk free so that an ongoing case doesn't become jeopardised.

Just as the central characters and their goals are resolving into focus the narrative of *Miami Vice* abruptly veers off in a different direction. Crockett gets an urgent call from Alonzo Stevens (John Hawkes), a police informant who Crockett and Tubbs turned over to the FBI several months previously. Stressing that the issue must be dealt with immediately, Stevens convinces Crockett to disengage from the sting operation at the club. Crockett moves from the constricted space of the club interior to the balcony, where he is cast against an overcast night sky tinted a luminous shade of purple, with pinpricks of artificial light emanating from the city's skyscrapers and office blocks stretching behind him into the far distance. Shots of Crockett framed in front of the immense Miami skyline are intercut with wide tracking shots showing Stevens' car speeding through the highways of the city as he frantically explains the unenviable situation that he's been thrust into: FBI agent John Fujima (Ciarán Hinds) used Stevens to set up a drug transfer been several high-ranking members of the Aryan Brotherhood and a team of undercover agents. However, at some point in the lead-up to the transfer, a Columbian cartel leader found out about Stevens' connection to the FBI. The cartel kidnapped his wife Leonetta and threatened to kill her with a C-4 necklace bomb unless he divulged the names of all the FBI agents working on the case. Stevens caved under pressure and provided the cartel with the information they requested. Now, Stevens is planning to pick up Leonetta so they can both flee the city together – he is terrified of facing further repercussions from the cartel, the Aryan brotherhood, and/or the FBI.

Hearing this, Crockett and Tubbs alert the rest of the team that they have to cancel the sting operation at the club to deal with the botched FBI transfer. The remainder of the film focuses on the fallout from Stevens' decision and the transnational drug trade and the sex trafficking ring and Neptune's place within it are dropped instantly and are not referred to again. Crockett calls Fujima's department to inform him about the complications, and although Fujima is cooperative to a certain degree, he refuses to divulge vital details about the upcoming deal. Because Crockett and Tubbs are not given access to all the information they request, they are powerless to stop the planned drug bust from spinning out of control. The key members of the Aryan Brotherhood meet with the undercover FBI officers in a parking lot positioned underneath an overground railroad track. At first, the meeting seems to go according to plan, with the dealers checking a satchel of money provided by the agents and declaring it to be legitimate. The lead dealer tells them that one of his associates will call them the following day to arrange, in detail, the time and place for the transfer. After both parties have re-entered their vehicles, the Brotherhood member abruptly turns back and asks, 'My brother, how long have you been working with the FBI?' Gunfire erupts on both sides, but only the FBI agents are terminally injured. The dealers seize the bag of money and flee the scene. Just as Tubbs and Crockett were unable to stop the further victimisation of No 3 at the hands of Neptune, they are here incapable of preventing the meeting from descending into carnage.

Crockett and Tubbs eventually catch up with Stevens and pull him over by the side of the freeway. The informant is a bundle of nerves. Stevens' erratic demeanour and clipped, stuttering speech indicate that he is desperate to escape the scene as fast as possible, but Tubbs pleads with him to stay put until they can put together a clearer overview of the situation. Stevens repeatedly yells that he's 'got to go home' and moves towards his vehicle, but Tubbs keeps him in place by assuring him that the FBI has already sent in agents to ensure Leonetta's safety. After Tubbs has said this,

Mann cuts to a silent shot of Stevens' beach house – a sizeable modernist structure with a sterile white colour scheme. Mann captures the image from a low angle, yet the walls of the house extend beyond the boundaries of the frame from all angles. The SWAT members seem dwarfed by the environment, appearing small and impotent within the composition. This, combined with Mann's decision to drain the image of sound (especially jarring in contrast to the cacophonic ambient sounds of the traffic on the highway), lends the shot a disquieting quality. The viewer instantly intuits that the feds are too late, and the damage has already been done. Mann cuts back to the argument taking place on the side of the road as an increasingly volatile Stevens again attempts to pull away Crockett and Tubbs, only calming down (slightly) when Tubbs takes out his phone to call the household. Mann then cuts to a brisk series of images which briskly communicates to the viewer all they need to know about Leonetta's tragic fate: a side view of the Stevens' home, with a pair of legs steeped in a pool of blood visible through a living room window, the upper half of the body covered by a curtain; a dejected agent inside the home, her gun lowered and her gaze directed toward the ground, speaking grimly into her monitor. Again, these shots are silent. The scene then returns to Tubbs on the phone call. He listens to the information fed to him (we do not hear the voice of the speaker on the other line), then sighs heavily and hangs up. Mann cuts to a brief reaction shot of Stevens' anguished face, and then back to a reverse angle on Tubbs as he tells him, euphemistically: 'You don't need to go home.'

The camera now adopts Stevens' perspective as he directs his attention first to Crockett, then to Rico, then to the highway. Mann racks focus so that so detectives become blurred as the road shifts into focus, visually articulating Stevens' emotional state as he realises the institution that promised to protect him has failed in the most catastrophic way possible. Feeling completely alone, Stevens decides that only death can end his unendurable torment. As the sound of an upcoming semi-truck enters the soundscape, Stevens steps into the centre of the road. Crockett rushes after him but stops as the truck passes right in front of his path. Crockett and Tubbs can only watch hopelessly as the vehicle speeds past them, a faint trail of blood spilling out from underneath its carriage. Just as Crockett and Tubbs lost control of the sting operation in the nightclub, here they lose control over the tragedy which befalls the Stevens family. The pair have attempted to protect life, but, in both cases, they prove insufficient.

This sequence of events unfolds over the first 15 minutes of *Miami Vice* and announces that Mann's feature will be a significantly different beast from its televisual predecessor – tonally, formally, narratively, and thematically. While the series became iconic for its garish clothing, pastel colour scheme, poppy visual style, and seductive depiction of wealthy lifestyles, the movie has a solemn atmosphere. *Miami Vice,* the series, is structured around a dichotomy between the luxury of Miami's surface streets and the barbarity of its criminal underside; in the movie, the two sides have blurred together to the point that they are inseparable. The lead characters struggle to find genuine contentment, either from their relationships with each other or from their work; the landscape of the city appears cold and hostile to the humans residing within it; and there is no respite from the constant grind of thankless police work. The only real points of connection between the reboot and its source material are the central location (though portrayed in a vastly different light) and the basic narrative concept (the perilous exploits of a police force based in Miami tackling mostly drug-related criminal enterprise by the shore). Though the protagonists of the film share their names with the characters from the original series, their personalities have been altered so much it is difficult to spot much correspondence between them. Unlike many reboots of '80s television series produced around the same time, *Miami Vice* is neither an exercise in nostalgia (like Todd Phillips' *Starsky and Hutch* (2004) and Jay Chandrasekhar's *The Dukes of Hazzard* (2005)) nor a tongue-in-cheek pastiche (like Phil Lord and Chris Miller's *21 Jump Street* (2014) and Seth Gordon's *Baywatch* (2017)), but a qualitatively new project that draws on a pre-existing model to update it for a new era. As Jean-Baptiste Thoret writes in his outstanding *Senses of Cinema* essay on the film, *Miami Vice* revitalises the broad framework of the show to reflect a 'post-urban (and post-human) world', a world that is 'fragmented and controlled', held together 'only by the financial flux that crosses it and the electronic images (surveillance cameras, radars, computer screens, etc) recreating the simulacrum.' Within this environment, 'there is no other logic than that of offer and demand, of movement in all directions imposed by economic private interests', and the overall effect is the impression of 'paradoxical movement: illusion of speed (or rather haste) but effect of being stuck.' (2007).

A large part of the radical aesthetic difference between the original series and the reboot is a due to Mann's virtuoso use of digital cinematography. As Blake Howard observes, 'the formal style of the film contends with the narrative and subverts the traditional espionage and action narrative models through a less classical form and perspective.' (2014). Building on the experimentation with digital technology conducted during the production of *Collateral,* Mann here connects his fascination with the aesthetic qualities of the form with his thematic preoccupation with post-industrialisation, surveillance culture, the de-materialisation of labour, and the rise of expansive communication networks. To elucidate Mann's treatment of these themes in *Miami Vice,* it is helpful to consider the essential material difference between digital and analogue forms of image production. Analogue filmmaking is based on a process of physically imprinting light values onto a fixed photo-sensitive chemical frame in the form of silver-halide crystals. Though an image captured with an analogue apparatus may certainly be abstract or impressionistic, it creates an isomorphic material link between the pro-filmic event that occurred before the lens and the resulting cinematic representation of that event. In contrast, the digital apparatus transforms light input into binary code – a series of mathematical data stored in a hard drive. While photographic recording produces a concrete physical record, digital images are disconnected from the real, existing as computerised abstractions with no indexical link to the pro-filmic. The digital is, therefore, a medium inherently based on abstraction and algorithmic calculation.

The curious double logic of digital imagery exists in its ability to at once register verisimilitude (due to its easy portability, its association with consumer-grade image-making practices, and its ability to capture images in low-lighting conditions) and its ability to be hyper-real (due to the ease of manipulating digital footage and of building complex CGI creations with incredible nuance). In *Miami Vice*, Mann draws on both aspects of digital imaging simultaneously. The use of digital recording equipment enabled Mann to bring his cameras in close proximity to his actors and to capture the Miami landscape with a minimal amount of artificial lighting. Though most studio features are now shot, edited and distributed using digital technology in the, in 2006, the format was primarily associated with news reportage and amateur filmmaking practices. *Miami Vice* was one of the first big-budget Hollywood features to pioneer the use of digital, and Mann chose to foreground the formal characteristics of the new technology which render it distinctive from photochemical film, rather than effacing them. The landscapes of Miami appear breathtakingly tactile and lived-in. Mann utilises the mighty light-capturing power of digital video to mount stunning deep-focus images of the city. Recurring shots of the Miami skyline are particularly awe-inspiring – every nuance of the clouds which hang overhead can be clearly perceived. The combat scenes are shot with an extremely close proximity to the action, every gunshot and smashed window registering with a real jolt. The handheld cameras feel more unmoored and spontaneous than in any other Mann project.

At the same time, *Miami Vice* does not aspire to documentary-like realism. Mann's aesthetic design captures fragments of the real yet simultaneously renders them impressionistic – through the elliptical and fragmented nature of his montage, through key moments which obscure the action through shadow, through the relentless speed of the camera. As Calum Marsh observes, 'The camera at once takes in more – more detail, more light, more of the city at night – and does more with it, the image somehow, as Beebe says, "otherworldly," remarkably clear and yet seemingly blurred with the texture of digital noise.' (2013). The deep-focus lenses applied to Mann's digital cameras subtly distorts the feature's sense of space, making everyday spaces appear cavernous. Rather than working around the graphic glitches produced by the apparatus, Mann embraces them to create painterly effects: colours smear together, bright lights are blown-out, familiar elements are rendered abstract. Aside from Crockett and Isabella's trip to Havana, the extreme pace of *Miami Vice* does not let up. The viewer is constantly bombarded with information as the rhythms of the plot accelerate, side characters are introduced and unceremoniously dropped, and ostensibly diametrically opposed categories blend together professional/personal, interior/exterior, artificial/natural.

Images collapse into one another through the hyper-rapid montage, just as identities and cultural boundaries do, and the individual struggles to remain afloat within the flux of information and capital just as they struggle to stay in the centre of Mann's compositions. The sensation of becoming subsumed by a 'cruel technological present', which Sharrett identifies as a central subject in Mann's oeuvre, is reinforced here through Mann's emphasis on the immateriality of the digital image (2002: 255). Crockett is adrift within the cruel forces of a hyper-technological present and consumed by a vague longing for a lost era in American history. Crockett may try to savour pockets of snatched time, brief reprises from the flux, but they inevitably disappear, dissipating and fragmenting like Mann's pixels, which swirl around an immaterial void, constantly breaking down and recombining to form new images.

On an aesthetic and a narrative level, then, *Miami Vice* fulfils what Sharrett describes as Mann's ongoing quest to 'encourage [...] the critical faculties of the audience, and look beneath the façade of the existing order of things.' (2002: 262). The world of *Miami Vice* is defined by porousness: of borders (characters cross from Miami to Columbia to Cuba in the blink of an eye), of spaces (all private spaces in the film are designed with large windows which blur the boundary between inside and outside) and of identities (the entire plot hinges on Crockett and Tubbs successfully performing their undercover personas as drug transporters for kingpin Arcángel de Jesús Montoya (Luis Tosar)). This task fundamentally warps their sense of what is authentic and what is not, or, as Tubbs eloquently phrases it near the end of the narrative: 'Fabricated reality and what's really up collapse into one frame.' As Mann explained during an on-set interview with *Empire Magazine*, one of his primary ambitions with the feature was to truly explore the sense of uncertainty that officers experience when immersed in an undercover investigation: 'I did some research into what people really do when they go undercover at a very high level. I realised that the show never really captured that, and nobody else has really dealt with it. It's very, very dangerous, very extreme. These guys fabricate an identity which is a projection of the self, very much like acting – only instead of getting reviews, you can get dead. It explores what happens when you go undercover so deeply in a fabricated identity that it becomes more real than who you started out being.' (Pelan, 2019).

The drug traffickers under investigation *Miami Vice* are part of a vast network that is just as omnipresent and technologically advanced as that of the law enforcers. Many members of Montoya's transatlantic drug ring take on bureaucratic roles- monitoring surveillance feeds, scanning computerised databases, researching potential new clients and collaborators, and tracking fluctuations in the stock market. The money generated by such work provides no joy; the dealers engage in these intricate procedures out of compulsion, just as their counterparts in the police force do, and are similarly troubled by the relentless pressure and never-ending nature of their work. The material trappings of affluence that appear alluring in the series – fast yachts, limousines, flashy suits and chintzy jewellery – are here reconfigured to serve as reminders of the suffocating artifice that characterises life in LA. For example, police informant Nicholas (Eddie Marsan) resides in an elegant, open-plan bachelor pad suspended upon a breath-taking shoreline containing a private bar stacked with exotic liquors. In theory, this apartment should be an embodiment of the splendour enjoyed by the city's *nouveau riche*. Instead, the space is presented as a claustrophobic echo chamber of Nicholas' own neuroses. Its monolithic windows appear like panoptic prison walls through which one is always on display. Nicholas' anxiety stems, in large part, from his dual identity, as he is tied to both the cops *and* the criminals: his freedom from the penitentiary relies on his ability to play the 'role' of drug trafficker, so that he may feed the information to the cops. Though he lives in luxury, Joplin emphasises the precariousness of his position when the police pile pressure on him to make contact with high-ranking members of Montoya's drug ring, threatening to throw him back into jail unless he cooperates with their requests.

While the television versions of Crockett and Tubbs are charismatic, energetic and traditionally heroic, the 2006 iterations of the characters exhibit a sense of weariness, disillusionment, and dissatisfaction which aligns them more closely to later Mann protagonists like Hanna, McCauley, Graham and Vincent. Like these other characters, they are solitary figures deeply troubled by their inability to connect with the people around them, and they are fundamentally unable to reconcile the demands of their chosen profession with their desire to maintain a satisfying personal life. The romantic relationship that develops between Crockett and Isabella – Montoya's lover and business partner – symbolises a potential escape route from the unceasing pressure of work in the city, comparable to the liberating female presence of Eady in *Heat* and Jesse in *Thief*; however, unlike in those films, Isabella does not occupy a position outside the professional sphere. Instead, she is just as committed to her work as Crockett and Tubbs are, though she works within a professional sphere that is on the opposite side of the law to theirs. The romance between Crockett and Isabella, then, does not represent a clash between the a consummate professional and a romantic figure inextricably connected to the domestic sphere like in so many earlier Mann films, and is more aligned with the bond that builds between two kindred spirits working within (ostensibly) opposed lines of business that forms the structural foundation of *Heat*. And, like in *Heat*, their relationship is destined to fail, as each character ultimately proves to be too closely tied to their professional role to abandon it. The romance that blossoms between them powerfully encapsulates film's thematic emphasis on performance, shifting identities and the porous line that separates cop from criminal. Crockett and Isabella meet under false pretences, as Crockett is assuming the role of another, complete with a fake backstory, hobbies, and ambitions for the future. For most of their courtship, Crockett successfully performs this fabricated identity – in fact, Crockett exploits the emotional and physical bond between them by using it to become more heavily integrated into the upper echelons of Montoya's network.

But, despite the element of performance that their romance is founded upon, the relationship that blossoms between Crockett and Isabella is infused with more genuine depth of feeling than any of the trivial connections either of them has within their own professional/social sphere. In the world of *Miami Vice*, all professional roles rely on a substantial degree of deception. Every character feels the need to adhere to complex rules and expectations related to cultural and social expectations. Crockett and Tubbs express no real sense of camaraderie throughout the film and are never seen together outside the boundaries of work (the one-time Crockett enters Tubbs' home, it is to discuss their upcoming infiltration operation). Though there is no real tension or hostility between them, their exchanges tend to be brief and to-the-point: their conversation never strays away from the topic of the investigation, and Crockett never honestly confesses the extent of his attachment to Isabella to him.

In *Thief*, the mafia boss Leo holds an enormous power over the city, but his level of influence seems quaint and insignificant compared to Montoya's drug network. Montoya is not restricted by geographical location, has access to incredibly advanced technological means, and who presides over a surveillance system through which he monitors the actions of his expansive hierarchy of workers. Montoya not only operates drug and arms running missions across the United States, South America, Europe, and the Caribbean, he runs his loads through varied locales to make the movement of his shipments more difficult for law enforcers – and rival gangs – to track. And Montoya accomplishes this with an extreme level of protection, operating primarily from his home sited atop a clifftop in Brazil, within which he surveys a never-ending stream of digital data. Leo builds a personal relationship with Frank, but Montoya only has one in-person interaction with Crockett and Tubbs.

After José Yero (John Ortiz) – one of Montoya's most loyal henchmen – has approved their request to serve as traffickers in the network, Crockett and Tubbs are transported via a series of labyrinthine car journeys that bring them to an isolated car lot. They are then taken out by guards and guided to the interior of a plush black vehicle, identical to several other cars lined up in the lot. Their meeting is brief. Maintaining a calm, collected demeanour, Montoya explains that the meeting has no purpose other than to allow him a chance to see the men who will be moving his product face-to-face. 'When you work for me,' Montoya warns them, with an eerily stilted cadence, 'You must do exactly what you say you will do. In this business with me, I do not buy a service. I buy a result. If you say you will do a thing, you must do exactly that thing. And you will prosper beyond your dreams.' Even within the vehicle, Montoya has access to a wall of surveillance monitors, through which he can observe the actions of everybody in his chain of command. He stresses that, whether or not they accept his offer – transport 3 kilos of cocaine from Columbia to Miami in return for a cut of 3 million dollars – it is 'unlikely' that they will never see him again. The fact that statement is made in front of the wall of monitors illustrates Montoya's methods of retaining control over his underlings. He will not physically or verbally threaten them, but he will make them feel as though his omnipresent camera-eye is *always* watching them. When they are in the vicinity of Montoya's vehicle, Crockett notices that his phone signal has been blocked – he cannot make calls, and his GPS signal cannot be tracked. Astounded by the technological capabilities of Montoya's gang, Tubbs comments, 'This is the kind of stuff that the CIA does in Baghdad.' The cops have never before witnessed a drug-trafficking operation as complex and technologically advanced as Montoya's, and they are shocked to discover that they have access to information-gathering technologies that can rival those of their own department.

This meeting with Montoya recalls the scene in *Thief* in which Frank meets Leo for the first time by the water. Like that sequence, this scene introduces the film's primary antagonist and sets up the stakes of the Faustian bargain the protagonist(s) enter, which will eventually ensnare them and bring about their downfall. Unlike Leo, however, Montoya takes on a more spectral, abstract role in the narrative. Whereas Leo develops a close personal relationship with Frank – first lowering his defences by appearing as a paternal mentor figure, then turning into his tormentor – Montoya retains a strictly professional, hands-off relationship with Crockett and Tubbs. Montoya is similarly omnipresent throughout the remainder of the narrative, but his influence is mostly glimpsed indirectly, through the behaviour vast network of employees and the effects of his decisions, rather than directly, as an embodied villain. There is no moment in *Miami Vice* comparable to the scene in the earlier film where Leo explosively lambasts Frank in a boiler room. Montoya is a source of overwhelming threat, but this threat is only communicated by his power to control others – he always appears subdued and level-headed, never feeling the need to raise his voice or engage in physical combat.

And, unlike in *Thief*, there is no scene in which Montoya receives his comeuppance. Whereas Frank is granted a chance to exact violent revenge on the individual who caused him so much grief, , Montoya is so insulated from the real-world consequences of his decisions that he is not even present at the climactic shoot-out between Tubbs, Crockett, Yero and several of his henchmen. Crockett and Tubbs may dispatch of Yero at the end of the film, but Montoya remains unscathed, and his criminal enterprise remains as strong as ever. When the feds burst through the doors of Montoya's hideout in the final act, they find it empty. Montoya has fled to an unknown location – he has cut himself off from all attachments in order to evade capture, fulfilling McCauley's 'heat' mantra that so many Mannian criminals are too emotionally vulnerable to commit to. Mann does not show the moment at which Montoya decided to run, but we are left to infer that his vast information-gathering network has warned him that the feds are zeroing in on his hideout, and Montoya has reacted accordingly. He can leave his life behind at the drop of a hat because he truly has no emotional connections to anyone or anything around him – criminals like McCauley and Vincent claim to lead this type of lifestyle, but their ingrained longing for companionship leads them to seek out interpersonal relationships. This is not the case with Montoya. His criminal network extends beyond national borders, so he does not have to be fixed in one single location to keep it running smoothly – he can therefore flee his residence while still running the enterprise as efficiently as ever. Montoya is a perfect symbol of the new type of crime syndicate bound to the contemporary digitised network society: from the comfort of his mansion, he constantly taps into streams of information through surveillance monitors, news stations, and financial models, allowing him to see the impact of his actions while remaining fundamentally, materially, removed from the effects on the ground; he exploits the resources of the Third World, and he uses his henchmen to deal with any physical conflict so that he may keep his hands clean.

When they later meet with Fujima to inform him of their preliminary findings, they tell him that the FBI's intel on the drug trafficking situation in Miami barely scratches the surface of what the dealers are actually capable of. As Tubbs explains, Yero is not the head of the ring as they initially thought, he is merely 'middle-management, part of a bigger transnational operation'. Montoya runs drugs across Columbia, China, the United States and Brazil, using a complex system of money laundering networks. Crockett and Tubbs then renegotiate the objective of their mission. Their original goal was to infiltrate the gang to identify who was behind the initial data leak, but they now plead with Fujima to allow them to go undercover for longer, to fully 'illuminate Montoya's operations from the inside'. After some initial resistance, Fujima agrees. But Crockett and Tubbs' new mission is destined to fail: the contours of Montoya's network are so vast, so sprawling, that tackling it in its totality proves to be impossible.

The first task undertaken by Crockett and Tubbs in their new personas takes them to Ciudad del Este, used by the gang as a transitional space positioned between their larger bases in Brazil, Paraguay and Argentina. After having made initial contact with Yero, Crockett and Tubbs are given instructions to meet with him face-to-face in a darkened, underground warehouse. Yero is captured in the centre of the frame, surrounded by armed guards. He makes Crockett and Tubbs sit on much smaller chairs on the opposite side of a large desk, and Yero's guards form a wall behind them. The pressure on Crockett and Tubbs is intense. The guards scrutinise every nuance of their behaviour so that they may pounce if either man allows for the mask of their fabricated identity slip for even a second. The room is sparsely decorated, with minimalistic blue-and-white walls and dilapidated grey flooring. A small series of white lights from the ceiling create the only points of illumination, throwing down beams of bright light, like spotlights. The effect is to make the room resemble a theatre stage, thus underlining the sense of theatricality that characterises this exchange as the two cops slip into their criminal roles. Although Crockett and Tubbs don't arouse suspicion at first glance, it appears that they may crack under the pressure when Yero presses them for more information about their backgrounds and their relationship with one another. Crockett and Tubbs skilfully navigate this aggressive line of questioning. They first claim that they are too concerned about the privacy of those they work for to reveal any personal information about other jobs, and then go as far as to accuse Yero of incompetence due to his inability to conduct background research on them himself. Tubbs asserts his authority by stating, emphatically, 'we're not here to audition for business, business auditions for us.' Sensing that Yero has not quite been convinced yet, Tubbs ups the stakes by accusing *him* of potentially having ties to the federal government. Crockett leans over and frisks Yero, before upping the stakes by pulling out a grenade and placing it on the table. The sense of unease that permeated the scene until this point dissipates as Crockett and Tubbs forcefully take charge of the situation. Their ability to control this high-pressure and high-stakes interaction illustrates Crockett and Tubbs' impressive ability to adopt the personas of criminals and, through these personas, influence others. Crockett and Tubbs repeatedly abandoned and/or wrecked missions during the first act, but here they are adept at controlling the course of events so that they come out on top. It is ironic, then, that Crockett and Tubbs prove to be more effective when adopting criminal roles than they are when carrying out their duties as officers of the law. As Yero finds himself at a stalemate with Crockett and Tubbs, a third node of power is introduced: Isabella, previously unseen, is heard from off-screen, giving firm orders to Montoya's henchman.

Even at this early moment in the narrative, Isabella is positioned as being 'separate' from the other members of Montoya's organisation. She sits in the corner of the room, bathed in shadow, a distant observer watching over the actions of the other participants. As Yero's control over the situation rapidly breaks down, it is up to Isabella to redirect the conversation back to business matters. When Isabella verbally interjects, Mann cuts away from the table, disrupting the established visual rhythm of the scene. Crockett glances over at her, and his gaze lingers for a few moments after Tubbs and Yero have resumed talking. Although the pair haven't yet interacted directly, it appears as though, at this moment, Crockett instinctively recognises that she is a kindred spirit – an isolated soul who is embroiled within a professional position that suffocates her yet she is incapable of leaving. For a brief moment, the relentless pace of the narrative slows down, and Mann lingers on a silent exchange of yearning looks.

In an attempt to re-assert his authority after momentarily being intimated by Crockett and Tubbs, Yero warns them of the sophistication of the surveillance technology he has access to: 'I run security into counter-intel, I get people to tell me what they don't want to say. And I have eyes everywhere. A part of what I do, you never want to find out about. Other people negotiate money and go, or no go, yes, no, maybe so. Not me.' Like Montoya, Yero recognises that, in the digitised network society, knowledge is power, and so Yero lauds his control over Crockett and Tubs by making them aware of the vast nature of Montoya's surveillance system. Yero stresses that, if he agrees to hire Crockett and Tubbs, he is going to keep them in the dark regarding the minutiae of the enterprise's operations. As Yero explains, he prefers to give as few details as possible when he is working with transporters. He will give them a time and a place to pick up the goods that need to be transported, and a time and place to drop them off – in other words, he provides the dealers with only the basic information they need to achieve their single task and no more. They will not be told who is buying the goods, and they will not be told about the larger deals and ambitions of the operation. The meeting ends inconclusively. Yero tells Crockett and Tubbs to return to their hotel room. If they get a phone call, it means that he has decided to go into business with them. If they receive no further correspondence from him, they should 'piss off back to where [they] come from.'

Miami Vice thus reconfigures the theme of the individual versus the network that has preoccupied Mann since the early stages of his career.

What differentiates *Miami Vice* from Mann's earlier work is that the characters no longer even entertain the possibility that they can lead a life of crime off-the-grid, free from any professional ties which compromise the individual's autonomy. In *Thief*, Frank is pressured by circumstance to strike a deal with the local mafia boss and abandon his principles to become part of a larger crime syndicate. At the end of the feature, Frank is faced with a binary decision to either return to the life of the isolated criminal or to remain tied to the mafia. In *Miami Vice*, no such opposition exists; the characters either belong to the sphere of professional law enforcement or the elaborately orchestrated drug-running syndicate – a criminal organisation that is presented as being as bureaucratic, technocratic and intricately run as the police. Every romantic and otherwise personal relationship depicted in the film is connected to one of these two spheres. Whereas Neil McCauley's relationship with Eady in *Heat* represents a genuine respite from the overwhelming pressures of his profession, Crockett's affair with Isabella is intricately tied to his work – he meets her during his infiltration mission and repeatedly rationalises his decision to his colleagues by claiming that maintaining a close relationship with her is necessary to obtain vital information about Montoya. *Thief*, *Manhunter* and *Heat* demonstrate the danger that arises when private and public spaces between too deeply intertwined. In *Miami Vice*, all these elements interpenetrate to the point of being indistinguishable. The dominance of globalised systems of private capital and corporate power is a central theme in *The Insider*. In that earlier film the spheres of journalism, scientific research, the law, and politics are connected and are all subject to the demands of the nation's most financially powerful institution. Such is the power of a monolithic, multinational corporation that any individual who threatens to challenge its all-consuming influence is likely to become the victim of multiple intertwined branches of societal violence – financial ruin, media smear campaigns, and even incarceration.

In *Miami Vice*, the power of technologically advanced, enormously wealthy monopolies has grown even further. On the one side, there is the pervasive influence of the FBI, a huge organisation that operates an expansive surveillance system which infiltrates into every area of life in Miami, on the other side, the technocratic transnational criminal empire of Montoya. Every character is embroiled within one of these systems. There is no possibility of resisting these networks in *Miami Vice*, there is only the possibility of the crossing over from one to another. The network of law enforcement and the network of drug smuggling, therefore, exist in a symbiotic relationship, and no character feels as though they can escape from the system in any real, tangible sense. Thoret perceptively describes Montoya's operation as being 'a state-within-the-state equally at ease in the transfer of funds on a grand scale as in the clinical execution of offenders.'

(Thoret, 2007). Isabella emphasises the sheer magnitude of Montoya's operation when she warns Crockett that: 'All that you see around you belongs to Jesus Montoya'. The criminal lifestyle does not offer the characters a way to escape from the crushing mundanity of 'legitimate' forms of work, as in the classical crime film; it instead entraps the criminal within another monolithic organisation in which the individual holds no autonomy over their profession and is treated as merely another node in the chain of command. Whereas Frank wanders off into the great unknown at the end of *Thief*, alone but totally in charge of his destiny, Crockett must return to the crushing grind of his police work, becoming absorbed, once more, in the suffocating structures and overwhelming pressures that he had longed to flee. Isabella, suffers a similarly bleak fate. For them, there is no choice.

Miami Vice is, then, Mann's most pessimistic work since *Heat*. *The Insider* and *Ali* suggest that the individual can obtain a personal victory over the vast corporate powers which shape American society, and *Collateral* celebrates the nobility of an individual who demonstrates concern and compassion for others within the vast, hostile environment of the city; there is no sense of optimism at all in *Miami Vice*. The closest that Crockett comes to experiencing pure joy is during his impromptu trip to Havana with Isabella at the midpoint of the film. This ten-minute sojourn sees the couple momentarily leave the city and attempt to establish a counter space where their relationship may flourish. During this sequence, the temporality of the feature slows down, the characters share intimate details about their respective childhoods (even though Crockett is 'in character', the information he tells Isabella about his relationship with his family seems to be sincere) and engage in genuinely sensual and mutually satisfying moments of physical passion. Significantly, this trip is introduced visually with an image of Crockett and Isabella travelling into the horizon on a speedboat. The image is framed from the perspective of Yero watching the couple go, his head and shoulder occupying the right side of the frame as Mann racks focus to shift the central focal point of the shot from Yero to the ocean. As Rybin argues, Crockett's relationship with Isabella is driven by a mutual desire to reach 'a kind of utopian transcendence from the worlds they both inhabit.' (2013: 207). Although this image captures the sense of freedom felt by Crockett and Isabella , the dominance of Yero in the frame indicates, from the outset, that the utopia they are pursuing is fragile. This careerist henchmen's loyalty to his boss will later lead him to inform him of Isabella's infidelity, thus causing the dissolution of their relationship.

On the speedboat, Isabella defiantly asserts that her identity is not tied to her professional or romantic ties to Montoya: 'I never do business in Cuba. And Jesus is not my husband. I am a businesswoman. I do not need a husband to have a house to live in.' Crockett instructs Isabella to steer while he removes his jacket, and then he fastens her seatbelt. After this brief moment of physical contact, Mann cuts to a wide shot of the ocean, the horizon in view and no sign of land in frame, reducing the boat to a small element on the bottom of the frame as it powers forward toward the horizon. Moving from the intimate to the expansive, this series of images links Crockett and Isabella's burgeoning romance to the broader sense of liberation from their social and professional roles which both parties secretly long for. A subsequent tracking shot following the boat's motion from left to right – this shot transitions seamlessly into a slow pan of the Havana skyline, which comes to rest on a close-up of Crockett and Isabella sitting in a nightclub. Unlike in the opening club sequence, the integrity of the space is preserved here, the shots are longer and more graceful, and it is easier for the viewer to orientate themselves within spatial contours of the location.

As they sit in a small diner the following morning, Crockett states, bluntly: 'This is a bad idea. And it has no future.' After making this statement, however, Crockett falsely reassures himself by saying 'Then there's nothing to worry about.' They embrace, seemingly at peace with the fact that, because of Isabella's strong ties to Montoya (more professional than romantic), their relationship will be necessarily short-lived. Yet, Crockett appears troubled by this knowledge, as he glances off-screen, absorbed in his own thoughts, rather than meeting her gaze. And even within this quasi-reprieve, business matters arise. At one point, Crockett waits for Isabella in the shower. Isabella approaches framed behind tinted glass. She appears as an abstract shape, as if an ethereal presence. However, when she enters, the line of conversation brings the couple crashing back down to reality. Crockett tells Isabella that he and Tubbs want a larger cut of the money they make from the transfers, and they want to form a permanent partnership with Montoya's gang. They won't be middlemen anymore, he tells her they will be partners, or they'll walk away. She puts him down, 'Your ideas are too big for your skin, and merely to propose this is a dangerous thing.' They then alternate between kissing and negotiating monetary figures. As they speak, a large mirror behind them visually multiplies the couple within the composition, emphasising the split nature of Crockett, who is simultaneously expressing his true feelings for Isabella and maintaining the performative identity of the criminal. Knowing that if this façade drops, he is likely to place his and Tubbs' lives in danger, Crockett cannot fully lose himself in the moment; this is the closest thing that Crockett has experienced to a reciprocal, emotionally authentic connection with another individual, but, because of the nature of his operation, he is still plagued by a sense of self-consciousness and a need to perform which prevents him from completely giving himself over to Isabella.

Crockett's trip back to Miami via speedboat is captured in a wide tracking shot that mirrors the earlier speedboat sequence. However, this time, the horizon does not appear as a vast open field. Instead, a line of tall silver and chrome buildings are visible in the background, signalling a return to normality and a curtailing of Crockett's freedoms. When Crockett returns to the dock, he is met by a frustrated Tubbs, who reminds him that his allegiance to the police, and to the case, means that this fling with Isabella cannot be sustained for much longer. The ocean symbolises the possibility of escape, of the horizon of possibilities that exist at the city's margins, and it has an irresistible pull to those who feel alienated within the structures of Miami. But, Crockett cannot find it within himself to leave behind the urban space entirely. To leave requires a bold leap into the unknown, and Crockett ultimately retreats into the only lifestyle he is familiar with. If Tubbs is thoroughly integrated into the rhythms of the hyper-modern cityscape (which brings him some degree of security, though not real fulfilment), then Crockett must struggle to reconcile his burning desire to flee this landscape and his socially conditioned belief that true escape is impossible.

Tubbs and Joplin's marriage can remain afloat because they both commit fully to the demands of the police force, and willingly become cogs in the system. They are co-workers and spouses; their domestic space is also the site where they conduct meetings related to their cases. On the other hand, Crockett transgresses the demands placed on him by his profession by pursuing a romance with Montoya's partner. Although Crockett attempts to rationalise the decision by telling Tubbs that he is using the relationship to gain greater access to the upper echelon of the trafficking network, Tubbs recognises that Crockett's attraction to Isabella runs far deeper than that: 'There's undercover and there's which way is up.' It may be Montoya's henchmen who ultimately force the couple to split up, but Crockett also receives a significant degree of condemnation from his colleagues at the force. This level of judgement contributes massively to the pressure placed on the couple and causes a rift in his working relationship with Tubbs. Although Tubbs certainly has moments in which he expresses his dissatisfaction with his work, he has accepted his place within modern society and within the police force. Tubbs is so immersed in his role that he cannot even conceive how he may embark on a different, more fulfilling lifestyle. Trapped within an environment where interior and exterior spaces merge together, and the omniscient eye of the surveillance camera seems to penetrate every area, Crockett and Isabella struggle to find spaces in which they can express their mutual attraction without being spotted by their adversaries on either side of the law. After Isabella lands in Miami via private plane, she and Crockett enter the backseat of a limo; the windows are tilted so they are blocked from view from passing pedestrians, and a partition is erected between them and the driver. The two make love in the back of the vehicle, moving along the freeway, as the sights of the city roll past. The passing crowds cannot see the interior of the vehicle, but they can look out upon them. This potent image underlines the fragile nature of their romance, suspended as it is, on the thin line that separates public life from private life, performance and authenticity. The pair will soon prove to tragically incapable of navigating this risky terrain, and the relationship dissolves as a result. Crockett and Isabella go to a rendezvous spot in a nightclub, where they meet with members of her professional sphere (Yero) and of his (Tubbs and Joplin). After some preliminary business talk, Yero disappears into the backroom while the others remain on the main dance floor. Mann then reveals that there is a series of surveillance monitors in the backroom, relaying visual information from every inch of the club. Yero pays close attention to the feeds as Crockett and Isabella begin to dance passionately, unaware that they are being subjected to the gaze of the CCTV camera. This dance scene is staged in a similar manner to the earlier sequence in which the pair danced in Havana: they are framed in profile, in a series of shallow-focus handheld shots which alternate between medium-shot two shots and close-ups. But here, Mann intercuts their motion with ominous shots of eyes observing them carefully: Yero's first, and then Joplin's and Tubbs'. Although Isabella and Crockett pretend to share a platonic working relationship, Yero believes that Crockett and Isabella are expressing genuine ardour on the dance floor.

The intimacy the pair enjoyed in Havana cannot, therefore, be recreated in Miami. It collapses under the weight of the intense scrutiny the members of their respective professional groups place them under. Neither the criminals nor the law enforcers will allow Crockett and Isabella to cross professional boundaries and form a genuine relationship with somebody from the opposing social group. Crockett and Isabella then go for a walk on a concrete bridge by the sea. It's night. The artificial lights of the city recede into the distance behind them, throwing purple and red shades onto the surface of the water – thus signifying the corruption of the film's symbol of liberation by the intrusion of man-made elements. She tells him: 'Once I had a fortune. It said "live now, life is short, time is luck".' Placed at this late point in the narrative, Isabella's aphorism registers as painfully poignant. Isabella reflects on both characters' need to focus fully on the present moment. They both struggle to keep up with the constant stream of information that determines the course of their professional lives. Any snippet of time they can set aside for themselves is, as Isabella phases it, 'luck', and it is inherently fleeting. Unbeknownst to them, as they speak, Yero is already kick-starting the chain of events that will lead to their separation. Their luck is rapidly running out.

Crockett and Isabella's mistake on the dance floor – of allowing their true feelings to slip through the cracks of their fabricated personas – has devastating consequences, not only for themselves but also for those around them. Just as a minor breach of information sealed Stevens' fate at the beginning of the film, now a tiny slip on the dance floor causes Crockett and Tubbs' infiltration operation to collapse. As the pair are preparing to set up a new transfer, they receive a call from a member of the Aryan brotherhood, informing them that they are keeping Joplin as a hostage. After placing the phone to Joplin's mouth so she can verify her identity, the Aryans tell Crockett and Tubbs that – because they now know that they cannot be trusted – the Brotherhood will be taking the reins: 'I will now tell you when and how this load will get dropped. This is happening our way.' Crockett and Tubbs are instructed to meet representatives from the Aryan Brotherhood by Miami River, at which point they will receive further instructions regarding how to handle their cargo. Crockett and Tubbs are, therefore, rendered powerless, forced to take instructions from another group and left in the dark regarding how the entire plan will unfold. And, like Stevens in the first act, Crockett and Tubbs are uncertain of how the information leak happened; unable to trace their steps back to identify the exact point at which Montoya's associates became aware of their duplicity, they become consumed by paranoia.

The entirety of the final act is characterised by chaos and confusion. Crockett calls Isabella, who reveals that she knows Yero has become suspicious of their relationship and, therefore, placed him under closer scrutiny. She does not, at this point, know about Crockett and Tubbs' connection to the police and she does not know that Joplin has been kidnapped. Unaware of the urgency of their need to retrieve Joplin, Isabella instructs Crockett and Tubbs to avoid meeting with the Aryan Brotherhood, as they are probably leading them towards a trap. Crockett and Tubbs, nevertheless, move forward, with little preparation, little idea of how they ended up in this situation, and little idea of how they will deal with Montoya's enterprise once Joplin has been rescued. For the first time since the opening sequence, the various members of the Miami Dade police work together once again to achieve a common goal – and, again, they fail to establish order. Olmos traces the call from the Brotherhood and retrieves a series of coordinates, which he uses to track down Joplin's whereabouts to a trailer park. A heavy rain descends upon the road in front of Crockett and Tubbs, obscuring the view through the windshield, morphing the city's lights into an abstract field of dark and shadow that seem to engulf the characters as they speed towards an uncertain fate. Recalling in the earlier sequence, which saw the federal agents storm Stevens' house in a futile attempt to rescue Leonetta, Mann drains the images of sound as he captures the advancement of the law enforcers towards the trailer in a series of brief tracking shots.

Gina rolls underneath the trailer sets up a video feed that allows her to monitor the activity inside the living room. Gina crouches outside the trailer and signals for the other two to surround it. The cops gather outside the front door, with Crockett and Gina strategically placed on either side of the entrance. Tubbs picks up a pizza box and knocks politely, pretending to be a delivery man. One of the Aryan brothers answers it and is immediately pulled to the ground by Tubbs. The other three law enforcers then burst into the trailer. The lead Aryan picks up the bomb detonator and stands in the centre of the room, claiming that Joplin will die instantly if they shoot him. Gina responds that her intricate training has prepared her for such a situation: 'What will happen is, I will put a round at 2700 feet per second into the medulla at the base of your brain. And you will be dead from the neck down before your body knows it. Your finger won't even twitch. Only you get dead. So tell me, sport, do you believe that?' Before he has a chance to respond, she already commits to the action – a swift, brutal motion which propels a splatter of blood across the back wall. He falls to the ground, motionless.

The police officers demonstrate an impressive level of skill, agility and adaptability in their work, but, like their first sting operation, the mission doesn't unfold as planned. One of Yero's men-on-the-ground calls him to inform him that Crockett and Tubbs didn't show at Miami River, and Yero correctly assumes that they have gone to retrieve Joplin. The cops are completely unaware that they have fallen into Yero's trap: Yero presses a button on his phone that sets off the detonator, destroying the trailer and seriously injuring Joplin. As Crockett and Tubbs sit over Joplin's unconscious body in a hospital, Tubbs, in a fit of rage, expresses an awareness of the nugatory nature of their profession: 'You know what gets me? The prospect of her losing her life. Of her losing her life over this bullshit line of work.' For the first time, Tubbs verbally expresses his dissatisfaction at the relentless, de-humanising nature of their jobs (separating the value of Joplin's life from her role in the system) and, by describing their profession in this way, makes explicit his frustration that their work will never be complete. Montoya's criminal network is too extensive and all-powerful for either of them to tackle it in its totality; no matter how many deals they intercept, no matter how many low-level collaborators they put away, the syndicate will remain operational. Tubbs, then, expresses at this point an understanding of what Crockett has been conscious of since the beginning: the societal system they are entangled within is cold and uncaring – so much so that if they are killed on duty their absence will barely register.

In the hospital's parking lot, Crockett gets a call from Yero. Yero maintains the illusion that he and Crockett are still business partners and disingenuously expresses concern for his safety, after hearing that 'some bad shit happened with those crazy whites at the trailer park.' Crockett does not call out Yero's lie, but he takes control of the discussion, demanding that

Yero arrange a final deal so they can return Montoya's cocaine and, then, cut themselves off from the syndicate for good. 'This is the only deal,' Crockett asserts to Yero, 'or else I offload your shit to some other buyer.' Like *Heat* and *Collateral*, *Miami Vice* ends at a space of transit. Crockett and Tubbs meet Yero at a shipyard at dusk. A group of Montoya's henchmen stand in front of an abandoned liner, upon which several more crew members are stationed, strategically positioned with weapons. The members of the Miami Dade arrive and form a parallel arrangement on the other side of the shipyard. Detective Lieutenant Martin Castillo (Edward James Olmos) is stationed behind them with a rifle, ready to respond if any of Montoya's henchmen get trigger-happy. Communicating through a voice transmitter, Castillo tells Crockett that he has a comprehensive view of the yard but is struggling to locate the exact locations of all Montoya's snipers. He advises Crockett to stall for time until he can gather more information. The two sides stand opposite one another, like mirror images. Mann alternates between wide shots of both groups, images taken from Castillo's viewfinder, searching across the levels of the liner, and snatches of the ambient space around the yard. Shots of and speedboats and the surface of the water, which previously symbolised mobility and liberation, now signify stagnancy and devastation: the sea's surface is barely visible in the shadows, and the boats sit motionless. It is clear that, no matter how this stand-off ends, the relationship between Crockett and Isabella (and, by extension, both of their dreams of escaping their stifling lifestyles) is over.

The stalemate ends when Yero brings out Isabella as a bargaining chip, taunting Crockett by telling him that they are now a couple: 'After I grow tired of her, I throw her away. Her head someplace, her legs somewhere else.' Upon seeing Isabella treated in this way, Crockett allows his emotion to cloud his reason. He steps forward ahead of the other officers and makes his own demands to Yero, throwing off the careful planning of the police. Crockett tells Yero that he will send one of their men over with the cocaine if Yero sends Isabella over with the money simultaneously; he doesn't trust anybody else. Despite some resistance from the henchmen, Yero signals for them to let her go – but he also makes it clear that before any transfer is made, both parties must check that the other one's goods are legitimate. The deal is agreed upon; Isabella and Olmos both tentatively walk across the yard, their movements captured in two rhyming, frontal tracking shots that frame them from the waist up. However, just as they are both reaching the centre, Castillo takes a shot against Montoya's sniper. This hit causes an eruption of gunfire from both sides, and Crockett shields Isabella behind a nearby vehicle as the situation descends into carnage. Droplets of blood splatter on the lens, metal is left smashed and dented, glass is shattered, bodies fall. Crockett stands up momentarily to spot Tubbs as he fires a fatal shot against Yero, and, as he does so, Isabella notices the badge visible on

Crockett's police uniform. The image slows as she walks towards him, first uncertainly, then furiously, exclaiming, 'Who are you?' Overcome by feelings of betrayal, Isabella tackles him to the floor. Crockett rolls them over to avoid the gunfire and then shoots one of the Brotherhood members. As the gunfight continues, Crockett leads Isabella into a police vehicle and transports her to a safe house by a port. As the pair drive away from the wreckage, Mann fades from a two-shot of their faces in profile to a tracking shot of the city lights, glimpsed as though out of a car window. It appears as though Crockett and Isabella are dissolving into the urban environment as their relationship – and the hope of escape it represented for both of them – dissolves.

The pair sit on the balcony, and Crockett explains to Isabella that he's making the necessary preparations to ensure their safety – but the only way to achieve this is for them to separate and never contact one another again: 'A man named Frank is going to come in a boat. He will run you into a Cariosaw Veno, and from there, you can find your way to Havana. And nobody will follow you. Including me.' The sky is overcast; the palm trees loom over their heads as though an oppressive weight is hanging over them. Although disappointed, Isabella puts up little resistance, instead reminding Crockett of her earlier aphorism: 'Remember, I said time is luck.' Crockett responds, definitively, 'Yeah. Luck ran out. It was too good to last.' As Crockett makes this final comment, affirming his earlier fatalistic outlook, Mann cuts to an image of the couple in profile, with only Crockett's face in focus. Isabella is framed behind him so that only her nose and chin is visible. She fades from our view, visually merging with the background of the image.

Mann then cuts to a close-up handheld shot panning across Joplin's arm in the hospital bed. Her fingers are interlaced with those of Tubbs, who watches over her attentively. As the camera comes to a halt, her hand twitches slightly. Mann rhymes this image with a shot panning right to left across the beach house. There is no sign of life here, only an empty chair, an unoccupied bed, an unused ashtray. The beach house symbolises absence, unfurnished with blank white walls. On the sand outside, Crockett silently watches Isabella disappear into the distance. The two no longer share the same frame. Mann alternates between a frontal one-shot of Joplin, gazing directly into the lens, and a corresponding one-shot of Crockett. Their eyes meet, just as they did during their first encounter in Yero's hideout. This time, they are forcefully pulled away from one another, though the two try to retain their reciprocal gaze for as long as possible. As the ship drifts away from the shore, Isabella walks across the length of the boat to remain in Crockett's line of vision for as long as possible. In lockstep, Crockett races across the shoreline to stay in hers. They cannot keep this up, however, and she slides away from his field of vision.

Crockett's decision to release Isabella is his final act of rebellion against the rigid restrictions of organised policing. Isabella works outside the boundaries of the law and harbours a large amount of information about Montoya's enterprise. This choice has multiple implications. On the one hand, it is an expression of defiance against his dissatisfying and demoralising line of work (why put himself through the pain of arresting somebody he cares for deeply to obtain information about a narcotics network that they are powerless to take down?). However, it is also a sign that Crockett has resigned himself to his place within the urban environment, even though it brings him no joy. He has become, like Tubbs, a man who is fundamentally dissatisfied by his circumstances but cannot imagine living in any other way. The presence of Isabella de-stabilised Crockett's sense of professional duty and his loyalty to the police throughout the narrative. If she were apprehended and kept as a source of information by the federal agents, she would continue to be a presence in his life, and he would continue to be led astray from his work on the force. It is easier for him to rid himself of Isabella, so he no longer harbours any illusion that he may embark upon a more utopian life. By sending Isabella away, Crockett abandons his only chance to escape the drudgery and alienation fostered by his work. Crockett is left alone on the shore, gazing into the distance at the horizon, a symbol of the better future he once dreamed of but now believes will forever remain just out of reach. After a short period of introspection, he returns to the police car and returns to the flux.

Mann intercuts Crockett's acceptance of his fate with images of Joplin waking from her coma. A napping Tubbs wakes with jubilation as Joplin's slight twitches turn into more complex movements, and she grabs his hand. Tubbs calls for a nurse as Joplin collects her mental bearings, and it is implied that she will make a full recovery. Because Tubbs and Joplin have fused their personal lives with their professional roles so thoroughly, their marriage can continue within the logic of the networked society. Their union poses no threat to the stability of the system, as they both willingly submit to its demands. Crockett and Joplin have learned to adapt to the system. Crockett and Isabella's romance cannot survive in this high-pressure environment because it involves transgressing against their respective social and professional roles. The closing image of *Miami Vice* is one of the most heartbreaking in all of Mann's work: Crockett is captured in a smooth, wide-angle tracking shot, first following his movement along the side of a van and then remaining in place as Crockett moves away from the foreground of the image, crossing a road and walking towards the entrance of the hospital. Mann does not show us what happens after Crockett walks into the building; all that matters is that we know he has decided to return to the flux.

Like *Thief*'s Frank and *Heat*'s Hanna, Crockett ends up on his own, but unlike them, he does not accept solitude as the price he must pay for retaining agency and control over his work. Instead, Crockett throws himself back into the organisation that treats him as a disposable cog, and re-establishes his empty social connections with Tubbs and Joplin. He is returning to the state he was in at the beginning of the feature, only now with a newfound certainty that escape is impossible. Although it is a mesmerising, formally accomplished work, *Miami Vice* is arguably the bleakest film in Mann's entire oeuvre, a feature which articulates a profoundly pessimistic view of life within a globalised, increasingly technocratic network society in which the forces of de-humanisation crush everything in their path and the individual can find little solace in their work or in their relationships. Fortunately, as the next few chapters will explore, Mann's following work revisits many of these themes but pay more consideration to the ways in which the individual may hold on to their autonomy and independence within such a social system.

The Last Outlaw:
Public Enemies (2009)

Although it shares thematic and formal characteristics with Mann's earlier work, the release of *Miami Vice* marked a watershed moment for the filmmaker. The enthusiastic embrace of the aesthetic possibilities of digital imaging, the sense of narrative fragmentation, the critique of computerised regimes of surveillance and control and the radical distortion of temporal and spatial relations distinguish *Miami Vice* from the Mann features that preceded it. From its very first set-piece, *Miami Vice* announces itself as something radically new, an experimental work which abstracts the familiar tropes and motifs of the crime genre to the point that they are nearly unrecognisable, and, in the process, launches a reflexive critique of the impact on digitisation on economic channels, labour practices, and social relations. Considering that *Miami Vice* is such an ultra-modern feature, in terms of its subject matter and its aesthetic form, it may seem strange that Mann decided to make a period piece immediately afterwards. Yet, although it may at first seem jarring to see a historical drama shot with state-of-the-art digital cameras, yet, when one considers the subject matter more closely, *Public Enemies* is firmly of a piece with the other features Mann directed over this period.

Public Enemies was shot entirely with HD digital cameras, and employs the same deliberately rough, handheld-heavy formal style Mann fine-tuned with *Miami Vice*. Yet, while the earlier feature draws upon the audio-visual vernacular of war reportage and surveillance footage, *Public Enemies* is rooted in the narrative conventions and visual signifiers of classical Hollywood gangster films. However, Mann does not directly imitate the aesthetic language of the 1930s gangster films, nor does he utilise the digital cameras in the service of a photo-realistic style. Indeed, *Public Enemies* is just as formally adventurous in its use of digital filmmaking technology as *Miami Vice*, and seeing Depression-era costumes, settings, props, behaviours and modes of speech reconfigured through Mann's HD apparatus lends the feature a deeply uncanny quality. Mann establishes a hyper-real approach which at once brings history closer than ever before (the nuances of Depp-as-Dillinger's face appear in greater detail in Mann's HD close-ups than could have been captured with a photo-chemical camera, and the reconstructions of '30s banks are rendered with greater clarity and depth than can be witnessed in contemporaneous narrative films or newsreels), while also rendering these elements unfamiliar. The images of the 1930s crafted by Mann appear so distinct from the actual visual artefacts of the period that the viewer is forced to reflect upon the technological apparatus through which the material was crafted. As Adam Gallimore observes, Mann's late features 'look as if they were shot on digital video rather than attempting to replicate the feel of film: the depth of field extends further, opening out the image to subjective focus, while action and movement often appears rather jarred or fragmented.' As a result of this stylistic choice, *Public Enemies* 'reframes the past through this lens of the present, resulting in a more direct engagement with the experience of history through its subjectivity and focus on immersion.' (2014: 5-7). The extensive use of hyper-detailed deep focus shots, tight close-ups in which the actor's faces nearly seem to bulge out of the frame, and pixelated abstraction, creates a constant tension between our immersion in the historical era depicted and our awareness of the ultra-modern apparatus.

Set at the height of the Great Depression, *Public Enemies* charts the final months in the life of John Dillinger, a young bank robber who became the subject of a highly publicised manhunt headed by J Edgar Hoover. In its portrayal of 1930s gangsterism, *Public Enemies* represents a radical aesthetic break from the original run of classical Hollywood gangster films of the period and from modern media texts which depict the era and milieu by adopting a formal language associated with traditional continuity editing – features such as Sam Mendes' *Road to Perdition* (2002) and Ruben Fleischer's *Gangster Squad* (2013), as well as the popular television series *Boardwalk Empire* (2010-2014) and *Peaky Blinders* (2013-2022). At the same time, these projects mobilise modern technologies to replicate the look and feel of traditional genre films while still tailoring the aesthetic to fit match contemporary audio-visual trends – ie for example, by employing colour grading and incorporating modern renditions of classical music.

Mann, in contrast, does not provide us with a warm nostalgic view of the period, nor does he present a comforting parable that offers a straightforward narrative of teleological evolution. Instead, the unusual combination of period elements and hyper-modern shooting methods encourages the viewer to think critically about the relationship between modern day society and the historical moment, and, therefore, to seek out the socio-political parallels that exist between the '30s in consideration and the contemporary era. Released in 2009, in the aftermath of the Bush administration's steady erosion of civil liberties (conducted under the guise of protecting the USA from a litany of external threats) and the crash of a financial system accelerated by digital technologies, the contemporary relevance of the events depicted in *Public Enemies* should be very apparent. Deborah Tudor perceptively observes that the de-familiarisation of the historical period through the use of high-definition digital video 'allows the narrative overall to function as a displaced version of post 9-11 USA.' This is evidenced through the emphasis Mann places on the 'corporatisation of crime' and the 'phenomenon of the Federal Bureau of Investigation using the hunt for 'public enemies' like Dillinger and Pretty Boy Floyd to justify its requests for more manpower and resources, and therefore to become a much more powerful, and pervasive law enforcement agency.' (Tudor: 2010). *Public Enemies*, therefore, has much in common with *Miami Vice* and *Blackhat* on a thematic level, as it explores the nascent surveillance state, the erosion of individual privacy, the fading of the outlaw mentality and the dominance of financial institutions.

In Mann's hands, Dillinger is turned into a prototypical Mannian figure: an idealistic loner who struggles to keep his cherished outlaw lifestyle afloat in an era of extreme techno-historical change. Like Crockett, he feels the acceleration of the society that surrounds him very acutely. Aware that the type of individualist criminality he represents cannot be sustained for much longer, Dillinger longs to grasp on to the precious moment and make the most of the small amount of time he has left. Dillinger desires to carve out a life away from the pervasive forces of encroaching modernity – a lifestyle of backroads, forest-dwelling hideouts, back alleys, whorehouses and forged identities – but as he is increasingly targeted by Hoover and Melvin Purvis'

(Christian Bale) newly developed methods of surveillance, it rapidly becomes painfully apparent, that there will soon be nowhere left to run.

What, then, is the relationship between *Public Enemies* and the classical gangster film? Mann not only recounts the biographical facts of Dillinger, but also revisits and repurposes the codes and conventions of this genre that was so integral to the early years of Hollywood narrative filmmaking. Produced in the era of Hoover's self-described 'war on crime', films like Howard Hawks' *Scarface* (1932), Raoul Walsh's *The Roaring Twenties* (1939), Michael Curtiz's *Angels with Dirty Faces* (1938) and Mervyn LeRoy's *Little Caesar* (1931) walk a fine line between celebrating the outlaw as a figure of resistance against the tyranny of an increasingly invasive state, and putting forth a socially reactionary worldview by placing their central gangsters into a moralistic narrative framework. In many of the American gangster films produced during this era, the excitement and freedom of the criminal lifestyle is ultimately punished by a spectacular fall -- resulting in either their arrest or death. Such a structure implicitly suggests that any attempt to live outside of the boundaries of 'legitimate' civilisation will inevitably result in self-destruction, and that the crimes of the rogue individual are of greater severity than the injustices perpetrated by the government. A seminal example of a film in this mould is *The Roaring Twenties*, in which the early success of a group of bootleggers headed by Eddie Bartlett (James Cagney) comes to a grinding halt with the onset of the Wall Street crash. Bartlett, formerly portrayed as an appealing, suave and sophisticated operator, is eaten away by bitterness and paranoia. His increasingly shabby appearance signifies his fall from grace, and he gradually finds that all of his former friends have turned on him. In the film's final act, Bartlett and his former associate George (Humphrey Bogart), now a gang leader, burst into all-out warfare, resulting in a final shootout that sees both men fatally wounded. The ending sees the lifeless bodies of the former bootleggers scattered around the cold street outside a church as the police swarm in, assessing the damage and taking into custody the few remaining members of George's gang. Panama (Gladys George), a former flame of Bartlett's who has since embraced 'legitimate work' in mainstream society, gazes over Bartlett's body, sobbing, before commenting that, 'He used to be a big shot.' This ending encapsulates the simultaneous sympathy for, and antipathy towards the figure of the gangster embraced throughout the genre (the tragedy of Eddie's downfall deserves to be mourned, and it is recognised that he is, to a certain degree, the product of a corrupt and hostile environment), while the presence of the cops as benevolent forces of stability signifies the necessity of maintaining social order. The initial portrayal of the criminal lifestyle as being an enthralling and inciting prospect, an escape route from the crushing drudgery of post-crash American society, is ultimately undermined by the suggestion that such a lifestyle is reckless, transient, and bound to result in tragedy. The final ruination of the protagonist, positions the gangster as an aberration who must ultimately be stamped out in order to re-establish the societal status quo. *The Roaring Twenties* may raise objections to the social problems which push individuals into gangsterism – such as the difficulty of achieving upward social mobility for the working class, wealth inequality, and the poor working conditions of those on the bottom rung of the social ladder. This makes the gangster a sympathetic anti-hero, but one who must ultimately pay for their transgressions so that the corrosive influence of criminality may be safely contained.

The plot of *Public Enemies* broadly falls in line with the narrative arc of the classical gangster film, as described above, as it charts the rise and fall of its central antihero as he breaks out of jail, pulls off a series of heists, evades the cops, starts a romance, and is finally gunned down on the street by federal officers. However, in *Public Enemies*, there is no indication that Dillinger's tragic fate is a form of karmic punishment for his criminal transgressions. As Rayner argues, 'While bearing a superficial resemblance to the defeat and negation of the classical gangster's rebellion, Dillinger's death in *Public Enemies* also appears both fated and sought, and conducive to a romanticised institutionalisation within popular culture and memory.' (2013: 158). Mann's portrayal of Dillinger's downfall is portrayed not as an inevitable result of his transgressions but as a frightening indication of the all-pervasive powers of a burgeoning authoritarian surveillance state that would only intensify over the decades which followed his death. Over the course of the feature, Hoover develops and expands his all-consuming electronic grid, not only combining all states under the banner of a single overarching legal system but also connecting together individuals and institutions through abstract electronic streams – wire-tapping, radio-waves, records of banking transactions etc. Such an environment is actively hostile to individual expression and personal autonomy.

Throughout *Public Enemies*, Mann dramatises the erosion of the utopian ideals upon which America was founded – self-determination, personal liberty, meritocracy – as Hoover's draconian instincts influence how he runs the nascent Federal Bureau of Investigation. In committing wholeheartedly to self-determination, agency, and mobility, Mann's Dillinger is treated not only as a charming and quick-witted gangster, but also as an authentic individual who heroically refuses to assimilate into an unjust social order. As Hoover's sprawling surveillance network increasingly collapses the boundaries between private and public spaces, makes the citizen the subject of constant monitoring by the state, flattens the frontier into a standardised mass, and places a disturbing amount of power into the hands of a few autocrats, Dillinger nobly refuses to compromise his outlaw lifestyle. The monumental, national-wide manhunt waged against Dillinger by Hoover reflects Hoover's surveillance network's startling level of power, even at this early stage of its development. Fitting in with the recurrent theme of Mann protagonists lost within a 'cruel technological present', Dillinger, placed in opposition to Hoover, appears as a remnant from a lost era, an honourable outlaw whose way of thinking about society and his place within it is antithetical to Hoover's view of the nation.

Public Enemies takes place before the total domination of the technologically-facilitated surveillance state, which characterises the diegetic environments of *Miami Vice* and *Blackhat*. Crockett and Hathaway are men who, thrust into 21st century America, must learn to adjust to the rhythms of advanced globalised techno-capitalism to remain afloat. In contrast, Dillinger is a man of the frontier who leads (temporally, at least) a life that is truly off-the-grid. Crockett and Hathaway are immersed within mainstream societal systems, whereas Dillinger is able to live on the margins of society, though over the course of the narrative, these margins are increasingly subsumed by Hoover's technological network. Dillinger ultimately finds it impossible to remain on the outskirts, but chooses to embrace his own death rather than becoming part of the system, as many of his more pragmatic associates do. It is not that Dillinger rejects all new technologies – he embraces the automobile, the media and the Tommy gun to build his mythology – but he gradually realises that the forces of the state are utilising all forms of modern technology to serve their own nefarious ends. And these forces come to perceive Dillinger as an aberration that must be snuffed out to ensure the smooth functioning of the new social system.

This is one of the central contradictions of Dillinger's character: he is a man enamoured with mass-produced art, but he is unaware (at least, at first) of its ability to function as propaganda which coerces the public into complying with legislation that goes against their best interests. Dillinger laps up the limelight when he realises that the American people, disenfranchised with the interconnected forces of the state, big business and financial institutions, admire him for pitting himself in opposition to these forces. He self-consciously constructs his identity according to the images he consumes from popular gangster films, imagining himself as the lead in his movie and mentally positioning his beau Billie Frechette (Marion Cotillard) as his glamorous gangster's moll. In an interview conducted ahead of the release of *Public Enemies*, Mann explained that he was drawn to Dillinger's story because of the outlaw's deliberate efforts to mould his public image, and his conscious resistance to state power: 'In his time he was very current and contemporary,' says Mann. 'He was popular for good reason. There had been 140 bank failures in Chicago, and most people blamed the banks. He had the sense to treat hostages well because he knew they would all be interviewed [...] Dillinger didn't "get out" of prison; he exploded onto the landscape. And he was going to have everything and get it right now. In assaulting the banks, and outwitting the government, it's as if he spoke for the people battered by the Depression. He was a celebrity outlaw, a populist hero.' For Dillinger, the act of bank robbery is an act of performance. The exquisite marble floors of the banks, often framed in overhead wide shots, appear like theatre stages, in which Dillinger acts out his carefully sculpted persona.

Hoover, however, is also aware of the immense potential of the mass media to shape public opinion. Throughout the narrative, Hoover and Purvis constantly appear in front of cameras and give press releases, monitoring newspaper columns and radio broadcasts After Hoover's proposal to the Senate Appropriations Committee to establish a centralised national bureau of investigation is rejected, his first reaction is to contact a series of prominent newspaper editors to shape the headlines to his favour. Hoover demands that the front pages attack the committee for failing to have the backbone to support his brave new plan. After he makes this demand, Hoover pointedly comments that he will not fight the battle to establish his bureau 'in this committee room', but 'on the front page.' By generating comfortable and easily consumable narratives through the combined forces of radio, cinema, and print, Hoover aims to socially condition the American people into a voluntary and active acceptance of his bureau and its intrusion into their everyday life. Hoover establishes and reinforces his narrative of a 'crime wave' sweeping America through these communication technologies, thus generating a perpetual atmosphere of paranoia that renders the public fragile and more willing to sacrifice their civil liberties.

Hoover recognises that, because of his status as a media icon, , a hunt against Dillinger would provide a powerful opportunity to demonstrate the power of his new techniques of law enforcement: a centralised, nation-wide system (as opposed to the earlier modes of police control, in which individual powers were delegated individually to each state), presided over by technologically adept bureaucrats who remain fundamentally distanced from any direct involvement in the work on the ground. Under his instruction, Dillinger is branded 'Public Enemy Number One', and his face is displayed in movie theatres and town halls all across the country. Early techniques of cinematic distribution, radio transmission, and image reproduction are utilised to weed out Dillinger from his hiding spots and turn him into electronic target to be methodically tracked down and then taken out.

Dillinger's love affair with the media is short-lived. He eventually discovers that the newspapers are prepared to turn on him at the drop of the hat; it is those like Hoover who truly hold the cards, and when the media-sphere is so intertwined with the state, the very publications which first transformed Dillinger into a cult hero ultimately turn out to be the cause of his undoing. Dillinger's complex relationship to the mass media is poetically encapsulated in the late sequence in which he watches the demise of Clark Gable on a theatre screen; Dillinger's final words are an allusion to the film *Manhattan Melodrama*, which he watches on the evening of his death, and indicate an awareness that he must inevitably suffer the same tragic fate that befalls the screen gangsters he – in part – models his persona on.

The type of gangsterism dramatised in *Public Enemies* should be differentiated from large crime syndicates and family-lead mafia dynasties. While those organisations are intricate and elaborately structured, concerned with familial histories, decades-long businesses relationships, cultural traditions, and social codes, the criminals who take centre stage in *Public Enemies* are idealistic wanderers – frontiersmen who are constantly in transit, have no established home, and consciously oppose monolithic corporate, state and financial powers. They do not have any ties to any wider institutions. In the narrative of *Public Enemies*, this worldview is represented not only by Dillinger, but also by Baby Faced Nelson (Stephen Graham), Machine Gun Kelly (Tommy Dallace), Pretty Boy Floyd (Channing Tatum) and Alvin Karpis (Giovanni Ribisi). Some of these figures play a substantial role in the narrative, while others are only referenced in passing, easy to miss if one is unfamiliar with the specific cultural context.

This distinction is vital because the gangster lifestyle as symbolised by wide-reaching, bureaucratic crime syndicates were not snuffed out in the same way that the romantic image of the frontier highwaymen was. To survive in the burgeoning surveillance state designed by Hoover, a criminal had to be assimilated within a much larger group, employ similarly technocratic methods of illegal activity, and, most importantly, arrange some kind of agreement with the local authorities, whose silence could be bought. Certain areas within the US even became known as being 'safe areas' for criminal enterprises due to the protection offered by the local police forces. However, the approach to criminality represented by these syndicates is fundamentally incompatible with Dillinger's entire philosophy of being. The sensation of freedom and absolute independence would dissipate if he were to join a highly organised syndicate with direct ties to the local authorities.

In direct opposition to Dillinger's sensibilities, there is a sense of bureaucracy to the way these syndicates conduct crime; they mirror the practices of financial institutions and big businesses. The ideology behind these syndicates is represented by the characters of Frank Nitti (Bill Camp) and Phil D'Andrea (John Ortiz). If Dillinger represents an anachronistic outlaw lifestyle, Nitti and D'Andrea represent the future of organised crime. During their first encounter, D'Andrea scoffs at Dillinger's desire to be adored by the viewing public. 'Every time I read about your bank jobs,' D'Andrea tells Dillinger, 'where you give customers back their money, you crack me up …' As these organisations were firmly integrated into the American capitalist system, they did not come under fire from Hoover in the same way that rebels like Dillinger and Nelson did. Their connection to 'official' institutions meant that they did not register as grand threats to the establishment in the same way that Dillinger did.

The guiding mentality of the syndicates is best encapsulated in a late scene, when a desperate Dillinger, who has already seen many of his former outlaw friends either arrested or killed seeks out syndicate leader D'Andrea for help. Dillinger finds D'Andrea in the backroom of a pawn store, presiding over a massive floor of men sitting at desks, tapping wires and taking phone calls. The room looks nearly identical to the surveillance centre of Hoover's bureau, in which a large team of agents listen to covertly recorded conversations and recorded significant information onto vinyl discs. D'Andrea schools a perplexed Dillinger on the new nature of organised crime in the city: 'Look around. What do you see? (...) You see money. Last month there were independent wire services letting bookies know who won the third race at sportsman park. 300 of them nationwide. Now there's only one. Ours. On October 23rd, you robbed a bank in Greencastle, Indiana. You got away with 74,802 dollars. You thought that was a big score? These phones make that every day. And it keeps getting made day after day after day. A river of money. And it keeps getting deeper and wider. Week in and week out. Month in and month out. Flowing right to us.' He then assures Dillinger that they can rest knowing that the cops will never come through the door because of the regular payouts they make to the local authorities. However, if the cops find out that the syndicate is aiding Dillinger – Hoover's designated 'Public Enemy Number One' – then they won't be so obliging

Mann cuts to several shots of Dillinger's concerned face in close-up, struggling to keep up with this new methodology of conducting crime. Both the sphere of criminality and the sphere of law enforcement are becoming more evolved and expansive through the power of new communication technologies. The vanishing of the frontier, and the utopian dreams and myths which came with it, is embodied by the attitudes of those like Nitti and D'Andrea; if, for Dillinger, money is treated as a means to an end, merely a necessity to keep leading his outlaw lifestyle, then for these two, money is an end-in-itself – they have little interest in the activities through which they obtain their funds, nor in what they do with the money after they've amassed it. The only logic that drives individuals like Nitti and D'Andrea is that of never-ending economic growth; this mentality is merely an extension of the logic of the capitalist state. As Patterson notes, the crime syndicates depicted in *Public Enemies* appear 'oddly corporate' in their organisation and in their ambitions (2009). This type of criminal does not oppose the monolithic power of the corrupt banking system – made painfully clear by the Wall Street Crash – like Dillinger does, they, instead, desire to utilise new technologies to engage in parasitic strategies of economic exploitation comparable to those of the financial giants.

There is no place for a rogue agent like Dillinger within a syndicate like this. Dillinger is too much of a renegade, too much of an individualist, for the syndicate to trust him to obediently comply with their operation. The cops won't break down the door of their hideout, D'Andrea tells Dillinger, 'Unless you're around, and they've got to come through that door, no matter what.' These new criminals aren't opposed to the cops; they're in cahoots with them. While Dillinger, like Frank and McCauley, truly values personal agency and liberty, Nitti and D'Andrea are shallow pragmatists. They are only interested in amassing as much money as possible, and will go to any lengths necessary to ensure their pockets are lined. Dillinger is an aberration in this new system; the syndicate won't associate with showmen who don't play by the rules. Phil tells Dillinger, 'So the syndicate's got a new policy. All the guys like you, Karpis, Nelson, Campbell – we ain't laundering your money or bonds no more. You ain't holing up in our whorehouses no more. No armers, no doctors, no safe havens, no nothing.' For Dillinger, being abandoned by the fellow outlaws who should, theoretically, support him in a time of need, is a deep betrayal.

Dillinger poetically articulates the transience of his lifestyle when he remarks to Frechette, during their first meeting, that everybody in Chicago seems to be 'all about where people come from. The only thing important is where somebody's going.' A bemused Frechette asks him, 'And where are you going?', to which Dillinger responds, 'Anywhere I want.' Though Frechette is initially attracted to this aura of mystery and absolute freedom that life with Dillinger offers, she later grows tired of his refusal to think beyond the present moment. After seeing Dillinger express amusement at a national newspaper headline which reads 'Wanted: John Dillinger: Dead or Dead', a disturbed Frechette lambasts him for failing to make plans for the future. Frechette admires Dillinger's idealism, but is disturbed at the lack of thought he has given to practically ensuring his survival: 'You don't think past today or tomorrow. And eventually, they will capture or kill you. And I don't want to be there when that happens.' Frechette's observation is astute; Dillinger plunges headfirst toward his inevitable demise and he pays little thought to how Frechette will be impacted by the loss of her lover. Dillinger offers her comfort, but his words are unconvincing: 'You ain't going nowhere. You hear me. I'm gonna die an old man in your arms. We're too good for them. They ain't tough enough, smart enough or fast enough. I hit any bank I want, any time. They got to be at every bank, all the time.' This is ironic, because this kind of all-consuming, nationwide surveillance is precisely what Purvis and Hoover are in the process of setting up.

Public Enemies tracks a similar narrative trajectory to that of *Heat* and *Thief*, in the sense that its central outlaw hopes to make enough money to retire from his life of crime and retire with Frechette. However, what distinguishes *Public Enemies* from these earlier films is that, here, the development comes very late in the narrative, and Dillinger seems only half-committed to the plan. While Frank and McCauley are defined by a profound sense of hollowness they feel while conducting their criminal activity, Dillinger genuinely loves what he does. He does not decide to quit his profession in a desperate attempt to fill an inner void, as they do, but because he knows that his criminal lifestyle is no longer sustainable within an urban environment that is evolving faster than he can keep up with.

Dillinger and Frechette discuss this plan to elope while sitting in front of Lake Michigan in the middle of the night; the composition renders the contours of the space difficult to make out, creating the impression that the two characters are perched against an abstract field of vision. The fact that this scene is framed like no other sequence in the feature makes this exchange appear as though it is a fantasy, removed from the rest of the narrative. Having witnessed many of his former associates killed, arrested, or subsumed into a syndicate, Dillinger tells Frechette that he'll retire after conducting one final, high stakes robbery, and then they'll move overseas. She asks him where they'll escape to, but Dillinger is clearly uncertain, replying with the vague answer that it will be somewhere 'off the map'. It is evident that this plan has been hastily devised, and, deep down, Dillinger knows it probably won't become reality. He offers these sweet words to Frechette but doesn't even seem to believe them himself. On an unconscious level, what he really desires is to continue to live the frontier lifestyle for as long as possible, and if this means that he must face his own annihilation in the process, then so be it. Very soon after this scene, Frechette is arrested by the Feds while Dillinger is waiting for her outside a liquor store. And as they place her into a police vehicle, Dillinger slowly drives away, emphasising that he prioritises the continuation of his gangster lifestyle over protecting Frechette. It's not that Dillinger has no genuine feelings towards Frechette – he views her as the perfect embodiment of the gangster's moll archetype and needs her to fulfil his dream lifestyle – it's that he can only conceive of a life with her if he can also live according to his principles.

Public Enemies, like *Miami Vice*, begins in *media res*: a long line of prison inmates walk in lockstep along the yard of Indiana State Prison, chained together by the ankles. The camera captures them in a series of static, wide shots, the massive outer wall of the prison taking up the upper portion of the frame. The men, dressed in cotton uniforms, are entirely silent, and their bodies move in perfect synchronisation, in accordance with the commands of the guards. The representation of the prison environment here represents a marked contrast from the establishing shots of the jail in the opening moments of *The Jericho Mile*. In the earlier film, the prison yard is a site where the different inmates express their own interests, hobbies, and gang affiliations; here, the prisoners have had their spirits broken, their wills crushed and subordinated into the greater whole strictly disciplined organisation of the maximum-security prison. One of the convicts collapses from the heat and the exhaustion of the activity, but the other men step around his body. He is an expendable casualty within this environment, which is indifferent to the lives of the men within its confines. During this scene, the men all blend into an indistinguishable crowd, but we will later recognise three of them as members of Dillinger's gang: Charles Makley (Christian Stolte), Homer Van Meter (Stephen Dorff) and Harry Pierpont (David Wenham).

Mann doesn't devote a lot of screen time to establishing pre-existing characters and relationships; the feature throws the viewer into the deep end and calls upon them to keep up with the ceaseless flow of action, from which details of narrative, motivation, backstory and sociological context emerge. The film's arc will track Dillinger's ascent to become one of the most famous men in America, an icon adorned and scorned in equal measure, but in this opening sequence, he is given a pointedly un-heroic introduction. He is first seen sitting in the back of a police vehicle, driven into the courtyard and then escorted to the entrance by a man who will later be identified as Red Hamilton (Jason Clarke), one of Dillinger's closest friends, posing as an officer. At first, we only see Dillinger through a series of small glimpses, his image obscured by the windows and exterior of the car. When he is forced out of the vehicle, he is framed as a minor figure dwarfed by a massive concrete wall.

The power dynamic established in these opening moments is soon upended, however. Mann cuts to a workstation within the jail. The men remain tightly monitored by the guards and initially appear as though they are an obedient group working in unison. But, then, Mann cuts in to a series of close-ups, revealing that the inmates are covertly communicating with one another through a series of minute glances and gestures. Through this subtle mode of communication, the inmates plan a rebellion against the guards. Dietrich enters the room with a box containing loaded Colt 45 automatics. Pierpont hides the weapon in his sleeve and then checks carefully to ensure that the security forces haven't noticed that the transfer has taken place. When they are certain that the staff have lowered their defences, Pierpont takes one of the guards by surprise and points the gun in his face. Dietrich and Van Meter physically restrain three other guards and line them up on the other side of the room. A commotion breaks out amongst the men, with several other inmates picking up clubs and battering rams to aid in the suppression of the guards.

In a holding cell located in another part of the prison, a guard named Turkney interrogates Dillinger. After some questioning, he realises that he has a pre-existing relationship with the mysterious new entrant. He squints as he examines Dillinger's face before asking him, 'Didn't you get paroled out of here a few months ago?' Dillinger reveals the truth: he had been sentenced for 14 years in Indiana State Penitentiary after robbing a grocer of $550, while intoxicated. He ended up serving only nine of those years, during which time he was trained in the art of bank robbery by older, more experienced convicts. Dillinger has snuck into the prison under the guise of being a new prisoner, but he hasn't been sentenced this time, which means that the guards have no legal power over him, and he is not obligated to obey their commands. Ecstatic at the prospect of putting these wardens in their place. Dillinger makes it clear that he will not accept insolence from the guard, stating that: 'A son of a bitch screw like you better address me as Mr Dillinger.' He then effortlessly breaks out of his cuffs and beats Turkney with the end of a Tommy gun. Hamilton then drops his performance and orders all the guards in the holding cell to open the gates leading to the yard.

The prisoners from the work station burst into the holding cell, guided by Dietrich and Van Meter. Dillinger checks that the escape path leading from the gate to the parked Pontiac is clear while the prisoners steal the clothes from the captive guards. Hamilton exits the building and walks back across the yard to the vehicle, getting poised to make a quick getaway. Dillinger emerges into the yard alone, framed against the concrete wall. Unlike the shot in which he entered the prison, the wall is now framed diagonally, and the sky is the most prominent element in the composition. Visually, this alteration of perspective signifies the extent to which Dillinger can assert his individuality within constricting circumstances and transform a place of dehumanisation into a site of emancipation. The viewer was initially lead to believe that Dillinger is being incarcerated, but it now becomes clear that he was, in fact, only assuming this role to gain access to the prison and lower the defences of the guards. While some other inmates allow their anger to get the better of them – beating and terrorising the guards as revenge for the injustice and disrespect they've experienced at their hands – Dillinger and his crew do not allow for their concentration to be broken. They carry out the escape mission as cleanly and swiftly as possible. It is immediately established that, in a direct, hand-to-hand combat situation, Dillinger is a master, and can easily overwhelm the wardens and police officers that seek to suppress him. Unfortunately, he will soon be pitted against a foe who does not carry out any of his dirty work directly – there is not even a single scene in the narrative which sees Hoover and Dillinger share a physical location, a formal choice which emphasises Hoover's fundamental distance from the prisoners he devotes his life to apprehending.

Making his way across the yard, Dillinger comes under fire from guards in the watchtowers. He sprints towards the Pontiac, and, after arriving at the vehicle safely, he fires strategically at central spots in the towers' structure. The guards cower, in turn. Seeing a pause in the fire from the watchtower, the rest of the escapees – some of whom haven't finished dressing in their new disguises – make a mad dash toward the road. Some are shot en route.

Hamilton starts the ignition as Manley, Ed Shouse (Michael Vieau) and Pierpont approach the vehicle. When he is close to the side door, Dietrich is shot in the neck by an unseen guard. Dillinger and Pierpont grab the now-paralysed Dietrich and attempt to lift him into the back of the vehicle as Hamilton speeds away from the gunfire. As they drive, the force of Dietrich's limp body leaning against the back door forces it open, and Dietrich collapses out of the side. Dillinger holds on to him desperately to prevent Dietrich from falling onto the road. As Dillinger grasps the man as tightly as he can, his body dragging across the ground, the two men do not exchange words. Dietrich realises he is dying, and his final gesture is simply to make firm eye contact with Dillinger. Mann alternates between two rhyming close-ups of the two men, their eyes locked in an overwhelming gesture of intimacy, before the life finally drains from Dietrich's body and Dillinger lets him go. He becomes an inanimate body on the roadside, and disappears from view as the getaway car continues onward.

The use of shot/reverse-shot here extends the duration of this moment of death and lends it a sense of incredible weight. This aesthetic tactic is rarely used in a film built on hyper-acceleration, a constantly roving camera, and the fragmentation of screen action. Despite Dillinger's most ardent efforts to extend his lifespan, it is too late: Dietrich fades into the realm of history as he disappears into the horizon. It's a powerful moment that encapsulates both the honour and the futility of Dillinger's struggle throughout the narrative – the struggle against time, against the dehumanising forces of modernity, against the forward march of societal development. Dillinger's chosen lifestyle necessitates constant movement, and a tragic consequence of this lifestyle is that there is little time to mourn those who get mortally wounded along his passage. Keith Uhlich describes the power of this moment in foreshadowing Dillinger's inevitable fate: 'Dillinger looks into the eyes of a wounded comrade as the spirit slips out of him, the loss taking a protracted, uncomfortable beat to register. He's now aware of his own death rattle, though that doesn't stop him from living it up until his last gasp.' (2009: 69).

On a more metaphorical level, the early death of the older gangster Dietrich creates a sense of distance between Dillinger and the older sphere of frontier outlaws, soon to be displaced by the twin forces of federal policing and criminal syndicates. Dillinger may wish to hold on to the style of outlaw criminality represented by Dietrich, but his efforts are in vain. After Dillinger's jailbreak, Mann introduces Purvis, who is similarly in the middle of carrying out a hyper-detailed and painstakingly executed operation – in this case, taking down the prolific bank robber Floyd. Purvis is a taciturn presence, a man who makes no extraneous movements and keeps firm control of his emotions as he stalks his target. Mann captures the chase in a series of smooth tracking shots, the camera moving in lockstep with the advancing lawman. In contrast to Purvis' methodical and punctilious motion, Floyd is clumsy and poorly coordinated, flailing around and shooting behind his back haphazardly. Mann cuts to a wide shot of Floyd thoughtlessly running into a field of grass, then back to a tracking shot of Purvis as he perches on the edge of the clearing. Now that he has a clear view of Floyd's motion, he puts the gun to his eye and yells, 'Floyd, halt!' When Floyd fails to respond to Purvis' command, Mann to a reverse angle from Purvis' perspective as he angles his weapon and fires a precise long-distance shot. Floyd is taken down with one brutal blow. Purvis walks towards the body and announces that Floyd is under arrest. Floyd makes an awkward attempt to pick up his gun, but Purvis quickly kicks it out of his hand.

The qualities of Purvis outlined in this opening scene – his professionalism, his ability to divorce his emotions from his work, his technical aptitude, his all-consuming focus – make him the perfect puppet for Hoover. Purvis is defined by his complete deference to authority: he follows Hoover's instructions without protest or hesitation, implementing his increasingly authoritarian policies without ever thinking too deeply about Hoover's disturbing motivations for seeking to implement these policies. At one point, Hoover tells Purvis, during a pep talk, 'As they say in Italy these days, take off the white gloves!' explicitly suggesting a connection between the totalitarian tendencies of Hoover's operation and the rise of fascism under Mussolini.

Unlike Hoover, Purvis is not an active proponent of fascist politics, but he is meek and malleable; he allows his ingrained sense of duty to his government to supersede any moral objections he may have to his boss's unorthodox practices. Under the guidance of Hoover, the FBI implements several pernicious information-gathering strategies, including the use of physical torture during interrogations, the unwarranted arrest of family members and friends of the wanted criminals, and wire-tapping civilian phone lines. Mann repeatedly implies that Purvis is not entirely comfortable with the more extreme commands given to him by Hoover, but he lacks the conviction to act on these concerns.

Because of this internal tension, it is fair to view Purvis as an antagonist while also recognising that he is a pawn used by grander socio-political influences that manipulate him to achieve heinous ends. In this sense, Purvis is comparable to Duncan Hayward in *The Last of the Mohicans* – he has unwavering faith in the rightness of the government he was raised to respect, and, because of this faith, he allows himself to be used as a pawn by noxious men interested only in consolidating their power and upholding an unjust establishment. Although Purvis does not get a chance to redeem himself, as Hayward does, a title card that appears just before the end credits indicates the extent to which his complicity in Hoover's project tormented him. As the card reveals, Purvis quit the FBI shortly after Dillinger's death, and he committed suicide not long after his retirement.

The internal contradiction at the core of Purvis' character is best encapsulated in the film's two torture scenes. In the first, a group of federal agents, following Hoover's orders, attempt to extract information on Dillinger's whereabouts from Charles Mackley (Christian Stolte), an associate of Baby-Faced Nelson. The associate has just been shot in the eye following a botched bank eye and lies in hospital, in agony, as the federal agents deny him medication. As Mackley repeatedly denies any knowledge of Nelson's recent activity, the agents push down on his head and forcibly open his eye socket. Purvis is not directly involved in the torture of this suspect, but he lingers in the hallway watching the events unfold and does nothing to intervene. As the superior officer of the men inflicting the torture, Purvis has the power to end Mackley's suffering whenever he desires, so his refusal to do so must be perceived as an *active* choice. A doctor even pleads with Purvis to allow him to give his patient the medicine necessary to put an end to his torment: 'The bullet entered the back of his head, it's resting over his right eye. His brain will be dead soon. He's suffering. I need to sedate him.' Purvis is not responsive to the doctor's appeal. Instead, he matter-of-factly threatens him with immediate arrest if he attempts to obstruct the 'interrogation' (as Purvis euphemistically calls it). Purvis maintains a detachment from the horrific actions inflicted by his employees, thus allowing him to deny ethical responsibility for the physical harm inflicted upon the suspect. Purvis' desire to distance himself from the torture suggests that, on some level, he considers the behaviour of the other men to be repulsive. However, he does nothing to stop them from taking place – thereby meaning that he is just as guilty as his officers.

Purvis takes on a similar approach during the second torture scene, in which Frechette is physically beaten after being arrested at the liquor store. Despite not being charged with any crime, Frechette is hit, humiliated, battered with a plank of wood, and threatened with murder unless she volunteers information about Dillinger's location. Throughout the scene, she is denied the right to use the bathroom or have a glass of water. Finally, Frechette tells them a convincing lie to end the abuse, temporarily: she gives the Feds a false address and tells them that's where she was planning to meet Dillinger. The agents go to this address, but when they realise they've been tricked, they return to the interrogation room, now even more incensed. When the agents find out they've been tricked, they return to the interrogation room. Breaking under the pressure, Frechette mocks her interrogator: 'You wanted to know where he is, you dumb flatfoot? You were too scared to look around. You walked right past him on State Street. He was at the curb in that black Hudson.' The interrogator is furious, and prepares to land a particularly vicious blow against Frechette. At this moment, Purvis passes the room. Finding Frechette in her weakened and distressed state, Purvis discharges his agent and offers to carry her to the bathroom. This act may seem, on the surface, to be a gesture of kindness towards a woman who his agents have mistreated, but, really it is merely a facile and disingenuous effort on his part to cleanse his conscience. After all, Purvis was the one who ordered his agents to subject Frechette to extreme methods of interrogation, even after witnessing the intense agony they caused in the hospital scene. And Purvis doesn't step in to end the torture until it is obvious that Frechette genuinely doesn't know where Dillinger is hiding (as she comments, 'He's way the hell away from here by now, isn't he?').

In contrast to the more explicitly villainous and emotion-driven Hoover, Purvis represents a more mundane, everyday type of evil that may be perpetuated by those who consider themselves to simply be carrying out instructions. The critique of state torture methods in *Public Enemies* creates a clear parallel between the totalitarian measures implemented by Hoover and the draconian policies administered by the Bush administration; the images of those close to Dillinger being sadistically abused in exchange for information can't help but call to mind images of Abu Ghraib and Guantanamo Bay – and, of course, both regimes rationalised their violent methods of enhanced interrogation through widespread propaganda programs which de-humanised the victims. The message that Mann articulates here is that when one is embroiled in unjust corrupt social system, it is the moral duty of the individual to actively stand up to injustice. To aid in their implementation of malicious practices and policies makes one directly responsible for the harm they end up causing, even if one passively expresses their disapproval of them, and so Purvis is a deeply morally compromised character.

Indeed, following the torture of Frechette, Purvis puts into play a strategy of coercion for information which may, at first glance, seem to be less openly heinous than physical abuse, but is, in actuality, just as noxious. Purvis arranges a meeting with Anna Sage (Branka Katić), a brothel owner who had a series of encounters with Dillinger in the past. Purvis threatens to deport her to Romania unless she helps the FBI organise a sting operation. She is given instructions to invite Dillinger to hide out in her establishment so that she can secretly pass on information about his movements directly to the Bureau. This will gradually break down Dillinger's defences, and then, when he is least suspecting it, the FBI may launch an ambush. Sage demands a 'guarantee' that, if she is willing to do this favour for Purvis, she will be able to remain in America for as long as she wants. Purvis is unwilling to grant this request but does tell her that if she fails to comply, he can promise that she will be on a boat to Romania 'within 48 hours'. Here, Purvis uses an ostensibly more 'humane' method of obtaining information on Dillinger, but it is, in its own way, just as malicious.

To further highlight the pusillanimous nature of Purvis' character, the climactic shooting of Dillinger does not take the form of a grand showdown. Dillinger is caught when he has his guard down (dressed in civilian clothes, crossing a pedestrian street, making his way back from a trip to the cinema). Purvis' agents drastically outnumber him, and the fatal blow lands while his back is turned. Furthermore, it isn't Purvis who delivers this shot, despite being present at the scene, but the Texan lawman Charles Winstead (Stephen Lang). Purvis does not register any sense of triumph or satisfaction, he instead looks on in shock as a large crowd of pedestrians gather around Dillinger's lifeless body, many of whom are distraught to see him perish in such a cowardly attack. Purvis looks at the commotion with a disquieted expression, troubled by the sense of dissatisfaction he feels after successfully carrying out the task he had dedicated his life to for such a long period of time. Winstead kneels down beside Dillinger and listens to his last words. Unable to hear them, Purvis pushes through the crowd and asks Winstead to relate them to him. Even this small shed of closure is denied to Purvis: Winstead, respecting Dillinger's privacy in death, lies to his superior officer and tells him that the words were too garbled for him to make out (in the next scene, we discover that Dillinger, in fact, told Winstead that his last words were only meant to be heard by Frechette, and Winstead chose to obey his final wish).

If the prototypical Mannian hero is totally committed to their own moral and ethical code – even if this commitment drives them to the edges of society, into solitude, or even into death – then Purvis represents the polar opposite of this figure. He is a man who willing to compromise his values so that his manhunt may be completed as quickly as possible. During his pursuit, Hoover demands that Purvis sets aside 'obsolete notions of sentimentality' to apprehend Dillinger by any means necessary; it's the kind of unreasonable request by a corrupt authority figure that Mann's protagonists usually challenge. Purvis, on the contrary, bows down to this pressure, and as much as he'd like to distance himself from the atrocities committed by his department, he cannot shield himself from the guilt.

The two-pronged structure of *Public Enemies* may recall *Heat*, in the sense that both films follow the pursued and the pursuer simultaneously, with the two lead characters meeting at one point in the middle of the narrative and then again at the climax. But, while *Heat* positions McCauley and Hanna as kindred spirits who share a near-identical ethical code, Mann underlines the differences between the moral constitution of Dillinger and Purvis. Indeed, the earlier film affords both Hanna and McCauley equal weight in the narrative, here the bulk of the screen time is preoccupied with Dillinger, and Bale's restrained, reticent performance as Purvis naturally draws the viewer's attention (and sympathy) towards Depp's charming outlaw. As

Rayner observes, there is a clear and deliberate contrast between the charismatic rakishness of Depp's performance and the understatement of Bale's: 'If Depp's characterisation of Dillinger presents him as a self-conscious performer, this is balanced by Bale's incarnation of Purvis as a man forced into an inimical role.' (2013: 156). This lopsided structure is not a flaw on Mann's part, but a deliberate choice that expresses the fundamental dissimilarities between the two men in terms of their personal motivations, public images, and attitudes towards the mass media. Dillinger becomes the heavily publicised face representing a form of criminality which Hoover seeks to eradicate – it is in Purvis' interest to spread Dillinger's image through as many communication channels as possible, so that the nation may witness the power of the federal crime-fighting network which finally brings the outlaw to justice. On the other hand, Purvis is a mere middle-man, a self-effacing figure who does not hog the limelight in the same way that either Hoover or Dillinger does.

In a similar manner to his treatment of Ali, Mann here approaches Dillinger as an individual who is, on the one hand, an introverted dreamer who values having personal space and time to reflect, and a performer who is deeply moved by the attention he receives from the wider public – and, in particular, the disenfranchised working class who view him as an aspirational figure of resistance against the oppressive US government. Yet, though Dillinger regularly performers to the cameras, he never quite feels comfortable at the mass media's ability to construct a falsified image of 'Dillinger', that is disconnected from his true experience.

Dillinger's complex attitude towards the proliferation of his image is expressed in a scene that occurs in the middle of the film. Sitting in a movie theatre with some friends and criminal associates, Dillinger is dismayed when a public service announcement announces him as 'Public Enemy Number One', accompanied by a monolithic image of his mugshot. The narrator implores the audience to inform the police of any information they may encounter regarding Dillinger's whereabouts and keep a watch in case they see anybody resembling the photograph looming over the auditorium. The lights come up, and the audience is then told to turn to the left and turn to the right, to emphasise that Dillinger could be anywhere – even within the theatre itself. The audience members follow the instructions. Dillinger remains still, his expression of concern growing into a sly grin as he realises that nobody in the crowd will pick him up on it. At this moment, Dillinger realises the paradox of having his image spread so widely across mass media channels: the more ever-present his visage is, the more unreal it seems to be. Dillinger remains undetected by the public in this scene because they are incapable of matching the gigantic, widely-circulated image of 'Dillinger' they see on the screen to the actual, flesh-and-blood individual sitting amongst them. Indeed, this specific image of Dillinger has been seen in various contexts throughout the film leading up to this moment, including in the FBI headquarters, on newspaper covers, and 'Wanted' posters.

A similar moment occurs towards the end of the film, wherein Dillinger again audaciously tests the relationship between his myth and his corporeal presence. When he is dropping Polly Hamilton (Leelee Sobieski) off at a police station to pick up her waitressing licence, Dillinger makes the impulsive decision to accompany her inside. As Polly waits in line, Dillinger's attention is drawn to the offices in the back of the building. He rides an elevator to an upper floor, surrounded by several men in full police uniform who remain oblivious to his presence. Exploring one of the second floor hallways, Dillinger comes across a door marked 'Detective Bureau Dillinger Squad'. He tentatively enters and walks through a series of empty offices, surveying many collected materials on himself and his associates. The scene climaxes as he approaches an organisational noticeboard that features a map with several of his regular hide-outs highlighted, handwritten notes with observations about his relationships and working methods pasted on, and many copies of his mugshot attached. Dillinger focuses on the most prominent image of his face, positioned in the centre of the board (significantly, the same photograph broadcast in the movie theatre). This time, Dillinger is not focused on anybody else's reaction to his image – he stares intently at the image itself. He gazes directly into his own eyes for an extended time, studying the image as though looking into a mirror. In this poignant moment, Dillinger reflects upon how his image has become detached from his own lived experience, becoming an autonomous icon that others project their own thoughts and opinions onto. He is starting to understand the magnitude of his iconography. His visage lies at the centre of a sensationalistic state campaign to push through draconian policing measures and shift the entire landscape of law enforcement. It's a lot for any individual to bear, and Dillinger can only respond by marvelling at the absurdity of the situation. Hearing the faint sound of a baseball broadcast, Dillinger turns a corner to find several bureau agents gathered around a radio. Not merely satisfied with exploring the building undetected, Dillinger goes one step further and calls out to the Feds to ask them what the score is. Still, they do not spot him – one of the officers casually turns to him and says that the Cubs are winning. Like the cinema-goers in the earlier sequence, the agents have become so immersed in the myth of Dillinger that they cannot even recognise the real man when he is right in front of them.

In this scene, Dillinger comes face-to-face with his image, but he responds with muted amusement; it is not until the final sequence at the Biograph Theatre that Dillinger truly seems to arrive at a true comprehension of what his image means to society and the position it will take in the annals of history. The Biograph scene is infused with a remarkable sense of portent. Although Dillinger is unaware of the importance of the night, the viewer knows that time is rapidly running out – we have seen Sage phone the FBI headquarters to inform them that she will be accompanying Dillinger to a movie theatre that night, adding that she will wear a white blouse with an orange skirt to make it easy for them to locate her and Dillinger in the crowd. Mann intercuts images of the federal agents carefully plotting their ambush (checking the cinema listings, stationing their cars around several theatres in the city, surveying possible escape routes) with images of Dillinger performing quotidian tasks (washing, shaving, picking an outfit). Throughout the sequence, Dillinger gazes at a photograph of Frechette stored in a timepiece, fantasising about the future he hopes to lead with his beau. Dillinger remains blissfully unaware that Purvis' grip is immediately closing in around him. His plans for the future will soon be cut short – the dreams he projected into an undefined future will remain dreams, forever unfulfilled. The dramatic irony which infuses this scene is expressive of the futility that has always defined his activity – like so many other Mann protagonists, Dillinger has always understood, on some level, that he will not be able to sustain his chosen lifestyle forever, but chooses to follow his instincts into his potential death, rather than compromise and lead a life that would require him to sacrifice his deeply-held values.

As Purvis' agents wait outside the theatre gates in black vehicles, Dillinger experiences his final moments on earth being immersed in an illusory spectacle of gangster life – a late-night screening of *Manhattan Melodrama*. The scene is one of the most powerful in all of Mann's work – a doomed protagonist whose visage has become public spectacle gazes upon a manufactured image of a gangster in a cinema space and finds a reflection of his struggles, aspirations and values. After the film-within-the-film begins, Mann alternates between close-ups of a receptive Dillinger in the audience and close-ups of the actors on-screen, bridging the gap between Depp-as-Dillinger and Clarke Gable as corrupt Casino owner Edward J 'Blackie' Gallagher. The use of close-ups collapses the difference between Dillinger and the diegetic cinema screen, heightening the sense of connection he feels to these popular images of gangsterism. The trajectory of Blackie in *Manhattan Melodrama* simultaneously offers Dillinger a point of identification and a tragic prophecy of events to come. Mann's editing radically condenses Van Dyke's film, first showing us a fragmented series of images that depict Blackie luxuriating in the glamourous criminal lifestyle of fixed sports games, gambling, gunplay, and drunken revelry. These images of jubilation soon serge into images of Blackie's slide into isolation and destitution. Blackie's long-term girlfriend Eleanor Packer (Myrna Loy), exasperated with his inability to commit to a stable life, walks out on him, delivering the devastating farewell: 'Bye bye, Blackie.' This moment strongly resonates with Dillinger, whose smile fades as he sees the door close behind Eleanor. It is evident from Mann's selection of clips from *Manhattan Melodrama* that Blackie is crushed by Eleanor's decision, but he feels unwilling to follow her out of the room because he knows that to provide Eleanor with the security and stability she desires would involve betraying his essential sense of self.

In the following clip, Blackie comes to an acceptance of his own death. At the end of *Manhattan Melodrama*, Blackie has been sentenced to death for murder, and he awaits his execution on death row. His brother Jim Wade, who has recently been elected district attorney, offers to intervene and commute the sentence – changing his punishment from execution to life in prison. Blackie thanks his brother but rejects the offer, telling him, 'Do you think you're doing me a favour by keeping me locked up in this filthy trap for the rest of my life? No thanks,' before voluntarily walking to the electric chair. Blackie is comfortable with this death because he's allowing it to happen on his own terms – he could have avoided this fate either by settling into a mundane life in mainstream society with Eleanor, or by taking the option of spending the rest of his days in a jail cell. Both of these choices are unacceptable to him, however – he pursued a particular way of life knowing that it was going to be short-lived, and now he must accept that it must inevitably come to an end. What's ultimately important to him is that he never compromised. As he passes the other inmates, he says to one of them the immortal line: 'Die the way you lived. All of a sudden. That's the way to go. Don't drag it out, living like that doesn't mean a thing.'

This piece of dialogue chimes with the transience and focus on the present moment that defines Dillinger's experience, and he is visibly emotionally affected by it. Dillinger no longer looks distraught as he did while watching Eleanor leave Blackie – his lips curl into that recognisable smile, and he seems to take pride in seeing his lifestyle be lionised on screen. Like Blackie, Dillinger acknowledges that the most important thing is that he lived exactly the way he wanted to live, evading the influence of both the state and the crime syndicate. And so, just as Blackie willingly walks to the electric chair, Dillinger comes to accept that the path he has chosen will inevitably lead to his demise. Ignatiy Vishnevetsky poetically sums up the emotional power of this sequence: 'It's an image communicating with another image [...] The film is about Dillinger's persona, totally: the way it shaped the whole world. I think there's something Utopian here, too: you live a life, and at the end they let you see the effects of everything you've done. You experience yourself.' (Kasman, Walker Knight and Vishnevetsky, 2009). Dillinger recognises that he can no longer survive within this environment, but he will go down in history as a cultural icon; he will be immortalised American legend through the transference of his visage to films, books, magazines, and other forms of media. At this moment, the man has fully given way to the image – his focus is no longer on self-preservation but on taking stock of how he will be remembered and how his image will become a symbol of liberty, agency and the counter-cultural spirit for future generations.

As he walks through the streets following the theatre screening, Dillinger intuitively turns backwards to meet Winstead's gaze head-on. Mann slows down the speed of the sequence, cutting between Dillinger's eyes in extreme close-up and the purposeful motion of Winstead angling his gun. Dillinger makes a move for the weapon in his trouser pocket, but, for once, he lacks agility and speed. Winstead fires a bullet which hits Dillinger directly in the back of his head and exits through his cheek. As Dillinger stumbles forward he is shot once more – this time in the back. Blood splatters all over the sidewalk. After Dillinger falls to the ground, the street becomes filled with pedestrians holding flares and photographers racing to capture the first image of the deceased outlaw – they are already transforming Dillinger's death into a spectacle for mass consumption.

The very final scene displays the transference of Dillinger from private individual to public myth. In a women's correctional facility, Frechette is brought out of her cell to meet an unexpected visitor – Winstead. 'They say you're the man who killed him,' a hostile Frechette tells him. 'So why did you come here? To see all the pain you've caused me?' Winstead is calm in the presence of her subordination, perhaps feeling guilty himself for the grief he inflicted upon those who shared personal relationships with the former 'Public Enemy Number One'. He tells Frechette was that the only reason he's seeing her is to honour Dillinger's dying wish: 'Tell Billie for me, bye bye blackbird.' While the preceding scene was almost entirely based on historical fact (Dillinger was really shot outside of the Biograph Theatre following a screening of *Manhattan Melodrama*), Dillinger's final words here are fabricated. However, this considerable twisting of the truth is fitting for a scene that dramatises the passing of Dillinger into the realm of public myth. These words are precious to Frechette because they were delivered off the record, kept secret from Purvis and Hoover, and, thanks to Winstead, retained for the ears of Frechette and Frechette alone. These words are not printed in the press and they are not recorded by wire-tappers to be entered into to the files of the FBI. They are private words delivered from one lover to another, containing a call-back to first time they met – in the Chicago ballroom, when they danced to Diana Krall's version of 'Bye-Bye Blackbird'. Dillinger is dead, and Frechette remains confined within the institution, but this final gesture of interpersonal connection represents Dillinger's final act of rebellion against the state, which systematically works to render all activity a matter of public record. Frechette maintains her composure, but tears run silently down her cheeks – she recognises the significance of this moment, of an expression of private affection within an increasingly de-humanising society, but, as she is under the surveillance of the guards, feels unable to express this grief openly.

Public Enemies, then, looks back to the 1930s to address the merging of public and private life, the increasing authoritarianism of the state, and intensifying methods of surveillance technologies prevalent within 21st century America. The feature's portrayal of a historical era in which epochal technological advancements allowed for state lines to be merged under a single federal policing system endowed with a frightening degree of power over ordinary citizens is filtered through a contemporary lens, so that the audience may perceive the parallels between the current moment and how subsequent iterations have intensified the worst tendencies established during Hoover's reign. If Dillinger's crew are perceived as public enemies by the state, it is because they committed to a substantial resistance to the control of the federal government, evading the ties to mainstream political and economic institutions which were increasingly consuming every element of American life – in contrast, the criminal syndicates were symbiotic to state power.

Dillinger holds on to this rapidly vanishing way of life for as long as he can, but ultimately, he is snuffed out to re-establish the balance of the system. Although the narrative ends with Purvis finally catching and eradicating Dillinger, the film ironically frames Dillinger as the victor and Purvis as a man whose decline began the minute he began his collaboration with Hoover. Dillinger can retain his individuality against the overwhelming forces of dehumanisation, and as a result, he transforms into a folk icon who continues to inspire; Purvis not only submits to these forces, he plays a substantial part in consolidating Hoover's power. Mann's feature recontextualises the tropes and conventions of the gangster film to reflect upon the socio-political landscape of America in the years following the financial crash and the mechanisms of control implemented using the need to maintain domestic security during the (seemingly) never-ending 'War on Terror' as a smokescreen – while simultaneously reflecting upon the mythologising of the 1930s gangster archetype and its continued appeal in modern society. The radical use of digital technologies deepens and enriches this dialogue between past and present, as contemporary filmmaking techniques associated with digital technologies (motion blur, blood and dirt on the lens, the incredible deep focus facilitated by HD technology, rapid rack focus, jerky handheld movement) pulls us out of complete immersion within the diegetic universe to encourage our contemplation of the act of mediation and the parallels between the 1930s and the present day – for it is only through an understanding of past systems of oppression that similar forms of injustice may be resisted in the modern world.

In the Realm of the Senses: *Blackhat* (2015)

If *Miami Vice* offers a deeply pessimistic portrait of an idealistic loner engulfed by the dehumanising structure of an expansive, sprawling surveillance society, and *Public Enemies* looks back to the 1930s to chart the origins of the systems that would later form the foundation of this 21st-century technological dystopia, then *Blackhat* presents an optimistic vision of how an individual may retain their agency and exercise power within these confines. At the time of writing this book, *Blackhat* stands as Mann's final completed feature, and in this writer's eyes, it represents the culmination of the formal and socio-political preoccupations that have been at the centre of his work since *The Jericho Mile*. While Mann's crime films tend to either present a lead character whose will is crushed by the overwhelming forces of an inhuman urban landscape (*Heat*, *Miami Vice*) or who chooses to retain their autonomy by completely turning their back on society (*Thief*, *Public Enemies*), *Blackhat* is unique in that it dramatises the efforts of an idealistic hero to resist institutional systems of control by repurposing the technological tools utilised to oppress everyday citizens. Dillinger is an anachronistic figure within the nascent network society, because his commitment to the outsider ethos proves increasingly difficult to sustain in an era of widespread surveillance and corporatised crime. Crockett is terminally unsatisfied by his life in hyper-modern Miami, and is temporarily drawn to the outsider lifestyle, but he ultimately lacks the conviction to commit to it. *Blackhat*'s Hathaway, on the other hand, is a figure who exhibits a non-conformist attitude but has also adapted – physically and intellectually – to survive within the strange new digitised landscape. Unlike in Mann's previous two features, in *Blackhat* there is a complex dialectic at play between panoptic modes of social control and synoptic strategies of dissent. Utilising his exceptional computer hacking skills, Hathaway breaks into and re-tools the technologies typically mobilised by the state and by large private corporations to assert his power and fight for his self-determined values.

Through the character of Hathaway, Mann merges the figures of the criminal and law enforcer so essential to his oeuvre. Hathaway was once a computer science student at the prestigious Massachusetts Institute of Technology, but was forced to drop out after an impulsive fight at a local bar landed him an 18-month jail sentence. Following his release, Hathaway's lack of formal qualifications, combined with his criminal record, made it difficult for him to find work at any major tech company, so he made money through illegal blackhat practices – primarily wholesaling and carding. Like Dillinger, Hathaway stresses that he never targets ordinary civilians, only monolithic corporations and financial institutions. After eight years of honing his blackhat hacking abilities, Hathaway was apprehended by the FBI and sentenced to 13 years in a high-security penitentiary.

Adopting an attitude comparable to *The Jericho Mile*'s Murphy, Hathaway views his lengthy prison sentence as an opportunity to commit to an intensive self-improvement program. As Hathaway phrases it, to ensure that the time he spends on the inside isn't robbed from him, he devotes every waking second to exercising '[his] body, and [his] mind'. The images that introduce Hathaway depict him performing press-ups in his cell, listening to music, and reading seminal books by post-structuralist philosophers – in essence, transforming the blank walls of his cell into a personal refuge in which he may engage in his favoured pursuits and pastimes. His circumstances change, however, when the FBI call upon him to use his considerable knowledge of malware programs to help them track down a cyber-terrorist.

After a malware virus is transmitted to a Chinese nuclear plant, causing the coolant pumps to become overheated and explode, the FBI, working in collaboration with the Chinese government, determine that the code was adapted from a Remote Access Tool (RAT) designed by Hathaway while he was still a student. After some persuasion from Captain Chen Dawai (Leehom Wang), an agent of the Chinese government's cyber warfare unit who happens to be Hathaway's former college roommate, the FBI agrees to place Hathaway on furlough so that he may help them apprehend the perpetrator(s). Hathaway is promised that his sentence will be commuted if he can successfully oversee the arrest of hacker responsible for the attack; but if he fails, or if he makes any attempt to escape, he will be sent back to prison and forced to serve the rest of his sentence.

Hathaway agrees to aid the bureau with their investigation into the hacking circle, and is placed under the close supervision of Dawai, Dawai's sister Chen Lien and FBI Special Agent Carol Barrett (Viola Davis),. Although Hathaway spends much of the narrative working alongside the FBI, he is ever truly one of them. He occupies an odd in-between position, suspended between liberation and entrapment: Hathaway's work must contribute to the larger project determined by the federal bureau (he is not legally allowed to work on any side projects he may personally be interested in pursuing), he is placed under the constant supervision of his three supervisors, and his motion is tracked at the head officers by a computerised ankle monitor. Hathaway, therefore, , may be physically removed from the confines of the prison, but he is placed under perpetual surveillance by the American government. Esther Muñoz González notes the fragile nature of Hathaway's position during the early stages of the narrative: 'The aesthetic of the governmental surveillance is shown on the screen of the FBI agents' mobile phones, where the real space of places is shown in its virtual portrait, and Hathaway is another "flow" located thanks to his ankle bracelet.' Hathaway's situation, therefore, reflects the transformation of the 'human subject' into 'an object captured and controlled by an increasingly improved surveillance system.' (2017: 226). Dawai and Lien are sympathetic toward Hathaway, but Barrett repeatedly reminds Hathaway of his outsider status and hangs the threat of re-imprisonment over his head. Ironically, Hathaway's only hope for achieving freedom requires him to first submit to the will of the authorities. The fact that the criminal being hunted is a blackhat hacker who re-appropriated code originally authored by Hathaway creates a sense of doubling between Hathaway and the cyber-terrorist, further underlining that Hathaway does not truly belong within the group of law enforcers.

Hathaway's ability to assert his own individuality against the whims of those who seek to place him under total state control is exemplified in an early scene which sees Hathaway negotiate the terms of his furlough with a representative of the US government. Led into a blank, whitened interrogation room that resembles a sensory deprivation chamber, Hathaway is handed a lengthy contract and pressured to sign before having an opportunity to read the fine print. Hathaway resists the agent's attempts to rush him, understanding how high the stakes of the case are, how valuable his contribution to it is likely to be, and that he is in a strong position to demand better terms. Reading that the initial conditions of the agreement offer to release him only for the period during which he will be working for the FBI, Hathaway tosses the contract back and tells the agent, emphatically, 'Both you and the US attorney can stick that document up your ass.' The agent, evidently shocked by Hathaway's self-confidence, incredulously responds 'Sorry?' At this point, Hathaway turns the tables on him and asserts power over the situation. 'Why are you apologising?' Hathaway asks, in a derisive tone. 'I insulted you, you said sorry. I'm not sorry. What are you sorry for?.' After Hathaway has voiced his counter-offer of an unconditional release if he can help the federal agents successfully identify the cyber-attacker, the interviewer makes a pitiful attempt to place Hathaway in a subordinate position, telling him 'this isn't a negotiation.' Without hesitating, Hathaway emphatically retorts that he 'just made it one.' In this scene, Hathaway takes a situation in which he may seem to be powerless and turn the tables on the figure of authority, taking charge of the interaction and making his demands known. Hathaway – who is inherently distrustful of authority – can easily recognise the methods used by the state to exploit and manipulate individuals, and here he demonstrates his capacity to resist these strategies.

Like *Miami Vice*, *Blackhat* sees Mann constructing an environment in which criminal enterprises employ vast technological systems just as – if not more – advanced than those utilised by the official bodies of law enforcement that attempt to track them down. Crockett is astonished to discover that Montoya employs similar surveillance and data harvesting mechanisms as the FBI do; Hathaway, in contrast, is one of the outlaws who recognise the huge potential of repurposing advanced technology to achieve his own objectives. The diegetic world of *Blackhat* is one in which almost all labour is performed at a distance, through the manipulation of abstract data that causes tangible material effects. This is an environment in which a few keystrokes can cause cataclysmic physical destruction in another continent, an environment in which nearly all human actions are digitally tracked and logged in the form of computerised data. As Ryland Walker Knight writes, *Blackhat* explores the possibility for the internet to be used as a tool 'to perpetrate crime at a remove but relying on the speed and microscopic anatomy of a computer, of code.' The feature meditates on 'the ability to use what looks like nothing to wreak havoc on what is manifest reality – to fabricate an effect upon the world -- as fast and as hidden as possible.' (2015). The opening sequence of *Blackhat* powerfully visualises the collapse of spatial and temporal boundaries in the era of digital networks: the first image is a vast wide shot of the planet earth, a glistening blue orb suspended within the monumental vacuum of space. Mann then cuts in closer, depicting the planet's surface as a vast grid of pulsating digital signals transported across national borders. The silence is replaced by a multi-layered arrangement of computerised notifications, dial tones, error messages and indecipherable chatter.

Mann's camera zooms in on one part of the glowing grid, and abstract reams of light gradually resolve into the more recognisable form of skyscrapers, roads and power lines. Our perspective is directed towards one specific glowing line as the camera moves in. We realise that it is transmitting electronic impulses to an offshore location. Mann then dissolves to a bird's eye perspective of a Hong Kong power plant – a complex structure comprised of cooling towers, high offices, and transmission lattices. This is the closest image so far to a classical establishing shot, and it initially seems as though Mann's perspective is going to rest at this level. But Mann keeps zooming inwards. The camera moves over a worker's shoulder, zeroing in on a series of numbers displayed on a digital screen. The camera zooms deeper into the screen and we find ourselves looking at the inside of the computer's mainframe: a space of whirling fans, interconnecting cables, and microchips. The apparatus tracks through one of these cables into a circuit board. The speed of the camera's motion increases as it is directed through another wire, which becomes illuminated by pulsing blue lights. Finally, the camera comes to a halt as the cable reaches a computer monitor. A miniature LED light is activated, and Mann cuts to the interior of a dim room containing multiple monitors, bookcases and hard drives. It is just as saturated with technological devices as the power plant's control room, but the décor marks it as a private space such as an apartment or den. A figure – whose face remains obscured by ambient objects in the foreground of the images – rapidly types a sequence of code at a desktop computer and then presses 'enter'. Mann's camera propels us back into the digital network, a reverse trajectory across the route we just witnessed – but this time, Mann alternates between images of the camera's motion through cyberspace and images of the power plant. These shots depict the plant rapidly plunging into a state of disarray: monitors indicate that the towers are overheating, pipes burst, water boils. And, then, the reactor explodes. Flesh burns, Medics arrive at the scene in hazmat suits, and employees are retrieved from the site on stretchers, screaming and writhing.

In this astonishing five-minute montage, Mann elegantly introduces the (ostensible) dichotomies which lie at the centre of the narrative: the immaterial vs the physical; distance vs proximity; direct action vs the abstract manipulation of digits. The actual actions of the unseen hacker (later revealed to be a middle-aged American named Sadak) appear pointedly un-cinematic, even though the material consequences of them are spectacular in scope: all he does is hit a few keystrokes from the comfort of his domestic space. As González observes, in these first images of Sadak, 'he seems Mr Nobody, invisible, hidden in a dark room with classical furniture and wooden walls.' Thus, the feature suggests that, '[h]e can be any one of those people who spend their lives in front of a computer screen.' (2017: 231) It is soon revealed that the ultimate aim of Sadak's attack on the plant was not the explosion itself but the impact of the blast on the financial markets. The scene depicting the destruction at the power station is followed by a series of roving tracking shots across an empty stock exchange building. As television monitors arranged around the room broadcast news about the cyber-attack, the digital display boards reveal that the market value of soy is going haywire. Mann's camera zooms into one of these displays and, again, enters the visually abstract realm of cyber-space. The camera, then, exits via a wire attached to Sadak's computer monitor. Sadak reclines in his seat and hits a few more keys on the board, expressing no emotional reaction whatsoever to the real-world violence he has inflicted in Hong Kong. The camera then transports us back through the computer system to the stock exchange floor. It is now packed with traders selling and buying their shares, responding frantically to the rapid fluctuations in the market. What is so unnerving about Sadak is that he expresses hostility towards human life, but that he is utterly indifferent to it. He does not relish in inflicting real-world trauma, he simply perceives it as being one component in a process that begins in abstraction (the stream of code which forms the basis for the malware) and ends in abstraction (the virtual stream of future-orientated values which form the foundation of the stock market).

Later into the narrative, it is revealed that there is a second, even more heinous component to Sadak's plan: Sadak intends to detonate an explosive that will destroy a dam in Malaysia, resulting in the flooding of several major tin mines. This will cause an international shortage of the material and allow Sadak to make a huge amount of money by cashing out his shares in tin production. Shockingly, this plan, which will have enormous global implications and involve many deaths, can be conducted by a single man from the comfort of his own home. In contemporary digitised society, *Blackhat* suggests, the criminal no longer needs to be a skilled fighter or an agile physical performer to wreak mass-scale havoc; Sadak can implement his momentous plan using blocks of computer code, inputted on his personal computer.

Blackhat communicates the concept of contemporary society as being based on interconnected streams of computational flows by visualising the networks on both the micro- and the macro-level: on the micro-level, Mann's camera repeatedly plunges into the minute space of computer chips and wiring, the digital apparatus taking on an impossible perspective as it takes on the viewpoint of binary coding being instantaneously transported from one digital device to another; on the macro level, the opening sequence visualises the globe as being little more than a network of computer signals, stretching across land and sea with no visible borders. Between these two levels, the surface-level physical world of people, cities and the natural environment is suspended in a fragile state. The material, geographical level of lived experience is increasingly enmeshed within computerised systems – economically, socially, politically. There is no longer any straightforward distinction between 'inside' and 'outside' the computer; the two realms are intricately intertwined such that any damage committed within one sphere has an immediate effect on the other. Mann himself described the nature of this new networked society very elegantly in an interview with *The New York Times*: 'It's almost like there's an invisible kind of exoskeleton above the layer in which we think our lives take place on planet Earth, that's made up of interconnectedness and data […] We're swimming around in it, and everything is porous, vulnerable and accessible.' (Ryzik, 2014). Within the diegesis of *Blackhat*, tangible and computerised experiences converge, computer mediation has subsumed work and social lives, and human behaviour takes on the properties of mechanic functions. To break away from the system seems to be impossible: a bank card and virtual ID is required to perform even the most essential tasks, from purchasing goods to booking a medical appointment, to entering certain buildings.

Blackhat powerfully taps into the widespread sense of paranoia that had come to dominate the collective attitude towards digital culture by the year 2015. The brave new world of expanded horizons, instantaneous communication and freedom of expression that the more optimistic sociologists of the 1990s predicted had, by this point, become tainted by the use of digital information technologies to expand state surveillance techniques, develop more efficient strategies of warfare, and accelerate precarious financial processes. In the wake of the 9/11 attacks and the subsequent series of seemingly never-ending imperialist wars that followed had given rise to an affective economy of collective anxiety regarding the influence of digital technology on our everyday lives. In contemporary Western societies, the threat of international terrorism is presented as not being tied to any single, fixed nation or organisation, it is presented as a perpetual risk that may spill over into real-world violence. As a result, the Western world seem to be constantly teetering on the edge of a mass destruction event, a feeling enforced by mass media channels which heighten the public's sense of anxiety so that governments may implement policies that erode civil liberties and rationalise immoral military action committed overseas.

If, in industrial society, there existed a split between public areas in which surveillance cameras were present (the factory, the street, the library, etc); in the contemporary age, the mass proliferation of digital devices into every aspect of lived has dissolved this barrier. In the current climate, virtually all citizens are plugged into the digital network constantly, and create online traces which are tracked and stored by myriad external institutions. In modern networked society, the hierarchy of control is not maintained by the forced gaze of cameras administered by the powerful to monitor the powerless; instead, citizens voluntarily purchase and subject *themselves* to the very devices used to monitor their actions. Thus, systems of control become disguised under the veil of active participation, as consumers are falsely led to believe they have agency over these devices, which, in fact, enable the state and various corporations to gather a vast amount of information on them to serve their own ends. With the manufactured, omnipresent threat of international terrorism, the ubiquity of digital devices is treated as offering an increased sense of security (through, for example, the high number of CCTV cameras in airports, information used for background checks, etc), when, in actuality, they only accelerate the collective paranoia.

The spectre of 9/11 infuses every moment of *Blackhat*, though there is only one direct reference to the event itself, which occurs near the end of the second act. While driving through the city at night in pursuit of a now-wanted Hathaway, Deputy United States Marshal Jessup (Holt McCallany) asks Barrett, intuitively, 'You don't have to answer this, but who did you lose on 9/11.' After a moment of silence, Barrett responds, 'My husband.' The dialogue is not elaborated upon because no more contextual information is necessary. All we need to know is that Barrett is personally connected to the intense sense of national trauma which followed the 9/11 attacks. This immense feeling of loss she experienced still motivates her, and has lead her to become an active participant in the spread of draconian government policies. The US state exploits her private grief to convince her to perform actions that only amplify her feelings of alienation and dissatisfaction, but, like Purvis in *Public Enemies*, she does not question the orders she receives from her superiors. When Barrett is gunned down by Elias Kassar (Ritchie Coster) shortly after this sequence, Mann cuts from a close-up of her face, the life slowly seeping out of her eyes, to a low-angle POV shot of the top of a nearby skyscraper – it appears like a luminous monolith dominating the skyline, extraordinary and daunting in equal measure. The fact that this is the final sight Barrett witnesses before she passes highlights the tragic futility of the cause she has devoted her life to: she has spent the past decade and a half acting to maintain an inhuman and indifferent technological system. She is ultimately expelled from the network, which continues to run, unaffected by this loss.

For Hathaway, the proliferation of digital devices is a double-edged sword. On the one hand, he becomes a victim of the systems of surveillance which, first, allowed him to be apprehended by the FBI and, then, tightly monitor his behaviour when he is furloughed; on the other hand, the accessibility and ease-of-access of advanced computing equipment allows Hathaway to eventually overcome the American government and hunt down Sadak on his own terms. The hacker figure is increasingly gaining currency within popular culture as a symbol of agency and self-determination. Lana and Lilly Wachowskis' *Matrix* series (1999-2022), Bill Condon's *The Fifth Estate* (2013), David Fincher's *The Girl with the Dragon Tattoo* (2011), Howard Franklin's *Antitrust* (2001) and the popular television series *Mr Robot* (2015-2019) are all recent works which have helped to cement the new archetype of the hacker-hero into the collective cultural consciousness. Mann has always sought to take prototypical figures from popular genre categories and critically interrogate them to determine what they reveal about the specific cultural context which produced them, from the frontiersman in *The Last of the Mohicans* to the gangster in *Public Enemies*, to the lawman in *Manhunter* and *Heat*. Here, Mann interrogates the appeal of the hacker as a genre hero in an era of ubiquitous computation. As Daniel Kasman observes, in the world of *Blackhat*, liberation is 'attainable by brilliant minds externalised and embodied by equally brilliant physique and prowess.' As such, 'this hacker seems a new kind of god.' (2016).

Over the 1980s and 1990s, hackers tended to be positioned within genre fiction as criminals, threats, and disrupters of the stability of social order. In recent years, hackers increasingly tend to be coded as subversive activists uncovering information typically concealed by the establishment; they utilise advanced technological means to upend traditional hierarchies of control. Due to the prominence within the cultural imagination of whistleblowers such as Edward Snowden, Julien Assange and Chelsea Manning, the hacker is increasingly being perceived not as a destabilising force, but a noble folk-hero dedicated to revealing the corruption and deception at the heart of official institutions. Nick Pinkerton notes the importance of this wider intellectual context to the viewer's perception of Hathaway, acknowledging that *Blackhat* was produced at 'a moment when the agency [the NSA] was very much in the news thanks to revelations of the scope of its global surveillance operation by whistleblower Edward Snowden.' (2018). Against the overwhelming dominance of plutocratic digital communication networks, the hacker stands as an icon of individual agency, intellectual curiosity, and ideological purity. Because they typically operate with consumer-grade technology, the hacker has often been associated with grassroots activism and ground-up political programs. By engaging in righteous acts of civil disobedience while also maintaining anonymity within the network, the hacker represents a positive example of how an individual may hold on to personal integrity within a world of accelerating digitisation. In Blackhat, we see a dialogue between the traditional idea of the hacker as an ominous threat and the newer idea of the hacker as an honourable vigilante through the ideological clash between Hathaway and Sadak. While Hathaway represents a type of hacker that pits themselves against an authoritarian state and only targets incredibly powerful institutions, Sadak's use of digital technology mimics the worst, most predatory instincts of the state – his only concern is for amassing personal wealth by playing the market system better than his competitors, and he doesn't care how many innocent civilians he harms in pursuit of this end-goal.

The valorisation of the hacker as a folk hero in 21st-century cinema comes with a substantial problem, however: the act of hacking is thoroughly un-cinematic. As Zara Dinnen notes, 'code itself appears antithetical to narrative cinema, conforming to the unnarratable conditions of the supranarratable' (2018: 1). Rapid typing, reviewing lines of code, bypassing firewalls – all these activities do not appear to be immediately captivating in visual terms. It involves inputting a series of symbols that form the basis for a programming language that can be read by a machine but appears abstract to human eyes. When inputted, the computer system then reconfigures this set of code to a different language known as 'object code', which activates an action within the mainframe. Computer coding is future-orientated; it involves programming a set of actions to be translated into instructions for a machine to execute. Only the first part of this complex series of actions involves human input; once the source code has been inputted, the machine must interpret the instructions and translate them, first into a series of symbols which can only be interpreted by other devices, and then into concrete action. As Dinnen continues: 'Programming a computer involves inputting a string of characters which will execute action. This does not happen magically all at once, but by layers of code each 'conversing' with the next layer until a discrete switch is moved in a circuit. Human programmers usually work in high-level (abstract) programming languages which are syntactically similar to natural languages; these are then compiled as 'object code' (2017: 15). The bulk of the process is conducted internally, by a machine or series of machines, without the necessity for human supervision. The intellectually comprehendible aspects of programming only provide the starting point of the operation; following that, the computer enters into dialogue with itself. The programmer/hacker relies on a digitised process that bypasses biological cognition to transform their input into observable results.

The vast majority of cinematic texts which deal with the concept of hacking side-step this issue by showing the hacker literally entering the virtual world of cyber-space: either by literally adorning virtual reality helmets which situate them within an intra-computer diegesis, or by visualising the activity of hacking through the metaphor of an embodied digital sphere being physically penetrated. These strategies allow filmmakers to dramatise the process of breaking into the immaterial sphere of the virtual, in concrete terms; in such a visual schema, computer code itself is not shown on screen, but is translated into a symbolic visual representation of digital space which aligns more readily with expectations of audio-visual dramaturgy. On the other hand, Mann does not resort to visual metaphors to render the realm of binary code more easily intelligible; the digital sphere is portrayed directly as streams of letters, numbers, and mathematical symbols manipulated and transmitted instantaneously. There is no metaphorical virtual 'world' within the computer monitors of *Blackhat* –

as there are in films like Joseph Kosinski's *Tron: Legacy* (2010) and Steven Spielberg's *Ready Player One* (2018) – only a constant stream of data which infiltrates our own, corporeal environment. When the camera 'moves' into the screen, all we see is a tangle of cables, tubes, and chips – not a window into another plane that resembles our own sphere of experience, but a piece of inanimate, intricately designed machinery which transports electrical signals across the globe.

Like *Miami Vice* and *Public Enemies*, *Blackhat* was shot with state-of-the-art HD cameras, and Mann does not attempt to efface the material/ontological nature of the technological apparatus. The visual scheme alternates between stunning deep-focus compositions and smeary, shallow focus handheld shots. What differentiates the visual style of *Blackhat* from that of the early film is that *Blackhat*'s aesthetic is smoother and more refined than the frenetic bombast of *Miami Vice*. The shots run longer, and the camera movements are more serene; the colour scheme is a more muted palette of silver, navy and emerald. If *Miami Vice*, made during an early stage of digital image proliferation, envisions the new visual regime as an overwhelming cacophony of rough, de-materialised sights and sounds, *Blackhat* responds to a society in which digital streams of audio-visual information have become fully integrated into the texture of everyday life. The diegetic world of the feature is suffused with digital monitors: computer screens, surveillance feeds, smartphones, motion advertisements, news broadcasts, and digital stock market displays. The colours that dominate the opening scene also bleed into the feature's physical environments, infusing the action with a subtle, hyper-real glow that constantly reminds us of the degree to which the material and the virtual have become intertwined.

Another characteristic which marks Hathaway as a noble outcast within the narrative of *Blackhat*, is the high degree of value he places on corporeal experience. Though he devotes much of his professional life to mastering digital technology, Hathaway is also deeply in tune with the needs of his physical body – as signalled in his stated commitment to a programme of self-improvement designed to 'work on [his] body and [his] mind.' While the FBI agents rely on abstract, perceptual labour in their investigations and Sadak carries out all of his attacks remotely, , Hathaway skilfully navigates the physical and the immaterial realms. Unsurprisingly, both the FBI agents and Sadak prove to be tragically ineffectual when they are they find themselves in a situation that requires physical action.

This is another major difference between the mentality of Hathaway and that of Sadak. Sadak projects himself into the world of cyberspace to such an extent that he believes he can transcend the limitations of the material sphere altogether. Sadak outlines his philosophy of life in an extended conversation with Hathaway near the end of the film: 'Sometimes wake up in the morning, and I don't even know who I am, where I am, in what country […]

If I stop thinking about anything, it disappears, it vanishes, it ceases to exist.' Sadak believes that the source of his power is the anonymity and spatial abstraction of cyberspace. Concealing his identity, location, and IP address through a VPN, Sadak could theoretically be anybody and could theoretically be anywhere. As a corporeal being Sadak is not a physically powerful or intimidating presence; he is not able to evade capture due to his of physical strength or agility. His ability to wreak havoc and avoid the authorities is based entirely on his capacity to manipulate binary code creatively and intelligently. Pointedly, Sadak remains off-screen for the vast majority of the feature. He is briefly visible during the opening sequence, but his visage is obscured by wires, computer monitors, and other miscellaneous objects; other than that, he is mainly glimpsed through virtual traces, such as the text message he sends to Hathaway under a false name and concealed IP address: 'Piss off and die ghostman.' While, as this book has explored, Mann's man-hunt films tend to be organised according to a mirroring structure wherein the law enforcer and lawbreaker figures occupy positions of more or less equal weight in the narrative, in *Blackhat*, Sadak functions almost as a structuring absence. Although his actions cause very real material effects, Sadak only appears as a physical figure very close to the finale. As such, he seems to be at once invisible and omnipresent.

Sadak does not directly, physically inflict violence upon others and is, therefore, able to mentally distance himself from the atrocities he creates through his malicious manipulation of computer code. The amount of time he spends immersed within cyberspace has rendered him emotionally detached from the world outside the digital databank. After Hathaway kills Elias, one of Sadak's close henchmen, in an act of self-defence, an unmoved Sadak responds by saying: 'Plenty of people die on this planet every day. What do you want me to do? Grieve? Because I knew him? He's not here anymore.' Sadak is pathologically incapable of considering the impact of these actions on other individuals because his mind is focused entirely on the virtual sphere; the outside world seems, to him, akin to a computer programme he is able to shape and control through his monitor.

Sadak, then, is representative of a new form of criminal, distinct from any other antagonist in Mann's work. *Miami Vice*'s Montoya uses advanced technology to consolidate his power, but his enterprise still structurally resembles a recognisable criminal syndicate; Sadak, on the other hand, never has to engage with the outside world. Sadak lacks even the most rudimentary moral code, is disconnected from any personal/professional relationships (to the extent that he does not care when one of his most loyal employees is killed in front of him) and strives to be totally anonymous. So inured is he from the material substance of life that he refers to murder as 'sub-symbolic stuff'. When so many people slip out of existence every day, Sadak believes that it is irrational to mourn a single life.

Sadak revels in his disconnection from the rest of humanity, believing that his total lack of concern for his fellow man is a sign of strength. Sadak prefers to contact his associates remotely, through coded messages. A Bluetooth transmitter is hidden within the shrubbery of a square in Hong Kong, set up so that it can transmit messages to three of Sadak's runners so long as they are physically present within a short range of the device. The messages are then deleted shortly after being read. When his henchman is killed, Sadak views it as the natural result of the weakest being weeded out of the population, emphasising the lack of personal connection he feels with those he works with. Totally immersed within the new regime of virtual criminality, Sadak exhibits feelings of alienation, isolation and indifference to human life more intense than any of Mann's other antagonists. Even *Manhunter*'s Dollarhyde, a pathological egomaniac wrapped up in his own fantasies of grandeur, makes an attempt to enter the social world of the through his romantic relationship with a co-worker. Hathaway pits himself against the powerful and makes a point of never targeting individuals; Sadak views damage to individuals as being acceptable collateral damage.

However, there is a massive dissonance between the all-powerful threat he presents himself as in the realm of cyber-space and the weak, frustrated and petulant man who lies behind the facade. In *Miami Vice*, Montoya refrains from engaging in physical labour or direct combat, but he, at least carries himself with an aura of gravitas and exudes an air of genuine authority. On the other hand, Sadak is clumsy, irritable, and poorly coordinated in speech and action. The first interaction between Sadak and Hathaway takes the pointedly unglamorous form of a phone call, and Hathaway easily takes charge of the dialogue. Sadak attempts to denigrate Hathaway as a 'glorified carder', but is rendered speechless when he hears the retort: 'A glorified carder holding your 75 billion.' Sadak attempts to lead Hathaway into an ambush. He convinces Hathaway to meet him at an abandoned parking lot, planting several of his henchmen around the area to strike when Hathaway's guard is down. But Sadak's plan falls apart when Hathaway spots, from a distance, Sadak's men waiting to ambush him, and he phones Sadak to plan a new meeting – stipulating that, this time, Sadak *must* come alone.

When Hathaway and Sadak finally met face-to-face in the film's climactic sequence, the confrontation is completely one-sided. During this meeting, the two men are totally cut off from the technological strategies of self-assertion that have previously been their speciality. While Hathaway enters the situation prepared to take on Sadak in one-to-one combat, Sadak relies upon the efforts of a few armed henchmen he has secretly organised to wait in strategic hiding spots around the surrounding religious procession. As Hathaway fights them off, Sadak sneaks behind him, brandishing a previously concealed blade. He stabs Hathaway once in the shoulder while his attention is focused elsewhere, and then slashes his arm. At this point, Hathaway collects his bearings and breaks away from Sadak's grip. Hathaway effortlessly avoids Sadak's feeble lunges before grabbing and breaking his arm. Sadak relinquishes his grasp on his weapon, and Hathaway removes a screwdriver from a hidden belt. He pierces Sadak's chest multiple times, leaving the body bloodied and lifeless on the ground. This is perhaps the most visceral scene of violence in Mann's entire body of work: Hathaway's thrusts are savage and unrelenting; the camera captures Sadak in a medium shot from the torso-up, keeping in frame his pained facial expression and the wounds inflicted upon his flesh. The audio design isolates the sound of the screwdriver puncturing Sadak's skin, emphasising the brutality of his actions.

The extreme nature of the physical carnage in this scene is necessary to articulate the fragility of the human body in contrast to the immaterial sphere of abstract code. The spectre of Sadak hangs over the film's first two acts like an invincible, God-like figure, yet, when he is removed from his computer monitor and forced to fend for himself within the corporeal world, he is easy to defeat. His only hope to beat a skilled athlete like Hathaway is to take him by surprise, but when Hathaway has gotten over the suddenness of Sadak's initial attack, Sadak cannot even manage to land a single counter-blow. Sadak, we come to realise, vastly overestimates his own significance. The true antagonist of *Blackhat* is the panoptic digital network itself, and it is far too large, complex and sprawling to be embodied by any single human villain. Sadak is, ultimately, merely a single player within the digital network. He does not hold control or ownership over the digital network; he merely logs in to it to redirect its flow of data and then profits from the chaos which ensues. Sadak is, ultimately, a biological organism like anybody else, with the same physiological needs and weaknesses as every other person. Though it is possible to kill Sadak, the virtual system will continue to run undisturbed. Individuals like Sadak may hack into the database to achieve their own mercenary ends, but they will never be able to exert complete control over the network. The final image of *Blackhat* re-affirms the continued dominance of the network over all areas of human life – Hathaway and Lien are captured by a multitude of surveillance cameras as they walk across the main lounge of an international airport, their images fed into a operations room monitored by several government agents.

The significance of mass media in constructing social and political narratives is a central theme in *Public Enemies*: Hoover recognises that if he wants to exert power over the population, he must first reconstruct the collective consciousness to align the people with his viewpoint. Newspapers, movie theatres, and radio broadcasts are used as primary instruments in Hoover's propaganda campaign against Dillinger. Hoover gathers a substantial archive of photographs and film reels, providing the FBI with a significant visual resource to either mine for information or to proliferate to the wider population, thus reducing Dillinger's ability to 'hide out' in public. Surveillance tactics are vital in this regard, as images are gathered, and transcripts of his private phone conversations are collected to provide the FBI with an up-to-date, constantly updated record of his movements. In *Blackhat*, Mann studies just how extensively the surveillance state has expanded in the intervening years. Monitoring systems are embedded within every possible environment. There is no longer any hope of escaping the gaze of the surveillance camera by physically removing oneself from its purview; the only way individuals may retain some semblance of true privacy is by using complex systems to scramble their digital footprint.

The slipperiness of identity and the ease with which it may be manipulated or stolen is yet another source of perpetual anxiety in the age of mass computation. When investment banker Gary Baker refuses to pass on confidential data about his company's recent activity to the FBI, Barrett pressures him into complying by threatening to launch a media campaign against him through the nation's major newspapers and television stations. Like Hoover, Barrett understands the power of the state to sway public opinion with a few carefully worded headlines. He recognises that she holds power to transform Baker into a public enemy overnight. The FBI, Barrett clarifies, don't even need to charge him. All they need to do is tell the media that he is refusing to assist with a state investigation into cyber-terrorism, and they will ensure that his reputation will be tarnished. Individuals in the network society are more than just their physical bodies and their identities; they are constituted from the streams of information which make up their digital footprint – whether this information has been voluntarily offered (through social media sites, etc) or gathered without their knowledge (through surveillance feeds). These are versions of our identities that exist entirely within the virtual realm, and though related to our actual actions, are also fundamentally disconnected from our experience as empirical beings. The institutions which have access to this data may selectively draw upon this digital footprint and use it to serve their own ends, even if this means destroying the lives of the individuals this data is connected to. This aspect of contemporary digital culture is dramatised in *Blackhat* not only through Barrett's threat to Baker but also through the FBI's constant monitoring of Hathaway, and Hathaway's decision to assume the identity of a senior NSA officer – using data gathered through hacking into his computer system – to access the Black Widow programme.

Despite not being an agent of the state, Sadak's technological aptitude grants him an enormous amount of surveillance power. During the early parts of the narrative, Sadak uses this power to deliberately lead the authorities astray and frustrate their attempts to hunt him. Shortly after being furloughed from jail, Hathaway deduces that a former employee of the FBI is now working for Sadak. Hathaway accesses the employee's confidential files and tracks him down to his apartment Once the team arrive, however, they find that he has been murdered. The viewer, like Hathaway, is lead to assume that Sadak somehow knew the FBI were heading to the man's apartment and killed him as a pre-emptive measure to ensure that they would not be able to gather information from him. Next to the bed upon which the lifeless body lies, a laptop sits with several web pages still left open. Hathaway scans the man's open email inbox to find details of a money transfer arranged that night in a nearby Korean restaurant. With permission from the FBI, Hathaway and Lien go to the location.

After waiting in the restaurant for several hours without spotting a single sign of suspicious behaviour, Hathaway intuitively turns his attention to a small surveillance camera mounted in the top corner of the main floor. Sensing that the two are being closely watched, Hathaway walks to a back room and finds a computer monitor displaying the surveillance feed from inside the dining room, angled so that his table is the primary focal point. Lien stands up to get a napkin, and the surveillance camera follows her in lockstep with her motion. Hathaway realises that a trap has been set up for the FBI, and he's fallen right into it. Sadak arranged for his henchman to be killed and for the laptop to be open with information about a false meeting place visible, so that he could lure the investigating officers into the restaurant. The extreme frustration Hathaway expresses at this moment is rooted in his realisation that he has become the subject of another regime of panoptic surveillance – in addition to that of the state, Hathaway has unwittingly become an object placed under observation by strategies of surveillance employed by Sadak. Bilge Ebiri notes the significance of this moment: 'By stringing us along in this manner, and presenting what at times seems like a wild goose chase that spans the whole planet, Mann exposes just how thoroughly technology has infiltrated our lives, and how vulnerable that makes us.' (2018).

A dialog box opens on the monitor, and Hathaway realises that a user whose identity is being obscured is trying to contact him. The username is 'sdksdk'. The user asks for Hathaway is, and in response, Hathaway replies with the pseudonym 'ghostman'. After a few moments of no communication, the simple reply is: 'Piss off and die ghostman.' As he has been following the trail of digital breadcrumbs carefully laid by Sadak, Hathaway has not only wasted time and resources, but he has allowed the cyber-terrorist to gather information about himself that may be used against him. Hathaway's identity is known to Sadak, but he is not aware of theirs, placing Sadak in a position of greater power at this moment in the narrative. Hathaway unplugs the computer, heads back to the restaurant's main floor, guides Lien by the arm, and tells her that they need to leave immediately.

Before they can reach the door, however, three intimidating men enter. Hathaway tackles them to the ground, easily, in front of shocked onlookers. As they lunge for him, he beats up one of them with the side of a table, the next by kicking his face, and the last with a broken beer bottle.

In *Public Enemies*, the rise of the surveillance state is presided over by Hoover, a paranoid megalomaniac who directs his personal anxieties outward, constructing a vast network of state control that transforms an entire nation into an echo chamber of his private neurosis. Still, in its infancy, the surveillance state at this point has a relatively simple top-down structure, with only a few individuals wielding power over this system. The centralised, hierarchal surveillance system detailed in Mann's prior film has expanded into a more dispersed, sprawling mass in *Blackhat*. In *Public Enemies*, there is a clear split between the state's technologically advanced means of law enforcement and the comparatively low-key tools that the criminals must rely on to survive; this asymmetrical access to state-of-the-art machinery essentially dooms Dillinger and his men to fall victim to the FBI's manhunt. In *Blackhat*, power relations are more complex and difficult to track. Despite only having access to consumer-grade digital devices (at the beginning of the narrative, at least), Hathaway is far more skilled with technology than anybody at the FBI. Furthermore, Sadak is capable of mobilising extremely advanced technological systems to pursue his own goals. The identity of Sadak remains obscure to the FBI even at the very end of the film – Hathaway can locate and take down Sadak only after he has broken free from the rigid rules and protocols of the FBI. The final act takes the form of a showdown between two wanted men struggling to remain undetected. Hathaway and Sadak do not have the advantage of great wealth, prestige or institutional power, but they have both developed an intricate understanding of how to navigate the digital infrastructure that underpins all aspects of modern life. An ability to respond intuitively to what Lien terms the 'rapid stream of decision-making' in cyber-culture, an intuition for the fluctuations of the market and an instinct for gaming the systems put in place to oppress individuals – these are the characteristics that unite Hathaway and Sadak. This is in marked contrast to the government officials who populate the narrative, who exhibit a bureaucratic knowledge of the system but lack the ambition or the intuition of these outlaws.

From the scene in the restaurant onwards, Hathaway must constantly be on guard – he knows that he is being monitored but doesn't know exactly how extensive the cyber-terrorist's surveillance network is, and, as such, he is unsure which digital devices he encounters may be feeding information to them. The strategies of data collection which Hathaway repurposes to extract money from banks and other financial institutions are now directed toward him, so he becomes subject to surveillance from the state and from

Sadak's criminal gang simultaneously. To align the viewer with Hathaway's state of paranoia, the film never explicitly states how Sadak is capable of capturing critical pieces of information; as in *Miami Vice*, several of the data breaches which drive the structure of the feature are never fully explained, and we are thus encouraged to view every computer device in the diegesis as a potential instrument in Sadak's overarching plan.

Over the final act of the feature, Hathaway regains control by cutting himself free from the grasp of the FBI, so that he may pursue Sadak on his own terms. This is process is catalysed by Hathaway's decision to break protocol to attain access to a computer program that allows him to read a heavily encrypted hard drive retrieved from the ruins of the power plant. Hathaway recalls that, following his own arrest, an advanced piece of NSA software named Black Widow was used to recover data that he had tried to eliminate from all servers. Hathaway believes that, if he had access to the same software, he may similarly be able to recover seemingly irretrievable information that Sadak tried to hide. Barrett reluctantly complies with Hathaway's request but adds that they will have to ask permission from the headquarters of the NSA first. This request is denied, as the intermediating agent refuses to allow such sensitive technology to be utilised by a team that includes a felon and several employees of the Chinese government. While Barrett accepts the decision, Hathaway recognises the necessity of breaking with protocol to prevent anybody else from becoming a victim of Sadak's attacks. He attaches a keylogger to an email he forwards to the NSA agent under a false name. In the email, Hathaway states that a security risk has recently been detected, and the agent needs to change his password to ensure the safety of the data on his system. The paranoid NSA agent is instinctively startled by the alleged security threat, and thoughtlessly complies with Hathaway's instructions – unknowingly supplying Hathaway with the vital information he needs to hack into the Black Widow program. Hathaway is fully aware of the scale of the consequences he will face if the NSA discovers that he has accessed the system. He gives the other members of his team the option to leave the room so they may conceivably deny involvement if the matter is ever brought to trial. Only Lien stays with him. The gamble pays off – Hathaway successfully uses Black Widow to uncover a series of high-resolution satellite photos of tin mines in Malaysia obtained by Sadak, pointing them to the cyber-terrorist's next target. However, when the NSA agent discovers that Hathaway has hacked his account, he does not care that his actions have uncovered valuable intel. He views the hack as being an unacceptable breach of the rules, and immediately calls for Hathaway's arrest.

Although Hathaway receives some degree of sympathy from Barrett and Dawai, their fear of facing severe repercussions overrides any sense of loyalty they feel towards him. Dawai defends Hathaway to a committee run by the Chinese government, arguing that the cyber security division requires the continued support of Hathaway to track down the cyber-terrorist ring. The Chinese state officials consider Dawai's perspective but are unwilling to destabilise trade relations with the US by refusing to extradite Hathaway. Similarly, Barrett briefly attempts to convince her superior officer, Pollack, that Hathaway acted in good faith, but Pollack is uninterested in listening to her rationale. For these characters, the maintenance of bureaucratic order is perceived to be more important than potentially saving lives. Barrett quickly gives up on her attempt to support Hathaway, and aids Pollack in tracking him down. They discover that Hathaway manipulated his ankle bracelet so that it only refreshes his location once every 24 hours shortly after his release from jail – a sign of Hathaway's innate suspicion towards the US authorities, even before he becomes targeted for the NSA data breach.

At a safe house, Dawai explains to Hathaway, in plain terms, that it would not matter if he and Barrett defended him in front of a federal tribunal. The NSA and the FBI need to sustain the illusion that their digital infrastructure is impenetrable, so they will gladly make a public example of Hathaway to prevent other individuals from trying to break through their defences. He tells Hathaway that the only viable option he has left is to run – he must remove his ankle bracelet entirely, cut ties with the FBI, escape the city, and avoid all mechanisms of state surveillance to evade detection. Considering the extent to which Mann has established the all-encompassing nature of the surveillance network, this challenge seems unsurpassable, and the final act of *Blackhat* is imbued with an intense sense of pressure – a sense that the omnipresent camera-eye is increasingly closing in, and all Hathaway can do is make the most of the dwindling time he has remaining as a free man.

Lien is the only one willing to accompany Hathaway in his new existence as a fugitive wanted by both the American and Chinese authorities. The relationship between Hathaway and Lien is mutually loving, egalitarian, and long-lasting in a way that is uncommon in Mann's cinema. This is because the romance is founded upon a bond of complete trust and honesty, as well as an ideological kinship and a desire to pursue a shared socio-political goal. Lien is, like Hathaway, highly dedicated to her work, and, although they initially belong to different sides of the law, like Crockett and Isabella in *Miami Vice*, their situations become aligned after they both remove themselves from the grid in their hunt for Sadak. Their relationship is visualised with remarkable sensuality and tactility; more than ever in Mann's body of work, romantic communication is articulated through stray glances and light touches. Their first moment of attraction is indicated shortly after Hathaway has been released from prison. Stepping onto an airport tarmac, Hathaway first seems overwhelmed by the great expanse of space that surroundings him. As Barrett and Dawai enter the plane,

Hathaway remains standing in place. Mann's camera adopts Hathaway's point-of-view, tracking from left to right across the runway. Mann then cuts across the 180-degree line to an extreme close-up of Hathaway, pushed into the right of the screen so that only half of his face is visible. Most of the frame is dominated by negative space, rendered an abstract field of navy and dark green by Mann's use of shallow-focus. The scene then cuts to a reverse angle, now framing Hathaway's head from behind. The tarmac is now visible in front of him, appearing hazy due to the high aperture. This sequence of images essentially freezes the forward drive of the narrative, and the rapid fluctuation of viewpoints and focal lengths makes this moment very disorientating. Hathaway's – and the viewer's – visual perception is confused, as Hathaway becomes overwhelmed by the mass of visual information. As Peter Labuza argues, 'When [Hathaway] first steps out onto the runway of an airport, he can only see material of greys and blacks, out of focus and without dimension. It's simply a mass. Then a hand grabs his arm, and everything becomes tangibly real.' (2016). Lien steps into the frame behind Hathaway, moves from soft focus to sharp focus, finally coming to be framed in a medium-close shot as she places a hand on Hathaway's shoulder. She asks Hathaway if he is alright, and Mann cuts to a profile view of them, now centred within the foreground of a composition with a wide depth-of-field. Hathaway nods and assures her that he is okay, and they both board the plane. It is not only Lien's compassion that centres Hathaway; the physical act of touch acts as a stabilising force. Later, Hathaway and Lien share an intimate moment in a taxi speeding through the centre of a high-tech metropolis. Again adopting Hathaway's gaze, the camera focuses on Lien's neck, then her hair, then her arm, in a series of close, roving handheld shots. Lien looks over to Hathaway, and he initially turns away in embarrassment, but as she establishes a flirtatious conversation with him, the visual scheme of the scene again breaks down to isolate individual parts of their bodies.

Within the largely de-materialised environments depicted in *Blackhat*, bodily intimacy is treated as being an act of resistance in itself. The intense sensual experiences that Hathaway seeks out with Lien are indicative of the significance he places on both the realm of the intellectual and the realm of the corporeal. This recognition of the importance of both spheres allows Hathaway to keep hold of his humanity within an environment which threatens to de-humanise him. It is only after Hathaway and Lien have consummated their relationship that they divulge information about their pasts, their family lives, and their respective cultures – providing grounding connection to personal and national histories of the kind that Sadak, in his ambition to dissolve into the sphere of abstract code, tries to eradicate. Hathaway even mentions to Lien that he would replay memories from his childhood to feel human while he was locked in prison. The inmates of *The*

Jericho Mile cover their cells with photographs and other memory totems to add a touch of homeliness to their surroundings, but Hathaway keeps the walls of his room blank. This is because he knows that if he displayed these images, the prison wardens would be able to gather information regarding who Hathaway is closest to and what memories he cherishes – information that may potentially be used against him in the future. Unlike Murphy, however, Hathaway does not mentally distance himself from others and try to forget his own past to survive on the inside; it is sufficient for Hathaway to keep his valued memories locked inside his mind as a source of private reverie.

This aspect of Hathaway's character becomes particularly apparent during the final act of the feature; after he has cut himself loose from the FBI's mechanisms of control, he cultivates a mode of existence which balances physical prowess, sensual pleasure and intense intellectual activity. He can finally defeat Sadak only by moving the conflict away from the abstraction of cyber-space to the concrete realm of bodies present in material space. As Kasman argues, 'Hathaway is at once virtual and real, a hybrid existence, and those that fall around him, friends and foes, fail to cross such boundaries.' (2016). The emphasis on human tactility, of the agony and the ecstasy of corporeal experience, poses an affront to the attempts of digital networks to quantify and store all human activity as disembodied data. Hathaway, however, does not wish to simply flee urban society – Hathaway is tech-savvy enough to realise that the immense grasp of the digital network will inevitably catch up with the rogue individual if their plan is merely to disappear into the margins. Instead, Hathaway must constantly manipulate and rework digital informational channels. Hathaway stages a revolt against the forces of de-materialisation through his own personal emphasis on physicality, but his fugitive lifestyle can only be sustained because of his ability to hack into bank accounts, scramble his digital footprint through VPN software, and reverse the panoptic gaze so that he can keep tabs on those attempting to hunt him down. This is not a contradiction in his character: he has achieved a healthy balance between digital and physical experience, and it is through navigating the two realms that he is able to retain his autonomy and authenticity.

Hathaway and Lien's final-act decision to break away from the systems of control implemented by the American and Chinese governments, then, is a transitional moment in the feature which sees the pair finally embrace their full potential. This shift is put into motion by a moment of severe personal tragedy. On the way to a collection point where Hathaway has arranged to board a private plane to escort him out of the country, Dawai and Hathaway tell Lien that it may be a better idea if she didn't accompany Hathaway to his dangerous new life. Both Dawai and Hathaway recognise the immense sacrifices that Lien would have to make if she agreed to lead a life on the run, and believe that it would be better for her if she wasn't thrust into these circumstances. Dawai and Hathaway clearly have good intentions here, but they fail to pay Lien due respect by attempting to make this decision for her. A despondent Lien storms out of the car, followed by Hathaway shortly afterwards. He embraces her in the foreground of the image, the vehicle visible but out-of-focus in the background. Hathaway explains that, because powerful agents are targeting him from both sides of the law, the only way he can survive is to completely reinvent himself, eradicate his old identity and cut ties with everybody he knew in his previous life.

This may seem, at first, to be a familiar scene in Mann's body of work: the moment at which the protagonist realises that his all-consuming commitment to his ideological programme and his ingrained desire to disengage from conventional social structures makes him an unsuitable life partner. There are similar scenes in *Thief*, *Heat*, *The Insider*, *Miami Vice* and *Public Enemies*. In these features, this realisation leads the protagonist to cut himself off from his romantic partner and either embrace the inevitability of his own death or resign himself to an existence of solitude. In *Blackhat*, however, something unexpected happens: Dawai's car explodes, forcibly severing the only powerful emotional connection Lien has to her old life. It's a shocking, intense moment. The tender exchange occurring in the foreground of the image suddenly becomes visually obscured by flashes of fire and rubble. As the attack happens, the image transitions to 120 frames per second, appearing as though the very fabric of the film's aesthetic design is breaking down. Hathaway pulls Lien away from the explosion and the two hide behind a steel pole positioned on the left side of the frame.

The explosion, it is revealed, was triggered by Kassar with two accomplices, who then begin to open fire in the middle of the street. Barrett and Jessup, who have just arrived at the scene in pursuit of Hathaway, get caught in the shower of bullets, and both collapse on the road. Again, it is left unclear exactly how or when Sadak bugged Dawai's vehicle – the absence of this information is another indication that Sadak, utilising his advanced mechanisms strategies of surveillance, can stay several steps beyond the FBI. Hathaway takes Lien by the hand and leads her through a subway station. They do not know how much information Sadak has gathered on them, but they know that they cannot risk taking the private plane that had been arranged to take them out of the country, in case Sadak has also figured out that they are headed to the vehicle. The pair also know that they cannot turn to the authorities, otherwise, Hathaway will immediately be incarcerated. With no clear path forward, they are forced to adapt to the situation. The two run into a nearby subway station, and, as they circle through the maze-like arrangement of claustrophobic tunnels, Hathaway emphasises the importance of thinking on their feet: 'We've got to grieve later, now we've got to survive.' If they are to remain alive and retain their freedom, it is imperative that they take down Sadak's gang without the help of the authorities – and they must do so while evading the gaze of the globalised surveillance system.

As Lien commits herself to Hathaway and the fugitive life, the two embrace in an empty subway cart – the setting blends the boundaries between private and public space, motion and stasis, signifying that the remainder of the narrative will force the pair to seek out pockets of privacy within an expansive grid of camera-eyes hunting them. As daunting as this initial step is, however, the pair feel a newfound sense of liberation and agency after shaking off the shackles of the professional/social roles they occupied in mainstream society. No longer expected to operate by the rigid rules and restrictions determined by their former employers, Hathaway and Lien are free to go wherever they want, be whatever they want, and employ any methods they deem necessary to stop Sadak's operation. Ultimately, only Hathaway and Lien have the ability to locate and eradicate Sadak; the members of the FBI and the Chinese Cyber-security Unit simply lack the vision and the ingenuity to take down a criminal so advanced.

Blackhat reconfigures the role of the action hero in the digital age, dramatises the negotiation between the material and the virtual that has become a fundamental part of lived experience, and articulates how contemporary modes of state control may be railed against. On the one hand, *Blackhat* points to the ways in which digital technologies have intensified panoptic surveillance, given rise to widespread feelings of alienation, and caused the widespread de-materialisation of many aspects of everyday life. When under the control of corrupt powers, new digital communication channels may be used for totalitarian purposes, eroding the rights of the citizens and collapsing the boundary between public and private experience. On the other hand, *Blackhat* also expresses a belief in the possibility of mobilising new technology to challenge this hierarchy of control. This possibility is embodied in the figure of Hathaway, a character who combines his individualist ethos with a strong socio-political conscience and sense of moral purpose. He utilises his preternatural technological skill to stand up to tyranny, whether represented by corrupt governments or criminal organisations that similarly use advanced technological systems to expand their base of power. Hathaway emerges as one of the most successful protagonists in Mann's entire body of work – he fulfils his professional and ethical mission without compromising his agency or detaching from the social sphere. Although the work depicted in *Blackhat* is abstract and theoretical, as opposed to the painstaking craftsmanship deployed in, for example, *Thief* and *Heat*, Hathaway can find a satisfying balance between his body and his mind, the virtual sphere and the embodied world.

At the end of the narrative, Hathaway and Lien are free to move across international borders, with an almost limitless amount of wealth at their disposal -- they access their funds from an encrypted bank account previously operated by Sadak, so there will be no trail of their outgoings. They have no obligations to anybody or any institutions other than themselves. The film's final sequence sees the pair traversing an airport terminal; their motion across the open space is captured in an elegant, wide tracking shot, emphasising their mobility. Yet, the very final image somewhat tempers the optimism of this ending. As Hathaway and Lien walk toward the foreground of the frame, Mann's camera gradually pulls back. The colour seeps out of the image as Mann reveals that they are being caught on a surveillance feed that is being relayed on a wall of monitors in a backroom of the airport. There is no indication that the security officers in front of the screen recognise either of them – the pair blend into the crowd within the airport, and the guards do not pay attention to them specifically – but the image is a final, bittersweet reminder that Hathaway and Lien must live out the rest of their days evading capture. The pervasive digital network is still intact – one false move will alert the authorities to their presence, and their self-fashioned utopia will crumble. Hathaway and Lien have, for the moment, achieved liberation, but *Blackhat* leaves us questioning whether they can sustain it forever, or whether it will prove to be transient. If Mann's criminal protagonists have repeatedly proven to be incapable of overcoming the system, then perhaps Hathaway comes the closest out of all of them to achieving true fulfilment, finding a way to keep hold of a mutually fulfilling personal relationship while still retaining control over his work *and* his ideological programme within the confines of a hyper-modern digital network society.

Filmography

The Jericho Mile (ABC Circle Films, 1979)

Producer: Tim Zinnemann
Cinematography: Rexford Metz
Screenplay: Patrick J Nolan, Michael Mann
Editor: Arthur Schmidt
Art Director: Stephen Myles
Music: Jimmie Haskell
Starring: Peter Strauss, Brian Dennehy

Thief (Mann, Caan Productions, 1981)

Producers: Jerry Bruckheimer, Ronnie Caan
Cinematography: Donald Thorin
Screenplay: Michael Mann, from the book *The Home Invaders* by Frank
Hohimer
Editor: Dov Hoenig
Production Design: Mel Bourne
Music: Tangerine Dream
Starring: James Caan, Tuesday Weld, Willie Nelson, James Blushi, Robert
Prosky, Dennis Farina

The Keep (Associated Capital, 1983)

Producers: Gene Kirkwood, Howard W Koch Jnr.
Cinematography: Alex Thomson
Screenplay: Michael Mann, from the novel by F Paul Wilson
Editing: Dov Hoenig, Chris Kelly
Production Design: John Box
Music: Tangerine Dream
Starring: Scott Glenn, Jurgen Prochnow, Ian KcKellen, Gabriel Byrne,
Alberta Watson, Robert Prosky

Manhunter (Dino De Laurentiis Entertainment Group, Red Dragon Productions, 1986)

Producers: Richard Roth, Michael Mann
Cinematography: Dante Spinotti
Screenplay: Michael Mann, from the novel *Red Dragon* by Thomas Harris
Editing: Dov Hoenig
Production Design: Mel Bourne
Music: The Reds, Michel Rubini
Starring: William Peterson, Kim Greist, Joan Allen, Brian Cox, Dennis Farina, Tom Noonan

L.A. Takedown (1989)

Producer: Patrick Markey
Cinematography: Ron Garcia
Screenplay: Michael Mann
Editing: Dov Hoenig
Production Design: Dean Taucher
Music: Tim Truman
Starring: Scott Plank, Alex McArthur, Michael Rooker, Xander Berkeley

The Last of the Mohicans (Morgan Creek, 1992)

Producers: Michael Mann, Hunt Lowry
Cinematography: Dante Spinotti
Screenplay: Michael Mann, Christopher Crowe, from the novel by James Fenimore Cooper
Editing: Dov Hoenig, Arthur Schmidt
Production Design: Wolf Kroger
Music: Trevor Jones, Randy Edelman
Starring: Daniel Day Lewis, Madeleine Stowe, Wes Studi, Jodhi May, Russell Means, Steven Waddington

Heat (Warner Bros, Regency, Forward Pass, Monarchy Enterprises, 1996)

Producers: Michael Mann, Art Linson
Cinematography: Dante Spinotti
Screenplay: Michael Mann
Editing: Dov Hoenig, Pasquale Buba, William Goldenberg
Production Design: Neil Spisak
Music: Elliot Goldenthal, Brian Eno, The Kronos Quartet
Starring: Al Pacino, Robert De Niro, Val Kilmer, Jon Voight, Diane Venora, Tom Sizemore, Mykelti Williamson, Ashley Judd, Amy Brenneman, Wes Studi

The Insider (Blue Light Productions, Forward Pass, Kaitz Productions, Mann Roth Productions, 1999)

Producers: Michael Mann, Pieter Jan Brugge
Cinematography: Dante Spinotti
Screenplay: Michael Mann, Eric Roth, from the _Vanity Fair_ article 'The Man Who Knew Too Much' by Marie Brenner
Editing: William Goldenberg, Paul Rubell, David Rosenbloom
Production Design: Brian Morris
Music: Lisa Gerrard, Pieter Bourke
Starring: Al Pacino, Russell Crowe, Diane Venora, Michael Gambon

Ali (Columbia Pictures, Forward Pass, Peters Entertainment, Initial Entertainment Group, 2001)

Producers: Jon Peters, James Lasiter, Paul Ardaji, Michael Mann, A Kitman Ho
Cinematography: Emmanuel Lubezki
Screenplay: Stephen J Rivele, Christopher Wilkinson, Eric Roth, Michael Mann
Editing: William Goldenberg, Stephen Rivkin, Lynzee Klingman
Production Design: John Myhre
Music: Lisa Gerrard, Pieter Bourke
Starring: Will Smith, Jon Voight, Mario Van Peebles, Ron Silver, Mykelti Williamson, Jamie Fox, Jada Pinkett Smith

Collateral **(Dreamworks SKG, Paramount Pictures, Parkes MacDonald Productions, 2004)**

Producers: Michael Mann, Julie Richardson
Cinematography: Dion Beebe, Paul Cameron
Screenplay: Stuart Beattie
Editing: Jim Miller, Paul Rubell
Production Design: David Wasco
Music: James Newton Howard
Starring: Tom Cruise, Jamie Foxx, Jada Pinkett Smith, Mark Ruffalo, Peter Berg

Miami Vice **(Universal Pictures, Forward Pass, Michael Mann Productions, 2006)**

Producers: Michael Mann, Pieter Jan Brugge
Cinematography: Dion Beebe
Screenplay: Michael Mann, based on the television series created by Anthony Yerkovich
Editing: William Goldenberg, Paul Rubell
Production Design: Victor Kempster
Music: John Murphy
Starring: Colin Farrell, Jamie Foxx, Gong Li, Naomie Harris, Ciaran Hinds

Public Enemies **(Universal, Relativity Media, Forward Pass, Misher Films, 2009)**

Producers: Kevin Misher, Michael Mann
Cinematography: Dante Spinotti
Screenplay: Ronan Bennett, Michael Mann and Ann Biderman, based on the book by Bryan Burrough
Editing: Paul Rubell, Jeffery Ford
Production Design: Nathan Crowley
Music: Elliot Goldenthal
Starring: Johnny Depp, Christian Bale, Marion Cotiillard, Billy Crudup

Blackhat **(Legendary Pictures, Forward Pass, Universal Pictures, 2015)**

Producers: Thomas Tull, Michael Mann, Jon Jashni
Cinematography: Stuart Dryburgh
Screenplay: Morgan Davis Foehl, Michael Mann
Editing: Joe Walker, Stephen E Rivkin, Jeremiah O'Driscoll, Mako Kamitsuna
Production Design: Guy Hendrix Dyas
Music: Harry Gregson-Williams, Atticus Ross, Leo Ross, Ryan Amon
Starring: Chris Hemsworth, Tang Wei, Viola Davis, Ritchie Coster, Holt McCallany, Yorick van Wageningen, Wang Leehom

Bibliography

'An Evening with Michael Mann, moderated by critic Bilge Ebiri'. (2016). Youtube video, added by BAMorg. [Online]. Available at: https://www.youtube.com/watch?v=1QtAbxh7shw [Last Accessed 12th December 2020].

Appelo, T. (2014). 'Legendary Newsman Mike Wallace "Detested" the *The Insider*, Michael Mann Reveals'. *The Hollywood Reporter*. Online. Available at: https://www.hollywoodreporter.com/news/general-news/legendary-newsman-mike-wallace-detested-734792/. [Last Accessed 1st August 2021].

Arnett, R. (2009). 'The American City as Non-Place: Architecture and Narrative in the Crime Films of Michael Mann'. *Quarterly Review of Film and Video*. 27(1). pp.44-53.

Arnold, G. (1981). 'The Thief Steals the Show'. *The Washington Post*. Online. Available at: https://www.washingtonpost.com/archive/lifestyle/1981/03/27/the-thief-steals-the-show/dceb2e25-d10f-4e78-a01e-a394a5e477d3/. [Last Accessed 2nd September 2021].

Canby, V. (1983). 'Film: McKellen in *Keep*'. *The New York Times*. Online. Available at: https://www.nytimes.com/1983/12/16/movies/film-mckellen-in-keep.html. [Last Accessed 12th December 2020].

Collins, K. A. (2019). 'The Insider at 20: As Alive With Style and Possibility as Ever'. *Vanity Fair*. Online. Available at: https://www.vanityfair.com/hollywood/2019/11/the-insider-al-pacino-20th-anniversary. [Last Last Accessed 5th March 2021].

Croce, F. F. (2009). 'Thieves and Enemies: Some Thoughts on Michael Mann's Evolution'. *MUBI Notebook*. Available at: https://mubi.com/notebook/posts/thieves-and-enemies-some-thoughts-on-michael-manns-evolution. [Last Accessed 5th September 2021]

Dinnen, Z. (2018). 'Cinema and the Unnarratability of Computation'. In *The Edinburgh Companion to Contemporary Narrative Theories*. Edited by Dinnen, Z. and Warhol, R. Edinburgh: Edinburgh University Press. pp. 158-173.

Doyle, K. (2006). 'Muhammad Goes to Hollywood: Michael Mann's *Ali* as Biopic'. *The Journal of Popular Culture*. 39 (3). p.383-406.

Dyess-Nurgent, P. (2014). 'The "MTV cops" of *Miami Vice* gave television a facelift, then succumbed to the ravages of age'. *The AV Club*. Available at: https://www.avclub.com/the-mtv-cops-of-miami-vice-gave-television-a-facelift-1798272156. [Last Accessed 5th January 2021].

Dzenis, A. (2002). 'Impressionist Extraordinaire: Michael Mann's *Ali*'. *Senses of Cinema*. Online. Available at: https://www.sensesofcinema.com/2002/feature-articles/ali. [Last Accessed 15th March 2021]

Dzenis, A. (2002). 'Michael Mann's Cinema of Images'. *Screening the Past*. Online. Available at: http://www.screeningthepast.com/issue-14-first-release/michael-manns-cinema-of-images/. [Last Accessed 12th February 2021]

Ebiri, B. (2018) 'The Pixelated Splendor of Michael Mann's *Blackhat*. *Oscilloscope*. Online. Available at: https://musings.oscilloscope.net/post/178954843321/the-pixelated-splendor-of-michael-manns. [Last Accessed 10th May 2021].

Elsaesser, T. (2000). *Weimar Cinema and After: Germany's Historical Imaginary*. New York, NY: Routledge

Feeney, F. X. and Duncan, P. (2006). *Michael Mann*. Cologne: Taschen.

Gaine, V. M. (2011). *Existentialism and Social Engagement in the Films of Michael Mann*. London: Palgrave Macmillan.

Gaine, Vincent M. (2009). 'We're on Flashdrive or CD-ROM: Disassembly and Deletion in the Digital Noir of *Collateral*'. *Networking Knowledge: Journal of the MeCCSA Postgraduate Network*. 2 (1). pp.1-13.

Gallagher, B. (2018). 'American Gigolo and the Rise of the Armani Generation'. *Grailed*. Online. Available at: https://www.grailed.com/drycleanonly/american-gigolo-rise-of-armani. [Last Accessed 5th January 2021].

Gallimore, A. (2014). '"We Ain't Thinking About tomorrow": Narrative Immediacy and the Digital Period Aesthetic in Michael Mann's *Public Enemies*.' *Scope: An Online Journal of Film and Television Studies*. 26. pp.1-23.

Garcia-Mainar, L. M. (2008). 'Say it with generic maps: Genre, identity and flowers in Michael Mann *Collateral*.' *Screening the Past*. Online. Available at: http://www.screeningthepast.com/issue-23-first-release/say-it-with-generic-maps-genre-identity-and-flowers-in-michael-mann%e2%80%99s%c2%a0collateral. [Last Accessed 10th May 2021].

González, E. M. (2017). 'Living In the Posthuman Network Society: Mobility and Surveillance In *Blackhat*'. *Journal of English Studies*. 15. pp.221-234.

Graham, P. (2005). '*Manhunter*'. *Chicago Reader*. Online. Available at: https://chicagoreader.com/film/manhunter/. [Last Accessed 12th January 2021].

Grossberg, L. (1988). 'Rockin' with Reagan, or the Mainstreaming of Postmodernity'. *Cultural Critique*. 10. pp.123-149.

Howard, B. (2014). 'What Makes A Mann?: Part 3 – Mann's Style: *Ali, Collateral & Miami Vice'. Graffiti with Punctuation*. Online. Available at: https://graffitiwithpunctuation.com/opinion/2014/05/01/makes-mann-part-3-manns-style-ali-collateral-miami-vice. [Last Accessed 12th July 2021].

Kasman, D. (2016). 'Michael Mann's *Blackhat*: The Modern Mythology'. *MUBI Notebook*. Online. Available at: https://mubi.com/notebook/posts/michael-mann-s-blackhat-the-modern-mythology. [Last Accessed 10th May 2021].

Kasman, D., Knight, R. W. and Vishnevetsky, I. (2009). 'A Conversation About Michael Mann's *Public Enemies'. MUBI Notebook*. Online. Available at: https://mubi.com/notebook/posts/frontiers-of-extinction-a-conversation-about-michael-manns-public-enemies. [Last Accessed 20th May 2021].

Knight, R. W. (2015). 'The Speed of Causality: Michael Mann's *Blackhat'. MUBI Notebook*. Online. Available at: https://mubi.com/notebook/posts/the-speed-of-causality-michael-manns-blackhat. [Last Accessed 10th March 2021]

Kracauer, S. (2004). [1947]. *From Caligari to Hitler: A Psychological History of the German Film*. Translated and Edited by Leonardo Quaresima. Princetown, NJ: Princeton University Press.

Labuza, P. (2016). 'Michael Mann's *Blackhat'. Labuzamovies.com*. Online. Available at: https://labuzamovies.com/2015/01/22/michael-manns-blackhat. [Last Accessed 10th May 2021].

Marsh, C. (2013). 'Blown Out: *Miami Vice'. Reverse Shot*. Online. Available at: http://www.reverseshot.org/archive/entry/552/miami_vice. [Last Accessed 20th March 2021].

Mattes, A. M. (2014). 'Action without regeneration: The deracination of the American action hero in Michael Mann's *Heat.' Journal of Popular Film and Television*. 42 (4). pp.186-194.

McCrisken, T. and Pepper, A. (2005). *American History and Contemporary Hollywood Film*. Edinburgh: Edinburgh University Press.

Ó Maoilearca, J. (2015). *All Thoughts Are Equal: Laruelle and Nonhuman Philosophy*. Minnesota: University of Minnesota Press.

Olsen, M. (2004).'Paint it Black'. In *Michael Mann – Cinema and Television Interviews*, 1980-2012. Edited by Sanders, S. and Palmer, R. B. Edinburgh University Press. pp.81-84.

Panagia, D. (2015). 'Film Blancs: Luminosity in the Films of Michael Mann'. *Film-Philosophy*. 19. pp.33-54.

Patterson, J. (2009). 'Number one with a bullet'. *The Guardian*. Online. http://www.guardian.co.uk/film/2009/jun/26/interview-michael-mann-public-enemies. [Last Accessed 11th May 2021].

Pelan, T. (2019). 'Take It to the Limit One More Time: Michael Mann's *Miami Vice*'. *Cinephilia & Beyond*. Online. Available at: https://cinephiliabeyond.org/miami-vice. [Last Accessed 22nd July 2021].

Phillips, K. R. (2003). 'Redeeming the visual: Aesthetic questions in Michael Mann's *Manhunter*'. *Literature/Film Quarterly*. 31 (1). pp.10-16.

Pinkerton, N. (2018). 'A Thousand Unblinking Eyes: A History'. *The Baffler*. Online. Available at: https://thebaffler.com/salvos/a-thousand-unblinking-eyes-pinkerton. [Last Accessed 10th May 2021].

Pinkerton, N. (2004). 'Night Vision: *Collateral*'. *Reverse Shot*. Online. Available at: http://www.reverseshot.org/reviews/entry/226/collateral'. [Last Accessed 1st May 2021].

Rayner, J. (2013). *The Cinema of Michael Mann: Vice and Vindication*. London: Wallflower Press.

Rybin, S. (2013). *Michael Mann: Crime Auteur*. Lanham: Scarecrow Press.

Ryzik, M. (2014). 'The Tech Changes, but Not the Crime'. *The New York Times*. Online. Available at: https://www.nytimes.com/2014/12/28/movies/michael-mann-prepares-his-new-film-blackhat.html. [Last Accessed 10th May 2021].

Saito, S. (2013). 'Michael Mann on Going Back to Chicago for *Thief*'. *The Moveable Fest*. Online. Available at: https://moveablefest.com/michael-mann-thief/. [Last Accessed 5th September 2021].

Sanders, S., Skoble, A. J., and Palmer, R. B. (2014).*The Philosophy of Michael Mann*. Kentucky: The University Press of Kentucky.

Sharrett, C. (2002). 'Michael Mann: Elegies on the Post-industrial Landscape'. In *Fifty Contemporary Filmmakers*. Edited by Yvonne Tasker. London and New York: Routledge. pp.253-263.

Smith, G. (1992). 'Wars and Peace'. *Sight and Sound*. 2(7). pp.10–14.

Sragow, M. (1999). 'All the Corporations' Men'. *Salon*. Online. Available at: https://www.salon.com/1999/11/04/mann_2/. [Last Accessed 5th March 2021].

Steele, I. K. (1993). '*The Last of the Mohicans*'. *The Journal of American History*. 80(3). pp.1179–1181.

Thoret, J. B. (2007). 'Gravity of the Flux: Michael Mann's *Miami Vice*'. *Senses of Cinema*. Online. Available at: https://www.sensesofcinema.com/2007/feature-articles/miami-vice/. [Last Accessed 1st July 2021].

Thoret, J. B. (2013) [2000]. 'The Aquarium Syndrome: On the Films of Michael Mann'. *Screening the Past*. Online. Available at: http://www.screeningthepast.com/issue-14-first-release/michael-manns-cinema-of-images/. [Last Accessed 12th February 2021].

Tucker, K. (2012). 'The Michael Mann interview part 1: *Miami Vice, The Jericho Mile, Luck*, and more'. *Entertainment Weekly*. Online. Available at: https://ew.com/article/2012/01/21/michael-mann-interview-luck-hbo/. [Last Accessed 2nd August 2021].

Tudor, D. (2010). 'Light bouncing: digital processes illuminate the cultural past'. *Jump Cut: A Review of Contemporary Media*. 52. Online. Available at: http://www.ejumpcut.org/archive/jc52.2010/deeDigitalCinematog. [Last Accessed 10th May 2021]

Uhlich, K. (2009). 'Public Enemies'. *Time Out New York*. 718. p.69.

Uhlich, K. (2011). 'Nazi Cuckoo: *The Keep*'. *Reverse Shot*. Online. Available at: http://www.reverseshot.org/archive/entry/1465/keep. [Last Accessed 16th December 2020].

Van Es, R. (2003). 'Inside and Outside *The Insider*: A Film Workshop in Practical Ethics'. *Journal of Business Ethics*. 48(1). pp.89-97.

Vishnevetsky, I. (2009). 'The First Ten Minutes of *Ali*'. *MUBI Notebook*. Online. Available at: https://mubi.com/notebook/posts/the-first-ten-minutes-of-ali. [Last Accessed 10th March 2021].

Vishnevetsky, I. (2013). 'Michael Mann twisted *Miami Vice* into something thrillingly new'. *The AV Club*. Online. Available at: https://www.avclub.com/michael-mann-twisted-miami-vice-into-something-thrillin-1798238074. [Last Accessed 1st July 2021].

Wildermuth, M. E. (2005). *Blood in the Moonlight: Michael Mann and Information Age Cinema*. Jefferson, N.C.: McFarland & Company.

Williams, T. (2007). '*Manhunter*'. *Senses of Cinema*. Online. Available at: https://www.sensesofcinema.com/2007/cteq/manhunter/. [Last Accessed 10th January 2021].

Wilson, F. P. quoted in Peterson, A. (2011).'Between The Lines feature interview F Paul Wilson'. *The Big Thrill*. Online. Available at: https://www.thebigthrill.org/2011/02/between-the-lines-feature-interview-f-paul-wilson [Last Accessed 12th December 2020].

About the Author

James Slaymaker is a film critic and filmmaker from Dorset, UK. His writing has been published in *Senses of Cinema, Little White Lies, MUBI Notebook, Film International, Bright Lights Film Journal, The Interactive Film and Media Journal, Sound on Sight, Vague Visages, Kinoscope, Alternate Takes, Popmatters, Tilt Magazine* and *McSweeney's*. He has also contributed chapters to recent books on Paul Schrader, experimental cinema, and Howard Hawks. As a filmmaker, his work has been spotlighted by *The Film Stage, MUBI, Fandor* and *Sight and Sound*, as well as premiering at the London DIY Film Festival, the Concrete Dream Film Festival, the Slow Film Festival, the InShort Film Festival and The Straight Jacket Film Festival. He is currently a PhD student at The University of Southampton, where his research focuses on the cinematic essay and digital culture. *Time is Luck: The Cinema of Michael Mann* is his first book.

Made in United States
Orlando, FL
04 August 2024

49925303R00153